FAMOUS AMERICAN ADMIRALS

Famous Admirals of America's Greatest Naval War (l to r)—Spruance, Mitscher, Nimitz and Lee—aboard the heavy cruiser *Indianapolis* in February 1945.
U. S. Navy Photograph

FAMOUS AMERICAN ADMIRALS

Clark G. Reynolds

A Norback Book

 VAN NOSTRAND REINHOLD COMPANY
NEW YORK   CINCINNATI   ATLANTA   DALLAS   SAN FRANCISCO
LONDON   TORONTO   MELBOURNE

Van Nostrand Reinhold Company Regional Offices:
New York   Cincinnati   Atlanta   Dallas   San Francisco

Van Nostrand Reinhold Company International Offices:
London   Toronto   Melbourne

Library of Congress Catalog Card Number: 78-9607
ISBN: 0-442-26068-7

Manufactured in the United States of America

Published by Van Nostrand Reinhold Company
135 West 50th Street, New York, N.Y. 10020

Published simultaneously in Canada by Van Nostrand Reinhold Ltd.

15 14 13 12 11 10 9 8 7 6 5 4 3 2 1

Library of Congress Cataloging in Publication Data

Reynolds, Clark G
    Famous American admirals.

    Includes index.
    1. Admirals—United States—Biography.   I.   Title.
V62.R48   359.3′3′10922 [B]   78-9607
ISBN 0-442-26068-7

Flag Rank in the U.S. Navy

The commanding officer of any naval squadron or fleet—two or more vessels—traditionally has been regarded as a "flag officer." That is, he is entitled to display his broad pennant or flag prominently from the mast of his "flagship" so that the other vessels can identify his location in the force. By the time of the American Revolution, the Royal Navy of Great Britain had firmly established four flag ranks, in order of seniority, Admiral, Vice Admiral, Rear Admiral, and Commodore (Army equivalents—General, Lieutenant General, Major General, and Brigadier General respectively), ranks also adopted for the new American nation by act of the Continental Congress on November 15, 1776. In lesser ranks also and practically every other aspect of the American navy, Britain provided the model.

However, the Continental Navy (1775–1783) and the early United States Navy (1798–1862) never commissioned any officers in these permanent flag ranks allowed by law, the highest officer grade being that of Captain. The reason lay in Americans' distrust of aristocratic-sounding titles reminiscent of the Royal Navy, a principal agent of oppression during the Revolution. Instead, the courtesy title of Commodore was bestowed upon each squadron commander, a title which he retained until his death, although it neither carried official status nor increased pay or any other administrative permanence. By act of the Continental Congress, Esek Hopkins was made "Commander-in-Chief of the Fleet," a unique title he held for only one year, during which time however he was usually addressed as Commodore, as were all other squadron commanders until the 1850's.

Congress in 1857 ruled that the designation of Commodore be replaced by the more cumbersome but seemingly more grandiose title of Flag Officer, and that each squadron commander be entitled to display the flag of a Vice Admiral or a Rear Admiral depending on length of service (20 years or more as Captain for the former, under 20 for the latter). Two years later Congress designated Charles Stewart as "Senior Flag Officer," but no rank of admiral existed in the Navy prior to the Civil War, and no one uniformed officer for that matter enjoyed supreme command at the top comparable to the General-in-Chief of the Army; the civilian Secretary of the Navy exerted direct control.

The Union and Confederate navies initially continued the flag practices of the prewar U. S. Navy, with the important difference that early in the fighting both sides gained naval heroes deserving special recognition through senior ranks, and the Union created four large blockading squadrons plus one substantial river command, all of which required a system of senior grades more realistic than the vague Flag Officer arrangement.

Therefore, the U.S. Congress, on July 16, 1862, created the formal ranks of Rear Admiral (two stars) for not more than nine active duty officers, the first being David G. Farragut of New Orleans fame, and Commodore (one star) for up to 18 individuals. The Confederacy, with its relatively small naval forces, allotted only four admiral's billets in April 1862. However, it made use of only two of them throughout the duration as special recognition for two particular heroes, with Franklin Buchanan of the *Merrimack (Virginia)* becoming Admiral in August 1862 and Raphael Semmes of the *Alabama* becoming Rear Admiral in January 1865.

From this time until World War II, Rear Admiral remained the normal senior permanent active duty rank in the U. S. Navy, a continuing reflection of the national bias against a large standing fleet and possible entrenched naval aristocracy.

In recognition of certain exceptional individual achievements, however, Congress enacted special legislation for more senior flag ranks on several occasions. For his victory at Mobile Bay, Farragut was given the rank of Vice Admiral (three stars), created by Congress for him in December 1864. Again, in July 1866, for Farragut's exceptional wartime services, Congress created the rank of Admiral (four stars) for him and elevated David D. Porter to be Vice Admiral. When Farragut died in 1870, Porter became Admiral and Stephen C. Rowan Vice Admiral. Congress then ruled in 1873 that both senior ranks would fall vacant upon the deaths of Porter and Rowan, which occurred in 1891 and 1890 respectively. However, in 1903 Congress created the unique rank of Admiral of the Navy especially for George Dewey for his victory at Manila Bay, and he remained the senior officer in the Navy until his death in 1917.

The rapid growth of the Navy in the years between the Spanish-American War and World War I necessitated higher grades than Rear Admiral. The rank of Rear Admiral, in two levels or "halves," completely replaced that of permanent Commodore in March 1899, the latter grade not reappearing again until World War II. But more significantly, on March 3, 1915, Congress elevated the commanders of the Atlantic, Pacific, and Asiatic Fleets, all Rear Admirals on the active list, to hold the temporary rank of Admiral, with each Fleet second-in-command to be temporary Vice Admiral. The next year the Chief of Naval Operations, newly created as senior post in the Navy, was also authorized to hold the temporary rank of Admiral. When the Atlantic and Pacific Fleets were succeeded by the United States Fleet in 1922, its Commander-in-Chief was also made a temporary Admiral.

Upon retirement, all flag officers reverted to Rear Admiral on the retired list. In 1930, however, Congress ruled that all retired officers be advanced to their highest World War I rank, and in 1938 former Chiefs of Naval Operations were authorized to hold the permanent full rank of Admiral on the retired list.

The expansion of the Navy prior to and during World War II finally led the nation and the Congress to accept the necessity for a large Navy with all the embellishments of permanent senior flag ranks, pay, and privileges. Consequently, on July 24, 1941, Congress empowered the President to promote as many Rear Admirals to temporary Admiral and Vice Admiral as necessary for the duration and that such individuals be retired in their highest grade held while on active duty. The rank of Commodore was also restored on a limited basis in 1943 for the duration.

Finally, to give adequate seniority to the highest U. S. Naval wartime commanders alongside their opposite numbers in the Royal Navy (Admirals of the Fleet) on the Combined Chiefs of Staff and in the major theaters of war, Congress in December 1944 created the rank of Fleet Admiral (five stars) for four officers to be held during their lifetimes. Three men were immediately appointed: William D. Leahy, Chief of Staff to the President and Chairman of the Joint Chiefs of Staff; Ernest J. King, Commander-in-Chief United States Fleet and Chief of Naval Operations; and Chester W. Nimitz, Commander-in-Chief Pacific Fleet and Commander-in-Chief Pacific Ocean Areas. Immediately after the war, Admiral William F. Halsey, Jr., was so promoted as an honorarium for wartime services rendered.

The flag system formalized during World War II has remained generally intact ever since. The only major change was the creation of the "tombstone" promotion in 1947. All officers below the full rank of Admiral were advanced one permanent grade upon retirement if they had been "specially commended for performance of duty before January 1, 1947, in actual combat." The chief effect was to enable Captains to be retired as flag officers, Rear Admirals, for the record (and their tombstones) but not for any increase in pension. This practice was discontinued by act of Congress in 1959. Also, the rank of Commodore was phased out in 1947 but restored again, 30 years later, in 1977, as an economy measure.

Below flag rank and squadron command in the U.S. Navy (patterned after the British) have been the principal commissioned ship's officers, notably the Captain (Army equivalent—Colonel) and the Lieutenant (Army equivalent—Captain). On the larger warships of the sailing period, senior lieutenants were required for specialized functions, resulting in several subordinate ranks: Master Commandant, or Master and Commander, was the most senior lieutenant, a grade which evolved during the nineteenth century into the rank of Commander (Army equivalent—Lieutenant Colonel), in line behind the Captain. The next lieutenant was the Lieutenant Commanding (unofficially, Lieutenant Commandant), a rank which eventually became Lieutenant Commander (Army equivalent—Major). Then came the Lieutenant, later Lieutenant (senior grade) (Army equivalent—Captain). All these lieutenants were qualified to command smaller warships.

Junior lieutenant grades also evolved: A specialized navigator was the Master, or Sailing Master, a rank which developed into Lieutenant (junior grade) (Army equivalent—First Lieutenant). The most junior grade has been that of Midshipman, an officer apprentice or naval cadet who upon successful completion of his schooling on board ship or at the Naval Academy was rated Passed Midshipman, which was changed finally to Ensign (Army equivalent—Second Lieutenant) to rank below Lieutenant (j.g.). During the nineteenth and early twentieth centuries both ranks existed, a Passed Midshipman being junior to Ensign. And briefly, during the 1880's, the Navy also flirted with a rank of Ensign (j.g.).

In addition to the Navy, the United States has had several other sea-related services (plus the U.S. Marine Corps), the major ones with ranks equivalent to those of the Navy. The U.S. Revenue Cutter Service appeared in 1789 and evolved with its lifesaving component into the U.S. Coast Guard in 1915. The U.S. Coast Survey, created in 1807, expanded first into the U.S. Coast and Geodetic Survey in 1878 and into the National Oceanic and Atmospheric Administration (NOAA) in 1970, nearly a century later. The U.S. Fish Commission was established in 1871, became the Bureau of Fisheries in 1903, and developed into the Fish and Wildlife Service in 1940, its ships officered by Naval personnel. Finally, the commercial and privately-owned merchant marine operated without peacetime controls until the establishment of the Maritime Commission in 1936 and its training component, the U.S. Maritime Service, in 1938. (Also adopting Navy ranks was the U.S. Public Health Service, established in 1798 to aid American merchant seamen.)

The only flag rank which applied to any of these several other agencies of the American sea-going establishment before the twentieth century was the honorary title of Commodore for the commanding officer of any assemblage of ships. Then, in 1919, Captain Commandant of the Coast Guard William E. Reynolds was given the temporary rank of Commodore in the U.S. Navy and in 1923 was appointed as the first Rear Admiral in the Coast Guard. The Coast and Geodetic Survey followed suit in 1936 by promoting its Director, Raymond S. Patton, to the rank of Rear Admiral; NOAA's first Rear Admiral in 1970 was Don A. Jones.

The Maritime Administration tended to rely on retired Navy admirals such as Emory S. Land or arranged to have its other senior officers made Commodore or Rear Admiral in the U.S. Naval Reserve. But during and soon after World War II, flag ranks were also established for the Maritime Service, the first USMS Commodore and Rear Admiral being its Commandant, Telfair Knight, in 1944 and 1946 respectively. The wartime expansion of the sea services also accounted for the first three- and four-star ranks outside the Navy; the Coast Guard Commandant Russell R. Waesche was made Vice Admiral in 1942 and Admiral in 1945. The Maritime Service appointed Knight as its first Vice Admiral in 1951.

In addition to flag officers of the American Navy, included in this book are one Coast Guard admiral, Waesche, and one of the Maritime Service, Richard R. McNulty, plus several Americans who achieved flag rank in navies other than the U.S. Navy: in the Russian, John Paul Jones; the French, Joshua Barney; the Mexican, David Porter; the Republic of Texas,

Edwin W. Moore; the Peruvian, John R. Tucker; and the Confederates, Franklin Buchanan, Raphael Semmes, Samuel Barron, French Forrest, George N. Hollins, Duncan N. Ingraham, William F. Lynch, John K. Mitchell, Josiah Tattnall and Tucker.

Finally, one should note that the fame of several of the Admirals and Commodores included in this work was achieved due to their earlier exploits before they reached flag rank.

Author's Note

The entry of each flag officer educated at the U. S. Naval Academy begins with the state from which he was appointed ("At Large" usually denotes a Presidential appointment for the son of a serviceman), followed by the class in which he graduated and finally (beginning with 1853) by his class standing (his place/total number of graduates).

Hull numbers of ships are given wherever possible for sake of reference, although the Navy did not officially begin its numbering system until 1920.

Abbreviations are used only after the full title of a command or billet has been spelled out in the same entry.

Wartime flag promotions were often to temporary rank, given herein, with promotions to permanent rank following a few years later and not included herein. Wherever known, actual month of promotion is given rather than the date to which the promotion was backdated.

Contents

Ainsworth, Walden Lee "Pug"

(November 10, 1886–August 7, 1960).
USNA (Minn.) 1910 (73/130).

Embarking upon a career as a surface line officer in ordnance and gunnery, Ainsworth served aboard the battleship *Idaho* (BB-24) and auxiliary cruiser *Prairie* (1910–14) before joining the battleship *Florida* (BB-30) for the Vera Cruz occupation and subsequent cruises (1914–17). During World War I, he served in the transport *DeKalb,* the captured liner *America,* and the armored cruiser *Frederick,* on the latter as gunnery officer. Following ordnance duty ashore at Charleston, West Virginia (1919–21), Lieutenant Commander Ainsworth was executive officer of the transport *Hancock* and the cruiser *Birmingham* (CL-2) before taking command of the destroyer *Marcus* (DD-321) in 1922. Ordnance and other shore duty at Pittsburgh and New York Navy Yard preceded his assignment to the Asiatic Fleet in 1926 as Destroyer Squadron gunnery officer aboard the flagship, destroyer tender *Black Hawk* (AD-9). He commanded the destroyer *Paul Jones* (DD-230) (1927–28) and then taught navigation at the Naval Academy. With these skills, he served as navigator of the battleship *Idaho* (BB-42) and the cruiser *Pensacola* (CA-24) with the Battle and Scouting forces respectively (1931–33). Shore duty in the Panama Canal Zone followed.

Commander Ainsworth completed the senior course at the Naval War College (1935–36) before reporting aboard the battleship *Mississippi* (BB-41) as executive officer (1936–38). Promoted to captain, he led the Naval ROTC unit at Tulane University prior to assuming command of Destroyer Squadron Two in the *Moffett* (DD-362) in the Caribbean in July 1940. In that capacity he patrolled the French Antilles following the fall of France and Atlantic waters against Axis submarines until the U.S. formally entered World War II. On December 20, 1941, he took command of the *Mississippi,* transferring with her from the Atlantic to the Pacific where on July 4, 1942, he was detached to become Commander Destroyers Pacific Fleet.

Promoted to rear admiral in December 1942, Ainsworth combined his genial personality and rigid disciplinary qualities to lead one of Adm. W.F. Halsey's cruiser-destroyer forces as Commander Cruiser Division Nine during the Solomon Islands campaign throughout 1943. With three or four light cruisers, including his flagship *Nashville* (CL-43) and up to ten destroyers, Admiral Ainsworth conducted many night bombardment raids against New Georgia and Kolombangara islands from January to July. On July 6 in the night battle of Kula Gulf, he led his Task Force 67 in capping the Japanese "T" and sinking two Japanese destroyers, although he lost one of his own cruisers. Six nights later his ships engaged another Japanese surface force in the battle of Kolombangara, sinking a Japanese cruiser though with considerable damage to his own force. These operations supported Halsey's landings in the central Solomons and continued into the northern Solomons until early 1944.

Shifting from the South to the Central Pacific and his flag to the cruiser *Honolulu* (CL-48), Admiral Ainsworth commanded a bombardment force of battleships and destroyers at the landings in the Marianas and Palau islands during the summer of 1944. His similar role during the assault on Leyte in October ended abruptly when his flagship was severely damaged by an aerial torpedo and he was appointed "type" commander of all cruisers and destroyers in the Pacific Fleet (October 1944–July 1945). Admiral Ainsworth's last duty (1945–48) was as Commandant, Fifth Naval District and Commander Naval Operating Base Norfolk. Upon his retirement in December 1948 he was advanced to vice admiral.

Ammen, Daniel

(May 16, 1819–July 11, 1898).

A boyhood friend of Ulysses S. Grant in Ohio, Ammen entered the Navy as midshipman from that state in July 1836, studying for three months at West Point where his brother Jacob (later General) taught. After initial service in the storeship *Relief* and frigate *Macedonian* (1836–38), he cruised the West Indies in the sloops of war *Levant* and *Vandalia* (1838–39) before joining the sloop *Preble* which took him to the Mediterranean Station (1840–41). Promotion to passed midshipman followed a tour at the Naval School in Philadelphia (1841–42). Then several short assignments culminated in his attachment to the storeship *Lexington* which supplied the Mediterranean Squadron. Ammen joined the sloop *Vincennes* for a tour with the East India Squadron (1845–47), after which he worked with the U.S. Coast Survey (1847–49, 1851–52). He returned to the Mediterranean aboard the frigate *St. Lawrence* (1850) and to South American waters to explore Paraguay's rivers with the steamer *Water Witch* (1853–54). Lieutenant Ammen served in the Brazil Squadron on the brig *Bainbridge* (1854–55) and at the U.S. Naval Observatory (1855–57) before going to the Pacific aboard the sidewheel steam sloop *Saranac* (1857–58) and then the Squadron flagship, the screw frigate *Merrimack* (1858–60). He was next ashore at the Naval Rendezvous at Baltimore (1860–61).

During the summer of 1861, Ammen participated in the North Atlantic blockade as an officer of the steam frigate *Roanoke* before taking command of the gunboat *Seneca* in September. He led this vessel in the successful attack on Port Royal, South Carolina, in November and in operations along the Carolina and Florida coasts until transferring briefly to command of the gunboat *Sebago* in August 1862. Commander Ammen brought the ironclad

Patapsco into commission in January 1863 and led her in the bombardments of Fort McAllister, Georgia, in March and the Charleston, South Carolina, forts in April before taking sick leave. He returned to the blockade of the latter port during the summer as aide to Adm. J.A.B. Dahlgren before ill health again forced him to withdraw from the fighting. Following brief service as commander of the screw sloop *Shenandoah,* Ammen boarded the merchantman *Ocean Queen* to escort 220 naval recruits from New York to Panama; when they mutinied en route, in May 1864, he led a small group in suppressing them, personally shooting two of the leaders. Command of the steam sloop *Mohican* followed in October, during which he participated in both attacks against Fort Fisher, North Carolina, and in the final operations against Charleston (1865).

After helping to recover naval equipment in North Carolina, Ammen brought the seagoing monitor *Miantonomah* into commission (1865–66), was promoted to captain in July 1866, served at Hartford, Connecticut (1866–67), and commanded the screw steamer *Piscataqua* (1867–69), flagship of the Asiatic Station. Profiting from his childhood friendship with the now President Grant, Captain Ammen spent the years of the Grant administration in Washington as Chief of the Bureau of Yards and Docks (1869–71) and Chief of the Bureau of Navigation (1871–78). Commissioned commodore in April 1872, he also served as secretary of the Isthmian Canal Commission (1872–76). He was promoted to rear admiral in December 1877 and retired the following June.

Admiral Ammen continued to serve the Navy, however. He actively supported the Nicaraguan canal scheme during the 1880's, invented a cask life raft which was adopted by the Navy, wrote two histories, *The Atlantic Coast* (1883) concerning the Civil War, and the autobiographical *The Old Navy and the New* (1891), and designed the experimental harbor defense "Ammen ram" *Katahdin* (1896).

Anderson, George Whelan, Jr.

*(December 15, 1906——). USNA
(N.Y.) 1927 (28/579).*

Chief of Naval Operations during the Cuban missile crisis, Anderson rose rapidly through the commissioned ranks in naval aviation, his keen mind always much in demand for major staff assignments. Following duty in the cruiser *Cincinnati* (CL-6) between the Far East and the North Atlantic (1927–30), he took flight training at Pensacola (wings, 1930), served successively in the aviation units of the cruisers *Concord* (CL-10) and *Raleigh* (CL-7) in the Atlantic (1930–33), and was a test pilot at Norfolk (1933–35) before joining Fighting Squadron Two on the aircraft carrier *Lexington* (CV-2). As lieutenant, he helped bring the *Yorktown* (CV-5) into commission (1937–39) and briefly flew patrol planes from Seattle with Patrol Squadron 44 (1939–40) prior to his assignment to the Plans Division, Bureau of Aeronautics, in Washington.

Anderson figured importantly in naval aviation during World War II in spite of his relatively junior rank. As lieutenant commander at the Bureau of Aeronautics (1940–43), he directed the mammoth mobilization and allocation program of the Navy's aircraft. Promoted to commander, he joined the new *Yorktown* (CV-10) as navigator and participated in strikes on Marcus and Wake islands (August and October 1943). Anderson served as a major adviser to Adm. J.H. Towers, his bureau chief at the beginning of the war, in the fighting against Japan, his official posts being Plans Officer to Commander Air Force Pacific Fleet (November 1943–March 1944) and Assistant to the Deputy Commander-in-Chief Pacific Fleet (March 1944–April 1945). As captain, he was aviation officer in the Strategic Plans Division on the staff of the Commander-in-Chief United States Fleet and Deputy Navy Planner on the Joint Planning Staff in Washington until the end of the war.

Captain Anderson's postwar duties at the Office of the Chief of Naval Operations included membership on the Joint War Plans Committee of the Joint Staff and on the joint U.S. defense boards with Canada and Brazil (1945–48). He commanded the Atlantic antisubmarine carrier *Mindoro* (CVE-120) (1948–49), received instruction at the National War College (1949–50), and served as Senior U.S. Officer in Plans and Operations to Gen. Dwight D. Eisenhower, Supreme Allied Commander in Europe (1950–52). He commanded the attack carrier *Franklin D. Roosevelt* (CVA-42) (1952–53), followed by a tour as Special Assistant to the Chairman of the Joint Chiefs of Staff, Adm. A.W. Radford (1953–55), during which (August 1954) he was promoted to rear admiral. Admiral Anderson then held key posts in the three major theaters of the Cold War. In the Pacific, he commanded the patrol force off Formosa (1955-56) and served as chief of staff to the Cincpac Joint Staff (1956–57) during a period of tense relations with Communist China. Promoted to vice admiral (May 1957), he was chief of staff to the Pacific commander, Adm. F. B. Stump (1957–58). In the equally tense Middle East, Anderson temporarily (at his own request) reverted in rank to rear admiral in order to command Carrier Division Six (1958–59), flagship *Saratoga* (CVA-60), which supported the Marine Corps landings in Lebanon in July 1958. Again as vice admiral, he fleeted up to be Commander Sixth Fleet and Commander Naval Striking and Support Forces, Southern Europe (1959–61). Promoted to admiral and appointed CNO (August 1961), Admiral Anderson climaxed his career by successfully leading the Navy in the thermonuclear arena, especially during the Cuban missile confrontation with the Soviet Union in October 1962.

In this top office, Admiral Anderson labored under the handicap of the overzealous Secretary of Defense Robert S. McNamara who constantly interfered with Anderson's directing of the naval blockade of Cuba and who then, in 1963, forced the Navy, against its wishes, to purchase the controversial TFX (F-111) airplane. So vigorous were Anderson's protests against McNamara's policies that the Admiral was asked to resign his post, which he did by retiring from the Navy (August 1963) and accepting the ambassadorship to Portugal (1963–66). Anderson's stand was vindicated when the TFX failed utterly to meet the needs of the fleet and was subsequently dropped from the Navy's inventory, while McNamara's continuing overcentralized controls seriously jeopardized the military's efficiency and effectiveness in the Vietnam War until he was finally removed from office (1967). Regrettably, Admiral Anderson had been professionally martyred for upholding his high standards. He had left the Navy at the relatively young age of 56 years.

His second wife was the widow of Rear Adm. William D. Sample, commander of the *Hornet* (CV-12) and of an escort carrier division in the Pacific war before his loss on a plane flight over Japan in October 1945. The youngest of his two Naval officer sons, Lt. Cdr. Thomas Patrick Anderson, flew over 200 combat missions in Vietnam (1966–68) and perished when his plane crashed while operating off the *Forrestal* (CV-59) in the Med in June 1978.

6

Austin, Bernard Lige "Count"

(December 15, 1902——). USNA
(S.C.) 1924 (89/523).

One of the most distinguished destroyer commanders of World War II, Austin spent his early career in ordnance and submarines. Brief postgraduate gunnery instruction led to his initial two years (1924–26) at sea aboard the battleship *New York* (BB-34) in the Pacific. Training in subs at Newport's Naval Torpedo Station and aboard the sub training vessel *Chewink* (AM-39) at New London, he operated out of Pearl Harbor on two consecutive two-year tours aboard the subs *R-10* (SS-87) and the *R-6* (SS-83). Lieutenant Austin taught in electrical engineering and physics at the Naval Academy (1931–34) before returning to sea aboard the *R-11* (SS-88). He served as executive officer of the Presidential yacht *Potomac* (AG-25) during the second half of 1937 and remained in Washington as Press Relations Officer for the Navy from the end of that year until August 1940. Transferred to belligerent England as a special naval observer at the American Embassy, he stayed there until America's official entry into the war.

In February 1942, Commander Austin took command of the destroyer *Woolsey* (DD-437), which led in the sinking of the *U-173* during the North African landings the following November. The next month he brought the *Foote* (DD-511) into commission and escorted a convoy to Casablanca during the spring of 1943 before moving to the Pacific in May as Commander Destroyer Division 46, flagship *Spence* (DD-512). Early in November, following the bombardment of Bougainville, Austin's destroyers were heavily engaged in the Battle of Empress Augusta Bay off that island. Austin shifted to the *Converse* (DD-509) and with the *Spence* performed brilliantly against a Japanese force at the Battle of Cape St. George later in the month. In December, promoted to captain, he assumed command of

Destroyer Squadron 14 and Destroyer Division 27, flagship *Bailey* (DD-492), and participated in the Marshalls operation the next two months. Austin joined the Pacific Fleet Destroyer staff as assistant chief of staff for operations and training in mid-April 1944 but two months later shifted to Adm. C.W. Nimitz's Pacific Fleet staff as assistant chief of staff for administration. In December he was promoted to commodore but reverted to captain upon his relief in October 1945.

Washington-based in the postwar years, Captain Austin served successively as Navy Secretary of the State-War-Navy Coordinating Committee, student at the National War College, and Assistant to the Assistant Chief of Naval Operations for Politico-Military Affairs. Following special duty in England, he took command of Service Squadron One, flagships the repair ships *Hector* (AR-7) and *Jason* (ARH-1), in January 1950 and six months later began to organize Service Squadron Three, flagships the destroyer tender *Piedmont* (AD-17) and then the *Hector,* the squadron which he commanded during the Korean War. He also led the Logistic Support Force at the Inchon landings. Transferred to the Office of the Chief of Naval Operations in May 1951 as assistant director, International Affairs Division, Austin was shortly thereafter promoted to rear admiral and made the Division's director in February 1952. He commanded Cruiser Division Two, flagship *Roanoke* (CL-145), in the Mediterranean (1954–55); served on the staff of the Supreme Allied Commander in Europe; directed the Joint Staff Office of the Joint Chiefs of Staff (1956–58) in the rank of vice admiral; and commanded the Second Fleet and Strike Fleet Atlantic, flagships the aircraft carrier *Intrepid* (CVA-11) and the command ship *Northampton* (CLC-1).

After a tour as Deputy CNO (Plans and Policy) (1959–60), Admiral Austin served as president of the Naval War College during his final four years of regular duty. He retired as vice admiral in August 1964 but continued on active duty as chairman of the Inter-American Defense Board in Washington (1964–67), as temporary officer with the Bureau of Naval Personnel (1967), and as senior naval officer investigating the loss of the nuclear submarine *Scorpion* (SSN-589) (1968).

Badger, Charles Johnston

(August 6, 1853–September 7, 1932).
USNA (At Large) 1873 (8/29).

Strategist and administrator of the World War I period, Badger came in the middle of a distinguished Navy lineage, his father being Commo. Oscar C. Badger (1823–1899), Union fleet captain during the attacks on Charleston in 1863, and his son Adm. Oscar C. Badger *(q.v.)*. He cruised in the Pacific aboard the screw sloop *Narragansett* (1873–75), off the Eastern seaboard briefly with the torpedo boat *Alarm* (1876) and the steam sloop *Monongahela*, on which he went to the Asiatic Station. Brief Bureau of Navigation duty (1879–80) was followed by short stints with the Coast Survey (1880–81), the screw sloop *Yantic* (1881–82), the Boston Navy Yard (1882–84), and the Bureau of Fisheries steamer *Fish Hawk*. As executive officer of the iron gunboat *Alert*, Lieutenant (j.g.) Badger participated in the Greely relief expedition to the Arctic in 1884, then took ordnance instruction at Washington. He joined the screw sloop *Brooklyn* off South America and transferred with her to the Far East (1885–89), returning to ordnance work at the Washington Navy Yard as lieutenant (1889–92, 1895–97). A short Naval War College course (1897) followed sea duty aboard the protected cruiser *Chicago* (1892–93) and unarmored cruiser *Dolphin* (1893–95) in the North Atlantic. Before and during the Spanish-American War, he was navigator of the cruiser *Cincinnati* (C-7) which had blockade, bombardment and convoy duty in the West Indies.

Lieutenant Commander Badger in 1899 inspected construction of the battleships *Kearsarge* (BB-5) and *Alabama* (BB-8), the next year becoming exec of the latter ship upon her commissioning and early service in the North Atlantic. Promoted commander in 1902, he spent a year at the Bureau of Equipment, after which he was appointed commandant of midshipmen

9

(1903–05) and later Superintendent (1907–09) of the Naval Academy. He commanded the protected cruisers *Newark* (C-1), training vessel at Annapolis (1905), and *Chicago,* flagship of the Pacific Squadron (1905–06), on the latter vessel being present during the great San Francisco earthquake of 1906 and directing all emergency naval parties ashore. Promoted captain in July 1907 and rear admiral four years later, Badger was briefly at the Bureau of Navigation (1907) and went on to command the *Kansas* (BB-21) (1909–11) in the Atlantic Fleet and that Fleet's second battleship division, flagship *Louisiana* (BB-19), for a cruise to European ports. Briefly Aid for Inspection (1911–12), he became commander-in-chief of the Atlantic Fleet, flagships *Wyoming* (BB-32) and *Connecticut* (BB-18), late in 1912 and carried out the naval demonstrations and landings at Vera Cruz during the Mexican crisis of 1914.

Admiral Badger in September 1914 joined the General Board of the Navy and quickly became a major force as chairman of its executive committee, establishing naval policy by advising the Secretary of the Navy with preparedness expansion programs and war contingency plans, especially involving antisubmarine measures. He also served concurrently on the Army-Navy Joint Board and had miscellaneous Navy board duties. Although he reached the mandatory retirement age of 62 in 1915, Badger was kept on active duty by a special act of Congress. With the passing of Adm. George Dewey as General Board president, no successor was appointed, leaving Badger as senior member during and after America's participation in World War I. In addition, in 1919 he became senior member of a board on naval aviation policy. He was finally relieved of all his duties at his own request in March 1921.

Badger, Oscar Charles

(June 26, 1890–November 30, 1958).
USNA (At Large) 1911 (29/193).

Office of the Chief of Naval Operations: National Archives

Prominent World War II-era battleship admiral, this son of the above began his naval career briefly in the battleship *Minnesota* (BB-22) in the Atlantic Fleet and the *Utah* (BB-31), from which ship in April 1914 he led a small landing party into Vera Cruz. Soon afterward he transferred to the new destroyer *Parker* (DD-48), and then the *Maine* (BB-10), both in the Atlantic. As lieutenant, he was in the commissioning crew of the *Arizona* (BB-39) from September 1916 to December 1917, when he reported to the *Allen* (DD-66) for antisubmarine operations out of Queenstown, Ireland. Lieutenant Commander Badger then commanded several vessels in quick succession: the *Porter* (DD-59) from January to June 1918, during which she severely damaged the *U-108;* the patrol boat *Sultana* (SP-134) at Brest in June and July; and from August to October the *Worden* (DD-16), as well as a task group of three American and three French destroyers.

After inspecting naval ordnance at Philadelphia (1919–21), Badger commanded the *Pruitt* (DD-347) for several months before reporting as gunnery officer first to Commander Destroyer Squadron 15, then to Commander-in-Chief Asiatic Fleet, Adm. Edwin A. Anderson, flagship the armored cruiser *Huron* (ACR-9). During the latter assignment he was also aide and Fleet personnel officer, and he directed that Fleet's relief efforts for earthquake-stricken Yokohama in 1923. Earning a reputation as an innovator in ordnance, Badger developed anti-aircraft systems at the Bureau of Ordnance's Fire Control Section (1923–25) with the result that he became chief of the Section (1928–31). He returned to the Far East as first lieutenant and gunnery officer of the *Maryland* (BB-46) (1925–28) and took command of the *Southard* (DD-207) from which he directed destroyers, submarines

11

and minelayers in successful antisubmarine detection measures and tactics (1931–32). Commander Badger was executive officer of the destroyer tender *Melville* (AD-2) in the Pacific, was on the staff at the Naval Academy (1933–36), and was exec of the heavy cruiser *Indianapolis* (CA-35) for two years. His last prewar tours were as student at the Naval War College (1938–39), secretary of the General Board (1939–40), and chief of staff to Adm. E. J. King, Commander Patrol Force, U.S. Fleet and Commander-in-Chief Atlantic Fleet, flagships *Texas* (BB-35) and *Augusta* (CA-31).

Captain Badger took command of the *North Carolina* (BB-55) in October 1941, aboard which he successfully experimented with increased anti-aircraft defenses. Although selected for rear admiral in April 1942, he took his ship to the South Pacific for the Guadalcanal operation and participated in the Battle of the Eastern Solomons in August. The next month he assumed flag rank as Commander Destroyers Atlantic Fleet but in December moved again, this time into the new key logistics post at the Navy Department: Assistant Chief of Naval Operations for Logistics Plans, also Director of Logistics Plans Division of the Joint Chiefs of Staff and Senior Logistics Adviser to the Combined Chiefs of Staff at the Quebec and Cairo conferences. Admiral Badger returned to the South Pacific in February 1944 as Commander Service Squadrons, in which post he remained until September supporting advanced American bases. The next month he became Commander Battleship Division 7, flagship *Iowa* (BB-61), participating in the Battle for Leyte Gulf and covering the fast carriers in the Philippines operations. Shifting his flag to the *Indiana* (BB-58), he directed a prelanding bombardment of Iwo Jima while with the carriers in January 1945 and served in the latter part of the Okinawa campaign aboard the *Iowa,* from which he commanded five battlewagons in a shelling of the Japanese coast during July. Shifting to the *San Diego* (CL-53), he directed the occupation of Yokosuka late in August.

In the postwar period Admiral Badger served briefly as Commander Battleship Squadron Two and ComBatDiv One, before his appointment in December 1945 as Commander Service Forces Pacific Fleet in the rank of vice admiral; as such he helped to demobilize the wartime Fleet and bases and assist in the atomic bomb tests at Bikini atoll. In April 1947 he became Commander Eleventh Naval District (as rear admiral) and the following February (as vice admiral) hoisted his flag aboard amphibious command ship *Eldorado* (AGC-11) at Tsingtao, China, as Commander Naval Forces Western Pacific (later Seventh Task Fleet) in the final stages of the Chinese Civil War. His resultant expertise on the Far Eastern crisis led to his recall to Washington as an adviser late in 1949. In May 1950 Admiral Badger took command of the Eastern Sea Frontier and Atlantic Reserve Fleet at New York City and the following May assumed additional duty as Naval Representative of the JCS to the United Nations Security Council. A fourth "hat" which he later received was that of NATO commander in the American Defense Area. He retired in July 1952 in the rank of admiral.

Bainbridge, William

(May 7, 1774–July 27, 1833).

Member of a distinguished New Jersey family, physically rugged and having an adventurous disposition, this giant of the early Navy received a sound education prior to fulfilling his youthful desires for a career at sea by joining a Philadelphia merchantman under the tutelage of its captain. Bainbridge was fifteen years old, and within three years he rose to officer's rank and chief mate, in which capacity he boldly rescued his ship from a band of mutineers. Rewarded with his own command at the age of nineteen, he traded in Europe as a neutral during the wars of the French Revolution. In 1796, commanding the *Hope* of four guns and less than a dozen men, Bainbridge was attacked by a British schooner twice his strength while en route from Bordeaux to St. Thomas but by a vigorous counterattack forced his assailant to strike its colors. On the homeward voyage, the British man-of-war *Indefatigable* forced the *Hope* to give up an alleged British deserter from its crew, the protesting Bainbridge promising retribution which he made good by seizing a British seaman from a British merchantman several days later.

Upon the creation of the Navy in 1798, Bainbridge received the commission of lieutenant commandant in August and command of the schooner *Retaliation* for convoy escort duty and commerce raiding in the West Indies against France during the quasi-war. As part of a three-vessel squadron, the *Retaliation* one day in September found herself alone and hopelessly outgunned, thus surrendering to the French frigates *L'Insurgente* and *Volontier*. Bainbridge, taken on board the latter, convinced the French to avoid closing with his consorts which now approached, the 20-gun

13

Montezuma and 18-gun brig *Norfolk,* on the pretext of their having much stronger armaments. Transferred to Guadaloupe as prisoner, Bainbridge used guile and false promises to convince the local French governor to release him and several other American captives. Promoted to master commandant and given command of the *Norfolk* in March 1799, he returned to the West Indies where he had notable successes escorting American convoys and capturing, destroying and blockading French vessels over the ensuing year. Upon the termination of hostilities, in May 1800 Bainbridge was promoted to captain in command of the 32-gun converted merchantman *George Washington.*

American commercial humiliation at the hands of the piratic Barbary states next consumed Captain Bainbridge's attention. Upon delivering the American tribute to the Dey of Algiers, Bainbridge was further humiliated by being forced to carry presents to the Sultan of Turkey at Constantinople. Nevertheless, he impressed the Turkish leaders sufficiently to obtain their protection of him from further Algerian demands, and upon his return to Algiers he even managed to secure the release of several enslaved French citizens, for which he was thanked by Napoleon. Taking command of the frigate *Essex* in May 1801, Bainbridge performed convoy escort and blockade services against hostile Tripoli until ordered home for refit during the summer of 1802. After construction duty ashore, he assumed command of the frigate *Philadelphia* in May 1803 and from August operated out of Gibraltar in taking a number of Barbary vessels until his ship ran aground on an uncharted reef in the harbor of Tripoli in October and he was taken prisoner. Communicating to Commo. Edward Preble, the squadron commander, his hope that his vessel should be destroyed before her conversion into an enemy cruiser, Bainbridge took satisfaction when Lt. Stephen Decatur, Jr., accomplished the daring feat early in 1804. Bainbridge played a key role in the subsequent peace settlement between the U.S. and Tripoli, was exonerated of blame in the loss of the *Philadelphia,* and for a time commanded the navy yard at New York.

Obtaining a furlough in order to recoup financial losses incurred during his confinement, Bainbridge reentered the merchant service (1805–08), during which he was saved from drowning by his black servant (he could not swim!). Recalled to active duty in March 1808, he commanded the frigate *President* and as commodore patrolled the southern coast of the U.S. before again engaging in merchant activities (1810–11). Hastening home from the Baltic on the eve of the War of 1812, he joined Commo. Charles Stewart in convincing Congress not to lay up the vulnerable Navy, then returned to duty as commandant of the navy yard at Boston (Charlestown). As captain of the frigate *Constitution* and commodore of a three-vessel squadron, late in 1812 Bainbridge sailed to the South Atlantic where in December in a furious battle the *Constitution* destroyed the British frigate *Java.* Twice wounded in the action, Commodore Bainbridge returned to Boston in February 1813 where he resumed command of the navy yard. With Boston blockaded and besieged by the British fleet, he exhibited great patriotic resolution in overcoming criticism of disgruntled Massachusetts merchants over his defense of the port in the national interest. He superintended construction of the 74-gun line-of-battle ship *Independence,* launched in June 1814, which became his flagship for the defense of Boston harbor.

An early advocate of a professional board of naval commissioners, established in 1815, Commodore Bainbridge in the summer of that year relieved the new Mediterranean Squadron with a second eight-ship squadron of his own to impress the recently-humbled Barbary states. His flag aboard the *Independence,* in November he returned to Boston where for the next three years aboard the same flagship he chafed at inaction and engaged in peacetime quarrels with Commodores Isaac Hull and Decatur, to whom however he acted as second in Decatur's fatal duel with Commo. James Barron (1820). Having been given command in November 1819 of the Mediterranean Squadron, Bainbridge sailed the following spring aboard the new 74 *Columbus,* serving in this capacity until mid-1821. In the face of rapidly deteriorating health, he served as President of the Board of Navy Commissioners (1824–27) and as commander of the navy yards at Philadelphia (1821–23, 1827–31) and Boston's Charlestown (1823–24, 1832–33).

Barbey, Daniel Edward

(December 23, 1889–April 11, 1969).
USNA (Ore.) 1912 (113/156).

Office of the Chief of Naval Operations: National Archives

Destined for wartime prominence as "Uncle Dan the Amphibious Man," Barbey began his naval career conventionally as a surface line officer during the Nicaraguan political disturbances of 1912 aboard the armored cruiser *California* and then during the Mexican crisis of 1914 as engineering officer of the destroyer *Lawrence* (DD-8), which he also commanded while she was in reserved status (1915–16). As engineering officer of the gunboat *Annapolis* (PG-10) he cruised off Central America and Mexico (1916–17) before becoming wartime executive officer of the destroyer *Stevens* (1918). Reporting to Cardiff, Wales, in January 1919, Lieutenant Barbey became Naval Port Officer there in July, transferring the next month to U.S. Naval Headquarters in London. In November he became Naval Port Officer at Constantinople, advancing in October 1920 to the posts of operations officer and flag secretary to Adm. M. L. Bristol, U.S. High Commissioner to Turkey, during which duty he was an American delegate to the Allied commission for control of trade with Turkey and an observer with the White Russian armies in the Crimea amidst the Russian Civil War.

After serving briefly aboard the cargo ship *Capella* (AK-13) (1922), Barbey operated in the Pacific as assistant engineering officer of the battleship *Oklahoma* (BB-37) prior to recruiting duty in Portland, Oregon (1923–25). Transferring to the Atlantic, he was engineering officer of the cruiser *Cincinnati* (CL-6) before joining the oil tanker *Ramapo* (AO-12) as executive officer (1927–28), a vessel which he later briefly commanded (1936). A lengthy tour followed as flag secretary to Adm. Samuel S. Robison, Superintendent of the Naval Academy (1928–31). Barbey commanded the destroyer *Lea* (DD-118), inspected ordnance at Mare Island (1933–35) and served as damage control officer of the battleship *New York* (BB-34) in the rank of commander. He commanded Destroyer Division 17 in the *Goff* (DD-247) in the Pacific (1936–37) before joining the War Plans Section of the Bureau of Navigation, during which tour he was promoted to captain and began to develop an interest in amphibious warfare from studying Japanese operations in China. He then commanded the *New York* in the Pacific (1940).

Captain Barbey, reporting in January 1941 as chief of staff to Adm. Randall Jacobs, Atlantic Fleet Service Force commander (which included the Fleet's amphibious forces), was ordered by Jacobs to organize a new amphibious force. He initiated landing maneuvers in primitive craft along the North Carolina coast during the summer and became such a pioneer in this neglected aspect of modern naval operations that he was made head of the Navy Department's Amphibious Warfare Section in May 1942. Starting virtually with nothing, he led in the development and tactical uses of the specialized landing craft, notably the Dukw, which would revolutionize naval warfare throughout World War II. Promoted to rear admiral at the end of 1942, in January 1943 Barbey reported to Australia as Commander Seventh Amphibious Force, Southwest Pacific. For several months, he had no equipment and only inexperienced personnel, but matters began to improve slowly from April 1943.

Admiral Barbey led his command as part of "MacArthur's Navy," the Seventh Fleet, throughout the Pacific counteroffensive, which began at Woodlark and Kiriwina islands off the southeast New Guinea coast in June 1943. In September his Force landed on the New Guinea coast at Lae and Finschhafen and in the spring of 1944 assaulted the north and northwest coasts, most dramatically around Hollandia. Gen. Douglas MacArthur was a demanding and polemical commander, but Barbey's affability enabled him to work effectively with his controversial chief. Following a brief visit to Washington to advise the Normandy amphibious leaders, he returned to his command for successful landings at Morotai in the Halmaheras in September 1944 and those of the Northern Attack Force at Leyte in October aboard his flagship, the amphibious command ship *Blue Ridge* (AGC-2). Promoted to vice admiral, he directed the San Fabian part of the Lingayen Gulf assault in January 1945 and subsequent operations around Luzon and in the southern Philippines and Borneo through the summer, being overall commander at Balikpapen.

In November 1945 Admiral Barbey became Commander Seventh Fleet and directed the ticklish tasks of landing American occupation troops in Korea and North China, transporting Nationalist Chinese forces into the North, training them in amphibious operations, and keeping his own units from becoming involved in the Chinese Civil War. In March 1946 he took command of the Atlantic Fleet's Amphibious Forces and in September the Fourth Fleet, returning to the Far East early in 1947 on a strategic fact-finding mission. Barbey's final active duties were as Commandant Tenth Naval District and Commander Caribbean Sea Frontier (1947–50) and Commandant Thirteenth Naval District (1950–51). He retired as vice admiral in June 1951 and published his wartime memoirs as *MacArthur's Amphibious Navy* (1969).

Barney, Joshua

(July 6, 1759—December 1, 1818).

By Rembrandt Peale: The Peale Museum, Baltimore

Longing for a career at sea since boyhood, Barney served briefly with a pilot in his native Baltimore (1771) before apprenticing to his brother-in-law aboard the merchant brig *Sidney* (1772–75), a vessel which after the sudden death of its captain he successfully commanded throughout 1775 in adventures which included transporting Spanish troops to and from North Africa. In October he became sailing master of the Continental sloop *Hornet* of Commo. Esek Hopkins' squadron but which fell out of that fleet's first expedition due to a collision with its tender. Transferring to the eight-gun sloop *Wasp,* during the spring of 1776 he engaged the 44-gun British frigate *Roebuck* and led the *Wasp*'s boat in John Barry's expedition against the *Nancy* in Delaware Bay. Commissioned lieutenant in the Continental Navy in June 1776, Barney three months later completed fitting out the sloop *Sachem,* of which he became second-in-command, and then engaged, captured, and became prize skipper of the British privateer brig *Three Friends,* taking it to Philadelphia. He embarked in October as lieutenant of the 14-gun brig *Andrea Doria* to the West Indies, overpowering the 12-gun sloop *Racehorse* in a furious battle and then the armed snow *Thomas,* of which he was prize master until captured in early January 1777 by the 20-gun 6th rate *Perseus.* Inactive ashore on parole, he was exchanged in October and made second lieutenant of the frigate *Virginia,* during which duty the following February he led the pilot schooner *Dolphin* in recapturing the sloop *Peggy* in the Chesapeake. In April 1778, however, the *Virginia* ran aground, the captain deserted her, and Barney was obliged to surrender the vessel, remaining captive until exchanged in August.

Barney took command of the privateer brig *General Mercer* in November 1778, sailing early in the new year to bludgeon the privateer brig *Rosebud* in battle and then capture the privateer *Minerva,* which he took to Philadelphia as a prize. Inactive ashore due to the British blockade, Barney did not have sea duty again until April 1780 when he became first lieutenant of the sloop *Saratoga,* which in September and October captured three vessels, the last being the privateer *Charming Molly.* As her prize master, Barney three days later struck his colors when confronted by the British 64 *Intrepid.* This third captivity by the British was his harshest, being spent for nearly a year in Old Mill Prison near Plymouth, England, before he escaped to France with the help of American sympathizers. Returning home late in 1781, he was soon made captain in the Pennsylvania state navy and given command of its 16-gun converted merchantman *Hyder Ally* to convoy merchant vessels in Delaware Bay. During this duty in April 1782 Barney successfully covered his convoy by brilliantly defeating and taking the stronger 32-gun frigate *General Monk,* originally an American privateer but now placed in Pennsylvania service as the *General Washington,* and with Barney as her captain. Operating for several months in the West Indies on convoy duty with the French and Spanish and in Delaware Bay capturing Tory sloops, the vessel entered Continental service in August as a transatlantic packet. She made three voyages to France (1782–84), Barney being the last ship's captain to be retired from the wartime Navy.

Barney engaged in several business enterprises in Baltimore, on the frontier and in the West Indies before being selected to command one of the nation's six new frigates in 1794. Offended by being placed on the list junior to Silas Talbot, he rejected this opportunity and instead accepted a captain's commission in the French navy *(Captaine de Vaisseau),* serving briefly in Holland during 1795 before resigning this commission to protest his junior status. Over the winter he purchased and sent to sea three French privateers which in due course brought him handsome profits. In March 1796 Barney was again commissioned into the French navy, this time as a senior captain and commodore *(Chef de Division des Armées Navales),* his flag in the new frigate *La Harmonie.* Basing at Santo Domingo (1796–98), he fought several actions, capturing enemy vessels and convoying friendly ones, was blockaded for some months in Chesapeake Bay, and suffered a broken thigh during a storm. Thereafter inactive, he was retired from French service on the first day of 1802 and returned to the United States.

In addition to subsequent commercial activities, Commodore Barney rejected an offer to command the Washington Navy Yard (1805) and twice ran unsuccessfully for Congress (1806, 1810) before the advent of the War of 1812. Commanding the armed schooner *Rossie,* he took several prizes during the summer and autumn of 1812. In July 1813 he presented a plan for the defense of Washington to the government, leading the next month to his commission as acting master commandant and appointment to command a flotilla of barges or row galleys then under construction to protect the seaward approaches to the capitol. Putting to sea in April 1814, this force of ten barges, one cutter and a gunboat successfully countered British thrusts until a landing in force in August. Ordered to fight on shore, Barney with some 450 men and five ships' guns mounted on carriages joined the militia for the defense of Washington. Barney personally directed the artillery at the battle of Bladensburg until the American position was overrun and the commodore wounded in the thigh and taken prisoner. Immediately paroled, in October he was promoted to captain in the U.S. Navy (not received until the following February) and returned to his flotilla command. His last services were carrying dispatches to the peace commissioners in Paris (1815) and as "Naval Officer of the Port of Baltimore" (1817–18).

Barron, James

(1769—April 21, 1851).

Chrysler Museum at Norfolk

Member of a distinguished Virginia seafaring family, Barron served as a midshipman to his father, Commo. James Barron (1730–1787) of the Virginia state navy during the latter part of the American Revolution, a war in which his uncles Richard and William were naval officers and his brother Samuel (1765–1810) also a Virginia naval midshipman. Like the latter, he was commissioned a lieutenant in the U.S. Navy in March 1798 and through conspicuous performance aboard the frigate *United States* in the quasi-war with France was advanced to captain fourteen months later. First commanding the armed ship *Warren* in the West Indies, Captain Barron commanded two flagships of the Mediterranean Squadron, the frigate *President* (1801–02) and the frigate *New York* (1802–03) in the Barbary wars. After commanding the inactive frigate *Chesapeake* (1803–04), he returned to the

20

Mediterranean as captain of first the frigate *Essex* (1804–05) and then the *President* (1805–06) operating against the Barbary states in the squadron of his brother, now a commodore.

Barron returned home shortly after his brother relinquished his command due to ill health, was appointed commodore at Norfolk in 1806, and hoisted his broad pennant aboard the refurbished *Chesapeake,* Capt. Charles Gordon, with orders to return to the Mediterranean as squadron commander. Perhaps not suited to combat command, Commodore Barron feuded with Commo. John Rodgers, was plagued by ship's officers loyal to Rodgers, and found his flagship ill-equipped and poorly manned upon leaving Norfolk for the Mediterranean in June 1807. Offshore, the vessel was intercepted by the British frigate *Leopard* which demanded the surrender of four suspected British deserters on the *Chesapeake.* Upon Barron's refusal, the *Leopard* poured several devastating broadsides into the *Chesapeake,* which was so unprepared to fight that only one token gun could be fired before the colors were stricken. The alleged deserters were taken off, and the hapless *Chesapeake* limped back to Hampton Roads, Barron suffering from several wounds. This incident, which worsened Anglo-American relations, ruined Barron's naval career. Arrested in December, he faced a court-martial trial presided over by Rodgers which found him negligent in preparing for battle and suspended him from active duty for five years without pay. Disgraced by the *Chesapeake* affair, Barron became a merchant captain in the West Indies and in Denmark, exiling himself there (1811–18) during which time however he busied himself with several mechanical inventions.

Upon returning to the United States, Commodore Barron found his application for reinstatement thwarted by his former peers, one of whom, Commo. Stephen Decatur, goaded him into a duel; in March 1820, seconded by Commo. J. D. Elliott, Barron killed Decatur in the exchange, while receiving a severe wound himself. Finally restored to duty, he held only shore commands, the navy yards at Gosport (1825–31) and Philadelphia (1824–25, 1831–37), over which period however he presided at the court-martial of Commo. David Porter (1825) and made several nautical inventions, including a drydock, windlass, metal blocks and pulleys, a ship's ventilator, a bomb vessel and a galley, though none of these were officially adopted by the conservative Navy already prejudiced against him. Commodore Barron also advocated steam and a steam-driven ram (1833–44) and became senior officer of the Navy in 1839, but aside from his brief governorship of the Philadelphia Naval Asylum (1842), he was kept in the ignominious status of "waiting orders" from 1838 until the end of his life. His nephew was Flag Off. Samuel Barron of the Confederate Navy *(q.v.).*

Barron, Samuel

(November 28, 1808—February 26, 1888).

Appointed midshipman in April 1812, to date from January 1, Barron was the youngest boy ever to enter the U.S. Navy, the reason being his family ties: his father was Commo. Samuel Barron (1765–1810), and his uncle, who adopted him upon his father's untimely death from ill health, was Commo. James Barron *(q.v.)*. Following shore duty at Norfolk Navy Yard (1816–20), young Barron joined the new 74 *Columbus* on her maiden voyage to the Mediterranean (1820–21), returned to Norfolk, deployed to the West Indies on anti-pirate duty in the frigate *John Adams* (1822–23), and returned to Norfolk followed by extended leave. Assigned to the frigate *Brandywine,* he was with her when she transported the Marquis de Lafayette to France prior to joining the Mediterranean Squadron (1825–26). Lieutenant Barron served for three years in the sloop of war *Lexington* (1826–29), returning home in the *Delaware,* 74.

Barron patrolled the coast of Mexico as captain of the sloop of war *Fairfield* (1831–32), flagship of the West Indies Squadron, Commo. J. D. Elliott, his uncle's second in the duel with Stephen Decatur. The next several tours alternated between Norfolk in his home state of Virginia (1836–37, 1840, 1844, 1849 on the receiving ship *Pennsylvania,* and 1854–57) and in the West Indies and South Atlantic on anti-pirate and anti-slaving patrols in the schooner *Enterprise* (1834), the sloop *Ontario* (1837–38), the West Indies flagships frigate *Constellation* (1840) and *Delaware* (1841–43), and the brig *Perry* (1847–48), which he commanded. Commander Barron saw ordnance duty ashore (1844–47, 1850) prior to commanding the *John Adams* off the African coast, engaged in protecting black Liberian settlers against raiding natives (1851–53). Promoted to captain in September 1855, Barron served on the Lighthouse Board (1857–58) before taking command of the screw frigate *Wabash*, flagship of the Mediterranean Squadron which protected American citizens against outrages in Syria (1858–59). Following extended leave, he rejoined the Lighthouse Board in February 1861.

Upon Virginia's secession from the Union in April 1861, Captain Barron resigned his commission in favor of a captaincy in the Virginia Navy (May) and then the Confederate Navy (June). Briefly serving as Chief of the Bureau of Orders and Detail, he took command of the naval defenses of Virginia and North Carolina, personally commanding Fort Hatteras, North Carolina, during its fall to Union attack in August 1861. Paroled soon afterward but not exchanged until the following summer, he returned to his command. In October 1862 Barron was appointed to build steam gunboats on the Tennessee and Cumberland rivers but was frustrated by Confederate reverses in that quarter. The next month he returned to Richmond in command of Confederate naval forces in Virginia waters. In August 1863 he was sent abroad as Flag Officer of all Confederate naval forces in Europe, charged with outfitting warships. After the Laird rams then building were seized by the British government, Flag Officer Barron concentrated his efforts on the raiders *Georgia* and *Stonewall.* Resigning his command in February 1865, he returned to Virginia to become a farmer. His son Lieutenant Samuel Barron, Jr. (1835–1891) served abroad with him and in the Confederate cruisers *Florida* and *Shenandoah.*

Barry, John

(1745—September 13, 1803).

Navy Department: National Archives

A native of Ireland who immigrated to Philadelphia a dozen or so years later, Barry commanded several merchantmen, the last being the Philadelphia ship *Black Prince* (1774–75), purchased for the Continental Navy, armed and renamed the *Alfred* in November 1775, its rerigging supervised by Barry as former master. Appointed captain in the Navy, Barry brought the brig *Lexington* into Continental service. In April 1776 the *Lexington* ran the British blockade of the Delaware River, engaged and captured the British tender *Edward* on the 7th and returned with her as a prize to Philadelphia, the first capture in battle by a Continental Navy vessel. Over the ensuing month, the *Lexington* escaped pursuing superior British naval units off Charleston and the Delaware Capes, engaging them during the latter operations. Again blockaded in Delaware Bay, Barry in June sent his boats along with those of other American warships to unload powder from the stranded Pennsylvania brig *Nancy,* which he then exploded by a delayed-action fuse, killing several enemy boarders. Again eluding the British, Barry in July took the Tory privateer *Lady Susan* and two months later the sloop *Betsy.* These activities entitled Barry to bear the title of commodore.

Placed seventh on the Navy's initial list of captains in October 1776, Barry assumed command of the uncompleted frigate *Effingham* at Philadelphia but then led his crew ashore as an infantry company, crossing the Delaware with General Washington and participating in the battles of Trenton and Princeton in December and January. Forced up the Delaware with the *Effingham* to avoid its capture during the British occupation of Philadelphia,

Barry reluctantly scuttled his vessel in November 1777. The following February he brazenly led four boats to capture three enemy vessels and destroy forage destined for the British army, an exploit dampened by his censure by Congress for mistreating one of its Naval committeemen. Barry did not assume another command until the frigate *Raleigh* during the summer of 1778, losing it, however, in September when forced to run aground in Penobscot Bay, Maine, by a British force, although he and his crew escaped overland. In November Barry was appointed to command a force of galleys to take St. Augustine in Florida, but the enterprise died for lack of vessels. In February 1779 he became captain of the Pennsylvania state brigantine *Delaware* and commodore of a five-vessel squadron operating in the West Indies, capturing the British sloop *Harlem* late in the year. He then engaged in privateering.

A close naval adviser of Secretary of War Henry Knox, Commodore Barry was given command of one of the Navy's five remaining ships, the Continental frigate *Alliance* at Boston in September 1780. Sailing in February for France, the *Alliance* took the brig *Alert* and on the return voyage several weeks later, during which Barry suppressed a mutiny, the vessel engaged and captured the brig *Mars,* two more brigs, and a snow. This cruise culminated in May when the *Alliance* hotly engaged and captured the sloops of war *Atalanta* and *Trepassey,* during which action Barry was wounded in the shoulder. The *Alliance* carried the Marquis de Lafayette to France early in 1782, the first of two such transatlantic voyages that year, the vessel taking nine rich prizes on the latter trip in August and September. Barry concluded his Revolutionary War service in the West Indies in an inconclusive gunnery duel between the *Alliance* and the frigate *Sybil* in March 1783, the last battle of the Continental Navy; the ship sailed thereafter to Newport, Rhode Island, carrying specie for Congress. The vessel finished its service carrying a cargo of tobacco to Holland, after which Barry returned to merchant service.

With the authorization of the six new frigates in 1794, Commodore Barry became senior captain and commander of one of them, the *United States,* which with Decatur's *Delaware* he took to the West Indies in 1798 for operations against the French. Initially returning to port for fear of hurricanes after one capture, Barry was ordered out again, only to indeed suffer heavy damage in an autumn storm. He assumed command of all American naval forces in the West Indies, taking one privateer and engaging French shore batteries at Guadaloupe in a mediocre cruise which ended in May 1799. Barry operated in the *United States* off the East coast during the summer and transported American diplomats to France in the autumn, returning again to command the Guadaloupe station (1800–01). Failing health hampered his ordnance and other duties during 1802 and prevented him from assuming command of the Mediterranean Squadron to fight Tripoli early in 1803. At the time of his death, Commodore Barry was senior officer of the U.S. Navy.

Belknap, George Eugene

(January 22, 1832—April 7, 1903).
USNA 1853/54 (N.H.)

Several weeks after his arrival at the Academy in 1847, future inventor Midshipman Belknap was assigned to the brig *Porpoise* for Mexican War duty engaged on anti-slaving patrols off the west coast of Africa (1847–50). After service (1850–53) aboard the frigate *Raritan* in Chilean waters during which (1851) he participated in a landing party to protect American citizens during a revolution, he returned to the Academy to complete his studies. He joined the Coast Survey vessel *Corwin* upon graduation (1854), transferring to the sloop *Falmouth* (1854–55) as acting master, after which he was promoted to lieutenant. He distinguished himself aboard the sloop *Portsmouth* (1856–58) while commanding a launch in the attack on the Canton, China, barrier forts in November 1856. He reported to the sloop *St. Louis* at Pensacola in 1859, operating with the Home Squadron, and in April 1861 commanded the ship's boats which reinforced Fort Pickens, Florida. Detached in October, Lieutenant Belknap the next month boarded the fitting-out screw steamer *Huron* and blockaded the coasts of South Carolina and Georgia from February to June 1862, when he brought home a prize and was promoted to lieutenant commander. He served as executive officer of the ironclad steamer *New Ironsides* (1862–64) in the same waters and participated in the intense bombardment of Charleston during April 1863. Shifting to the North Atlantic Blockading Squadron he commanded first the gunboat *Seneca* then the single turret monitor *Canonicus,* leading the latter in both attacks on Fort Fisher, North Carolina, December 1864 and January 1865; in the latter action the *Canonicus* took several hits but without serious effect. The vessel participated in the final operations against Charleston and in the search for the raider *Stonewall.*

26

An able diplomat and scientific investigator as well as ship handler, Belknap cruised with the Naval Academy practice squadron before assignment to the screw sloop *Shenandoah* late in 1865 for Brazil patrol and transit to the Far East, where in 1867 he took command of the screw sloop *Hartford,* flagship of the Asiatic Squadron, and directed operations against Formosa until detached in August 1868. At the Naval Academy until October and the New York naval rendezvous (1868–69), he had navigation duty at the Boston Navy Yard (1869–72) and command of the steam sloop *Tuscarora* (1872–74) during which he engaged in submarine cable surveys in the North Pacific; he invented a specimen-collecting cylinder for ocean research and was the first to utilize piano wire for taking soundings, from which he made a number of discoveries about the ocean floor. He was a founder of the U.S. Naval Institute (1873) and wrote prolifically in *The United Service.* Promoted to captain in January 1875, he commanded the receiving ship *Ohio* at Boston (1874–75), the navy yards at Pensacola (1876–80) and Norfolk (1883–85) and the Pacific Squadron screw gunboat *Alaska* (1881–83). Following important diplomatic work in Chile in 1881, Belknap— promoted to commodore in June 1885—served as superintendent of the Naval Observatory (1885–86), commandant of the Mare Island Navy Yard (1886–89) and as commander-in-chief of the Asiatic Station (1889–92), whose flagships were the screw sloops *Omaha* and *Marion.* Named rear admiral in February 1889, he finished his active service as president, Board of Inspection and Survey (1893–94). Though he retired early in 1894, Admiral Belknap continued naval activities as a director of the Massachusetts Nautical Training School, chairman of a coaling station board during the Spanish-American War, and as adviser to the Navy on several matters up to the time of his death while on temporary duty at Key West.

Bell, Henry Haywood

(April 13, 1808–January 11, 1868).

U. S. Signal Corps: National Archives

Civil War leader Bell joined the Navy as midshipman from his native North Carolina in August 1823 and later married a Virginia woman. He served in the sloop *Erie* in the Mediterranean (1823–26) and the Caribbean (1827), transferring there to the schooner *Grampus* for anti-pirate work (1828–29). After tours of duty during the 1830's and early 1840's during which he served aboard the sloop *Vincennes* as acting sailing master, the frigates *Constellation* and *United States,* as well as aboard the sloop *Marion* and the Hunter-wheel steam sloop *Union,* Lieutenant Bell commanded the latter vessel (1843–45). He returned to serve in the *United States* in the Mediterranean, then commanded the brig *Boxer* in African waters. Detached in May 1848, he served at the navy yards of Philadelphia, Norfolk, and New York prior to his promotion to commander in 1854 and command of the screw sloop *San Jacinto,* flagship of the East India Squadron (1855–58). In that capacity, Bell personally led part of the initial assault which took the first of the barrier forts near Canton, China, in November 1856. He then served ashore at Annapolis and in New York State until the outbreak of the Civil War.

Commander Bell chose to remain loyal to the Union and became Assistant Inspector of Ordnance in June 1861 before going to sea as fleet captain of the West Gulf Blockading Squadron the following January. In this capacity he was Flag Officer D. G. Farragut's chief of staff during the attack on New Orleans in April and May 1862, in which he commanded one of the three divisions of vessels which reduced Forts Jackson and St. Philip. He then personally raised the Stars and Stripes over that city. Promoted commodore in August, he remained with the West Gulf Squadron,

28

commanding it from August 1863 on the screw steamer *Pensacola* until he was relieved in February 1864. As Inspector of Ordnance at the New York Yard during the spring and summer of 1864, Commodore Bell took command of the Asiatic Squadron in July 1865, in which capacity he campaigned against Chinese pirates in the flagship screw sloop *Hartford*. He was promoted to rear admiral in July 1866 and placed on the retired list the following April. Remaining on duty until his relief could arrive, Admiral Bell drowned when his barge capsized as he was about to pay a courtesy call on the American minister at Osaka, Japan.

Benson, William Shepherd

(September 25, 1855–May 20, 1932).
USNA (Ga.) 1877 (36/45).

The future first Chief of Naval Operations completed his Academy requirements aboard the flagship of the South Atlantic Squadron, the screw sloop *Hartford* (1877–79), and received his ensign's commission following duty on the last training cruises of the old frigate *Constitution* in the Atlantic (1879–81). Benson operated with the North Atlantic Squadron aboard the screw gunboats *Alliance* (1881–82) and *Yantic* (1882–84), participating in the abortive relief party to recover the Greely polar expedition during the summer of 1883. He then had varied duty with the Advisory Board (1884–85), the Hydrographic branch office at Baltimore (1885–86) and the Fish Commission steamer *Albatross* (1886–87). Lieutenant (j.g.) Benson circumnavigated the globe while aboard the unarmored cruiser *Dolphin* (1888–90), taught ordnance at the Washington Navy Yard (1893–94) and had several tours on the faculty at the Naval Academy, including the summer training cruises (1890–93, 1896–98, 1901–03). As lieutenant, he was attached to the

U.S. Coast and Geodetic Survey principally aboard its vessels *Blake* and *Bache* (1894–95, 1896), and returning to the *Dolphin* participated in a Guatemalan survey (1895–96). After brief duty aboard the receiving ship *Vermont* at New York (1898), he reported to the cruiser *Chicago,* flagship of the North Atlantic Station (1898–99), during which he cruised to the Mediterranean and participated in a show of force at Tangier.

Although he had missed seeing action during the Spanish-American War, Lieutenant Commander Benson held increasingly important posts in the expanding Navy of the Theodore Roosevelt years. He was aide to Adm. Norman von H. Farquhar, Commander-in-Chief North Atlantic Station, flagship the armored cruiser *New York* (ACR-2) and then the new battleship *Kearsarge* (BB-5) (1899–1901). He served with the recommissioned battleship *Iowa* (BB-4) in the North Atlantic and the Mediterranean (1903–05). Promoted to commander, he was lighthouse inspector at Charleston (1905–07), then commandant of midshipmen at the Naval Academy (1907–08), from which his son H. H. J. Benson graduated in 1909 and who eventually brought the battleship *Washington* (BB-56) into commission as her captain in 1941, retiring later as a commodore. Benson commanded the protected cruiser *Albany* (CL-23) patrolling the Pacific coast of Central America (1908–09). In July 1909 he became chief of staff to the Commander-in-Chief of the Pacific Fleet, Admiral Uriel Sebree, flagship the armored cruiser *Tennessee* (ACR-10), in the rank of captain, and made a voyage with the First Division to the Far East. After some months with the Naval Examining Board and commanding the reserve battleship *Missouri* (BB-11) at Boston, Captain Benson reported as prospective commanding officer of the new battleship *Utah* (BB-31) in October 1910. Commissioned the following August, the *Utah* operated with the Atlantic Fleet, acting briefly (1912–13) as flagship with Benson also as a division flag officer.

After two years as commandant of the Philadelphia Navy Yard with additional duty supervising three naval districts, Benson became Chief of Naval Operations in May 1915 with the rank of rear admiral. He organized the new and ill-defined office, centralizing much of the Navy's administration, and prepared the fleet for war, although he was hampered by Secretary of the Navy Josephus Daniels' strong prejudice against an overcentralized Navy high command. Advanced to the full rank of admiral in February 1916, Benson found little interference from the civilian leadership once the U.S. entered World War I in April 1917 and proved to be a reliable if humorless and undramatic administrative manager of the wartime Navy. He went abroad to improve Allied naval planning during the autumn of 1917 and again one year later to help conclude the naval aspects of the Armistice. Admiral Benson continued in 1919 as the principal American naval adviser at Versailles, where he served ably in insisting upon equal American naval power alongside the irritated British to the point where in fact he was accused of being anti-British. He retired in the rank of rear admiral in September 1919 but was advanced on the retired list to his wartime rank of admiral in 1930.

Admiral Benson rendered exceptionally distinguished postwar service as chairman of the United States Shipping Board (1919–21) and then as a commissioner of it (1921–28) and trustee of the Emergency Fleet Corporation (1920–21), during which tasks he championed a strong merchant marine and navy. His son Francis W. Benson graduated from the Academy with the Class of 1917 and rose to command a transport in the Solomons campaign during World War II and retire as rear admiral.

Berkey, Russell Stanley "Count", "Berk"

(August 4, 1893——). USNA (Ind.)
1916 (5/177).

The battleship *New York* (BB-24) was fittingly World War II leader Berkey's first duty assignment (1916–20), for he would devote his career to the surface line. In addition, after the ship participated in World War I as part of the British Grand Fleet, her new skipper in January 1919 became Capt. W. V. Pratt, with whom Berkey would be closely associated during his junior officer years. When Admiral Pratt became Commander Destroyer Force Pacific Fleet in November 1920 he took Lieutenant Berkey with him as aide and flag secretary, on flagship the cruiser *Charleston* (CA-19). After service as executive officer of the new destroyer *Selfridge* (DD-30) (1921–22) and assistant to the commandant of midshipmen at the Naval Academy, Berkey returned in June 1923 as aide (first as flag secretary, then division radio officer, finally flag lieutenant) to Pratt, who had become Commander Battleship Division Four, Battle Fleet, flagship *Arizona* (BB-39) and then *New Mexico* (BB-40). In June 1925 Pratt was relieved by Adm. Louis R. de Steiguer, and Berkey remained till November when he went to the light cruiser *Concord* (CL-10) in the Atlantic as gunnery officer, achieving high battle scores (1926–27).

Lieutenant Commander Berkey rejoined Admiral Pratt as a summer student in 1927 at the Naval War College, where Pratt was president, then resumed his role of aide and flag secretary to the Admiral in the latter's posts of Commander Battleship Divisions, Battle Fleet (1927–28), flagship *West Virginia* (BB-48); Commander-in-Chief Battle Fleet (1928–29), flagship *California* (BB-44); Commander-in-Chief United States Fleet (1929–30), flagship *Texas* (BB-35); and Chief of Naval Operations (1930–32). Berkey returned to sea as commanding officer first of the gunboat *Panay* (PR-5) on the Yangtze Patrol (1933–34) and then of the destroyer *Smith Thompson* (DD-212) in the Pacific. He was Port Director of the Norfolk Navy Base (1936–38) prior to service as a senior student at the Naval War College (1938–39). He then became Commander Mobile Target Division One of the fleet's Base Force in the Pacific, with his flagship *Dorsey* (DD-117) and other high-speed vessels of his command towing targets for the big ships (1939–41).

Commander Berkey brought the ammunition ship *Lassen* (AE-3) into commission in March 1941 and commanded her in both oceans until the end of October. Two months later he reported to the American Naval Base in Iceland as assistant commandant, remaining there during a crucial phase of the Battle of the Atlantic until October 1942. Captain Berkey helped fit out, then took command of the light cruiser *Santa Fe* (CL-60) upon her commissioning the next month. During the spring and summer of 1943 this vessel participated in the Aleutian Islands campaign, then provided gunfire and anti-aircraft cover during the northern Solomons and Gilbert Islands operations in November and December. Promoted during the latter month to rear admiral, Berkey took command of Cruiser Division 15 and Task Force 75 in the Southwest Pacific, flagship *Phoenix* (CL-46), providing bombardment services during MacArthur's landings through September 1944, at Cape Gloucester, the Admiralties, in New Guinea at Hollandia, Wakde-Sarmi, Biak and Noemfoor, and at Morotai in the Moluccas.

Although Admiral Berkey's title was in due course enlarged to Commander Cruisers Seventh Fleet and Commander Task Force 74, his cruiser-destroyer task group remained largely unchanged in the Leyte-Philippines operations and comprised the right flank at the battle in Surigao Strait in October 1944. He spent the rest of his wartime sea duty in this capacity providing fire cover for many landings in the Philippines and Borneo between December 1944 and July 1945: Mindoro, Lingayen, Corregidor, Zamboanga, Cebu, Tarakan and Brunei Bay, at the latter two aboard the flagship *Nashville* (CL-43), long a veteran of his force. Overdue for shore duty, in July Admiral Berkey took charge of the Navy Department's new Civil Liaison Section in Washington, and then surveyed the Shore Establishment (1946–47) and commanded the New York Navy Yard (1947–48). In January 1948 he took command of the Navy's support forces in the Far East and in July was promoted to vice admiral and Commander Naval Forces Far East. Admiral Berkey served as Commander Seventh Fleet, flagship *Toledo* (CA-133), from August 1949 to March 1950 and as Chief of Information during the summer of 1950, retiring due to physical disability in September in the full rank of admiral.

Biddle, James

(February 18, 1783—October 1, 1848).

One of the prominent Biddles of Philadelphia, War of 1812 fighter Biddle was nephew of the late Commo. Nicholas Biddle *(q.v.)* and brother of the commodore's namesake, the erudite but controversial president of the Second Bank of the United States. Educated at the University of Pennsylvania, he and his other brother Edward in 1800 became midshipmen aboard the new frigate *President*. Cruising the West Indies, however, Edward died of fever. James then operated against the Barbary pirates aboard the frigates *Constellation* (1802–03) and *Philadelphia* (1803), on which latter ship he was taken prisoner along with Capt. William Bainbridge when it ran aground off Tripoli. Released after 19 months, Lieutenant Biddle commanded *Gunboat No. 1* at Charleston (1805–06), surveyed the harbor there, served ashore at Philadelphia (1806–07), took leave to command a merchant ship to the Far East (1807–08), and then returned to Philadelphia and the Delaware flotilla which helped to enforce President Jefferson's embargo (1808–09). Over the next three years he saw duty aboard the *President,* the brig *Syren* as commanding officer, the frigate *Constitution* and the sloop of war *Hornet* carrying dispatches to American diplomats in France where early in 1812 he was received by Napoleon.

Biddle's most distinguished service occurred in the War of 1812, commencing with his assignment to the sloop *Wasp,* sister ship of the *Hornet*. In October the *Wasp* engaged and captured the sloop *Frolic,* during which action Biddle inspired the crew, led the boarding party, and personally cut down the British colors. With Biddle as prize captain, the *Frolic* and the *Wasp* were then taken by the enemy 74 *Poictiers*. After his parole early in 1813, Biddle was promoted to master commandant to command a Delaware Bay gunboat but received a larger award, command of the *Hornet,* at the end of April. The *Hornet* sortied from New York with two frigates, only to be chased into New London by a superior British force in June, to stay there for a year and a half. The *Hornet* finally slipped past the British blockade in November 1814 to go to New York, taking a merchant prize en route. Leaving New York in January 1815 with plans to rendezvous with other vessels off Tristan de Cunha in the South Atlantic, Biddle instead met the large British brig *Penguin* in March and in a furious cannonade took and scuttled her, though Biddle himself was severely wounded. Passing into the Indian Ocean, the *Hornet* encountered then outran the British 74 *Cornwallis* late in May. Upon his return to New York two months later, Biddle learned of the war's end and of his promotion to captain in February.

After duty ashore, Captain Biddle took command of the sloop *Ontario* in May 1817 and was ordered to proceed to the Columbia River and lay claim to the Oregon territory for the U.S. En route he visited Valparaiso, then in the grip of Chile's war for independence, and managed to obtain the release of several American merchant ships which had been seized. In August 1818 he raised the flag at Astoria, as ordered, then returned home via Monterey, California, and Valparaiso, arriving in April 1819. Next shore-based at Philadelphia, Biddle commanded the frigates *Macedonian* and then *Congress* as commodore of the West India Station (1822–24) and the *Macedonian* again in the southeast Pacific (1826–28). As commodore of the Mediterranean Squadron in the frigate *Java* (1829–32), he helped to negotiate the first commercial treaty between the U.S. and Turkey (1829).

Commodore Biddle, after an extended respite as governor of the Naval Asylum at Philadelphia (1838–42), assumed command of the East India Squadron in April 1845, his flag in the 74-gun ship-of-the-line *Columbus.* After negotiating this country's first treaty with China at the end of 1845 and acting as head of legation until April 1846, he unsuccessfully attempted to open Japan to commercial intercourse in July. Ordered to proceed to California to take temporary additional command of the Pacific Squadron for initial operations against Mexico, Biddle arrived at Monterey in March 1847 and acted as senior naval officer present until he departed for home two months later. Arriving at Norfolk in March 1848, he was detached from both squadron commands and given leave, during which he passed away.

Biddle, Nicholas

(September 10, 1750—March 7, 1778).

By James Peale: Naval Historical Center

One of the few American naval figures to have served in the British navy, Philadelphian Biddle had first gone to sea in 1763, been a merchant seaman (and a shipwrecked one at that in 1765), and held the commission of midshipman in the Royal Navy (1770–73), notably aboard H.M. sloop *Portland.* In 1773 he and the slightly younger Horatio Nelson, destined for legendary fame as Britain's greatest admiral, served as coxswains aboard the *Carcass* in a polar expedition sponsored by the Royal Geographical Society. Resigning to serve the American cause, Biddle briefly commanded the Pennsylvania state galley *Franklin* (1775) before assuming command of the Continental brig *Andrea* (or *Andrew*) *Doria* in December 1775 in the rank of captain. In March 1776 the vessel participated in Commo. Esek Hopkins' capture of New Providence, Bahamas, and in April took two small British warships off Montauk before driving away the 6th rate *Glasgow.* Operating out of New England during the spring and summer, Biddle's ship took many prizes, the military stores of which were thus transferred to General Washington. Off Newfoundland, the *Andrea Doria* captured two transports carrying 400 British army Highlanders, a large number of whom volunteered to fill out her crew as the original crewmen were detached to be prize crewmen.

Captain Biddle's impressive successes earned him command of the Navy's first frigate, the 32-gun *Randolph* of Philadelphia, in June 1776. Dispatched to the West Indies early in 1777, the ship suffered damages in a storm, was repaired at Charleston, then operated successfully against British shipping in the Caribbean. One triumph was over a three-vessel convoy plus its 20-gun escort, all which Biddle took into Charleston, wherein the *Randolph* was then blockaded by a superior enemy force. The State of South Carolina formed a four-vessel squadron to join the *Randolph,* with Biddle as commodore, which sortied late in February 1778. Instead of encountering British merchantmen, in March Commodore Biddle came up against the third-rate 64-gun ship-of-the-line *Yarmouth.* Hoisting her colors, the *Randolph* opened the battle with a broadside. Biddle was wounded but directed the close 20-minute engagement propped in a chair until his vessel literally exploded. He and all but four of his 315-man crew died in the action.

Blandy, William Henry Purnell "Spike"

(June 28, 1890–January 12, 1954).
USNA (Del.) 1913 (1/139).

Navy Department: National Archives

A superior expert in gunnery and ordnance from his Academy days where he excelled, Blandy served an unusually long initial tour (1913–18) in the battleship *Florida* (BB-30), including landing at Vera Cruz in 1914 and operating with the British Grand Fleet and on convoy escort during World War I, leaving the ship in November 1918 in the temporary grade of lieutenant commander. After short tours at U.S. Naval Headquarters in London and at the Bureau of Ordnance (BuOrd) (1918–19), he took advanced training in ordnance at Annapolis and the Naval Gun Factory, contributing many innovations in gun design, manufacture and fire control, notably the development of the standard one-man salvo-firing gun director. Blandy returned to sea as assistant fire control officer of the *New Mexico* (BB-40) (1921–22), then spent two years with the Asiatic Fleet aboard the cargo ship *Vega* (AK-17) as executive officer, in communications at Cavite, aboard the destroyer *Pruitt* (DD-347) and as gunnery and torpedo officer of

36

that Fleet's Destroyer Squadrons, flagship *Stewart* (DD-224), which included Tokyo relief work following the great earthquake of 1923.

His quick mind, efficiency and great industry, combined with his genius in gunnery, destined Blandy to rise through choice assignments to the top of the "Gun Club," the ordnance element and heart of the interwar Navy. Consequently, he served as Head of the BuOrd's Gun Section, as gunnery officer of the *New Mexico* (1927–29) which excelled in battle efficiency competition, and as gunnery officer on the staff of Adm. Lucius A. Bostwick, Commander Battleship Divisions, Battle Fleet (1929–30), flagship *West Virginia* (BB-48). After extended attaché duty in Brazil (1930–34), Commander Blandy commanded the *Simpson* (DD-221) then Destroyer Division 10 of the Battle Force (1935–36), flagship *Pruitt* (DD-347), afterward heading the Gunnery Section for surface ships, aircraft, and submarines in the Division of Fleet Training (1936–38) prior to assuming command of the target ship *Utah* (AG-16) in training the Navy's bomber pilots for offensive work and in developing the fleet's anti-aircraft defenses. He was promoted to captain in September 1939, returning to BuOrd the following June to coordinate all the defensive phases of anti-aircraft ordnance. In February 1941 he reached the top, being appointed over one hundred more senior officers to be Chief of the Bureau in the rank of rear admiral, the youngest (age 50) line admiral at the time.

Admiral Blandy's World War II service remained in ordnance, first administrative, then operational. As Bureau Chief, he led the production of the Navy's wartime weapons arsenal, notably in anti-aircraft systems, particularly the 40mm Bofors and 20mm Oerlikon guns, and the proximity fuze. Detached in December 1943 he assumed command of Amphibious Group One of the Pacific Fleet and participated in the Kwajalein operation early in 1944. Hoisting his flag in the converted amphibious command ship *Frémont* (APA-44), he commanded the floating reserve during the Saipan and Peleliu assaults in June and September. In November Admiral Blandy became Commander Amphibious Support Force (Task Force 52), flagship *Estes* (AGC-12), the first post specifically created to handle prelanding operations. As such, he led battleships, escort carriers, cruisers, minesweepers, gunboats, mortar and rocket ships and underwater demolition teams prior to the landings at Iwo Jima (February 1945) and most of these vessels before and during the Okinawa operation and capture of Kerama Retto (March and April). In July 1945 he became Commander Cruisers and Destroyers Pacific Fleet.

With the advent of atomic weapons, Admiral Blandy as the Navy's leading ordnance expert became its senior officer in matters involving these "special weapons" with his appointment in November 1945 as Deputy Chief of Naval Operations (Special Weapons) in the rank of vice admiral. In addition, he returned to sea early in 1946 as Commander Joint Army-Navy Task Force One aboard the *Mt. McKinley* (AGC-7), directing the atomic bomb tests at Bikini atoll in the Marshall Islands in July. Detached in November, the next month he assumed command of the Eighth Fleet in the Atlantic. In February 1947 he was promoted to admiral and made Commander-in-Chief Atlantic Fleet, a post he held for three years. Late in 1947 Admiral Blandy was considered for appointment as Chief of Naval Operations alongside Admirals D. C. Ramsey and Louis E. Denfeld but lost out to the latter. He retired in February 1950, but served briefly later as head of the Naval Reserve Evaluation Board (1953–54). His son-in-law, Vice Adm. John M. Lee, commanded the Seventh Fleet amphibious forces early in the Vietnam War.

Bogan, Gerald Francis "Gerry"

(July 27, 1894–June 8, 1973). USNA 1916 (Ill.) 26/177.

Navy Department: National Archives

The pugnacious Bogan, a boxer and scrapper during and after his Academy days, preceded his career in naval aviation with several routine duty assignments afloat and ashore: the battleship *Vermont* (BB-20); enlisted men's instructor at the Great Lakes Naval Training Station (1916–17); gunnery officer on the cruiser *Birmingham* (CL-2) in the first troop convoy to France and in convoy-escort operations out of Gibraltar for the rest of World War I; the destroyer *Stribling* (DD-96) in the Mediterranean (1919); engineer and executive officer of the *Hopewell* (DD-181) in the Caribbean; executive officer of the *Broome* (DD-210) in European and Asiatic waters (1920–21); and commanding officer of the Russian Island U.S. Naval Radio Station, Vladivostok (1922). He then instructed in electrical engineering and physics at the Naval Academy (1923–24).

Lieutenant Bogan entered flight training at Pensacola in August 1924 and received his wings the following March, returning twice later to that base in command of landplanes and Squadron One (1928–30), as superintendent of aviation training (1936–37), and as exec of the air station (1937–38). He saw extensive service on the Navy's three aircraft carriers in the Pacific during the formative years of carrier aviation: with Fighting Squadron One on the *Langley* (CV-1) as executive officer (1925–26) and commanding officer (1926–28); with Fighting Three on the *Lexington* (CV-2) and again the *Langley* (1930–31), winning extraordinarily high gunnery and bombing awards; as skipper of Fighting One again, this time on the *Saratoga* (CV-3); flight test officer at Anacostia (1932–34); and duty on the *Lexington* as assistant air officer (1934–35) and air officer (1935–36). In the rank of commander, he joined the *Yorktown* (CV-5) as navigator (1938–39), then exec (1939–40). He helped to establish and then commanded the wartime naval air station at Miami, Florida (1940–42).

Captain Bogan commanded the *Saratoga* in the South Pacific from October 1942 until June 1943, serving during the summer as naval air commander of the Tenth Fleet as the tide was turning against the Germans in the Battle of the Atlantic. In October 1943 he became Commander Fleet Air Norfolk, being promoted to rear admiral two months later. In January 1944 he hoisted his flag aboard the escort carrier *Fanshaw Bay* (CVE-70) as Commander Carrier Division 25 and led an escort carrier task group during the Saipan landings in June until his flagship was damaged by a bomb hit. The next month he became ComCarDiv 4 and Commander Task Group 58.4, flagship *Essex* (CV-9), in the final operations in the Marianas.

Admiral Bogan immediately became a premier task group commander in the Fast Carrier Task Force. In the Philippines campaign and the Battle for Leyte Gulf during the autumn of 1944 he commanded TG 38.2 aboard the *Intrepid* (CV-11) until late November when this vessel was badly damaged by two Japanese bombs. Transferring his flag to the new *Lexington* (CV-16), he directed his carrier planes in strikes in the Philippines, the South China Sea and around Formosa until granted leave at the end of January 1945. Recalled prematurely by his commander, Adm. M. A. Mitscher, who was anxious to have him available for any emergency, Bogan reported on standby status aboard the *Franklin* (CV-13) in March, only to have it disabled by enemy bombs several days later. Shifting to the *Randolph* (CV-15), he remained on call during the Okinawa campaign and led TG 38.3 during the carrier strikes against the Japanese homeland in July and August.

Appointed Commander Fleet Air Alameda in October 1945, Admiral Bogan was promoted to vice admiral the following February as Commander Air Force Atlantic Fleet. Relieved in July 1948, he became embroiled in the unification dispute then wracking the Navy with the result that his career was shortened as punishment. His last command was of the First Task Fleet (1949–50), he retiring in February 1950 in the rank of vice admiral. Though most of his contemporaries pronounced his name with the accent on the second syllable, he in fact accented the first.

Bowling, Selman Stewart

(April 26, 1906——   ). USNA (Ind.)
1927 (55/579).

Navy Department: National Archives

Although Bowling's claim to fame was in PT boats, he spent most his career in much larger warships, starting with the cruiser *Memphis* (CL-13) in the Atlantic, Caribbean and Pacific (1927–28), then the destroyer *Truxtun* (DD-229), transferring at the end of 1929 to the new river gunboat *Mindanao* (PR-8) of the South China Patrol Force. He reported aboard the *Louisville* (CL-28), commissioned in 1931, for service in American coastal waters, moved to the destroyer tender *Dobbin* (AD-3) and then the *Noa* (DD-343) for West coast service. Having done experimental work in radios on the *Dobbin,* Lieutenant Bowling studied applied communications as well as general line subjects at the Postgraduate School at Annapolis (1934–36), reported to the battleship *Maryland* (BB-46) as radio officer in July 1936 and to the flagship *Tennessee* (BB-43) of Battleship Division Two as staff radio officer in January 1938. The following September he moved to the *Colorado* (BB-45) as electrical officer, ending his Pacific Battle Force duty in June 1940 by transferring to the Executive and Planning Section, Enlisted Personnel Division, Bureau of Navigation.

Lieutenant Commander Bowling joined the staff of Adm. R. K. Turner, Commander Amphibious Force South Pacific, flagship *McCawley* (AP-10), in July 1942 as communications officer for the arduous Guadalcanal campaign, but shifted in mid-November to motor torpedo boat (MTB or PT) training at nearby Tulagi, later at Melville, Rhode Island. He directed the fitting out of Motor Torpedo Boat Squadron 21 at the New York Navy Yard, brought it into commission in April 1943, and took it to the Southwest Pacific for the New Guinea campaign in November, replete with the biggest, most athletic PT-boat skippers he could find! After successful operations against Japanese coastal shipping, Commander Bowling became Commander Motor Torpedo Boat Squadrons Seventh Fleet in February 1944, a post he occupied for the duration. He continued the New Guinea fighting in his PT-boat tender flagships *Portunus* (AGP-4) and *Hilo* (AGP-2). Moving up with the Morotai assault temporarily aboard the *Oyster Bay* (AGP-6) in September, he was Commander Task Group 70.1 at the Leyte landings and the surface battle in Surigao Strait in October. He thereafter braved kamikaze attacks in the Philippines area and assisted importantly in air-sea rescue operations. He shifted his flag from the *Hilo* to the *Cyrene* (AGP-13) in January 1945, based at Samar, and with 212 PT boats and eleven tenders helped to clear the Philippines of small Japanese craft for the rest of the war. Promotion to captain occurred in March, and from late August to November his command was designated as MTB Squadrons Philippine Sea Frontier to help police the Japanese surrender activities in those waters.

Captain Bowling worked at the Bureau of Naval Personnel (1945–48), initially in the Liberated Prisoners of War Section but most of the time as head of the unit which developed and then implemented the Officer Personnel Act of 1947. He was a student at the National War College until mid-1949, thereafter commanding the attack transport *Cavalier* (APA-37) in the Pacific until July 1950 and acting as aide to Under Secretary of the Navy Dan A. Kimball until the end of 1951, at which time he joined the staff of the above College. Reporting as Commander Destroyer Squadron 13, flagship *Blue* (DD-744), he patrolled Korean and Formosan waters (1953–54) and ended his naval career with the Office of the Assistant Secretary of Defense (Manpower and Personnel). He was retired in February 1957 in the rank of rear admiral.

Bristol, Mark Lambert

(April 17, 1868–May 13, 1939). USNA (N.J.) 1887 (5/44).

One of the Navy's most successful diplomats and ordnance specialists, Bristol operated with the wooden steamer *Galena* off New England (1887), twice aboard the gunboat *Yantic* (1887–88, 1890–91), and in the Coast Survey vessel *McArthur* (1888–90), being commissioned ensign in 1889. After brief duty on the converted bark *Monongahela* (1890), he went to the Far East with the gunboat *Petrel* (1891–94) as a watch and division officer, then shifted to the eastern Pacific and the gunboat *Alert* (1894). His gunboat and torpedo work continued ashore at Norfolk's equipment department (1895), and he taught on the schoolship *St. Mary's* at New York (1895–96). Bristol joined the battleship *Texas* in 1896, was promoted to lieutenant (j.g.) the next year, and fought at Guantanamo Bay and the Battle of Santiago. He transferred to the Washington Navy Yard as lieutenant in 1899 and briefly to the battleship *Massachusetts* (BB-2) in 1901 before reporting later that year to the *Kearsarge* (BB-5) as aide to the commander-in-chief of the North Atlantic Fleet, Adm. Francis J. Higginson. After a year as head of the Bureau of Ordnance's torpedo branch, in 1905 he acted briefly as fleet gunnery officer for the European Squadron, flagship the armored cruiser *Brooklyn* (ACR-3), followed by miscellaneous ordnance work.

Lieutenant Commander Bristol in 1905 became aide and ordnance officer to North Atlantic Fleet commander Adm. R. D. Evans, flagship *Maine* (BB-10), in which capacity he engaged in much ordnance experimentation and improvements, notably the design of gun sights. In 1907 he transferred to the *Connecticut* (BB-18) as executive officer for the global cruise of the "Great White Fleet" and inspected ordnance at the Newport torpedo station (1908–11). Returning to the Far East, he commanded the monitor *Monterey*

(BM-6) for a year, then (1912–13) the protected cruiser *Albany* (CL-23) which won several gunnery awards. It was during his patrols off revolution-torn China that he first displayed his keen diplomatic tact by handling well a delicate situation at Swatow. Jumped to the rank of captain and appointed Director of Naval Aeronautics in 1913, he developed an expertise in aircraft to match his knowledge of gunnery and torpedoes, serving also on the National Advisory Committee on Aeronautics (1915) and as commander of the air station at Pensacola. In 1916 he assumed command of the experimental aviation station ship cruiser *North Carolina* (ACR-12), which the next year convoyed troops to Europe. After duty at the Naval War College, Captain Bristol commanded the *Oklahoma* (BB-37) in the Atlantic Fleet from March to October 1918 although he was promoted to rear admiral in July. Commander of the U.S. naval base at Plymouth, England, during the autumn, he also acted briefly as U.S. naval member of the Inter-Allied Naval Commission dealing with the Armistice.

Admiral Bristol's close association with Turkey began in January 1919 when he was given command of a Naval detachment to protect American interests in the Middle East. His flag initially aboard the *Pittsburgh* (ACR-4), he found himself immediately embroiled in the general international chaos of the region and adopted a steadfast policy of strict unilateral American neutrality and humaneness which discouraged the dismember-ment of Turkey by the great powers, encouraged the settlement of the Graeco-Turkish war, and won over Turkish friendship for this country. To clarify his diplomatic status, the U.S. government in August 1919 designated Bristol as U.S. High Commissioner to Turkey with he eventually shifting his flag ashore to Constantinople. He helped to evacuate refugees from the Crimea during the Russian Civil War, brought food relief to Greek, Turkish, and Armenian refugees, and participated in the multilateral investigation of the Greek occupation of Smyrna, all these activities over the years 1919 to 1922. One of three American representatives at the Lausanne Conference (1922–23), Bristol in the permanent rank of rear admiral, with his flag in the gunboat *Scorpion* (PY-3), attempted to restore U.S.-Turkish diplomatic and trade relations but was not finally successful until 1927, at which time he returned home to the acclaim of the State Department and the government in general.

Because of his tremendous success, Admiral Bristol was made Com-mander-in-Chief Asiatic Fleet with the rank of admiral in mid-1927 to try to reach a settlement of the civil war raging in China. His flag again in the *Pittsburgh,* he protected American interests in the Far East for two years but was unsuccessful in the diplomatic sphere. Reverting to rear admiral, Bristol joined the General Board in 1929 and became its chairman in March 1930, a post he occupied until his retirement in May 1932 as rear admiral.

Buchanan, Franklin

(September 17, 1800—May 11, 1874).

Library of Congress: Naval Photographic Center

Remembered chiefly for his command of the *Merrimack* and as senior officer in the Confederate States Navy, Marylander Buchanan enjoyed a long and distinguished career in the prewar U.S. Navy. Warranted as midshipman in January 1815, Buchanan cruised in the Mediterranean aboard the new frigate *Java*, Capt. Oliver Hazard Perry (1815–17). He served on the new 74 *Franklin*, flagship of the Mediterranean Squadron (1817–20), then took a year-long furlough to be mate on a merchant ship to China (1821–22), followed by other sporadic leaves. Lieutenant Buchanan delivered a frigate to the Emperor of Brazil (1825), served on the sloop *Peacock* in the Pacific, joined the new sloop *Natchez* for anti-pirate work in the Caribbean (1827–29), and then transferred to the frigate *Constellation* for another Mediterranean cruise (1829–31). Inactive for over a year, he returned to the Mediterranean Squadron aboard its flagship, the *Delaware*, 74 (1833–34), tested ordnance at Philadelphia and was commander of the receiving ship at his native Baltimore (1837–39).

Assigned to the South Pacific Squadron as flag lieutenant to Commo. Alexander Claxton, flagship frigate *Constitution*, in 1839, Buchanan also served aboard the sloop *Falmouth* before promotion to commander in September 1841. He commanded the sidewheel steam frigate *Mississippi* (1842) and the sloop *Vincennes* (1842–44) in the Caribbean searching for slavers and pirates. Called upon by Secretary of the Navy George Bancroft to draft a proposal for the new Naval Academy at Annapolis, he submitted it during the summer of 1845, whereupon he became its first—and very effective—Superintendent (1845–47). He brought the sloop *Germantown* into commission in March 1847 and led it in Mexican War operations against

Alvarado, Tuxpan and Tabasco and on general blockade duty, the ship serving as Commo. Matthew C. Perry's flagship for three months, returning home early in 1848. While commanding the naval rendezvous at Baltimore (1849–51), Buchanan continued to serve the early Academy, after which he assumed command of the steam frigate *Susquehanna* (1852–55). Commodore Perry wore his flag in this vessel in the expedition which opened Japan in 1853. After several months on the Board of Efficiency, Buchanan was promoted to captain in October 1855 and had miscellaneous duties prior to commanding the Washington Navy Yard (1859–61).

Captain Buchanan resigned from the Navy in April 1861 but tried in vain for reinstatement when his native Maryland failed to secede. Commissioned captain in the Confederate Navy in September, he became Chief of the Bureau of Orders and Detail until the following February when he assumed command of the Chesapeake Bay squadron, flagship the revolutionary converted ironclad *Virginia* (ex-*Merrimack*), whose conversion he superintended. Flag Officer Buchanan led this vessel in its attack on the Union blockading force in Hampton Roads in March 1862, destroying or sinking the frigates *Congress* (of which his brother McKean was an officer) and *Cumberland* and three small steamers. Wounded by shore batteries during the action, he relinquished command to Lt. Catesby ap R. Jones, who then fought the famous duel with the *Monitor* the following day. He was promoted to admiral in August, and in 1863 he assumed command of the naval defenses of Mobile. There he hoisted his flag in the new ironclad *Tennessee,* which he also commanded, and accompanied by three wooden gunboats engaged the Union fleet in the Battle of Mobile Bay in August 1864. His vessel heavily damaged and isolated and he again severely wounded, Admiral Buchanan surrendered to Adm. David G. Farragut, remaining prisoner until exchanged in February 1865 just as the war was ending.

Bulkeley, John Duncan

(August 19, 1911——). USNA.
(Texas) 1933 (395/432).

Navy Department: National Archives

The most renowned PT-boat leader of World War II, Massachusetts- and New Jersey-raised Bulkeley took a one-year Depression-era delay before commissioning and shipping out in the cruiser *Indianapolis* (CA-35) on both coasts, then the transport *Chaumont* (AP-5), the old gunboat *Sacramento* (PG-19) and the aircraft carrier *Saratoga* (CV-3). As lieutenant (j.g.) he commanded Submarine Chaser Division Two in February and March 1941, then as lieutenant Motor Boat Submarine Chaser Squadron One. In August he took command of Motor Torpedo Boat Squadron Three, the only one in the Philippines when the war began. From December 1941 to April 1942 he and his few PT boats heavily engaged the Japanese in the futile defense of these islands, in March evacuating Gen. Douglas MacArthur aboard *PT-41*, with Bulkeley and others finally being flown out to Australia at the last moment. Stationed at the MTB Squadron Training Center at Portsmouth, Rhode Island, during the summer of 1942, Lieutenant Commander Bulkeley took command of MTB Squadron Seven, which reached the Southwest Pacific in February 1943, and led it in the New Guinea campaign throughout that summer. He was hospitalized from September 1943 to March 1944.

Bulkeley brought MTB Squadron Two into commission in March 1944 and prepared it for special missions to the enemy-held English Channel coast in conjunction with the Normandy landings before his transfer in May to command of PT Squadron 102, which during and after D-Day screened invasion vessels in the Bay of the Seine, France, and shelled German shore installations. In mid-July he assumed command of the destroyer *Endicott* (DD-495) which with 22 American and British PT boats in his charge created an amphibious diversion off the southern French coast, his own ship sinking two German corvettes in one surface action in August. Convoy escort in the Mediterranean followed, and early in 1945 the *Endicott* provided part of President Franklin D. Roosevelt's escort to the Yalta conference. Commander Bulkeley reported to Staten Island to outfit the *Stribling* (DD-867) in August 1945, assuming command of her upon commissioning the next month, basing thereafter at Key West. After duty at the Naval Academy (1946–48) he served as executive officer of the amphibious command ship *Mt. Olympus* (AGC-8) on the Eastern seaboard. Brief instruction at the Armed Forces Staff College in Norfolk (1949–50) was followed by service as Chief of the Weapons Division of the Military Liaison Committee to the Atomic Energy Commission.

Promoted to captain in 1952 Bulkeley commanded Destroyer Division 132 during and after the Korean War (1952–54), flagships *O'Brien* (DD-725) and *Harry E. Hubbard* (DD-748). Remaining in the Far East as chief of staff to Commander Cruiser Division Five (changed to Three), Adm. Ralph E. Wilson, flagships *Helena* (CA-75) and *Rochester* (CA-124), he then served on the Joint Staff of the Joint Chiefs of Staff in Washington (1956–58) and commanded the fleet oiler *Tolovana* (AO-64) on the West coast. He thereafter commanded Destroyer Squadron 12, flagship *Davis* (DD-937), in the Atlantic and Caribbean (1959–60); the naval weapons base at Clarksville, Tenn.; and from December 1963 the Naval Base at Guantanamo Bay, Cuba, in the rank of rear admiral. He withstood Cuba's pressure to cut off water to the base in early 1964 and remained in command there until June 1966. Admiral Bulkeley commanded Cruiser-Destroyer Flotilla Eight and Carrier Task Group 60.2 in the Mediterranean, flagships the guided missile cruiser *Columbus* (CG-12) and the destroyer tender *Shenandoah* (AD-26), after which in 1967 he became President of the Board of Inspection and Survey for an extended period. He retired on the first day of 1974 in the rank of rear admiral but remained in that post.

Burke, Arleigh Albert "Thirty-One Knot"

(October 19, 1901——). USNA
(Colo.) 1923 (71/413).

Navy Department: National Archives

The Navy's most famous destroyer squadron combat commander and a very young Chief of Naval Operations at the height of the Cold War, Burke began his career with a lengthy tour (1923–28) aboard the battleship *Arizona* (BB-39) in the Pacific, during which he attended torpedo school at San Diego. Following a year aboard the auxiliary *Procyon* (AG-11), flagship of the Battle Fleet's Base Force, he continued with postgraduate education in explosives at Annapolis (1929–30), and in engineering at the University of Michigan (M.S. 1931) and the Washington Navy Yard (1931–32). He was assistant gunnery and main battery officer of the heavy cruiser *Chester* (CA-27) again in the Pacific, where he remained on the staff of the Base Force (1933–35) before joining the Bureau of Ordnance in Washington. In June 1937 Lieutenant Burke became executive officer of the new destroyer *Craven* (DD-382), engaging in experimental torpedo work and operating along the West coast and in the Caribbean. Promoted to lieutenant commander in 1939, he commanded the *Mugford* (DD-389), flagship of Destroyer Division 8 in the Pacific, with which he excelled in gunnery competition.

Because of his abilities in ordnance, Burke spent much of World War II in such work ashore and afloat. As an ordnance inspector at the Washington Navy Yard from August 1940 until January 1943, he chafed at not being able to obtain sea duty. Finally awarded command of DesDiv 43, he hoisted his flag in the *Waller* (DD-466), which in March 1943 blew up a Japanese destroyer in battle while escorting a cruiser force in the central Solomons. In May he shifted to command of DesDiv 44, flagship *Conway* (DD-507), on board which he received wounds while escorting convoys in the Solomons. Captain Burke took over Destroyer Squadron 12 in August 1943 and then

DesRon 23 two months later, the latter coming to be known as the "Little Beavers" after their insignia based on the comic strip cowboy Red Ryder's sidekick. In addition, Burke commanded one of the squadron's two divisions, No. 45, his flag in the *Charles Ausburne* (DD-570). In the van at the Battle of Empress Augusta Bay, Bougainville, in early November 1943, Burke brilliantly distinguished himself in leading several torpedo attacks which sank a number of Japanese warships. At the end of the month he repeated his performance at the Battle of Cape St. George, New Ireland. During December 1943 and February 1944, Burke's squadron continued escorting American amphibious forces in the South Pacific and carried out bombardments, notably of Kavieng. The final score of "Little Beavers" sinkings was one enemy cruiser, nine destroyers, one submarine and several smaller vessels, plus some 30 planes shot down.

At the end of March 1944 the Squadron joined Task Force 58, escorting the fast carriers, and Burke became chief of staff to the force commander, Adm. M. A. Mitscher, flagships *Yorktown* (CV-10) and later *Lexington* (CV-16), in the rank of commodore. As such he participated in the landings at Hollandia and Saipan and in the battles of the Philippine Sea and Leyte Gulf throughout the spring, summer, and autumn of 1944, making many flights over the targets and becoming an indispensable adviser to Mitscher. During the first half of 1945 this role of assisting the now Commander First Fast Carrier Force Pacific Fleet increased, and Mitscher's failing health led the latter to depend even more on Burke during Task Force 58's participation in the Iwo Jima and Okinawa operations and the air strikes against Japan's home islands. During May kamikazes disabled the successive flagships *Bunker Hill* (CV-17) and *Enterprise* (CV-6), with Burke supervising the transfers of the staff, finally to the *Randolph* (CV-15). In July and August Commodore Burke headed an anti-kamikaze research unit at Casco Bay, Maine, and later in the year directed the research and development division at the Bureau of Ordnance. He returned to Admiral Mitscher again as chief of staff of the Eighth Fleet and then the Atlantic Fleet (1946–47) until the Admiral's death.

Reverting back to captain with the phasing out of the rank of commodore, Burke served on the General Board (1947–48) and commanded the light cruiser *Huntington* (CL-107) on a good will cruise to the Mediterranean and South America via African ports during the second half of 1948. Throughout 1949 he had the controversial duty at the Navy Department of being head of Op-23 which focused the Navy's battle against the Air Force to obtain part of the nuclear weapons mission. But he managed to escape punishment through the good offices of the new Chief of Naval Operations, Adm. Forrest Sherman, who early in 1950 appointed him Navy secretary to the Defense Department's Research and Development Board. Promoted to rear admiral, Burke in September 1950 became deputy chief of staff to Adm. C. T. Joy, Commander Naval Forces Far East, engaged in the Korean War. In May 1951 he was appointed Commander Cruiser Division Five, but in July went ashore as a United Nations delegate to the truce talks at

Panmunjom, North Korea, where he was very effective. At the end of the year Admiral Burke became Director of Strategic Plans in the Office of the CNO, which he held until March 1954, transferring then to the command of CruDiv Six, flagship *Macon* (CA-132), in the Atlantic Fleet. In January 1955 he assumed command of that Fleet's Destroyer Force.

In May 1955 President Eisenhower surprised the Navy by nominating the 53-year-old Burke for the post of Chief of Naval Operations, bypassing 87 active duty officers senior to him as well as the rank of vice admiral. Confirmed in August, he took over in the full rank of admiral and held the office for an unprecedented six years (1955–61), during which time the Navy was involved in the Quemoy-Matsu incidents, the Suez crisis, the Lebanon landings, the Laotian troubles, and the Caribbean disorders. Most importantly, Admiral Burke acted as a major force on the Joint Chiefs of Staff in developing the Navy's Polaris submarine missile program and in keeping it under Navy control; he also utilized the new *Forrestal*-class attack carriers in a nuclear deterrence role. He retired in August 1961.

Byrd, Richard Evelyn, Jr.

(October 25, 1888–March 11, 1957).
USNA (Va.) 1912 (63/156).

Office of the Chief of Naval Operations: National Archives

Achieving ultimate fame as a polar explorer, Byrd developed into that work via the Navy and naval aviation and carried out most of it under Navy auspices. Already a member of the prominent Byrd family of Virginia and seasoned by three years at the Virginia Military Institute (1904–1907) and one at the University of Virginia (1907–08), Ensign Byrd saw his first regular one-year tour of duty aboard the new battleship *Wyoming* (BB-32), followed by brief tours with the reserve battleship *Missouri* (BB-11), the armored cruiser *Washington* (ACR-11) during which tour he twice performed rescues from drowning, and the dispatch ship *Dolphin* (PG-24). He suffered a leg injury which caused his untimely but mandatory retirement in March 1916 in the rank of lieutenant (j.g.). Recalled two months later but restricted from standing long watches, he was an instructor with the Rhode Island Naval Militia (1916–17) and then organizer of the Commission of Training Camps with the Bureau of Navigation.

After almost a year of flight training at Pensacola, Byrd became Naval Aviator No. 608 in April 1918 and the following August assumed command of all American naval air forces in Canada and their air stations at Halifax and North Sydney, Nova Scotia. He returned to the Navy Department in Washington as lieutenant at the end of World War I to devise aerial navigation instruments and plans for the 1919 flight of the NC transatlantic flying boats, which he accompanied to their departure point in Newfoundland. He himself crossed the Atlantic in a dirigible in 1921, spending the ensuing year in England helping to complete the construction of a dirigible for the U.S. Assigned to the Bureau of Aeronautics, he participated in the establishment of Naval Reserve air stations at Chicago and Boston. Lieutenant Commander Byrd organized and commanded the Naval Flying Unit of the Navy-MacMillan polar expedition to Greenland in 1925, returning afterward to the Bureau. Byrd's naval career, already unusual due to his early injury, ceased to be "normal" when he requested and was granted leave in 1926 to lead an "Aviation Arctic Expedition" to the North Pole.

On May 9, 1926, Byrd and Chief Machinist's Mate Floyd Bennett (1890–1928) flew 1360 miles from Spitsbergen over the North Pole and back—the first to achieve the feat. In January Congress awarded both men the Medal of Honor and by special Act promoted Byrd to commander on the retired list. Five months later Byrd and four others flew a large plane 4100 miles across the Atlantic, having then to ditch dramatically in the French surf during poor weather. Returning to the Bureau, in the spring of 1928 he lost the invaluable services of his assistant Bennett who succumbed to pneumonia on the eve of Byrd's first expedition to Antarctica.

Byrd established his Antarctic base camp, which he named Little America, in December 1928, and on the following November 28–29 he and three companions became the first men to fly over the South Pole, leading in December to a special Act of Congress designating him rear admiral on the retired list. Relieved of all active duty in October 1931, he commanded two expeditions to the Antarctic (1933–35, 1939–41) aboard the screw steamer *Bear,* during the latter as commander of the U.S. Antarctic Service, making many discoveries of mountain ranges and other topographical features.

Admiral Byrd assisted the War Department in developing cold weather clothing (1941–42) before reporting for wartime service with Adm. E. J. King's office. From May to August 1942 he headed a special board to the South Pacific which hastened naval base construction there and for the rest of World War II undertook one special mission to Europe and two more to the Pacific, being present at the surrender of Japan. In 1946–47 he led the Navy's 13-ship, 4000-man expedition—the largest to date—to Antarctica, Operation Highjump, during which he made 64 aerial mapping flights of the coastline. He was relieved of all active duty in September 1947 but served temporarily with the Office of the Chief of Naval Operations (1949–51) while participating in international refugee relief. Designated Officer in Charge, U. S. Antarctic Programs in October 1955, Admiral Byrd initiated and accompanied Operation Deep Freeze to the Antarctic (1955–56) as part of the International Geophysical Year (1957–58). He received the Medal of Freedom in February 1957, three weeks before his death.

Calhoun, William Lowndes "Uncle Bill"

(July 13, 1884—October 19, 1963). USNA (Fla.) 1906 (13/116).

Navy Department: National Archives

The premier logistics commander of the war in the Pacific, Calhoun began his varied career in ordnance, aboard the cruiser *Chattanooga* (C-16) in the Far East (1906–08), where he joined the battleship *New Jersey* (BB-12) of the "Great White Fleet," cruising home with her but then returning to the Pacific and the armored cruiser *Maryland* (ACR-8), eventually as her gunnery officer and briefly as chief engineer (1909–13). After duty inspecting ordnance and instructing naval militia in the Connecticut area, he spent the latter part of 1915 training in submarines in both oceans aboard the *Columbia* (C-12) and monitors *Tonopah* (BM-8) and *Cheyenne* (BM-10). Lieutenant Calhoun fitted out the sub *L-7* (SS-46) up to the day of her commissioning in December 1917 at Long Beach, California, concurrently inspecting naval machinery contracting firms in the Los Angeles and San Francisco regions, instructing naval militia at Los Angeles and Santa

Barbara, and commanding the militia training ship *Farragut* (TB-11). He then commanded Submarine Force Division One, which became Submarine Flotilla One, in the Atlantic war zone, in December 1918 also taking over the sub base and naval air station in the Panama Canal Zone. After a month with the Cruiser Force, in May 1919 he became the award-winning gunnery officer of the *Mississippi* (BB-41).

Frustrated from joining the fitting-out *California* (BB-44) as her gunnery officer, Commander Calhoun became inspector of ordnance at Mare Island (1921–23) and commanding officer of the destroyer *Young* (DD-312), which was wrecked in September 1923 at Point Honda, California, the responsibility for which he was exonerated. Attached briefly to the destroyer tender *Melville* (AD-2), he served as navigator of the *Maryland* (BB-46), returning thereafter to his former Mare Island inspector's post (1925–27). Commanding Destroyer Division 31, pennant in the *Farragut* (DD-300), with battle efficiency awards in both oceans, he took the senior course at the Naval War College (1929–30) and headed the Navigation Department at the Naval Academy. Captain Calhoun commanded the old armored cruiser *Rochester* (ACR-2) during her final cruise with the Yangtze Patrol (1932–33); was chief of staff to Commander Base Force, U.S. Fleet, Adm. Henry H. Hough, at San Diego; remained there with the Eleventh Naval District (1934–37); and finally served for several months aboard the *California* as her commanding officer. In January 1938 he became chief of staff to Commander Battleships, Battle Force, Adm. Edward C. Kalbfus, flagship *West Virginia* (BB–48), being promoted to rear admiral the following November.

Admiral Calhoun, after attending the advanced course at the Naval War College, in December 1939 became Commander Base Force, U.S. Fleet (changed to Base Force, Pacific Fleet, in February 1941), with additional duty from August 1941 as Commander Train Squadron Two. With the beginning of hostilities in the Pacific, he became Commander Service Force Pacific Fleet in the rank of vice admiral and in which capacity he successfully directed, from Pearl Harbor, the entire logistics effort (except for aviation) in the war against Japan, including the revolutionary and crucial at-sea replenishment squadrons. In March 1945 Calhoun transferred to command of the backwater South Pacific Area, the logistics of which he had personally established during the trying Guadalcanal campaign of late 1942. Relieved in October, he spent several months as Inspector General of the Navy and then as General Inspector of the Western Sea Frontier, retiring in April 1946. He was advanced to full admiral in January 1954.

Callaghan, Daniel Judson

(July 26, 1890–November 13, 1942).
USNA (Calif.) 1911 (39/193).

Navy Department: National Archives

Beginning a career in gunnery and heavy line-of-battle ships on the armored cruiser *California* (ACR-6), Callaghan cruised in the Pacific and participated in Navy-Marine Corps landings in troubled Nicaragua late in 1912. Moving to the destroyer *Truxtun* (DD-14) in the summer of 1913, he patrolled the Mexican Pacific coast (1914–16), becoming the ship's skipper in March 1916 in the rank of lieutenant (j.g.). Transferring in November to the protected cruiser *New Orleans,* he performed convoy escort services to Europe (1917–18) before going to the Asiatic Station first as engineer officer then executive officer. Two years with the Bureau of Navigation (1918–20) were followed by duty as assistant fire control officer of the new battleship *Idaho* (BB-42) on the West coast. Lieutenant Commander Callaghan remained on that coast at San Francisco with the Board of Inspection and Survey, Pacific Coast Section (1923–25), followed by one year as first lieutenant of the *Colorado* (BB-45) on the U.S. Fleet's cruise to the South Pacific. He then joined the *Mississippi* (BB-41) as engineer officer (1926–28) before returning to the inspection and survey section at San Francisco. His inordinantly long sea duty with battleships was climaxed by assignment (1930–33) as gunnery officer on the staff of Adm. Richard H. Leigh, successively Commander Battleships Battle Force, Commander Battle Force, and Commander-in-Chief U.S. Fleet, on the latter staff as training officer.

Commander Callaghan was exec of the NROTC unit at the University of California (1933–36); exec of the cruiser *Portland* (CA-33) in the Pacific; and operations officer to Adm. J. K. Taussig, Commander Cruisers Scouting Force (1937–38). In July 1938 he reported as Naval Aide to President Franklin D. Roosevelt, receiving promotion to captain the following

54

October, and remained in that post until May 1941, at which time he assumed command of the *San Francisco* (CA-38). Following his participation in Pacific carrier raids early in the war, he was advanced to rear admiral in April 1942 and became chief of staff to Adm. R. L. Ghormley, Commander South Pacific Force, flagship *Argonne* (AG-31), in which capacity he helped to plan the Guadalcanal landings. In October he left the staff to assume command of the fire support task group protecting the beachhead at Guadalcanal. Ironically, Admiral Callaghan, a native of San Francisco, had begun his service in a ship named for his home state, had spent the better part of his career at or near his home city, had commanded that city's namesake ship, and now hoisted his flag in the same vessel. The next month he led his cruisers and destroyers into the Naval Battle of Guadalcanal, where he perished from direct hits on his flagship by Japanese heavy fleet units.

Bureau of Naval Personnel: National Archives

Caperton, William Banks

(June 30, 1855—December 21, 1941).
USNA (Tenn.) 1875 (30/47).

Pacific Fleet commander during World War I, Caperton served initially aboard the sidewheel steamer *Powhatan* in the North Atlantic prior to and after his commissioning as ensign in 1878 and with the training frigate *Constellation* (1878), the screw frigate *Tennessee* (1879–80), and the Coast Survey (1880–83). He spent the recommissioned screw sloop *Ossipee*'s entire Far Eastern tour on board (1884–87), then inspected steel for "the New Navy" at Pittsburgh and Washington, D.C. (1887–91). Lieutenant Caperton helped to bring the double-turreted monitor *Miantonomoh* into commission for East coast cruising (1891–93), spent six months with the *Vesuvius,* and

55

instructed midshipmen as an officer of the training screw steamer *Essex* (1894–95). After short periods at the Office of Naval Intelligence and the Naval War College, he was in the commissioning crews of both the armored cruiser *Brooklyn,* including her maiden voyage to Britain (1896–97), and the schooner-rigged gunboat *Marietta* (which accompanied the *Oregon* on her famous run around South America during the war with Spain), becoming executive officer in August 1898. Detached the following October, he spent some time at the Washington Navy Yard before reporting as exec of the training cruiser *Prairie* (1901–04).

Lieutenant Commander (since 1899) Caperton was then caught up in the rapid expansion of the Theodore Roosevelt navy, studying at the Naval War College, inspecting lighthouses on the Mississippi, and being promoted to commander, all in 1904. He took command of the protected cruiser *Denver* (C-14) in April 1907 in the Far East, then the battleship *Maine* (BB-10) in July 1908 in the midst of the fleet's global cruise, shortly thereafter achieving the rank of captain. Caperton spent four years (1909–13) ashore with the Lighthouse Board (as secretary), the Naval War College, Naval Examining and Retiring boards, and the Narragansett Bay Naval Station (as commanding officer). While in the latter capacity, in March 1913 he was elevated to rear admiral. The following November he reported aboard the *Alabama* (BB-8), his flagship in his new post commanding the Atlantic Reserve Fleet. One year later he took command of the Atlantic Fleet's Cruiser Squadron (later Force), flagships the armored cruiser *Washington* (ACR-11) off Vera Cruz and the gunboat *Dolphin* (PG-24), participating on the latter as naval commander in the suppression of the Santo Domingo revolt of May 1916.

Two months later Admiral Caperton became Commander-in-Chief Pacific Fleet in the full rank of admiral, flagship *Pittsburgh* (ACR-4). In this capacity he kept patrols off the East coast of South America during World War I then returned to the West side until relieved in April 1919, retiring in June. Throughout 1918 and 1919, before and after his retirement, he was active in cementing American relations with Brazil. Retired as a rear admiral, in 1930 he was advanced to admiral on the retired list.

Carney, Robert Bostwick "Mick"

(March 26, 1895——). USNA (At Large) 1916 (58/177).

Navy Department: National Archives

The future Chief of Naval Operations and son of Lt. Cdr. R. E. Carney (1868–1935) joined the destroyer tender *Dixie* (AD-1) after graduation and cruised with her to Queenstown, Ireland, in June 1917, war having commenced. The next month he transferred to the destroyer *Fanning* (DD-37) as gunnery and torpedo officer for convoy work and participated in the sinking of the *U-58* in November. In the first crew of the *Laub* (DD-263) in March 1919, Lieutenant Carney participated in tracking the flight of the NC flying boats, patrolled European waters, journeyed to Constantinople to engage in refugee food relief, and moved into the Pacific, in the final months as skipper. He remained in that ocean first as executive officer then commanding officer of the new *Reno* (DD-303) (1920–21), transferring to the *Rathburne* (DD-113) for its Asiatic cruise (1921–23). Briefly aboard the *Delphy* (DD-261) for Battle Fleet exercises in the Pacific, he then taught navigation at the Naval Academy (1923–25). Battleship duty followed, for six months as plotting room officer of the *Mississippi* (BB-41), then as flag secretary to Adm. Louis R. de Steiguer, successively Commander Battleship Division Four, flagship *New Mexico* (BB-40) (1925–26); Commander Battleship Divisions, flagship *West Virginia* (BB-48); and Commander-in-Chief Battle Fleet, flagship *California* (BB-44) (1927–28).

Lieutenant Commander Carney went to the Division of Fleet Training in Washington (1928–30), returned to sea as gunnery officer of the cruiser *Cincinnati* (CL-6) in both oceans, and returned to Washington to command the receiving station of the Navy Yard, acting additionally as war plans officer of the Yard and the Naval District (1933–35). Following command of the *Buchanan* (DD-131) in the Battle Force, he brought the *Reid* (DD-369) into commission in the rank of commander (1936–37). He then commanded the cargo ship *Sirius* (AK-15) which kept Midway Island supplied, afterward serving in the Shore Establishments Division at the Navy Department (1938–40), during which he helped mobilize the Navy's PT boats and subchasers. He was exec of the *California* before reporting to Commander Support Force, Atlantic Fleet, Adm. Arthur L. Bristol, Jr., in March 1941 as operations officer, then chief of staff, flagship *Prairie* (AD-15), in which capacity he developed convoy and antisub air defense techniques in the Battle of the Atlantic. This duty lasted until September 1942 when he was promoted to captain, bringing the *Denver* (CL-58) into commission the following month. Taking her to the South Pacific, he bombarded several of the Solomon Islands, laid mines and helped destroy two Japanese destroyers between January 1943 and the landings at New Georgia in June. Promotion to rear admiral came the next month.

Admiral Carney served as chief of staff to Commander South Pacific Force (later Commander Third Fleet), Adm. W. F. Halsey, Jr. *(q.v.),* from July 1943 to the end of World War II, playing a key role in the Solomons victories, the neutralization of Rabaul, the capture of the western Carolines and Philippines, the Battle for Leyte Gulf, and the final summer operations against Japan's home islands. After accompanying Halsey home in September 1945, he became Deputy Chief of Naval Operations (Logistics) as vice admiral in February 1946, handling the difficult task of maintaining fleet fiscal soundness during demobilization and acting during the spring of 1949 as senior naval member of the Armed Forces Petroleum Board. In April 1950 he took command of the Second Fleet, flagship *Missouri* (BB-63), at Norfolk, but the following November moved up to be Commander-in-Chief U.S. Naval Forces in the Eastern Atlantic and Mediterranean, headquarters London, with the accompanying rank of admiral. In July 1951 Carney was given additional duties as deputy to Gen. D.D. Eisenhower, Commander-in-Chief Allied (NATO) Forces in the Mediterranean and of Allied Naval Forces in Southern Europe, flagships first *Mt. Olympus* (AGC-8), then *Adirondack* (AGC-15), amphibious command ships at Naples. The latter post was changed in March 1953 to Commander Naval Striking Forces Southern Europe. Detached in July, the next month Admiral Carney became Chief of Naval Operations, a post he occupied during the tense Russo-American thermonuclear balance until his retirement from active duty in August 1955. His son, R. B. Carney, Jr., rose to be a general officer in the Marine Corps.

Carter, Samuel Powhatan

(August 6, 1819–May 26, 1891). USNA (Tenn.) 1846.

The only American admiral ever to be a general in the Army, Carter became midshipman in 1840, cruised the Pacific in the new sloop *Dale* (1840–43), the Great Lakes on the steamer *Michigan,* and in the West Indies aboard the frigate *Potomac* before going to Annapolis in 1845 as a member of the first graduating class, returning there several times during his career: as assistant professor of mathematics (1850–53), as acting master aboard the practice ship *Preble* (1852), as assistant to the executive officer (1857–59), and as commandant of midshipmen (1870–73). During the Mexican War, he served in the ship-of-the-line *Ohio* against the Mexican Gulf coast (1846–47) and at the Naval Observatory (1847–48), then accompanied the new frigate *St. Lawrence* to Europe (1848–50). Carter helped to supply the Brazil Station as acting master of the storeship *Relief* (1853–54) and was promoted to master in 1854 and to lieutenant in 1855. The latter year he sailed in the screw frigate *San Jacinto* for the Far East via the Cape of Good Hope on the first American diplomatic missions to Siam and Japan and participated in the battles against the barrier forts at Canton, China, late in 1856. He brought home the invalids of the East India Squadron the next year and sailed on the first voyage of the screw sloop *Seminole* to the Brazil Station during the summer of 1860, returning home one year later.

Loaned to the Army, with Navy Lt. William Nelson of Kentucky, in July 1861 to command border citizens loyal to the Union, Carter proceeded to raise East Tennessee troops as colonel of the 2nd Tennessee Infantry Regiment and then act as brigadier general of volunteers. He commanded a brigade of Tennessee troops at the battle of Mill Springs (Logans Cross Roads), Kentucky, in January 1862, and a few months later was permanently commissioned as a general officer in the volunteer army and promoted to lieutenant commander in the Navy. He continued to command a brigade in the Army of the Ohio throughout the war, his most notable action being a very successful cavalry raid during the Murfreesboro campaign at the end of 1862. Given command of a division in the District of Beaufort, North Carolina, in March 1865, General Carter fought at Wilcox's Bridge that month, then transferred to a division in the XXIII Corps for Gen. W. T. Sherman's final operations in North Carolina. He was brevetted major general of volunteers and promoted to commander in the Navy for his war services, a happier fate than that which had befallen his brother Naval officer Maj. Gen. Nelson, shot and killed in a personal quarrel with another general.

Mustered out of the Army early in 1866, Commander Carter brought the sidewheel steamer *Monocacy* into commission that year and took her to the Far East where the vessel helped to strengthen American trade relations with Japan. In 1869 he transferred to the Philadelphia Navy Yard and was promoted to captain the same year. As skipper of the screw gunboat *Alaska* (1873–75), Carter operated in European waters, then had examining board duty (1876) and service on the Lighthouse Board (1877–80). He was promoted to commodore in 1878, retired three years later, and elevated to rear admiral on the retired list in 1882—alone as both general and admiral in the United States Army and Navy (although see also Raphael Semmes).

Carter, Worrall Reed "Nick"

(January 11, 1885–July 22, 1975).
USNA (Me.) 1908 (169/201).

Navy Department: National Archives

Born at sea aboard the American ship *Storm King,* in the ocean in which he would one day lead part of the Navy's logistical effort against Japan, Carter had an early career in the first submarines. Following an initial three-year tour aboard the battleship *Minnesota* (BB-22) in the "Great White Fleet" and the Atlantic Fleet, Ensign Carter reported in April 1911 to the sub tender *Castine,* in November took command of the sub *C-5* (SS-16) on the East coast, and the following September took over the *D-3* (SS-19), operating in the Caribbean. As lieutenant (j.g.) he studied mechanical engineering at the Postgraduate School at Annapolis and at Columbia University (M.S. 1915). In August 1916 he brought the *L-11* (SS-51) into commission as her commanding officer for Atlantic Fleet duty, leaving her in June 1917 to teach mechanical engineering aboard the sub tender *Fulton* (AS-1) at New London. Seven months later he joined the staff of Commander U.S. Naval Forces in Europe, Adm. W. S. Sims, as aide for submarine detection devices. Lieutenant Commander Carter joined the *Nevada* (BB-36) as engineer officer in January 1919 but transferred to the Norfolk Navy Yard the following August.

Promotion to commander followed his service as executive officer of the Fleet Base Force flagship *Procyon* (AG-11) (1922–23) and the *Mississippi* (BB-44) in the Pacific and Caribbean. Attached to the Brazilian Navy afloat (1925–26), Carter went ashore at the Office of Naval Intelligence, then the naval air stations at Norfolk and Pensacola before taking command of the destroyer *Osborne* (DD-295) in the Atlantic in September 1927. Two years later he joined the Engineering faculty at the Naval Academy. Carter commanded the converted hydrographic survey vessel *Nokomis* (PY-6) in

61

the Caribbean (1931–33) before reporting to Norfolk where he became exec in February 1934. Detached in September 1936, he commanded the cruiser *Marblehead* (CL-12) in the Pacific until the spring of 1938, during which duty he was promoted to captain. He then commanded the naval base at Guantanamo Bay, Cuba (1938–40) and the sub base and Submarine Squadron Four at Pearl Harbor. In January 1941 he became chief of staff to Commander Battleships Battle Force, Adm. Walter S. Anderson, flagship *Maryland* (BB-46), where he remained until September 1942.

Captain Carter's experience in base commands led to his wartime assignment to key logistics posts for the duration. In October 1942 he took command of the Navy's Advanced Base in the South Pacific theater and spent the summer of 1943 in the final stages of the Aleutians campaign. In October he began to organize Service Squadron Ten for the Central Pacific offensive, bringing it into commission for the Marshalls operation in January 1944. Based at Majuro atoll, which Carter commanded following its capture the next month, this Squadron supported the fast carriers and amphibious forces in the advance to the Marianas, Carter shifting his headquarters to Eniwetok. Promoted to commodore in June, he hoisted his flag in the destroyer tender *Prairie* (AD-15) late in the summer for the Philippine operations, moving up to Ulithi atoll in October. Expanding his logistics effort for the Iwo Jima and Okinawa campaigns, Commodore Carter shifted his flag to the barracks ship *Ocelot* (IX-110) at Leyte in May 1945, remaining there successfully supplying the Fifth/Third Fleet until Okinawa was secured. Relieved at the end of July, he reported to the Bureau of Naval Personnel where he concluded his active duty late in 1946. He retired in the rank of rear admiral in February 1947 but returned to active service two years later to write the history of the Pacific Fleet's wartime logistics, *Beans, Bullets, and Black Oil* (1953).

Naval Historical Center

Case, Augustus Ludlow

(February 3, 1813—February 17, 1893).

One of the few distinguished flag officers of the post-Civil War "dead period" Navy, New Yorker Case received his midshipman's appointment in April 1828 and participated in the only cruise of the frigate *Hudson* (1828–31) on anti-slave patrol off Brazil. Returning to the New York Navy Yard, he reported to the sloop *St. Louis,* aboard which he cruised the West Indies (1832–33), returning again to New York for training which led to his appointment as passed midshipman (1834). He did coast survey and exploration work, in the former aboard the schooner *Experiment* (1836), in the latter with the South Sea Surveying and Exploring expeditions (1837–42) aboard the bark *Pioneer,* the storeship *Relief* and the sloop *Vincennes.* Lieutenant Case served aboard the frigate *Brandywine* in the East Indies (1843–45) prior to Mexican War duty with, successively, the dispatch boat *Mahonese,* the brig *Porpoise,* the frigates *Raritan* and *John Adams* and the sloop *Germantown,* all along the Mexican Gulf coast. From the *Porpoise* he landed with the Army at Vera Cruz early in 1847 and on the second day took over direction of troop, ammunition and supplies unloading of the landing forces at the beach. The *Porpoise* took Laguna, after which Case led 26 men in a "bungo" mounting one 42-pounder carronade upriver to capture and hold Palisada against enemy cavalry.

Shifting to the Pacific aboard the *Vincennes* (1849–51), Case stayed with that squadron to command the sloop *Warren* (1852–53). During lighthouse inspection duty at New York (1853–57), he was promoted to commander. After bringing the screw steamer *Caledonia* into commission, he led her in the show of naval force against Paraguay early in 1859. Ordered to the staff of Flag Off. S. K. Stringham as assistant in the Bureau of Detail in March

1861, he accompanied that officer the following month to the North Atlantic Blockading Squadron as fleet captain, flagship the steam frigate *Minnesota,* serving three successive flag officers, Stringham, L. M. Goldsborough and S. P. Lee (1861–62). Among the Squadron's achievements were the captures of Forts Clark and Hatteras, Roanoke Island, Sewall's Point, and Norfolk, plus general blockading. Promoted to captain, in January 1863 Case assumed command of the steam sloop *Iroquois,* continuing in the blockade of the North Carolina coast. After special duty in Washington, he served at the New York yard again (1864–65) and then as fleet captain, European Squadron, Adm. Goldsborough, flagship the screw frigate *Colorado* (1865–66).

Commodore (as of December 1867) Case again inspected lighthouses in the New York area, after which he was made Chief of the Bureau of Ordnance (1869–73). Promoted to rear admiral in May 1872, he took command of the European Squadron the next year, flagships the steam frigates *Wabash* and *Franklin.* During the diplomatic crisis with Spain over the "*Virginius* affair" in 1873–74, Admiral Case commanded the combined European, and North and South Atlantic squadrons for less-than-impressive tactical maneuvers and a show of force at Key West. This event, the Navy's only major operation between the end of the Civil War and the advent of the "New Navy" in the 1880s, climaxed Case's career, and he retired in February 1875.

Chadwick, French Ensor

(February 29, 1844–January 27, 1919).
USNA (W.Va.) 1865 (5/31).

Navy Photo from Harper's Weekly

An eminent naval scholar originally inspired as a boy by James Fenimore Cooper's history of the Navy, Chadwick served on anti-Confederate raider patrol during the summer of 1864 midshipman cruise aboard the screw gunboat *Marblehead* before graduating in November. After drilling recruits at the Brooklyn Navy Yard, he reported the next April to the sidewheel steamer *Susquehanna* in the Gulf and South Atlantic, and in November 1866 to the screw sloop *Juniata* as ensign, then master for more service in the South Atlantic. Brief duty on the training frigate *Sabine* and the new screw sloop *Tuscarora* in the South Pacific was accompanied by rapid promotions to lieutenant and lieutenant commander (1867–69). Chadwick participated in negotiations for the possible annexation of Santo Domingo, and then had torpedo duty during the spring of 1870 prior to joining the screw sloop *Guerrière* of the Mediterranean Squadron (1870–72). He taught mathematics at the Naval Academy before becoming executive officer of the sidewheeler *Powhatan,* flagship of the North Atlantic Squadron (1875–78).

Lieutenant Commander Chadwick in 1878 embarked upon ten years of intensive work on naval doctrine, that year concluding a valuable study of the training of seamen in foreign navies following a tour in Europe. In mid-1880 after brief duty at the Brooklyn Navy Yard he reported to the Third Lighthouse District in order to study the uses of lighthouses and two years later to London to observe foreign navies. In October 1882, attached to the new Office of Naval Intelligence, Chadwick became America's first naval attaché and remained at the London embassy for an unheard-of tour of seven years—a tribute to his mental powers and superior performance. A key contributor to the U.S. Naval Institute *Proceedings,* he was promoted to commander early in 1885 but did not return to sea until April 1889 when he brought into commission the new gunboat *Yorktown* (PG-1) for a two-year cruise in the Mediterranean. Late in 1891 he returned to Washington for board duty establishing the civil service system at the Navy's yards and to inspect ships at New York. In August 1882 he became Chief, Office of Naval Intelligence.

Chadwick began four years as Chief of the Bureau of Equipment in June 1893, at the end of which tour he studied the Navy's drydocks, was promoted to captain and was given command of the armored cruiser *New York* (ACR-2), flagship of the North Atlantic Squadron. In March 1898 Captain Chadwick concluded his role in the investigation of the destruction of the battleship *Maine* and assumed additional duty as chief of staff to the Squadron commander, Adm. W. T. Sampson. His vessel bombarded Spanish positions at Matanzas and San Juan, Cuba, before participating in the Battle of Santiago in July. Routine training missions followed during 1899, and in January 1900 he reported to the Naval War College, becoming its president in October and assuming collateral duty as Commandant, Second Naval District, in March 1903. Promoted to rear admiral in October, he ended his career as Commander-in-Chief South Atlantic Squadron, flagship *Brooklyn* (1904) (ACR-3). He retired in February 1906.

Admiral Chadwick, a prolific writer and profound thinker during the golden age of American naval philosophy as well as a student of military history, wrote three volumes late in life on the events surrounding the Spanish-American War (1909–11).

Chauncey, Isaac

(February 20, 1772–January 27, 1840).

By Gilbert Stuart, U. S. Naval Academy Museum: Naval Photographic Center

A merchant captain of the *Jenny* at the tender age of 19, Chauncey altered his youthful career from merchant to naval service with his commissioning as lieutenant in September 1798 and his position as first lieutenant aboard the frigate *President* the following year for a West Indian cruise in 1800 against the French. Operating in the Mediterreanean against Tripoli and on convoy, he commanded the frigates *Chesapeake* (1802–03) and *New York,* the ship which he saved from fire in a magazine explosion in April 1803. Promoted master commandant in May 1804, he led the frigate *John Adams* in heavy bombardments of Tripoli in August and September 1804, participating in one of them aboard the Mediterranean Squadron flagship frigate *Constitution.* Chauncey was detached the next year, promoted to captain in April 1806, and furloughed to command a merchantman to the East Indies. He returned to the Navy for an extended tour commanding the New York Navy Yard (1807–12).

Given command of the naval forces on Lakes Ontario and Erie in September 1812, Commodore Chauncey organized a force of some twenty warships, his flagship the schooner *Madison,* with accompanying base and logistical facilities, headquarters at Sackett's Harbor on Lake Ontario, New York. With his vessels in 1813 he supported the Army's victories at York and Fort George, and that August and September engaged and damaged the British squadron under Commo. Sir James L. Yeo on that lake. However, he failed to make the battles decisive, although he captured several vessels throughout the year. Again in 1814 he did not exploit his thin superiority on Lake Ontario, for which inaction he was nearly relieved. Chauncey concluded a treaty with Algiers while in command of the Mediterranean

Squadron, flagship the ship-of-the-line *Washington* (1816–18), which remained his flagship during his command of New York (1818–20). He was a Navy Commissioner (1821–24), again commandant at New York (1825–32) and thereafter a Commissioner, in which capacity he ended his career and life finally as president of the Board of Navy Commissioners (1837–40).

Commodore Chauncey's son, Commo. John S. Chauncey (1800–1871), commanded the screw steamer *Susquehanna* in the capture of Forts Hatteras and Clark, North Carolina, in August 1861.

Christie, Ralph Waldo

(August 30, 1893——   ). USNA
(Mass.) 1915 (160/179).

A World War II commander of submarines, Christie served only briefly in the battleship *New Jersey* (BB-16) and the armored cruiser *Montana* (ACR-13) in the Atlantic (taking torpedo instruction on the latter) before entering submarine training in January 1917 aboard the sub tender *Fulton* (AS-1) at New London. He joined the sub *C-1* (SS-9) six months later for wartime patrols, taking command of her the following January for the duration. In February 1919 he reported to the converted *Camden* (AS-6), flagship of the Atlantic Fleet's Submarine Flotilla, transferring briefly to command of the *R-6* (SS-83) in August 1920. Following this was postgraduate work in ordnance engineering at Annapolis (1920–21) and in mechanical engineering in torpedoes at M.I.T. (M.S. 1923). After commanding the experimental *S-1* (SS-105) during the summer, Lieutenant Christie went to the Philippines to command first the *Rainbow* (AS-7) in December, then the *S-7* (SS-112) in April 1924, and finally in September the destroyer *John D. Ford* (DD-228).

This successful Asiatic duty led to command of the sub base at Cavite (1925–26).

Lieutenant Commander Christie served at the Naval Torpedo Station at Newport; as torpedo repair officer of the *Argonne* (AS-10) in the Battle Fleet (1928–30); briefly aboard the *Holland* (AS-3), flagship of that Fleet's submarine divisions; and again at the Newport torpedo station (1931–33). He commanded the new large sub *Narwhal* (SS-167) on the Pacific coast before joining the commissioning crew of the aircraft carrier *Ranger* (CV-4) as navigator (1934–36) in the rank of commander. After heading the Torpedo Section, Bureau of Ordnance, in January 1939 he took command of Submarine Division 15, flagship *Snapper* (SS-185), operating mostly around Hawaii, and in December 1940 of Submarine Squadron 20, later redesignated SubRon Five, flagship *Griffin* (AS-13). Moving from Panama to Brisbane, Australia, early in 1942 Captain Christie's subs patrolled Southwest Pacific waters, with Christie in August becoming Commander Eastern Australia Submarine Group, Task Force 42. In November he was promoted to rear admiral, returning at the end of the year to be inspector of ordnance at the Torpedo Station at Newport for the first two months of 1943.

Admiral Christie became Commander Submarines Southwest Pacific (Task Force 51) and Commander Allied Naval Forces West Australia in March 1943, and he thereafter directed the Allied unrestricted submarine warfare campaign against Japanese shipping in that theater, also minelaying, supplying Filipino guerrillas, and maintaining contacts with Allied agents. In January 1944 he went on a war patrol to the Makassar Strait aboard the *Bowfin* (SS-287), in June provided boats to scout for the Fifth Fleet's Battle of the Philippine Sea, and in the autumn used wolf packs to support the liberation of the Philippines and provided lifeguard boats for Third Fleet operations. Relieved at the end of the year, Admiral Christie commanded the Navy's base at Bremerton from February 1945 till January 1948. He then commanded U. S. Naval Forces in the Philippines (1948–49) and served as General Inspector of the Western Sea Frontier prior to his retirement in August 1949 in the rank of vice admiral.

Clarey, Bernard Ambrose "Chick"

(May 4, 1912——). USNA (Iowa)
1934 (278/463).

Naval Photographic Center

One of the few distinguished submarine commanders of World War II to achieve four-star rank, Clarey served in only one surface line billet, aboard the cruiser *Milwaukee* (CL-5), before becoming a submariner in early 1937. Operating out of Pearl Harbor on the sub *Nautilus* (SS-168) until July 1941, he then transferred to the *Dolphin* (SS-169) as executive officer, engaging Japanese planes during the attack on Pearl Harbor and thereafter reconnoitering the Marshall Islands. Lieutenant Clarey brought the *Amberjack* (SS-219) into commission as her exec in June 1942 and made one successful war patrol to Guadalcanal, delivering supplies and personnel and sinking two enemy merchant ships. After staff duty with Submarine Division 81, he began preparing for sub command by patrolling in the South Pacific as navigator of the *Peto* (SS-265) during the spring of 1943 and by additional training at New London. Reporting in August to the *Pintado* (SS-387), under construction at Portsmouth, Lieutenant Commander Clarey brought her into commission on the first day of 1944 and took her on four war patrols between May 1944 and April 1945. On the first, into the Philippine Sea, as flagship of Capt. Leon N. Blair's wolf pack, *Pintado* sank two merchantmen and a troop transport of one convoy. On the second, into the East China Sea, Clarey in August nailed the big 19,000-ton tanker *Tonan Maru No. 2*. On the third patrol he led his own wolf pack, "Clarey's Crushers" with *Jallao* and *Atule*, to participate in the October operations relative to the Leyte landings, his boats sinking the light cruiser *Tama* and then lesser vessels during November and December.

With eight ships of nearly 43,000 tons in all to *Pintado*'s credit, Commander (since February 1944) Clarey left the boat in April 1945, two months later becoming assistant strategic plans officer to Commander Submarines Pacific Fleet, Adm. C. A. Lockwood. From December 1945 to April 1946 he served with the Secretary of the Navy's Committee on Reorganization, then with the office of the Naval Inspector General. He was flag secretary to Commander Submarines Atlantic Fleet, Adm. James Fife (1947–49), and then Assignment Desk Submarine Officer at the Bureau of Naval Personnel. Following wartime duty as exec of the *Helena* (CA-75) bombarding North Korean coastal positions in the summer and autumn of 1951, in May 1952 he took command of Submarine Division 52, flagship *Catfish* (SS-339), operating along the California coast. Captain Clarey had duty at the Navy's Far Eastern desk (1953–55), studied at the National War College, and was chief of staff to Commander Submarines Pacific Fleet, Adm. E. W. Grenfell (1956–58). After brief deep-draught command of the oiler *Hassayampa* (AO-145) during the Quemoy-Matsu crisis of 1958, he became—in January 1959—Director of the Military Personnel Policy Division in the Office of the Assistant Secretary of Defense (Manpower, Personnel, and Reserves).

During this duty, in July 1959, Clarey was promoted to rear admiral and in February 1961 moved up to be Director for Military Personnel in the same office. Service as ComSubsPac between July 1962 and June 1964, during which he brought the Polaris boats into that ocean, led to his promotion to vice admiral in the latter month. Advanced to Deputy Commander-in-Chief and chief of staff Pacific Fleet to Adms. T. H. Moorer and Roy L. Johnson, Admiral Clarey remained in that post for two years, helping to mobilize the Fleet for the Vietnam War before assuming command of the Second Fleet and the Atlantic Striking Fleet in August 1966. The following June he became Director of Navy Program Planning, terminating this job in January 1968 with his appointment as Vice Chief of Naval Operations in the full rank of admiral. Finally, in December 1970, Admiral Clarey became Commander-in-Chief Pacific Fleet and thereafter directed the Navy's final operations in the Vietnam War. He retired in October 1973.

Clark, Charles Edgar

(August 10, 1843–October 2, 1922).
USNA (Vt.) 1864 (15/29).

"Clark of the *Oregon*" entered the Navy at the outbreak of the Civil War, graduating in October 1863 to the screw sloop *Ossipee* on blockade duty off the Texas coast. He played a conspicuous role commanding one of her gun divisions at the Battle of Mobile Bay in August 1864, returning afterward to the Texas blockade. The next year he reported aboard the sidewheel steamer *Vanderbilt,* flagship of the Pacific Squadron, and in 1867 to the sidewheeler *Suwanee* in the same waters and was stranded for some time ashore when that vessel was wrecked on Vancouver Island, July 1868. Lieutenant Commander Clark's next duties were with the Portsmouth receiving ship *Vandalia* (1868–1869), the decommissioned screw sloop *Seminole* at Boston, the monitor *Dictator* in the North Atlantic as navigator (1869–70), and the Naval Academy (1870–73). He served as executive officer of the monitor *Mahopac* at Key West (1873–74) and then with the steam sloop *Hartford,* the sidewheel gunboat *Monocacy* and the screw sloop *Kearsarge,* all in the Far East (1874–77), going ashore at the Boston Navy Yard (1877–80). Promoted commander in 1881, he joined the schoolship *New Hampshire,* flagship of the Apprentice Training Squadron, first as exec (1881–82) then commanding officer (1882–83), with brief torpedo duty afterward.

Commander Clark performed hydrographic surveys off the West coast of North America as skipper of the iron screw steamer *Ranger* (1883–86) and ashore completing his reports (1886–87). A lighthouse inspector at Chicago (1887–91), he had ordnance duty at Mare Island (1891–93) before commanding first the steam sloop *Mohican* and a small squadron on Bering Sea patrol enforcing anti-pelagic sealing and fishery treaty provisions (1893–95), then the receiving ship *Independence* at Mare Island (1895–96). Promotion to captain was accompanied by command of the monitor *Monterey* (BM-6) out of Mare Island (1896–98) and in March 1898 command of the battleship *Oregon* (BB-3) at San Francisco. Captain Clark took his ship in a dramatic and much celebrated 67-day "race" around the Horn to the Caribbean to reinforce the fleet blockading Spanish Cuba, arriving in late May. The *Oregon* supported the Marine landings at Guantanamo Bay and fought at the Battle of Santiago Bay in early July, pounding several Spanish warships and running aground the cruiser *Cristóbal Colón*. This led to Clark's appointment a few days later as chief of staff to Commo. John C. Watson for one month, commanding the Eastern or "Flying" Squadron, flagship the protected cruiser *Newark* (C-1). After leave for health reasons, he was Captain of the Yard, League Island, Philadelphia (1899–1901) and Governor of that city's Naval Home (1901–04). He was awarded prize money for his success at Santiago but he donated it in toto to the widows and orphans of Spanish seamen lost in the battle. Promoted to rear admiral in June 1902, Clark concluded his career as a member of the General Board and president of the Naval Examining and Retirement boards (1904–05), his own retirement occurring in August 1905. His autobiography is *My Fifty Years in the Navy* (1917). Admiral Clark was father-in-law of Adms. C. F. Hughes (*q.v.*) and Samuel S. Robison (1867–1952), Commander-in-Chief United States Fleet in 1925–26.

Clark, Joseph James "Jocko"

(November 12, 1893–July 13, 1971).
USNA (Okla.) 1918 (47/199).

Probably the first flag officer with strong Indian blood, one-eighth Cherokee, and renowned as a fighting air admiral in the Pacific and Korean wars, Clark graduated early for wartime convoy escort aboard the armored cruiser *North Carolina* (ACR-12) (1917–18), during which he suffered a serious leg injury and had to be hospitalized. He helped bring the destroyer *Aaron Ward* (DD-132) into commission in April 1919 in time to stand picket duty for the flight of the NC flying boats, then assisted in commissioning the *Aulick* (DD-258) in July for a voyage to Hawaii. Lieutenant Clark cruised the troubled Baltic, Adriatic, Black and Eastern Mediterranean seas as engineering officer of the *Brooks* (DD-232) (1920–21), at the end of which he commanded her on the Eastern seaboard prior to joining the *Bulmer* (DD-222) as executive officer for more duty in unsettled Turkish waters (1922–23). After teaching navigation at the Naval Academy, he underwent flight training at Pensacola, earning his wings in 1925 but remaining there for advanced training until transferring to San Diego in July as flight officer of Utility Squadron One. Clark served with the aviation units on the battleships *Mississippi* (BB-41), *Pennsylvania* (BB-38) and *New York* (BB-34) (1926–28), doubling on the latter two as staff aviator to Commander Battleship Division Two, Adm. Montgomery M. Taylor. He was then exec of Naval Air Station Anacostia, D. C., and personal pilot of Adm. W. A. Moffett.

Lieutenant Commander Clark commanded Fighting Squadron Two on the aircraft carrier *Lexington* (CV-2) (1931–33) and was aeronautical member of the Board of Inspection and Survey, senior aviator then air officer of the *Lexington* (1936–38), and exec of the air station at Pearl

Harbor and Commander Patrol Wing Two in the rank of commander. He inspected naval aircraft at the Curtiss-Wright factory at Buffalo, New York (1940) and served as exec first of the new air station at Jacksonville (1940–41) then of the *Yorktown* (CV-5) in the Atlantic and on her Pacific raids against Marcus and the Gilbert Islands early in 1942. Promoted to captain, Clark brought the escort carrier *Suwannee* (ACV-27) into commission in September and led her during the North African landings in November and on her subsequent voyage to the Pacific. He then commissioned the new *Yorktown* (CV-10) in April 1943, attacking Marcus, Wake, the Gilberts and Kwajalein between August and December and participating in the subsequent seizure of the Marshall Islands. He was promoted to rear admiral and made Commander Carrier Division 13 in February 1944.

Admiral Clark commanded Task Group 58.1 against the Japanese at Truk, the Carolines, Hollandia, Palau, the Marianas, the Bonins, and the Volcanos from February to August 1944 and at the Battle of the Philippine Sea in June, flag in the *Hornet* (C V -12). As ComCarDiv 5 he commanded the same task group in the Iwo Jima and Okinawa operations, including strikes on Japan, February to June 1945. He was Chief of Naval Air Intermediate Training at Corpus Christi, then Assistant Chief of Naval Operations (Air) (1946–48) before commanding CarDiv Four and Task Force 87, flagships *Philippine Sea* (CV-47) and *Midway* (CVB-41), for two cruises to the Mediterranean (1948–50). Admiral Clark, after commanding the naval air bases on the West coast, in October 1951 took command of CarDiv Three and TF 77, flagship *Bonhomme Richard* (CV-31), operating against North Korea. The following March he was promoted to vice admiral and given command of the First Fleet as a prelude to taking over the Seventh Fleet in May, flagships *Iowa* (BB-61), *Missouri* (BB-63) and *New Jersey* (BB-62). He directed the Fleet through the last year of the Korean War, introducing effective close air support measures known as the "Cherokee strikes." Admiral Clark relinquished his command and retired in December 1953 in the full rank of admiral. He later published his autobiography, *Carrier Admiral* (1967).

Conner, David

(c. 1792—March 20, 1856).

One of the Navy's two premier commanders in the Mexican War (the other being M. C. Perry), Conner began his career as midshipman aboard the frigate *President* on the East coast (1809–10), took leave for two merchant cruises, and then reported—in August 1811—to the sloop *Hornet* at Washington. When this vessel engaged and took the British privateer *Dolphin* in July 1812 in the western Atlantic, he was made prize master of the latter, only to be recaptured several days later. Immediately exchanged and returned to the *Hornet,* he participated in the capture and subsequent foundering of the brig *Peacock* in February 1813, risking his own life to help rescue her crew. Commissioned lieutenant the following July, Conner was severely wounded in the victory over the brig *Penguin* in the South Atlantic in March 1815 but remained attached to the *Hornet* for another two years. As first lieutenant of the sloop *Ontario* for Commo. James Biddle's voyage to Oregon (1817–19), he went to hometown Philadelphia for naval rendezvous and receiving ship duty, where he assumed command of the new schooner *Dolphin,* with which he protected American interests off the west coast of South America (1821–24). In 1825 he returned to Philadelphia in the rank of master commandant and four years later commanded the sloop *Erie* in the West Indies, but facial neuralgia stemming from his war wounds rendered him inactive ashore thereafter (1831–34).

In command of the sloop *John Adams* in the Mediterranean, Conner became captain in 1835, only to be placed in "on leave" status again for his poor health until becoming a Navy Commissioner (1841–42). After only four months as the first Chief of the new Bureau of Construction, Equipment, and Repair, he resigned at the end of 1842 again for health reasons. This leave was terminated late in 1843 with his appointment to command of the Home Squadron as commodore, flagship the frigate *Potomac,* his responsibilities extending from the waters off Newfoundland to those of northern South America. Ordered to Mexican waters during the Texas crisis in the spring of 1844, he thereafter returned with his squadron to its normal patrols until ordered to reconcentrate in the Gulf of Mexico in March 1845. With the outbreak of war in May 1846 he imposed a blockade of the Mexican Gulf coast, basing chiefly in an anchorage south of Vera Cruz. Supporting the army on land, the squadron—sometimes with different flagships—seized several coastal towns over the ensuing year. Commodore Conner's normal two-year tour was extended in spite of his delicate health and somewhat cautious leadership, and the arduous blockade in the tropical heat and disease further weakened his constitution. The crowning achievement of his career occurred with the successful assault on Vera Cruz in March 1847, Commodore Conner in the frigate *Raritan* working effectively with his Army counterpart, Gen. Winfield Scott. He finally relinquished command on the 21st, rejected an offer to resume his old bureau post because of his fragile health, commanded the Philadelphia Navy Yard (1849–50), and served as president of the Board of Examiners (1851–55), prior to being placed on the reserve list in September 1855.

Navy Department: National Archives

Conolly, Richard Lansing

(April 26, 1892—March 1, 1962). USNA (Ill.) 1914 (59/154).

Amphibious commander during World War II, Conolly entered active duty in the Mexican crisis of 1914 aboard the battleship *Virginia* (BB-13), but was detached to the armored cruiser *Montana* (ACR-13) for instruction in torpedoes during the summer of 1915, and again to the *Vermont* (BB-20) as torpedo officer for the following spring. Joining the destroyer *Smith* (DD-17) in May 1916 he spent World War I on escort duty out of Brest, France, during which he salvaged a torpedoed transport. Lieutenant Conolly helped to bring into commission (1918–20) as executive officer successively the *Foote* (DD-169), *Worden* (DD-288), and *Hunt* (DD-194). His study of electrical engineering at Annapolis and Columbia University (M.S. 1922) and elsewhere preceded his Pacific battleship duty aboard the *Mississippi* (BB-41) (1922–24) and *New York* (BB-34), on the latter as assistant engineering officer. He taught electrical engineering at the Naval Academy (1925–27) and was engineer officer of the cruiser *Concord* (CL-10) and commanding officer of the *Case* (DD-285) (1929–30) and the *DuPont* (DD-152), all in the Atlantic-Caribbean area. Duty as student and then instructor at the Naval War College followed (1931–33).

Commander Conolly in May 1933 became flag secretary and aide to Adm. Harris Laning, Commander Cruisers Scouting Force, flagship *Chicago* (CA-29), in the Pacific and Caribbean. He reported as navigator of the *Tennessee* (BB-43) in April 1935, returning to the Naval Academy (1936–38) to teach electrical engineering, then seamanship and navigation, part of the time as acting department head. As captain he commanded Destroyer Division Seven, flagship *Blue* (DD-387), and Destroyer Squadron Six, flagship *Balch* (DD-363), part of Adm. W. F. Halsey's force escort prior to and during the early months of the Pacific war, including the Doolittle raid on Tokyo. Detached at the end of April 1942, he joined Adm. E. J. King's command staff at the Navy Department, being promoted to rear admiral in July. Early in 1943 he reported to the Atlantic Fleet Amphibious Force, becoming Commander Landing Craft and Bases, Northwest African Waters in March, flagship seaplane tender *Biscayne* (AVP-11), moving up from Algerian ports to Bizerta, Tunisia, in May, preparatory to the invasion of Sicily.

Admiral Conolly began his amphibious combat career in July 1943 commanding Task Force 86, one of the three invasion transport forces at Sicily, and then amphibious elements under overall British command for the Salerno, Italy, assault in September, still from the *Biscayne*. Transferred the next month to the Amphibious Forces in the Pacific Fleet, he boarded his flagship for the duration, the new amphibious command ship *Appalachian* (AGC-1), at San Diego late in November as Commander Group Three, Fifth Amphibious Force. As such, he led Task Force 53 in the capture of Kwajalein in the Marshall Islands, January and February 1944, and maintained it as a floating reserve during the Saipan landing in June. Redesignated Commander Group Three, Amphibious Forces Pacific Fleet in July, Conolly landed and supported the Marines at Guam that month after directing prelanding bombardments. Leading an amphibious group, he landed Army forces at Leyte in October and at Lingayen Gulf in January 1945. After a much-deserved rest, he began to plan the invasion of Japan but then instead directed the occupation of northern Japan in October.

Promoted to vice admiral in December 1945, Conolly served briefly as Deputy Chief of Naval Operations (Operations) and the next month moved over to be DCNO (Administration). In August 1946 he went to Europe to advise Allied foreign ministers at Paris and London, and late in September became Commander U.S. Naval Forces Europe (and Commander Twelfth Fleet to the end of the year), flagship *Houston* (CA-30), in the rank of admiral. His title twice changed: in March 1947 to Commander U.S. Naval Forces, Eastern Atlantic and Mediterranean; and in November 1947 to Commander-in-Chief of the same, a post he occupied until mid-1950. Reverting in rank to vice admiral, Conolly was president of the Naval War College from the end of 1950 until November 1953 when he retired in the rank of admiral.

Bureau of Ships: National Archives

Coontz, Robert Edward "Senator"

(June 11, 1864–January 26, 1935).
USNA (Mo.) 1885 (28/36).

A key figure in directing the post-World War I Navy, Coontz spent several of his initial years enforcing sealing and fishing laws in the Bering Sea as an officer of iron screw tug *Pinta* (1887–90, 1891–93), preceded by precommissioning training (1885–87) aboard the steam sloops *Mohican* and *Juniata,* the screw steamer *Galena,* and the new protected cruiser *Atlanta,* generally along the Atlantic seaboard and in Latin American waters. On one occasion he participated in a naval demonstration off revolution-torn Panama and on another with four Marines captured 125 armed Indians near Sitka, Alaska. Briefly at the Naval Observatory (1891), Ensign Coontz served on the old Great Lakes sidewheel steamer *Michigan* (1893–94) and had miscellaneous duties chiefly in the Bureau of Navigation (1894–96), culminating with his promotion to lieutenant (j.g.) and assignment to the cruiser *Philadelphia* (C-4), flagship of the Pacific Station (1896–97). Duty with the Coast and Geodetic Survey and its vessel *Patterson* preceded his reporting to the protected cruiser *Charleston* (C-2) in 1898; this vessel seized Spanish Guam, participated in the final operations against Manila, and fought in the Philippine Insurrection. Promoted lieutenant in 1899, he returned from the latter struggle with the protected cruiser *Boston,* then went to the Massachusetts schoolship *Enterprise* (1899–1901).

Lieutenant Coontz, senior watch officer on the final cruise of the *Philadelphia* off Panama (1901–02), trained personnel on the screw gunboat *Adams* along the Pacific coast (1902–04), then served briefly with the gunboat *Wheeling* (PG-14) and the auxiliary cruiser *Buffalo* also in the Pacific. Promoted to lieutenant commander in 1905, he had inspection duty at Seattle and at the Bureau of Equipment (1905–07) and became executive officer of the new battleship *Nebraska* (BB-14) for the world cruise of the "Great White Fleet" and Atlantic Fleet duty. As commander, Coontz was commandant of midshipmen at the Naval Academy (1909–11) and led the summer cruise of 1911 to Germany before reporting to the Board of Inspection and Survey for Ships. Appointed Naval Governor of Guam and commandant of its naval station in April 1912, Coontz was promoted to captain two months later. He commanded the *Georgia* (BB-15) (1913–15) during the Mexican and Haitian disturbances of 1914 and the Puget Sound Navy Yard and Thirteenth Naval District throughout World War I (1915–18), rendering valuable services in ship construction and repair. His success there, particularly as a negotiator with organized labor, earmarked him for rapid promotion to the top.

Promoted rear admiral in September 1918, Coontz was acting Chief of Naval Operations while Adm. W. S. Benson was in Europe and commanded Division Seven of the Atlantic Fleet, flagship *Arizona* (BB-39), from January to June 1919, shifting to the *Wyoming* (BB-32) to escort the NC flying boats expedition and then to go to the Pacific. Initially reporting to command that Fleet's Division Six, in September he became second-in-command of the Pacific Fleet, flagship *Nevada* (BB-36). He was appointed Chief of Naval Operations and member of the Joint Board in the rank of admiral in October and served in these capacities for four years, playing a leading role in the Washington Naval Conference force reductions of 1921–22 and in the creation of the United States Fleet in 1922. In August 1923 Admiral Coontz became Commander-in-Chief of that Fleet, flagship the cruiser *Seattle* (CA-11), taking most of it on a cruise to Australia during the summer of 1925. Appointed Commandant Fifth Naval District and of Naval Operating Base Norfolk in October, he reverted in rank to rear admiral and retired in June 1928. Two years later he published his memoirs, *From the Mississippi to the Sea,* and was advanced to the full rank of admiral on the retired list. He then wrote *True Anecdotes of an Admiral* (1934).

Admiral Coontz's family was henceforth largely a Navy one: son Lt. Kenneth L. Coontz (1897–1926) convoyed troops to Europe in the *Chattanooga* (C-16) during World War I; grandnephew Lt. (j.g.) Curtis W. Howard was shot down while operating from the carrier *Yorktown* (CV-5) during the Battle of Midway; nephew Rear Adm. Guy B. Helmick commanded the attack transport *Kittson* (APA-123) from commissioning late in 1944 until the middle of the Okinawa campaign; grandson Capt. Robert J. Coontz commanded the destroyer *Wedderburn* (DD-684) off Vietnam (1967–68); and cousin Rear Adm. Levering Smith directed the Polaris, Poseidon and Trident strategic missile projects during the 1970's.

Coye, John Starr, Jr.

(April 24, 1911—   ). USNA (Del.) 1933 (124/432).

Naval Photographic Center

One of the Navy's most accomplished submarine commanders of World War II, Coye served aboard the cruiser *Northampton* (CA-26) in the Pacific before helping to outfit the destroyer *Monaghan* (DD-354) as assistant engineer for duty in both oceans (1935–36). After sub training at New London in the first half of 1937, he was engineering officer of the sub *Shark* (SS-174) in the Pacific until October 1940. Joining the *R-18* (SS-95) prior to her recommissioning in January 1941, he patrolled the Panama Canal area during the summer and thereafter operated out of New London on North Atlantic patrols. In April 1942 he assumed command of the *R-18*, shifting his base to Bermuda for the summer and thereafter to training chores in the West Indies and then New England until detached in April 1943. Lieutenant Commander Coye took command of the *Silversides* (SS-236) in June and led her on six war patrols, between October 1943 and May 1944, sinking 14 Japanese vessels totaling over 38,000 tons. Among the most notable engagements was his attack on a heavily protected Japanese convoy and escape from an enemy sub attack near the Palau Islands at the end of 1943 and beginning of 1944. Also by his actions, his boat was instrumental in the rescue of the damaged *Salmon* (SS-182) off Kyushu, Japan, in October 1944,

Salmon with *Trigger* and *Silversides* comprising the wolf pack known as "Coye's Coyotes."

Commander Coye left the *Silversides* in December 1944 to instruct in submarine command at New London (1945–47), then served as operations officer in the Pacific to Commander Submarine Squadron One, Capt. Arthur H. Taylor, flagship *Becuna* (SS-319), and as Commander Submarine Division 52, flagships *Tilefish* (SS-307) and *Greenfish* (SS-351) (1948–49). He attended the Armed Forces Staff College before joining the staff of the Commander Operational Development Force, Adms. Maurice E. Curts and Frederick I. Entwistle, at Norfolk (1950–52). After commanding the submarine tender *Fulton* (AS-11) at New London, Captain Coye led SubRon Eight from there (1953–54), flagships *Crevalle* (SS-291) and *Dogfish* (SS-350), attended the Naval War College, and was operations officer then chief of staff for plans, operations, and readiness to Commander Second Fleet/Commander Striking Fleet Atlantic, Adm. Charles Wellborn, Jr., flagship the command ship *Northampton* (CLC-1). He then commanded the *Rochester* (CA-124), flagship of the Seventh Fleet in the Pacific, before reporting as assistant director of the Navy's Strike Warfare Division (1959–61). Promoted to rear admiral in July 1961, Coye in September took command of the naval forces in the Marianas and in January 1963 of Amphibious Group Three, flagship the amphibious command ship *Eldorado* (AGC-11). He served as deputy chief of staff to the Commander-in-Chief Allied Forces Southern Europe, Adms. Charles D. Griffin and J. S. Thach (1964–66), and as Commander Training Command, Atlantic Fleet, before retiring in August 1968 in the rank of rear admiral.

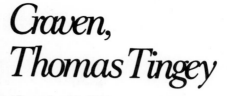

Craven, Thomas Tingey

(December 20, 1808—August 23, 1887).

Grandson of Commo. Thomas Tingey (1750–1829), for 27 years commandant of the Washington Navy Yard, and son of Navy purser and storekeeper Tunis Craven, New Hampshire-appointed Midshipman Craven began his Naval career in 1822, initially in the Pacific aboard the frigate *United States* (1823–26) and the sloop *Peacock* (1826–27), the latter vessel's career ended from damage received by a collision with a whale! As passed midshipman, he was sailing master of the sloop *Erie* in the West Indies (1828–29), which led to promotion to lieutenant in 1830. He then joined the schooner *Boxer* on the Brazil Station (1832–33, 1834), interrupted by duty with the new sloop *Peacock* on a diplomatic mission to Arabia. After serving on the receiving ship at New York (1835–36), Craven returned to the West Indies with the frigate *John Adams* (1837–38); was first lieutenant of the sloop *Vincennes,* flagship of the Wilkes expedition to the South Seas (1838–39); and rejoined the *Boxer* off the coast of Chile. In 1840 he reported to New York to study steam propulsion and the bomb gun, briefly commanding the receiving ship at Buffalo before joining Perry's flagship frigate *Macedonian* on anti-slave patrol on the African Station in March 1843. The following November he reported as commanding officer of the hermaphrodite brig *Porpoise* in the same squadron until her return to New York twelve months later.

After extended leaves and duty in that port city broken only by Mexican War service aboard the ship-of-the-line *Ohio* in the Pacific (1847–48), Craven acted as executive officer of the razee *Independence,* flagship of the Mediterranean Squadron, for several months during 1849. Reporting to the Naval Academy as commandant of midshipmen in June 1850, he instituted

83

the summer training cruise and therein commanded the practice steamer *Hancock* the following summer. At the end of 1852 he was promoted to commander, serving as commandant of mids till 1855 and again 1858–60, interrupted by his command of the frigate *Congress,* flagship in the Mediterranean. In April 1861 he assumed command of the naval rendezvous at Portland, Maine. Promoted captain in June, Craven took command of the Potomac Flotilla in the sidewheel steamer *Yankee* for the early dark days of the Civil War, transferring in December to command of the screw sloop *Brooklyn* of the West Gulf Blockading Squadron. He directed his ship in the capture of New Orleans and the initial operations against Vicksburg until June 1862. Two months later he took over the steam frigate *Niagara,* then under repairs at New York, and brought her into commission late in 1863 in the rank of commodore. In June 1864 he sortied in the *Niagara* to search for Confederate cruisers in European waters, capturing the screw steamer *Georgia* off Portugal in August. The same month Commodore Craven suffered a personal loss when his youngest brother, the distinguished Cdr. T. A. M. Craven (born 1813), went down with his ship, ironclad *Tecumseh,* in the Battle of Mobile Bay. More misfortune followed in April 1865 when the commodore refused to risk the wooden *Niagara* and her wooden consort *Sacramento* in engaging the Confederate ironclad *Stonewall,* for which he was severely condemned, detached from his command, and court-martialed as overcautious.

Excused from his sentence after a one year suspension without pay by Secretary of the Navy Gideon Welles, Commodore Craven in July 1866 took command of the Mare Island Navy Yard and then in August 1868 of the North Pacific Squadron, flagship the screw sloop *Ossipee,* preceded by promotion to rear admiral in October 1866. Returning to Mare Island in April 1869, he retired the following December but served throughout most of 1870 as port admiral of San Francisco. Of Admiral Craven's three sons who graduated from the Naval Academy, one, John E. Craven, retired as commodore and fathered Navy engineer Henry S. Craven, who in turn produced Vice Adm. Thomas T. Craven (1873–1950) who, because of his work in creating the Navy's first aircraft carrier, the *Langley* (CV-1), earned the sobriquet "Father of the Flattop."

Dahlgren, John Adolphus Bernard

(November 13, 1809–July 12, 1870).

Naval ordnance inventor Dahlgren sailed in the merchant brig *Mary Beckett* prior to his appointment as acting midshipman (Pa.) in 1826. He participated in the final cruise of the frigate *Macedonian,* in the Pacific (1826–28), had a tour with the sloop *Ontario* in the Mediterranean, and studied law while assigned to the Philadelphia Navy Yard (1833). Attached to the fledgling U.S. Coast Survey, he made important mathematical and astronomical contributions (1834–36), but the work seriously impaired his eyesight and required extended leave at home and in Europe, where he studied rocketry. His malady corrected in 1842, Lieutenant Dahlgren reported again to Philadelphia then to sea duty with the Mediterranean Squadron as flag lieutenant to Commo. Joseph Smith aboard the new frigate *Cumberland* (1843–45), during the tour of which he invented a percussion lock. In 1845 he reported to the Washington Navy Yard for work in rockets, but before the year was out he had been given control of all ordnance work at the Yard. Dahlgren then organized and upgraded the Navy's ordnance program, writing extensively on ordnance matters and inventing many types of cannons. His most famous, the 11-inch cast-iron smoothbore "Dahlgren gun," was designed in 1851, although it was not adopted for shipboard use until he demonstrated its effectiveness on a special cruise of the training sloop *Plymouth,* which he commanded, in 1857–58. He was promoted to commander in 1855.

Stationed at the Washington Navy Yard since 1845, Commander Dahlgren assumed command of it at the outbreak of the Civil War, taking on the additional post of Chief, Bureau of Ordnance in July 1862, promotion to captain following shortly thereafter. His vital prewar and wartime accomplishments in arming the Navy were rewarded by Congress granting him an additional ten years of active duty and promotion to rear admiral in February 1863.

In July Admiral Dahlgren took command of the South Atlantic Blockading Squadron, flagship the ironclad steamer *New Ironsides,* operating in combination with the Army against Charleston and which then succeeded in closing that port to blockade runners. He personally led a naval support force up the Broad River in November 1863, another up the St. John's River, Florida, in February 1864, and yet another up the Stone River against Charleston in July. In the meantime he lost one son, Col. Ulric Dahlgren, in a daring cavalry raid on Richmond, Virginia, while another son, later Capt. Charles B. Dahlgren, as executive officer of the sidewheel steamer *Gettysburg* participated in the assaults on Fort Fisher, North Carolina, several months later. Admiral Dahlgren, his flag in the sidewheeler *Harvest Moon,* cooperated with Gen. W. T. Sherman in the investment of Savannah in December, occupied the evacuated Charleston the following February, and stepped down from his command during the summer of 1865. He commanded the South Pacific Squadron, flagship the sidewheeler *Powhatan* (1866–68), and again served as Chief of the Bureau of Ordnance (1868–69) and as Commandant, Washington Navy Yard (1869–70), where he died. In addition to his writings on ordnance, he was the author of numerous essays on various subjects relating to the sea and the Navy.

Admiral Dahlgren's brother was sailor of fortune William DeRohan (1819–1891), who dropped the family name over a dispute with brother John. He refused to serve in the Union navy for fear of coming under the latter's command but had been a captain or admiral in the navies of Ottoman Turkey, revolutionary Argentina, Chile, and Italy, and a reserve commander in the Royal Navy.

Dale, Richard

(November 6, 1756—February 26, 1826).

By John Ford: Naval Historical Center

Son of a shipwright and nephew of a merchant captain, early naval hero and Virginian Dale began his merchant career as a seaman in 1768, rising to chief mate over the next seven years. In 1776 he became a lieutenant on one of his state's warships, only to be captured and imprisoned, whereupon he joined the Tory forces. After receiving a serious wound in battle, he sailed for Bermuda aboard the Tory privateer *Lady Susan* and fell prisoner to the Americans in battle with the brigantine *Lexington,* being appointed midshipman in the Continental Navy the very same day, July 27, 1776. Remaining with the *Lexington,* Dale participated in cruises to the West Indies and then Europe, where many prizes were taken before the vessel was trapped by superior British forces and compelled to surrender in the summer of 1777. Twice escaping Old Mill Prison, England, he eventually reached L'Orient, France, early in 1779 and joined the frigate *Bonhomme Richard* as first lieutenant to Capt. John Paul Jones. Dale commanded that vessel's gun deck and played a prominent role in her victory over the *Serapis* in September, an action in which he again received severe wounds.

Dale operated in the North Atlantic with the frigate *Alliance* (1779–80) and then the sloop *Ariel* (1780–81). As first lieutenant of the frigate *Trumbull,* he was wounded in action and captured by the *Monk* and the *Iris* in August 1781, but upon his exchange in November he returned to duty as mate and then captain of the privateer *Queen of France* (1782–83), with which he took several prizes. A successful merchant skipper of East Indiamen until the quasi-war with France in 1798, Dale interrupted this activity when appointed captain in the new naval force of 1794, spending some months supervising a frigate's construction at Norfolk. His last merchant command, the *Ganges*, was converted into a 26-gun warship which he commanded uneventfully during the summer of 1798. In a dispute over rank with Thomas Truxtun, he resigned his commission to command a privateer to the Orient in 1799 but returned two years later as commodore of the nation's first overseas battle force, five vessels led by his flagship, the new frigate *President*. Commodore Dale ineffectually blockaded belligerent Tripoli, a mediocre performance which led to his recall and resignation in December 1801. During the War of 1812 he participated as a civilian in helping to improve the defenses of Philadelphia.

Davis, Charles Henry

(January 16, 1807—February 18, 1877).

U. S. Signal Corps: National Archives (Brady Collection)

A prominent scientist as well as wartime admiral, Davis left Harvard College after two years in 1823 to become midshipman (Mass.) and reported to the schooner *Dolphin* off western South America via the frigate *United States*. On the *Dolphin*, he sailed to the South Seas and Hawaii (1825–26) in the successful search for the mutineers of the American whaler *Globe*. He operated in the West Indies with the sloop *Erie* (1827–28), then transferred as sailing master to the sloop *Ontario* for Mediterranean duty (1829–32). Returning to the Pacific, Lieutenant Davis served as flag lieutenant to Commodores John Downes and Alexander S. Wadsworth, successive commanders of the Pacific Station, flagship the sloop *Vincennes* (1833–35). From the receiving ship at Boston, he reported as lieutenant to the razee *Independence* in 1837 and enjoyed a diplomatic cruise to the Baltic and Russia before arriving on the Brazil Station to help enforce American neutrality in the Franco-Argentine war. Detached in 1840, he then had duty ashore at Boston where he earned his degree in mathematics from Harvard and in 1842 married the sister of the eminent Harvard astronomer Benjamin Peirce.

Loaned to the U.S. Coast Survey, Lieutenant Davis directed hydrographical studies of the New England coast for several years and in 1849 became the first superintendent of the new Nautical Almanac Office, based at Harvard where the annual *American Ephemeris and Nautical Almanac* was published. Working closely with his brother-in-law and colleagues, Davis made the office the fountainhead of the nation's first true scientific community. Promoted to commander in 1854, he commanded the sloop *St. Mary's* in the Pacific (1856–59), helping to save William Walker's "filibustering" party in Nicaragua. He returned to his *Almanac* post, advancing the cause of American science to the point where he could ultimately help found the National Academy of Sciences (1863). With the outbreak of the Civil War, Davis played a key role in shaping the Navy's early war plans and officer assignments from the new Bureau of Detail. Studying the problems of blockading the South Atlantic coast, he assisted in planning and organizing the Hatteras and Port Royal expeditions, leading part of the latter as fleet captain to Flag Off. S. F. DuPont. This was in November 1861, the month of his promotion to captain, and the following February he returned to the Navy Department.

Due to his genius for organization and leadership, in May 1862 Davis became flag officer and commander of the gunboat flotilla on the Upper Mississippi. With five gunboats he destroyed the Confederate flotilla in the naval battle of Memphis in June and accepted the surrender of that city. He then assumed command of all naval forces on the upper river and joined Flag Off. D. G. Farragut's siege before Vicksburg. But Farragut regarded Davis as too cautious and did not retain him after the summer. Promoted commodore and made Chief of the Bureau of Navigation in July, he did not assume that post until November, rising to the rank of rear admiral in February 1863. Although he served afloat and ashore in normal postwar flag commands—of the South Atlantic Squadron, flagship the new screw sloop *Guerriére* (1867–69), and the Norfolk Navy Yard (1870–73)—his first love was science and navigation. Admiral Davis therefore served on the Lighthouse Board (1873–74) and most notably as superintendent of the U.S. Naval Observatory (1865–67, 1874–77), where his son (*q.v.*) was stationed at the time. He died on duty.

Davis, Charles Henry (Jr.) "Shaky"

(August 28, 1845–December 27, 1921).
USNA (Mass.) 1865 (23/31).

Bureau of Ships: National Archives

Son of the above and a distinguished scientific officer in his own right, Davis graduated early with his class in November 1864 but finished the Civil War only in the receiving ship at New York. He cruised on the European Station aboard its flagship, the screw frigate *Colorado* (1865–67), was briefly on the sidewheel steamer *Augusta* and with the South Atlantic Squadron, and served with the new screw sloop *Kenosha* (renamed *Plymouth)* in European waters (1869–70) in the rank of lieutenant commander. He was with the sloop *Portsmouth* in the South Atlantic before shore duty at Norfolk (1871–72), returning to the former sea station aboard the new screw sloop *Omaha.* Davis joined the staff of the Naval Observatory (1876–78) for astronomical and geodetic activities similar to those of his father. Undertaking work in determining longitude with submarine cables in the Atlantic aboard the surveying ship *Guard* in 1878, he compiled his findings in published monographs while assigned to the Bureau of Navigation over the next several years, including a brief time with the iron screw tug *Palos* in the Far East in 1882.

Rewarded for his scientific work by promotion to commander in 1885, Davis remained at the Washington Navy Yard until given command of the training ship *Saratoga* (1887–89) and the screw corvette *Quinnebaug* (1889). He directed the Office of Naval Intelligence (1889–92) and brought the cruiser *Montgomery* (C-9) into commission for North Atlantic operations (1893–96). After sitting with the Board of Inspection and Survey, he followed in his father's footsteps as superintendent of the Naval Observatory (1897–1902), a tour interrupted by his bringing into commission the converted auxiliary cruiser *Dixie,* with which he received the surrender of

Ponce, Puerto Rico, from the Spanish in July 1898. Promoted to captain in November 1899, Davis remained at the Observatory until he assumed command of the battleship *Alabama* (BB-8) in 1903 in the North Atlantic. Elevated to rear admiral in 1905, he served on the international commission which investigated the Anglo-Russian Dogger Bank incident, after which he took command of a division of the North Atlantic Fleet which became the Second Division the next year, flagship *Georgia* (BB-15). Admiral Davis last commanded the Second Squadron of that Fleet, rushing relief to earthquake victims at Kingston, Jamaica, in January 1907. He retired the following August, having published several scientific volumes during his career.

Decatur, Stephen (Jr.)

(January 5, 1779—March 22, 1820).

By John W. Jarvis, Bureau of Ships: National Archives

One of the early Navy's greatest heroes, Decatur was the son of the distinguished Revolutionary War privateer captain (1752–1808) who became a captain in the new U.S. Navy in 1798 just as the son joined the frigate *United States* as midshipman. In the quasi-war with France (1798–1800), the elder Decatur first led the armed merchantman *Delaware* and then the new frigate *Philadelphia* on successful cruises, culminating in command of the West India Squadron (1800), in which his son rose to lieutenant while aboard the *United States*. After a brief period with the brig *Norfolk* in 1800, Lieutenant Decatur served as first lieutenant successively of the frigate *Essex* off Tripoli (1801–02) and the frigate *New York* for a voyage across the Atlantic (1802–03). He supervised construction of the brig *Argus* and commanded her on her maiden voyage to the Mediterranean during the autumn of 1803. Already a dashing, popular and headstrong officer who participated more than most of his peers in the practice of dueling, Decatur transferred to command of the schooner *Enterprise* in the Mediterranean in November and six weeks later captured the Tripolitan bomb ketch *Mastico* which was renamed *Intrepid* and pressed into service. Given command of this prize in order to destroy the captured American schooner *Philadelphia* anchored off Tripoli, he led the raid in February 1804 and achieved complete success. The event brought him instant fame and promotion to captain.

Rejoining the *Enterprise,* Decatur enhanced his reputation during the American bombardment of Tripoli in August 1804. Commanding one of two gunboat divisions and personally leading two boarding parties, he captured both vessels but narrowly escaped death in the hand-to-hand fighting. Over the ensuing two months he led his three gunboats in four more bombardments of Tripoli before shifting to command of the frigate *Constitution,* undergoing overhaul at Malta, late in September. Two months after that he moved to command of the frigate *Congress,* which he led in the final stages of the war and during the diplomatic negotiations (in which he participated) with Tunis. He returned home and left the *Congress* in December 1805. Decatur commanded the flotilla of gunboats in the Chesapeake (1806–07), directing their construction at Norfolk, which base he commanded for a time, and at Newport, Rhode Island. Early in the summer of 1807 he took command of the gunboats in the Norfolk area and of the frigate *Chesapeake* with the rank of commodore. As such he patrolled the coast enforcing President Jefferson's embargo, although he shifted to the *United States* as captain and commodore in February 1809, returning to Norfolk in May where he again added its gunboats to his command. During this duty he sat on the court-martial of Commo. James Barron (1808) and on the court of inquiry over the "*Little Belt* affair" as its president (1811).

With the outbreak of the War of 1812, Commodore Decatur joined the senior Commo. John Rodgers at New York in June in a sortie which took seven British prizes, followed by another expedition out of Boston in October, his flagship engaging the British frigate *Macedonian* off Madeira and taking her in a display of brilliant tactics and gunnery. He brought his prize back to the United States in December, only to be blockaded in port by a superior British fleet. Given command of the frigate *President* and all naval forces and defenses (mainly a small squadron) at New York in mid-1814, Decatur attempted to run the blockade the following January only to be temporarily grounded during a storm. The *President,* incurring serious damage, was overtaken and captured by the four-ship British squadron but not before her guns had first pounded the frigate *Endymion,* though suffering many casualties herself, including Decatur. Paroled immediately, he went back to New London. With the renewal of war against Algiers in March 1815, Commodore Decatur made a fast crossing from New York with a nine-ship squadron to the Mediterranean, flagship the new frigate *Guerriére,* the next month engaging and taking the Algerian flagship frigate *Meshuda,* driving the brig *Esteido* ashore, and applying a blockade to

92

Algiers, which thereupon hastily concluded peace. After receiving damage reparations from Tunis and Tripoli, he sailed home with his squadron during the autumn.

Commodore Decatur reported as one of the three members of the Navy's Board of Commissioners at the end of 1815, only to become the focus of much criticism over the final diplomatic activities with the Barbary pirate states as well as festering personal resentments by Commo. William Bainbridge and Commo. Barron, who finally mortally wounded him in a duel.

Dewey, George

(December 26, 1837–January 16, 1917).
USNA (Vt.) 1858 (5/15).

Bureau of Ships: National Archives

Hero of the Spanish-American War, Dewey as midshipman joined the steam frigate *Wabash* for Mediterranean duty (1858–59), then cruised to the West Indies in the sidewheel steamer *Powhatan* and the screw sloop *Pawnee* (1860) and in January 1861 became passed midshipman, in February master and in April lieutenant. He joined the sidewheel steam frigate *Mississippi* in May as a youthful executive officer, in the role of which he assisted in the capture of several blockade runners and distinguished himself during the investment of New Orleans late in April 1862. Remaining there for the next several months, the *Mississippi* moved upriver against Port Hudson, Louisiana, in March 1863, only to run aground and be pounded by Confederate shore batteries until she had to be set afire to prevent capture. Dewey shifted ashore to be prize commissioner at New Orleans, and then in the summer returned to sea to be exec of the steam sloop *Monongahela*, Adm. D. G. Farragut's flagship, against the same objective. He moved to the

Charleston blockade aboard the screw sloop *Brooklyn* after the fall of Port Hudson and in November brought into commission the new sidewheel gunboat *Agawam* for service in the James River. Dewey became exec of the steam frigate *Colorado* in the autumn of 1864 and participated in the attacks on Fort Fisher, North Carolina. Promoted to lieutenant commander in March 1865, he served as exec of the screw sloop *Kearsarge* in the closing days of the war and over the ensuing year.

After service aboard the screw sloop *Canandaigua* again as exec, Lieutenant Commander Dewey rejoined the *Colorado,* flagship in European waters, as flag lieutenant to Adm. L. M. Goldsborough. He taught at the Naval Academy (1867–70), during the last year as aide to the Superintendent, Adm. J. L. Worden, and twice commanded the sloop *Narragansett* (1870–71, 1873–75) in the Pacific, in the interim commanding the hospital ship *Supply* in a relief voyage to aid victims of the Franco-Prussian War and serving at the Boston Navy Yard and the Newport torpedo station. Appointed to commander in April 1872, he was lighthouse inspector at New York (1875–77) and thereafter Lighthouse Board member, and later (1878–82) its secretary. Following command of the screw sloop *Juniata* on a lengthy circumnavigation of the globe cut short for him by serious illness, Dewey returned home for promotion to captain in September 1884 and command of the uncompleted unarmored cruiser *Dolphin.* Transferred the following March to command of the screw steamer *Pensacola* in European waters and the Atlantic coast, he became Chief of the Bureau of Equipment in July 1889, a post from which he resigned in June 1893 in order to return to the Lighthouse Board. President of the Board of Inspection and Survey from November 1895, he was promoted to commodore the following February and in November 1897 given orders to take command of the Asiatic Station.

Commodore Dewey hoisted his flag in the protected cruiser *Olympia* at Nagasaki, Japan, in January 1898, moved his squadron to Hong Kong in February, and upon the opening of hostilities with Spain in late April departed for Manila Bay. On May 1 he attacked and destroyed the Spanish squadron there without the loss of a single American sailor, and two weeks later he was promoted to rear admiral. In August army forces arrived, but Manila surrendered after a short naval bombardment. Advanced to the rank of admiral in March 1899, the first since Porter, Dewey retained command of the Asiatic Station until October. In March 1900 he became president of the newly-created General Board, and as such lent his tremendous prestige to it for the rest of his life as it struggled successfully to become an effective policy advisory body of senior admirals to the Secretary of the Navy. In March 1903 Congress commissioned Admiral Dewey in the specially-created rank of admiral of the Navy, unique in the Navy's history, to date from March 1899. He published his *Autobiography of George Dewey* in 1913 and remained on active duty until his death in his 79th year on the eve of America's entry into World War I.

Deyo, Morton Lyndholm

(July 1, 1887—November 10, 1973).
USNA (N.Y.) 1911 (189/193).

A career gunnery man, Deyo appropriately began on the battleship *Virginia* (BB-13), two years later joined the commissioning crew of the destroyer *Duncan* (DD-46), then the armored cruiser *Washington* (ACR-11) and the *Jenkins* (DD-42), all Atlantic Fleet vessels. A plank owner of the *Allen* (DD-66) in January 1917, he participated in coastal convoy work till May, when he transferred to training duty as instructor at Boston. At the end of the year Lieutenant Deyo went to the troop transport *Northern Pacific* for carrying elements of the American Expeditionary Force to Europe. After helping to commission the transport *Pretoria* in England early in 1919, he returned with her to the United States where in July he brought the *Morris* (DD-271) into service as her commanding officer, operating over the ensuing year as part of the Adriatic Detachment. Aide to the Commandant of the First Naval District at Boston, Adm. Herbert O. Dunn (1920-21), and participant in the fitting out of the cruiser *Detroit* (CL-8) (early 1923), Lieutenant Commander Deyo served on the staff of Adm. Samuel S. Robison, military governor of Santo Domingo (1921-22), as aide, and then as flag lieutenant when that admiral was Commander Battle Fleet, flagship *California* (BB-44) (1923-25), and Commander-in-Chief U.S. Fleet, flagship *Seattle* (CA-11) (formerly his old ship *Washington*).

Deyo taught seamanship and then leadership at the Naval Academy (1926-29) before commanding the *Sloat* (DD-316), taking her out of commission and assuming command of her replacement *Upshur* (DD-144) in 1930. He was student then staff member of the Naval War College, moving to the *Milwaukee* (CL-5) as executive officer at the end of 1934.

Commander Deyo was operations officer to Adm. H. E. Yarnell, Commander-in-Chief Asiatic Fleet, flagship *Augusta* (CA-31) (1936–39); Assistant Hydrographer of the Navy; and aide to Secretaries of the Navy Charles Edison and Frank Knox (1940–41). In April 1941 as captain he took command of Destroyer Squadron 11, flagship *Sampson* (DD-394), and led the first American-escorted convoy to Iceland the following September. He reported to Brazil in February 1942 to command the auxiliary transport *Monticello* (AP-61) until June, and the next month he took command of the *Indianapolis* (CA-35) which he led in the Aleutian Islands throughout the summer, bombarding Kiska. Detached in December, he was promoted to rear admiral and made Commander Destroyers Atlantic Fleet, flagship the destroyer tender *Denebola* (AD-12) at Casco Bay, Maine. In 1944 he shifted his flag to the aircraft carrier *Ranger* (CV-4) in preparation for the Normandy landings.

Admiral Deyo, his flag in the *Tuscaloosa* (CA-37), commanded a fire support group during the D-Day assault and against German-held Cherbourg in June 1944, and then did the same in the southern France landings during August, returning with his flagship to Philadelphia the next month. Moving immediately to the Pacific, he assumed command of Cruiser Division 13, flagship *Santa Fe* (CL-60), from November supporting carrier operations in the Philippines, at Iwo Jima and against Tokyo. In March 1945 he took command of Task Force 54, the sprawling gunfire and support force for the Okinawa assault and beachhead, flagships *Tennessee* (BB-43) and briefly *Birmingham* (CL-62). Returning to California in May, Admiral Deyo again hoisted his flag in the *Santa Fe* and sortied to strike Wake Island in August, but the war ended. Pressing on to Japan, he directed the landing of occupation forces on Kyushu and western Honshu, flagship *Ralph Talbot* (DD-390). In charge of the Northern Japan Force occupying northern Honshu and Hokkaido during the autumn, he relinquished command of CruDiv 13 at the end of November. Admiral Deyo headed a board on postwar training centers early in 1946, commanded the First Naval District from April 1946 as well as the Boston Naval Base from June 1947 until his retirement in the rank of vice admiral in August 1949.

Donaho, Glynn Robert "Donc"

(March 25, 1905——   ). USNA (Texas) 1927 (538/579).

Celebrated World War II submarine skipper, Donaho had only one tour in surface ships—the battleship *California* (BB-44)—prior to ordnance instruction at Edgewood arsenal, Md., and submarine instruction at New London, both in 1930. Engineer of the sub *S-12* (SS-117) out of Panama (1930–33) and of the training sub *R-3* (SS-80) at Annapolis and Guantanamo Bay (1933–34), he returned to New London for training duty on the *R-13* (SS-90) and to Annapolis for postgraduate study (1935–37). Lieutenant Donaho served on the staff of Capt. Francis W. Scanland, commanding Submarine Squadron Four, flagship *Argonaut* (SF-7), as radio and sound officer, out of Pearl Harbor, and in May 1940 reported to the *R-14* (SS-91) training at New London and Key West, first as executive then commanding officer. In November 1941 he transferred to the *Flying Fish* (SS-229), bringing her into commission as skipper the next month, and took her on six war patrols throughout the Pacific from May 1942 to November 1943, sinking at least five Japanese cargo vessels (confirmed) but suffering from defective torpedoes. Promoted to commander in July 1943, he taught at New London at the end of the year before taking over Submarine Division 222 at Hawaii as well as the *Picuda* (SS-382) in July 1944. With his and two other boats, he commanded wolf pack "Donc's Devils" which during August and September sank over 64,000 tons of enemy shipping (13 vessels) in the South China Sea area. He returned to his administrative command in October and was promoted captain in April 1945.

Captain Donaho was operations officer to Adm. John F. Shafroth, Commander Battleship Squadron Two, flagship *South Dakota* (BB-57), for the final operations off Japan, May to October 1945; director of the

Recruiting Division in the Bureau of Naval Personnel; commander of the Submarine Group San Diego and Submarine Squadron Three (1948–50); assistant in the United Nations matters at the Navy Department; and student at the Naval War College (1950–51). After heading the Navy's Foreign Military Aid Branch, he commanded Destroyer Squadron 17 and Division 171, flagship *Gregory* (DD-802), in the last months of the Korean War and afterwards in the Pacific (1953–55), and served throughout most of 1955 as chief of staff to Commander Seventh Fleet, Adm. A. M. Pride, flagships the cruisers *Helena* (CA-75) and *Rochester* (CA-124), the amphibious command ship *Eldorado* (AGC-11), and the *St. Paul* (CA-73). In February 1956, shortly after assuming command of the Subic Bay naval base, he was promoted to rear admiral. Command of Destroyer Flotilla Three followed (1957–58), flagships the tenders *Frontier* (AD-25) and *Hamul* (AD-20) at Long Beach, and then duty at the Office of the Chief of Naval Operations as Director of the Logistics Plans Division and then (1959–62) Director of Naval Administration under the Vice CNO. Admiral Donaho served as Naval Inspector General before his promotion to vice admiral in August 1963 and afterward as Commander Fleet Activities Command. In June 1964 he took command of the Military Sea Transportation Service in Washington and remained at this post until he retired from active duty in April 1967.

DuBose, Laurence Toombs

(May 21, 1893–July 11, 1967). USNA (Ga.) 1913 (75/139).

A leading surface commander in World War II, this native of Washington, D.C., cruised off politically-troubled Haiti and Mexico while aboard the battleship *Connecticut* (BB-18), going on to the *Texas* (BB-35) (1916–17), then the training battleship *Alabama*(BB-8), as wartime engineering officer. Following duty at the Bureau of Navigation (1918–19), he helped to bring the destroyer *Kane* (DD-235) into commission as her executive officer for an extensive Baltic-to-Mediterranean cruise. In August 1921 he assumed command of the light minelayer *Lansdale* (DM-6) for service in the Caribbean, taking her out of commission in April 1922 and becoming aide to the Atlantic Fleet's Mine Squadron One commander, Capt. W. D. Leahy, flagship *Shawmut* (CM-4). Administrative duty at the Bureau of Aeronautics (1923–26) preceded DuBose's billeting as navigator of the cruiser *Richmond* (CL-9) in the Atlantic, Caribbean and China waters. He then taught at the Naval Academy in seamanship and later economics and government (1929–32, 1934–37), in between which tours he commanded the *Schenck* (DD-159) primarily in the Pacific.

Commander DuBose joined the *Brooklyn* (CL-40) at her commissioning in September 1937 as executive officer and served in both oceans, going on to the Naval War College's senior course (1939–40) and thereafter remaining on the faculty until April 1942. He took command of the heavy cruiser *Portland* (CA-33) just in time to take part in the Battle of Midway in June and in all of the major battles of the early Guadalcanal campaign from August to November: the landings, the Eastern Solomons, Santa Cruz, and the Naval Battle of Guadalcanal. Although seriously damaged in the latter action, the *Portland* scored hits on the battleship *Hiei* and blew up the destroyer *Yudachi*. Captain DuBose brought his injured ship home for repairs and was detached in May 1943 to assume the rank of rear admiral and post of Commander Cruiser Division 13, flagships *Brooklyn* until August, *Birmingham* (CL-62) and *Santa Fe* (CL-60) thereafter. In this capacity, he led fire support groups during the landings at Sicily, Bougainville, the Gilberts and the Marshalls, then shifted to fast carrier cover for the first Truk strike, the Marianas and Leyte where his cruisers finished off the Japanese carrier *Chiyoda*. He was relieved in November 1944.

Admiral DuBose presided over the Naval Examining Board for the first three months of 1945 before reporting in April as chief of staff to Commander Naval Forces Europe, Adm. H. R. Stark, a tour he completed in August, at which time he returned briefly to the Bureau of Naval Personnel. He commanded the Sixth Naval District and naval base at Charleston from November 1945 until May 1948 when he became Commander Battleships-Cruisers Pacific Fleet, with additional temporary duty from the following August to January as Commander First Task Fleet. DuBose stayed in the Pacific Fleet as Commander Cruisers-Destroyers (1949–51) and in March 1951 became Deputy Chief of Naval Operations (Personnel) and Chief of the Bureau of Naval Personnel in the rank of vice admiral. His final service was as Commander Eastern Sea Frontier and Commander Atlantic Reserve Fleet. He retired in June 1955 in the full rank of admiral.

DuPont, Samuel Francis

(September 27, 1803–June 23, 1865).

U. S. Signal Corps: National Archives (Brady Collection)

The Naval member of the DuPonts of Delaware who obtained his midshipman's appointment from President James Madison in December 1815, DuPont shipped out to the Mediterranean aboard the ship-of-the-line 74 *Franklin* and then the sloop *Erie* (1817–20), returning to the Philadelphia Navy Yard until sent to combat pirates in the West Indies and to perform diplomatic tasks in the South Atlantic aboard the frigate *Congress* (1822–24). Made sailing master of the new 74 *North Carolina,* he cruised again to the Mediterranean with this flagship, there served briefly on the schooner *Porpoise* (1826–27), and after two years at his home returned to that sea aboard the sloop *Ontario* (1829–32). Made lieutenant in 1826, DuPont was executive officer of the sloop *Warren* and the frigate *Constellation,* then commanding officer of the schooner *Grampus* and the *Warren,* all in the Gulf of Mexico (1835–38). Again in the middle sea force aboard its flagship-of-the-line *Ohio,* he returned with her to Boston (1838–42), following which he was promoted to commander and assigned to the Bureau of Ordnance. Given command of the brig *Perry* in 1843, he fell ill in the South Atlantic and had to return home. Two years later he briefly helped to found the U.S. Naval Academy before taking command of the *Congress,* now flagship of the Pacific Squadron.

After the outbreak of the Mexican War, in July 1846 Commander DuPont assumed command of the sloop *Cyane* with which he cleared the Gulf of California of Mexican naval forces over the ensuing two years, ferrying Captain John C. Frémont's battalion to the seizure of San Diego, cooperating with other army forces in the capture of La Paz, San Blas, and Guaymas and led a landing party to take Mazatlán and San Jose. Detached at Norfolk in October 1848, he made a report for improvements to the Naval Academy to which he was appointed Superintendent, then rejected in the autumn of 1849, but he continued to examine midshipmen periodically. He commanded the receiving ship at Philadelphia (1850–52), during which he examined the role of steam propulsion in the national defense. Appointed also in 1851 to the board on lighthouses, he played an active role thereon for the next six years. A naval reformer, he drew severe criticism for his role on the Efficiency Board, which accused over 200 officers of being downright ineffective in 1855, the year of his promotion to captain. DuPont commanded the new frigate *Minnesota* on her maiden voyage to China (1857–59), where he observed and learned from the Anglo-French amphibious assaults in the Arrow War. At the end of 1860 he took command of the Philadelphia Navy Yard.

With the outbreak of the Civil War Captain DuPont dispatched naval units to protect Union troops landing at Annapolis and in May 1861 became senior member of a strategy board to plan the blockade of the South, still commanding at Philadelphia until September. Thereupon made commander of the key South Atlantic Blockading Squadron, flagship the steam frigate *Wabash,* as flag officer he directed the bombardment of the forts before Port Royal, South Carolina, in November, resulting in the fall of that place and then of Beaufort, South Carolina. His forces cooperated with army units in taking Fort Pulaski and other Georgia and Florida outposts during March and April 1862, and in July he was elevated to rear admiral. DuPont established effective blockading stations around 13 Southern oceanic terminal points and one before Charleston, South Carolina, the latter port proving impossible to close. Assigned ironclads, including his new flagship *New Ironsides,* and a force of monitors whose effectiveness against coastal forts he doubted, in April 1863 Admiral DuPont led them in a bombardment of Charleston's Fort Sumter, only to be decisively repulsed. Criticized by the public, he requested relief under political pressure, in the interim his Squadron capturing the major Confederate ironclad *Atlanta* in Wassaw Sound, Georgia. Relieved in July, he became inactive and served in only one more official capacity, on a promotion board in March 1865, before his death.

Durgin, Calvin Thornton

(January 7, 1893–March 25, 1965).
USNA (N.J.) 1916 (127/177).

Navy Department: National Archives

Although Durgin spent virtually his entire career in naval aviation, he did not enter flight training at Pensacola until September 1919, following prewar and wartime tours on the battleships *Minnesota* (BB-24) and *Connecticut* (BB-18) in the Atlantic Fleet, the destroyer tender *Dixie* (AD-1) and destroyer *Kimberly* (DD-80) out of Queenstown, Ireland, and as engineer officer of the *Craven* (DD-70) along the East coast. Receiving his wings in May 1920, he remained at Pensacola instructing in seaplanes for two months, going on to the naval air station at Hampton Roads and then the squadrons with the aircraft tender *Aroostook* (CM-3) (1921–22). Lieutenant Durgin spent one year each studying aeronautical engineering at the Naval Postgraduate School, Annapolis, and the Massachusetts Institute of Technology (M.S. 1924), plus several additional months studying elsewhere. He was assigned to the Naval Aircraft Factory at Philadelphia for two years, spending the summer of 1925 at the Bureau of Aeronautics' Material Division. He flew with Observation Squadron Two on the aircraft carrier *Langley* (CV-1) and the unit of the *New Mexico* (BB-40) until September 1927.

Lieutenant Commander Durgin commanded the Observation Wing and Observation Squadron One, Aircraft Squadrons (1927–28), on the *West Virginia* (BB-48), then the Observation Wing of Battleship Divisions and Observation Squadron Five, and acted as aviation aide to Commander Battleship Divisions Battle Fleet, Adm. W. V. Pratt, continuing as aide to Adm. Pratt when the latter fleeted up to be Commander-in-Chief U.S. Fleet, flagship *Texas* (BB-35), in 1929. Durgin was thereafter attached to the Ship Movements Section, Office of the Chief of Naval Operations (1930–32), the

103

Saratoga (CV-3) and Naval Air Station Norfolk (1934–36), the last year as its executive officer. He reported to the fitting-out *Yorktown* (CV-5) in September 1936, remaining with her through commissioning until May 1938. Commander Durgin served as exec of the aircraft tender *Wright* (AV-1) till May 1939, when he became her commanding officer, transferring in June to command of the Utility Wing, Base Force, flagship the tender *Rigel* (AD-13), all on the West coast. He reported to the Bureau of Aeronautics in June 1940, serving initially with the Plans Division, then as head of the Flight Division.

Captain Durgin assumed command of the *Ranger* (CV-4) in May 1942 and participated in covering the North African landings the following November. Promoted rear admiral the next February, he became Commander Fleet Air Quonset Point, Rhode Island, as such successfully helping to train new carrier crews as they joined the Atlantic Fleet. In June 1944 he took command of the Anglo-American Task Group 88.2, flagship the escort carrier *Tulagi* (CVE-72), and provided air cover for the southern France landings in August. Transferring to the Pacific Admiral Durgin became Commander Carrier Division 29 in October and two months after that Commander Escort Carrier Group. From the *Makin Island* (CVE-93), he supported the landings at Lingayen Gulf in January and Iwo Jima in February and March 1945. His dogged success in this tedious duty against continuous kamikaze attacks was repeated off Okinawa from March through June. Earmarked to direct escort carrier air support for the invasion of Japan, he remained at his post through the surrender until relieved in November. After respite surveying the continental shore establishment, Admiral Durgin commanded the naval air stations of the Eleventh and Twelfth Naval Districts in California (1946–48) and Fleet Air Jacksonville (1948–49). He became Deputy Chief of Naval Operations (Air) in May 1949 with the rank of vice admiral and in March 1950 Commander First Fleet, with which he cruised from the West coast to the Western Pacific. The following January Durgin reverted in rank to rear admiral with his appointment as President of the Board of Inspection and Survey. He retired in the rank of vice admiral in September 1951 to become president of the State University of New York Maritime College, Fort Schuyler, a post he held until 1960.

Eberle, Edward Walter

(August 17, 1864–July 6, 1929). USNA (Ark.) 1885 (21/36).

Bureau of Ships: National Archives

Son of a Confederate Army major in Texas, future Chief of Naval Operations Eberle played a prominent role in early 20th century technical matters as well as fleet development and administration. Prior to his commissioning as ensign he served in three vessels off the west coasts of Latin America—the steam sloops *Mohican* (1885–86) and *Shenandoah* (1886) and the iron gunboat *Ranger* (1886–87). He charted the same waters from the Bering Sea to the Straits of Magellan aboard the Fish Commission steamer *Albatross* (1887–90) then had ordnance duty at the Washington Navy Yard (1890–91). He joined the steam sloop *Lancaster,* flagship of the Asiatic Squadron (1891–93), and stayed with that force on the sloop *Marion* (1893–94) enforcing sealing laws. After duty at the Naval Academy, Lieutenant (j.g.) Eberle reported to the battleship *Oregon* (BB-3) on the eve of her commissioning in July 1896, participated in her "dash" around the Horn during the spring of 1898, and commanded her forward turret at the Battle of Santiago, Cuba, in July. Transferring to the Asiatic Squadron, the *Oregon* participated in the Philippine Insurrection, and Eberle was briefly (May 1899) flag lieutenant to Capt. Albert S. Barker, temporary commander of the Squadron, flagship the cruiser *Baltimore* (C-3).

After reporting to the Naval Academy as aide to the Superintendent, Cdr. Richard Wainwright, Lieutenant Eberle wrote the first modern gunnery and torpedo manual for the fleet, and in addition he became an expert in mines. Gunnery officer of the *Indiana* (BB-1) (1901–02), he again (1903–05) served as flag lieutenant to Admiral Barker, first the Commandant of the New York Navy Yard then Commander-in-Chief North Atlantic Fleet, flagship *Kearsarge* (BB-5), during which duty he helped install the first telegraphs on

American warships and compiled instructions and codes for the first naval radio communication system. As lieutenant commander, Eberle followed a brief tour at the Naval War College with duty on the Board of Inspection and Survey as recorder (1905–07), and then the *Louisiana* (BB-19) as executive officer. He accompanied the latter vessel as part of the "Great White Fleet" as far as San Francisco, where he assumed command of that base's training station. In the rank of commander, he commanded the inactive cruiser *Milwaukee* (C-21) before taking the gunboats *Wheeling* (PG-14) and *Petrel* around the world as skipper of the former (1910–12), at the end of which cruise occurred his promotion to captain. After organizing the Atlantic Torpedo Flotilla, he pioneered the tactical use of the smoke screen of mine warfare vessels and of aircraft as antisubmarine weapons. After a mission to Europe, he hoisted his broad pennant in the armored cruiser *Washington* (ACR-11), which he also commanded, and directed a force off Santo Domingo during revolutionary struggles there during 1914.

Captain Eberle commanded the Washington Navy Yard and Gun Factory (1914–15), during which tour he brought uniformity to naval armament construction, and then distinguished himself as wartime Superintendent of the expanding Naval Academy (1915–19). He was promoted to rear admiral in February 1918 and commanded the Atlantic Fleet's Battleship Division Five, flagship *Utah* (BB-31) (1919–20), and BatDiv Seven, flagship *Arizona* (BB-39). He assumed command of the Pacific Fleet, flagship *New Mexico* (BB-40), in June 1921 with the accompanying rank of admiral. With the reorganization of the Navy in December 1922, his title became Commander-in-Chief Battle Fleet. He is credited during this tour with initiating aircraft operations from battleship turrets for gunnery spotting and also with improved fire control. In July 1923 Admiral Eberle became Chief of Naval Operations, in which role his diplomatic tact proved important during U. S. naval expeditions to revolution-wracked China and Nicaragua. He stepped down in November 1927, at which time he became chairman of the executive committee of the General Board, a post he held until his retirement the following August in the rank of rear admiral. In addition to his tract on torpedoes and gunnery, as a young officer Eberle authored several articles on his experiences in Cuba and the Philippines.

Elliott, Jesse Duncan

(July 14, 1782—December 10, 1845).

By David Edwin: Navy Department

One of the most controversial flag officers of the sailing Navy, Elliott received his midshipman's warrant in 1804 and shipped out aboard the frigate *Essex* for two years of Mediterranean operations against the Tripoli pirates. After brief duty with the schooner *Vixen,* he joined the frigate *Chesapeake* only weeks before her pounding in June 1807 by the British frigate *Shannon* which created an international crisis. During assignment (1809–11) to the frigate *John Adams,* laid up in ordinary, he was promoted to lieutenant and was cruising in the North Atlantic aboard the brig *Argus* at the outbreak of the War of 1812. Transferred to Lake Erie, Elliott raised and commanded a small squadron and jointly led an army-navy night raid in October which took two British ships at Fort Erie, earning him command of the new corvette *Madison* on Lake Ontario and subsequent promotion to master commandant. In August 1813 he took command of the brig *Niagara* and led her as second-in-command of the squadron under Commo. Oliver Hazard Perry at the Battle of Lake Erie the next month. Elliott's lack of aggressiveness early in the action was contrasted later by a distinguished performance, leading to a stormy debate over the ensuing years of his life. After supporting the Army up the Detroit River, he succeeded Perry in command of the squadron at the end of October.

Assigned to command the new sloop *Ontario* in March 1815, Elliott operated against Algiers in the Mediterranean before returning to Norfolk late in the year for extended shore duty. A master at intrigue, he followed his promotion to captain in April 1818 by engineering the feud and duel between Commodores Stephen Decatur and James Barron, which culminated in the former's death, Elliott acting as second to Barron. Captain

Elliott served on a commission to establish navy yard sites (1818–22), returned to Norfolk, then (1825–27) commanded the frigate *Cyane* off Brazil. Rejecting the proffered admiralcy of the Brazilian Navy, he had miscellaneous shore duties at Philadelphia and New York before taking command of the West Indian Squadron in 1829, flagship the new sloop *Peacock*. As such, he helped to thwart the Spanish from reclaiming Mexico, sent a landing force to assist in the suppression of the slave revolt of Nat Turner in Virginia, and was President Andrew Jackson's choice to lead the naval demonstration off Charleston during South Carolina's nullification crisis in 1832. Commodore Elliott commanded the navy yards at Charleston, South Carolina (1832–33) and Charlestown, Massachusetts (1833–35), prior to commanding the Mediterranean Squadron, flagship the frigate *Constitution* (1835–38). Charged with mismanagement by several subordinates, he was suspended from duty (1840–43), during which time he farmed. In December 1844 he assumed command of the Philadelphia Navy Yard, going on leave one year later, upon which he died.

Evans, Robley Dunglison "Fighting Bob"

(August 18, 1846–January 3, 1912).
USNA (Utah) 1864 (10/29).

Bureau of Ships: National Archives

Battleship captain in the Spanish-American War and prominent flag officer in the Theodore Roosevelt era, Virginia-born Evans spent his adolescence in Washington, D. C., longing for the sea. In 1860, he fought and was wounded by Indians on his journey to Utah to secure his Academy appointment. As midshipman he served on anti-privateer service aboard the sloop *Marion,* and in October 1862 reported aboard the sidewheel steamer *Powhatan* as acting ensign in the blockade of Charleston, then cruised the West Indies

108

(1863–64) and participated in both attacks on Fort Fisher, North Carolina. During the second, in January 1865, he gallantly led a company of Marines, for which he was commended by his seniors; however, he received four wounds and thus was granted medical retirement at the Philadelphia Navy Yard (1865–66). As lieutenant, he was briefly at the Naval Observatory and then the Washington Navy Yard in ordnance, during which time he appealed for reinstatement to active status. This was approved in January 1867, and fourteen months later he was advanced to lieutenant commander.

Evans served on the Asiatic Station (1868–70) aboard the flagship screw steamer *Piscataqua* (renamed *Delaware* in mid-cruise), protecting American interests during the Japanese civil war. He then returned to the Washington Navy Yard before moving to the Naval Academy (1871–72). Sailing to the European Station on the screw sloop *Shenandoah* (1873), he soon transferred to the screw sloop *Congress* (1874–76). After brief signal duty in Washington, he assumed command of the training ship *Saratoga* during which tour he was promoted to commander. Routine assignments followed in naval equipment at Washington (1881–82), as lighthouse inspector (1882–86) and as secretary of the Lighthouse Board (1888–89, 1893–94), and as chief inspector of steel for the new "ABC" cruisers (1886–87). Commander Evans commanded the screw sloop *Ossipee* briefly (1889), and after leave and furlough commanded the gunboat *Yorktown* (PG-1) (1891–92), during which tour in 1891 he demonstrated off Valparaiso in the diplomatic altercation with Chile, and in 1892 enforced restrictions on pelagic sealing in the Bering Sea at the head of a flotilla, and making several captures of illegal British sealers. Promoted to captain in June 1893, he commanded the armored cruiser *New York* (ACR-2) at the Kiel Canal dedication (1894) and brought the nation's first battleship, *Indiana* (BB-1), into commission in November 1895, training with her off New England until he was detached in December 1896 for more duty on the Lighthouse Board.

Captain Evans took command of the *Iowa* (BB-4) in March 1898, and with it he opened the Battle of Santiago in July, setting afire the Spanish cruisers *Maria Teresa* and *Oquendo,* helping to sink the destroyer *Pluton,* and chasing aground the cruiser *Viscaya* and destroyer *Furor.* Relieved in September, he served on the Board of Inspection and Survey, eventually as its president (1898–1902), being promoted to rear admiral in March 1901. In January 1902 he commanded the squadron which received Prince Heinrich of Prussia, acting also as his aide, flagship *Illinois* (BB-7). In March Evans became senior squadron commander of the Asiatic Station, taking command of that Station in October, flagship *Kentucky* (BB-6). He made several innovations in gunnery during this tour of duty, which ended in March 1904, then returned to the Lighthouse Board as chairman, also serving with the General Board. Admiral Evans in March 1905 hoisted his flag in the *Maine* (BB-10) as Commander-in-Chief North Atlantic Fleet, shifted to the *Connecticut* (BB-18) in April 1907, cruising to the Mediterranean as well as along the Atlantic seaboard. In December 1907 this force left Hampton Roads for the Pacific as the "Great White Fleet," but illness forced Evans to relinquish command upon reaching the West coast in March. Transferred to General Board duties in May 1908, he stayed on following his retirement in August, finally being detached in January 1910.

Admiral Evans wrote two volumes of memoirs, *A Sailor's Log* (1901) and *An Admiral's Log* (1910), and was the brother-in-law of Adm. H. C. Taylor. Evans' son, Capt. Franck Taylor Evans (1875–1934), was a distinguished destroyer commander.

Farragut, David Glasgow

(July 5, 1801–August 14, 1870).

Bureau of Ships: National Archives

America's most famous naval hero and the senior Union naval leader was known during the Civil War principally for his victories at New Orleans and Mobile Bay. Farragut was a first-generation native American from the South. His father, George Farragut (1755–1817), of Spanish Minorca, served Spain and Russia as a young naval and merchant sailor before becoming a privateer lieutenant for the American colonies in 1776 and a first lieutenant in the navy of South Carolina in 1778. As such, George built galleys for the defense of Charleston and Savannah, commanded one in battle, fell prisoner to the British, was exchanged, and returned to privateering in which activity he was severely wounded. After much success as a wartime cavalry officer in the Carolinas and a postwar frontier militia officer in Tennessee, he became sailing master in the Navy in 1807, commanding *Gunboat II* at New Orleans. The family cared for Sailing Master David Porter, father of Master Commandant David Porter commanding the New Orleans naval station; when in 1808 the elder Porter died in the Farragut home, the younger Porter adopted David Farragut in gratitude. In December 1810 the latter was

110

appointed midshipman from Tennessee, and the following August he embarked in the frigate *Essex* under Porter's command. His father remained in the Navy until 1814 (fighting the next year however in the Battle of New Orleans); his brother Lt. William A. C. Farragut retired after service in the War of 1812; and his own name was destined to be linked with the Porters thereafter.

Midshipman Farragut performed admirably on the *Essex* against the British in the Atlantic and Pacific and at the age of twelve (!) commanded the prize *Alexander Barclay*, one of several vessels taken. When *Essex* was captured after a savage battle at Valparaiso, Chile, in March 1814, he became prisoner of the British until exchanged in November and ordered to the brig *Spark* at New York. Farragut then saw service on three successive flagships of the Mediterranean Squadron (all ships-of-the-line) and as aide to two commodores; the *Independence* and Commo. William Bainbridge (1815) (a few weeks then on the frigate *Macedonian*), the *Washington* and Commo. Isaac Chauncey (1816–18), and the *Franklin* (1818–20). He spent nine months of 1817–18 studying with his former naval schoolmaster Charles Folsom, then consul at Tunis, and served as acting lieutenant of the brig *Shark* in 1819. After several weeks at New York, he had duty at Norfolk (1821–22) and aboard the frigate *John Adams* in anti-pirate work, partly with Commodore Porter again and his "Mosquito Fleet" (1822–25). In that force, attached to the schooner *Greyhound*, Farragut led a landing party against pirates on the Cuban coast in July 1823; transferred to the Navy's first active steam warship, the sidewheel gunboat *Sea Gull*, as executive officer; and served briefly as skipper of the schooner *Ferret*, all three assignments concerned with battling Cuban pirates.

Having failed his initial examination for promotion to lieutenant, Farragut finally achieved that rank in January 1825, spent the summer with a court of inquiry in Washington, and joined the new frigate *Brandywine* in August for her transport of the Marquis de Lafayette to France prior to her deployment in the Mediterranean. Reporting at the end of 1826 to the receiving ship *Alert* at Norfolk, the port which had become his permanent home, he began the frustrating phase of his generation of naval officers, that is, waiting to secure one of the few available sea-going billets. These tours included the sloop *Vandalia* on the Brazil Station (1828–29) as exec, the receiving ship *Congress* at Norfolk, the frigate *Java* (1831–32), exec of the sloop *Natchez* (1832–33) off Charleston during the nullification crisis, the schooner *Boxer* in the West Indies (1834), commanding officer of the sloop *Erie* (1838–39) during the Franco-Mexican imbroglio, and exec of the ship-of-the-line *Delaware* (1841–42), flagship of the Brazil Station. Farragut was promoted to commander early in the latter duty, September 1841, and remained off Brazil as captain of the new sloop *Decatur* (1842–43). Shore-bound again, he was exec of the ship-of-the-line *Pennsylvania* at Norfolk (1844), then her skipper, and he urgently requested duty in the Gulf of Mexico to utilize his wide experience there in the event of war with Mexico. However, it was all in vain following the outbreak of that war until March

1847 when he was given command of the sloop *Saratoga,* only to be assigned monotonous blockade duty off Tuxpan following a dispute with Commo. M. C. Perry. The vessel was decommissioned in February 1848, with her skipper returning to Norfolk as second-in-command until 1850.

Commander Farragut had ordnance duty involving the drawing up of a new regulations manual at Washington (1851–52) and Norfolk (1852–54), part of the time as assistant inspector of ordnance. In August 1854 he was assigned the considerable task of creating and commanding a navy yard at Mare Island, San Francisco, and in September 1855 he was promoted to captain. Detached in May 1858, he brought the screw sloop *Brooklyn* into commission the next January, taking her to the Gulf to observe the revolution in Mexico until relieved in October 1860. Back at Norfolk at the height of the secession fever, he responded to Virginia's secession in April 1861 by removing his family from Norfolk to New York state. A Southerner by birth, residence and marriage, he declared his loyalty to the Union but could not escape the suspicions of his peers. His first Civil War duty from September to December, therefore, kept him relatively idle: membership on a retirement board at New York City. But on the recommendation of his late guardian's son, Cdr. D. D. Porter, in January 1862 the Navy appointed him to command the West Gulf Blockading Squadron with orders to take New Orleans.

Flag Officer Farragut, flagship the screw sloop *Hartford,* mounted the attack against Forts Jackson and St. Philip, guarding the lower approaches to the port, in mid-April 1862, destroyed the defending Confederate squadron, and achieved victory by the end of the month by advancing up the Mississippi as far as the defenses of Vicksburg. For this brilliant success, in July Congress enacted legislation enabling Farragut to be promoted to rear admiral, the U. S. Navy's first admiral. Running the batteries of Vicksburg in late June, Farragut's fleet could not take the city due to lack of troops, and returned to New Orleans one month later. Operating actively against Port Hudson and Vicksburg in conjunction with Gen. U. S. Grant's army between March and July 1863, at which time both places finally surrendered, Farragut's ships kept most of the Gulf coast actively blockaded and thereafter focused upon Mobile. After a brief respite at New York between August and January 1864, Admiral Farragut returned to the Gulf to move against Mobile, his flag still on the *Hartford.* After gradually strengthening his fleet, he attacked Forts Morgan and Gaines, braved the obstructing torpedoes (mines), and defeated the defending Confederate squadron in the Battle of Mobile Bay in August. The forts surrendered before the end of the month, and Farragut was selected to lead the attack on Wilmington, North Carolina, but was relieved of this task for reasons of health, it being given to Porter.

Admiral Farragut's achievements were rewarded by promotion to vice admiral—again, the Navy's first—in December 1864, while a Confederate naval threat to Grant's base on the James River in Virginia led to Farragut's being given command there late in January 1865. When the threat failed to materialize, early in February he was relieved and sent to Washington on special duty. With the end of the war, he served briefly as president of the Board of Visitors at the Naval Academy, followed in July 1866 by his elevation to the full rank of admiral—again, a unique advancement. Selected in April 1867 to command the European Squadron, he hoisted his flag on the screw frigate *Franklin* for a good-will tour of European ports which ended back in New York in November 1868. Assigned to command the naval station there, Admiral Farragut stayed for only two weeks in April 1869, and then traveled to Mare Island. During the summer of 1870, on a visit to the Portsmouth Navy Yard, New Hampshire, on the dispatch boat *Tallapoosa,* he passed away.

Fechteler, William Morrow

(March 6, 1896–July 4, 1967). USNA (At Large) 1916 (18/177).

Navy Department: National Archives

Son of Rear Adm. Augustus F. Fechteler (1857–1921), who commanded a battleship division of the Atlantic Fleet during World War I (1915–18), the younger Fechteler followed his father immediately into battleships aboard the wartime *Pennsylvania* (BB-38), the Atlantic Fleet's flagship, remaining on board from August 1919 as aide to the fleet commander, Adm. Henry B. Wilson. He transferred to the destroyer *Barney* (DD-149) in July 1921 in the same fleet and the following January to the Naval Academy as regimental officer. While he was there, an airplane crash claimed the life of his brother, Lt. Frank C. Fechteler (1897–1922). The surviving Lieutenant Fechteler was executive officer of the gunboat *Isabel* (PY-10) on the Yangtze Patrol (1924–26) and the *Shirk* (DD-318) in the Pacific, returning to the Academy to teach electrical engineering (1927–29). As lieutenant commander, he served for one year as flag lieutenant to Commander Battle Fleet, Adm. Louis M. Nulton, flagship *California* (BB-44), in May 1930 becoming assistant gunnery officer on the *West Virginia* (BB-48). During the summer of 1932, he was flag secretary of Adm. J. R. P. Pringle, commander first of Battleship Division Three, flagship *Arizona* (BB-39), then of Battleships Battle Force on the *West Virginia*. Following service with the Division of Fleet Training at the Navy Department (1932–35), he commanded the *Perry* (DD-340).

Commander Fechteler spent one year (1936–37) as gunnery officer of the Scouting Force, Adm. William T. Tarrant, flagship the cruiser *Indianapolis* (CA-35), before joining the Postgraduate School staff at Annapolis. In December 1939 he reported to Adm. Milo F. Draemel, Commander Destroyer Flotilla One of the Battle Force, as operations officer, his boss the next summer being Adm. Robert A. Theobald, flagship *Raleigh* (CL-7). He advanced the following September to the staff of Commander Destroyers, Battle Force, Adm. Draemel, flagship *Detroit* (CL-8), becoming chief of staff in December when he fought at Pearl Harbor. Promoted to captain, in February 1942 Fechteler returned to Washington as Assistant Director, and later Director, of the Officer Personnel Division where he mobilized the Navy's wartime officer manpower until July 1943. He assumed command of the *Indiana* (BB-58) in August, participating in the Marcus Island raid that month and the Gilbert Islands operations in November and December. Promotion to rear admiral followed in January 1944, with his assignment as Deputy Commander Seventh Amphibious Force, flagship *Reid* (DD-369), in the Southwest Pacific. In this post he led the April landings at Humboldt Bay and those during May at Wakde-Sarmi and Biak, all in the New Guinea offensive. He shifted his flag to the transport *Henry T. Allen* (AP-30) as Commander Amphibious Group Eight to direct the Noemfoor and Sansapoor landings in July and August. Admiral Fechteler led one of the two attack groups at Morotai in September; the next month the assault group at San Ricardo, Leyte Island, in the Philippines; and in January 1945 one of the groups at Lingayen Gulf and other Luzon beaches. In February he landed the Army at Palawan and was planning for the Cebu operation in March when ordered to Washington as Assistant Chief of Naval Personnel, as such playing a key role in demobilizing the wartime Navy.

Admiral Fechteler's administrative talents and command experience resulted in his rapid advancement to senior billets in the postwar Navy. In January 1946 he became Commander Battleships and Cruisers Atlantic Fleet in the rank of vice admiral, returning to Washington thirteen months later to become Deputy Chief of Naval Operations (Personnel), a post he held for three years during the tumultuous unification period. During 1948 he also chaired the Armed Forces Personnel Board which concerned itself with possible subversion in the military during the "Red scare" of that time. Promoted to admiral, Fechteler in February 1950 assumed command of the Atlantic Fleet, and during the spring he directed the largest amphibious exercise since the war in the Caribbean. He also served as chairman of

NATO's North Atlantic Regional Planning Group and in February 1951 was designated to become NATO's first Supreme Allied Commander North Atlantic Region. Admiral Fechteler did not fill the post, however, for in August he was selected to be Chief of Naval Operations upon the untimely death of the incumbent, Adm. Forrest Sherman. His selection having been made partly because of his having remained generally aloof from the 1949 "revolt of the admirals" against the Air Force, he recognized the supremacy of aviation within the Navy by appointing a distinguished naval aviator, Adm. Donald B. Duncan, as his Vice CNO.

Admiral Fechteler led the Navy during the last two years of the Korean War and the revitalization programs of new construction which accompanied the war effort. In August 1953 he stepped down, only to be named Commander-in-Chief Allied Forces Southern Europe, a vital Cold War command billet. He remained in that post until July 1956 when he retired, serving briefly thereafter as a special committeeman examining security matters for the Secretary of Defense.

Felt, Harry Donald "Don"

(June 21, 1902——   ). USNA (Kans.)
1923 (152/413).

Navy Department: National Archives

Pacific Area commander during the height of the Cold War, Felt had sea duty first aboard the battleship *Mississippi* (BB-41) (1923–25) and the destroyer *Farenholt* (DD-332) in the Pacific and Caribbean before training as a naval aviator at Pensacola (1928–29) and returning to the Battle Fleet with Scouting Squadron 3-B on the Navy's first carriers, *Lexington* (CV-2), *Saratoga* (CV-3) and *Langley* (CV-1) (1929–31). Promoted to lieutenant, he taught flying at Pensacola (1931–34) and spent several months helping to outfit the heavy cruiser *Minneapolis* (CA-36) prior to joining Scouting 10-S (later VS-11-S) on the *Houston* (CA-30). This ship took President Franklin D. Roosevelt from Annapolis to the Pacific where the vessel remained (1934–36) and midway in the tour Felt became senior aviator. Reporting to Naval Air Station San Diego (North Island) in June 1936, he served for a year with Utility Squadron 2-F attached to the seaplane tender *Wright* (AV-1) and two years in the engine overhaul department first as assistant then superintendent. Lieutenant Commander Felt assumed command of Bombing Two on the *Lexington* in June 1939 in the Pacific, and several days after Pearl Harbor he transferred to command of the *Saratoga*'s air group with his promotion to commander occurring in January 1942. He helped cover the Guadalcanal landings in this capacity and in the same month of August led an air strike which sank the Japanese carrier *Ryujo* at the Battle of the Eastern Solomons.

Commander Felt became *Saratoga*'s air officer in October 1942, commanding officer of Daytona Beach Naval Air Station in January 1943 and of NAS Miami the next month, and a member of the American naval mission to the Soviet Union in March 1944, with promotion to captain taking place in July 1943. Command of the escort carrier *Chenango* (CVE-28) followed in February 1945 with heavy involvement in the Okinawa campaign from March through June, and Magic Carpet service returning servicemen home during the autumn. Detached in January 1946, Captain Felt went ashore to the Office of the Chief of Naval Operations and then the National War College as a student (1947–48) and had more carrier duty as skipper of the *Franklin D. Roosevelt* (CVB-42) in the Atlantic and Mediterranean. Reporting to the staff of the Naval War College in mid-1949, he became chief of staff there the following spring, with promotion to rear admiral in January 1951. Two months after that he took command of the Middle East Force in the Persian Gulf, flagships *Duxbury Bay* (AVP-38) and *Greenwich Bay* (AVP-41), returning to the Navy Department in October for the duration of the Korean War as assistant director of the Strategic Plans Division.

Admiral Felt engaged in antisubmarine operations as Commander Carrier Division 15, flagship *Rendova* (CVE-114) (1953–54) in the Pacific, and in the attack mode as ComCarDiv Three, flagships *Essex* (CVA-9) and *Philippine Sea* (CVA-47) (spring 1954) in the South China Sea. For two years he was Assistant Chief of Naval Operations (Fleet Readiness), culminating in his promotion to vice admiral and appointment in April 1956 to command the Sixth Fleet, flagships *Newport News* (CA-148) and *Salem* (CA-139). In September Felt became Vice CNO in the rank of admiral in which capacity he promoted the limited war capability of the Navy in the midst of the nuclear arms race of the Cold War. Thus prepared, in July 1958 he became Commander-in-Chief United States forces in the Pacific and Far East and U.S. Military Adviser to the Southeast Treaty Organization, headquarters Pearl Harbor, and employed these forces in the Quemoy-

Matsu tension that year, the Laotian crisis, and in the buildup of the early stages of the Vietnam struggle. Admiral Felt retired from the Navy in July 1964. His son, Captain Donald Linn Felt, became a naval aviator and commanded the *Midway* (CV-41) in the Western Pacific during 1977.

Fiske, Bradley Allen

(June 13, 1854–April 6, 1942). USNA (Ohio) 1874 (2/30).

Naval Historical Center

Naval inventor, administrative reformer and intellectual, Fiske supplemented his normal ship and shore duty assignments by studying electricity, wireless telegraphy and ordnance during his spare moments from the very beginning of his career to well beyond his retirement. During his first tours aboard the screw steamer *Pensacola* in the Pacific (1874–77) and the screw sloop *Plymouth* in the Atlantic (1877–78) he devised a boat-lowering-and-detaching mechanism (patented in 1878) as well as a typewriter and other non-naval instruments. He continued his theoretical thinking and experiments while at New York and the receiving ship *Colorado* (1878–79, 1880–81), sidewheel steamer *Powhatan* (1879–80) and gunnery training ship *Minnesota* (1881–82) there, then went on leave to complete his first book, *Electricity in Theory and Practice* (1883), which went through 21 subsequent editions. Promoted to master in 1881—changed to lieutenant (j.g.) two years later—Fiske was given the extraordinarily important task of installing the ordnance on the protected cruiser *Atlanta,* the first modern warship of the "New Navy," launched in 1884 and commissioned after two years. Attached to the Bureau of Ordnance, he incorporated his own invention of an engine order telegraph, while experimenting with wireless systems (1882). After completing his work on the *Atlanta* during the shakedown cruise in 1887, he was promoted to lieutenant and charged with helping to install the guns on the new dynamite-gun cruiser *Vesuvius* (1888). His energetic mind developed a stadimeter for measuring ranges by a two-mirror system (1889), an electric range finder, a flashing light communication system, and a practically flawless naval telescope sight (1890). He incorporated all of these into the new cruiser *Baltimore* (C-3), commissioned in 1890, on which Fiske installed the first shipboard telephone system. He also invented an electric ammunition hoist (1892).

Needless to say, Lieutenant Fiske's improvements were looked upon with critical misgivings by conservative-minded senior officers and the Bureau of Ordnance, but in nearly every instance his works proved successful and in the case of his telescopic gunsight, revolutionary. This short-sighted professionalism of his elders prompted Fiske to associate himself with several other officers of his generation of like mind to try to reform the administrative and educational hierarchy of the Navy through intellectual forums such as the U. S. Naval Institute and its published *Proceedings*, to which he became a key contributor. He served on the gunboat *Yorktown* (PG-1) during its demonstration at Valparaiso, Chile, in 1891 and with the *San Francisco* (C-5), flagship of the South Atlantic Squadron, during its near-collision with the rebelling Brazilian Navy in 1894. Throughout much of the 1890's Fiske developed a shipboard electric communication system, as well as an electric semaphore (1896), a submarine detection system (1899), and a device for controlling moving vehicles by radio (1900), he being stationed at New York (1894–95) and at the Bureau of Ordnance (1895–96). During the war with Spain he completed a two-year tour as navigator of the gunboat *Petrel* (PG-2), which participated significantly in the Battle of Manila Bay. In December 1898 he transferred to the same post on the monitor *Monadnock* for the initial stages of the Philippine Insurrection. Later, in 1899, following promotion to lieutenant commander, Fiske continued to fight these rebels as executive officer of the *Yorktown*. He then became an ordnance inspector at Brooklyn and recommended improvements in the automotive torpedo.

Promoted commander in 1903 and captain four years after that, Fiske served as exec of the battleship *Massachusetts* (BB-2) in the North Atlantic (1902–03), at the Naval War College and in miscellaneous ordnance inspection duties (1903–04), and on the naval wireless telegraph board (1904) before commanding three vessels: the *Minneapolis* (C-13) (1906) and the coast defense monitor *Arkansas* (BM-7) (1906–07), both for training midshipmen at Annapolis, and the armored cruiser *Tennessee* (ACR-10) (1908–10). He also recruited at New York (1907–08). By the time he was advanced to rear admiral in 1911 after a year on the General Board and Army-Navy Joint Board, Fiske had become a major leader in the modern Navy, although his advanced technical and administrative ideas made him a controversial figure. For example, after being the first admiral to leave and return to a ship by airplane (1911), he capped his career of invention at this

118

time by creating the torpedo-launching plane and its aerial torpedo (1912). Admiral Fiske commanded the Fifth, Third and First divisions of the Atlantic Fleet during 1912, respective flagships *Washington* (ACR-11), *Georgia* (BB-15) and *Florida* (BB-30). After a few weeks as Aid for Inspection, in February 1913 on the eve of World War I he was appointed Aid for Operations (and he returned to the Joint Board), the highest post in the Navy.

Unfortunately, the issue of preparedness for war brought Admiral Fiske into conflict with Secretary of the Navy Josephus Daniels and led Fiske to resign his post in May 1915. However, this did not occur before he had persuaded Congress—against Daniels' opposition—to create a new post for his successor, that of Chief of Naval Operations. After a year of languishing at the Naval War College, he retired from the Navy in the rank of rear admiral upon reaching the mandatory retirement age in June 1916. Nevertheless, the next year he was recalled to continue work on his torpedo plane, and he had temporary active duty later as well (1920, 1924, 1925). Admiral Fiske became ever more prolific during his unusually long tenure as president of the Naval Institute from 1911 to 1923 (still unequalled), during which time he wrote five books: *War Time in Manila* (1913), *The Navy as a Fighting Machine* (1916), the autobiography *From Midshipman to Rear Admiral* (1919), *The Art of Fighting* (1920), and *Invention: The Master Key to Progress* (1921). His last major invention (of over sixty!) was an early microfilm-type reader (1921).

Fitch, Aubrey Wray "Jake"

(June 11, 1883—May 22, 1948). USNA (Mich.) 1906 (110/116).

Navy Department: National Archives

Victor of the Battle of the Coral Sea, Fitch spent over half his career in the surface line and torpedo warfare before converting to naval aviation in 1930. Duty aboard the armored cruiser *Pennsylvania* (ACR-4) inaugurated his career, cruising from the Atlantic to the Asiatic Fleet, where he transferred to the destroyer *Chauncey* (DD-3) (1907–08) then the Philippine station ship *Rainbow* (AS-7) and the gunboat *Concord* (PG-3), which sailed to Guam at the beginning of 1909. After several months in the Atlantic battleship *Minnesota* (BB-22), he received torpedo training aboard the experimental torpedo ship *Montgomery* (C-9). He instructed crewmen of the new *Delaware* (BB-28) aboard the Norfolk receiving ship *Franklin* and joined that battleship upon her commissioning in April 1910. Lieutenant (j.g.) Fitch handled discipline and taught physical education at the Naval Academy (1911–13) before participating in the fitting out of the *Balch* (DD-50) through her March 1914 commissioning and initial Atlantic Fleet operations. Aside of several weeks aboard the *Duncan* (DD-46) and commanding the *Terry* (DD-25) in reserve, in September 1914 he joined the Atlantic Fleet staff on the *Wyoming* (BB-32) and the following January became fleet athletic officer and aide to the commander, Adm. F. F. Fletcher, and skipper of the tender *Yorktown* (PG-1). Leaving the latter in April 1917, he remained for five more months as aide for athletics to the next Fleet commander, Adm. H. T. Mayo.

Lieutenant Commander Fitch served with the wartime British Grand Fleet as gunnery officer of the *Wyoming* (1917–19) and at the Naval Academy, and subsequently inspected ordnance at Hingham, Massachusetts, and Frenchman's Bay, Maine, before (1920–22) commanding a

120

division of Atlantic destroyer minelayers (redesignated Mine Squadron One and later Division One of that Squadron) along with its successive flagships *Luce* (DD-99) and *Mahan* (DD-102). Adviser to the Brazilian Navy at Rio de Janeiro (1923–27), he spent six months as executive officer of the *Nevada* (BB-36) and two years as commanding officer of the Pacific storeship *Arctic* (1927–29). As a 46-year-old pilot, Commander Fitch served at San Diego's naval air station before commanding the seaplane tender *Wright* (AV-1) (1930–31) and then in the rank of captain the aircraft carrier *Langley* (CV-1) in the Pacific. He commanded Naval Air Station Hampton Roads (1932–35) and was chief of staff to Commander Aircraft Battle Force, Adm. Frederick J. Horne, flagship *Saratoga* (CV-3). Skipper of the *Lexington* (CV-2) in the Pacific (1936–37), Captain Fitch attended the senior course at the Naval War College and then commanded NAS Pensacola (1938–40). In April 1940 he took command of Patrol Wing Two at Pearl Harbor, being promoted to rear admiral in July and transferring to command of Carrier Division One, flagship *Saratoga,* in November.

During World War II Admiral Fitch figured prominently as a senior naval aviator, being junior to Adm. F. J. Fletcher in the abortive Wake Island Relief Expedition of December 1941 and at the Battle of the Coral Sea in May 1942 (his title since March being Commander Air Task Force). His flag aboard the *Lexington,* he directed air operations in the latter victorious action though losing his flagship. The next month he returned to the *Saratoga* and in September became Commander U.S. Naval Air Forces Pacific Fleet but later in the month took over the same role in the South Pacific, for two years successfully directing Allied land-based air support in the Guadalcanal and Solomon Islands campaigns. In December 1943, Fitch was promoted to vice admiral and in August 1944 appointed Deputy Chief of Naval Operations (Air) in Washington. Twelve months later he returned to the Naval Academy as Superintendent, the first aviator to do so, with additional duty as Commandant Severn River Naval Command. From January to March 1947 he served in the Office of the Undersecretary of the Navy and thereafter as senior member of the Naval Clemency and Inspection Board. In July 1947 Admiral Fitch retired from the Navy in the full rank of admiral.

Fletcher, Frank Friday

(November 23, 1855—November 28, 1928). USNA (La.) 1875 (14/32).

A developer of torpedo ordnance and senior commander at the 1914 Vera Cruz affair, Fletcher fulfilled his precommissioning cruise obligation on the steam sloop *Tuscarora* laying a transpacific oceanic cable (1875) and on the sloop *Portsmouth* in the Eastern Pacific (1875–76). He remained in these waters as ensign on the screw sloop *Lackawanna* (1876–77) before going to the Paris Exhibition of 1878 with the sloop *Constellation* and having a regular tour of duty to Korea on the steam sloop *Ticonderoga* (1878–81). With the Washington receiving ship monitor *Passaic* (1881–82), he went to the Hydrographic Office as master in 1882 and as lieutenant (j.g.) the next year, and journeyed with Lt. Cdr. C. H. Davis *(q.v.)* to the west coast of South America to chart telegraphic locations. After inventing a shipboard lighting device to help prevent collisions at sea, he cruised the Mediterranean in the steam corvette *Quinnebaug* (1884–87) before performing ordnance work at the Washington Navy Yard (1887–91), during which he became lieutenant, and at other locales in the eastern United States (1891–92). All these tours promoted ordnance manufacturing in this country. Author of several essays in the U.S. Naval Institute *Proceedings,* Lieutenant Fletcher commanded the torpedo boat *Cushing* (TB-1) at the Newport torpedo station, introducing the torpedo into U. S. naval operations (1892–95), and operated with the armored battleship *Maine* on her maiden cruise in the North Atlantic (1895–96), after which he returned to the torpedo base at Newport until the outbreak of the Spanish-American War. From May to early July 1898 he served as assistant chief of the Bureau of Ordnance and briefly with the auxiliary cruiser *St. Louis.* He then brought the auxiliary gunboat *Kanawha* into commission and commanded her throughout her brief career in the Caribbean until October, when he took command of the patrol yacht *Eagle* for three years of survey work off Cuba. He became lieutenant commander in March 1899.

Promoted to commander in 1904 after a three-year tour utilizing his expertise in torpedoes as ordnance inspector in charge at the Newport station, Fletcher was a member of the torpedo vessels board before reporting to the new battleship *Ohio* (BB-12) in March 1905. He sailed on her to the Asiatic Station where she became flagship and he, in May, chief of staff to Adm. William M. Folger. In November he transferred to command of the cruiser *Raleigh* (C-8) in that squadron until early 1907, followed by several months at the Naval War College, nearly a year on ordnance board duty as well as service on the General Board at Washington, and promotion to captain in May 1908. Credited with several ordnance inventions, he commanded the *Vermont* (BB-20) during the global voyage of the Atlantic Fleet (1908–10) and served as Aid for Material to the Secretary of the Navy to help reorganize the Navy (1910–12), during which—in October 1911—he was advanced to rear admiral. Admiral Fletcher then successively commanded the several divisions of the Atlantic Fleet with various flagships: the Fourth (1912–13), the Second (1913), the Third (1913–14) and the First (1914). In the latter capacity from February 1914 he commanded the naval forces off the Mexican east coast, flagships *Florida* (BB-30) and later *Arkansas* (BB-33), and in April directed the landings at Vera Cruz and the ensuing occupation. The following September he assumed the title of Commander-in-Chief Atlantic Fleet, flagships *Wyoming* (BB-32) and *New York* (BB-34), and vastly improved the gunnery performance of the Fleet through his new techniques. Promoted to the rank of admiral in March 1915, he relinquished command in June 1916 and went to the General Board where he rendered invaluable service during World War I. He was also a member of the War Industries Board and the Army-Navy Joint Board. Admiral Fletcher retired in November 1919 in the rank of rear admiral, but he later advised the League of Nations on disarmament and in 1925 was a member of the President's Aircraft Board.

Fletcher, Frank Jack

(April 29, 1885–April 25, 1973). USNA (Iowa) 1906 (26/116).

Office of the Chief of Naval Operations: National Archives

Task force commander at the Coral Sea, Midway, and Guadalcanal, Fletcher spent his career in the surface line, first in the Atlantic with the battleships *Rhode Island* (BB-17) and the *Ohio* (BB-12), and with a year aboard the converted yacht *Eagle* in the Caribbean (1907–08) before serving several months on the *Maine* (BB-10) along the East coast and on the Norfolk receiving ship *Franklin*. Torpedo duty followed in the Philippines on the destroyer *Chauncey* (DD-3) (1909–10), which he commanded (1912), operating there with the *Dale* (DD-4) in the interval. Transferring to the *Florida* (BB-30) at the end of 1912, he was present at the Vera Cruz affair of April 1914, directing refugee evacuation on the passenger ship *Esperanza*. Two months later Fletcher went to the armored cruiser *Tennessee* (ACR-10) but soon left to be flag lieutenant and fleet signal officer to the Atlantic Fleet commander, his uncle Adm. F. F. Fletcher, flagships *New York* (BB-34) and *Wyoming* (BB-32). In the Naval Academy's Executive Department from the autumn of 1915, he was gunnery officer of the training ship *Kearsarge* (BB-5) during the wartime spring and summer of 1917 and skipper of the patrol boat *Margaret* (SP-527) prior to European coastal patrol on the *Allen* (DD-66) early in 1918 and from May to the fall as commanding officer of the *Benham* (DD-49).

After helping to outfit the *Crane* (DD-109) and the *Gridley* (DD-92), Commander Fletcher brought the latter into commission as her skipper in March 1919, and left a month later to head the enlisted personnel detail section of the Bureau of Navigation. After three and a half years there he reported to the Asiatic Fleet where he first commanded the *Whipple* (DD-217), then the gunboat *Sacramento* (PG-14), and finally the submarine base at Cavite as well as the sub tender *Rainbow* (AS-7). Service at the Washington Navy Yard followed (1925–27), and then duty as executive officer of the *Colorado* (BB-45) in the Pacific (1927–29) and as a senior student at the Naval War College (1929–30) and Army War College (1930–31). Captain Fletcher was chief of staff to Adm. Montgomery M. Taylor, Commander-in-Chief Asiatic Fleet, flagship the heavy cruiser *Houston* (CA-30), during the Manchurian crisis and was thereafter (1933–36) aide to Secretary of the Navy Claude A. Swanson. He commanded the *New Mexico* (BB-40) in the Battle Force (1936–37), served on the Naval Examining Board in Washington and then as Assistant Chief, Bureau of Navigation. As rear admiral he left the Bureau in September 1939 to go to the Pacific in command of Cruiser Division Three, flagship *Concord* (CL-10), shifting to CruDiv Six, flagship *Astoria* (CA-34), in June 1940, with which he was at sea in Hawaiian waters during the Pearl Harbor attack.

Admiral Fletcher commanded the abortive Wake Island Relief Expedition in December 1941 before taking command of the Scouting Force's cruisers and CruDiv Four on the last day of the year. However, several days later he hoisted his flag on the aircraft carrier *Yorktown* (CV-5) as commander of Task Force 17. This force raided the Gilbert and Marshall island groups in February 1942 and New Guinea in March. The next month his larger title became Commander Cruisers Pacific Fleet, but still as commander of TF 17 he led the repulse of the Japanese fleet at the Battle of the Coral Sea in May 1942 and at the Battle of Midway in June, losing the flagship *Yorktown* in the latter engagement. Sharing the credit for both victories with others, Fletcher was promoted to vice admiral in late June and was soon made CTF 6, flag in the *Saratoga* (CV-3), to direct the Guadalcanal landings in August. As officer in tactical command in that and subsequent supporting operations he suffered heavy combat losses following questionable tactical decisions, and he received a slight wound when his flagship was torpedoed at the end of August. Detached from his command, he became Commandant Thirteenth Naval District and Commander Northwestern Sea Frontier in Seattle in November, being relieved of the former post the following October, the latter in April 1944 becoming the Alaskan Sea Frontier. From that month until the end of hostilities Admiral Fletcher also commanded the relatively inactive North Pacific Force and Ocean Area. He occupied northern Japan in September 1945 and in December joined the General Board, serving as its chairman from May 1946 until his retirement twelve months later in the rank of admiral.

Fluckey, Eugene Bennett

(October 5, 1913—). USNA (Ill.)
1935 (107/442).

Submarine leader Fluckey had prewar Pacific tours of duty in the battleship *Nevada* (BB-36) and destroyer *McCormick* (DD-223) (1936-38) before training in subs at New London and being assigned to the sub *S-42* (SS-153) based at Panama. In June 1941 he transferred to the *Bonita* (SS-165) in the same waters, patrolling the Pacific side on five war patrols until August 1942. A graduate student in naval design at Annapolis until November 1943, Lieutenant Commander Fluckey took further instruction at New London prior to making a war patrol in the Pacific aboard the *Barb* (SS-220) early in 1944 as her prospective commanding officer. From April 1944 until August 1945 he brilliantly led this boat on five war patrols which helped to devastate Japanese merchant shipping, sinking nearly 75,000 tons (14 vessels) of it in addition to a frigate and the escort carrier *Unyo* in September 1944. His total was over 95,000 tons, the highest for a skipper in the Pacific. During the summer of 1945 the *Barb* made submarine history by bombarding Japanese coastal positions with rockets! After helping to launch the *Dogfish* (SS-350) in the fall of 1945, he worked on unification of the armed forces with Secretary of the Navy James V. Forrestal, was briefly in the War Plans Division, and in December became personal aide to the Chief of Naval Operations, Adm. C. W. Nimitz.

Commander Fluckey commanded the *Halfbeak* (SS-352) out of New London (1947–49), established the Atlantic Submarine Naval Reserve, served as flag secretary to Adm. James Fife, Atlantic submarine commander (1950), and had attaché duty at Lisbon (1950–53). Commander Submarine Division 52, flagship *Catfish* (SS-339), at San Diego, he was captain thereafter of the sub tender *Sperry* (AS-12) in the Pacific (1954–55) and commander there of Submarine Squadron Five, flagship *Nereus* (AS-17). Captain Fluckey headed the electrical engineering department at the Naval Academy (1956–58), attended the National War College, and served on the National Security Council (1959–60), and in July 1960 he was promoted to rear admiral. He was made Commander Amphibious Group Four, flagships the amphibious command ships *Pocono* (AGC-16) and *Mount McKinley* (AGC-7) in the Caribbean; Commander Task Force 88 and Deputy Commander South Atlantic Force, flagship the dock landing ship *Spiegel Grove* (LSD-32), giving relief to riot-torn Zanzibar (mid-1961); president of the Naval Board of Inspection and Survey (1961–64); Commander Submarine Force Pacific Fleet; and Director of Naval Intelligence (1966–68). Admiral Fluckey finished his career by returning to Lisbon as Commander Iberian Atlantic Command and Chief of the Military Assistance Advisory Group, Portugal (1968–72). He retired as rear admiral in August 1972.

Foote, Andrew Hull

(September 12, 1806–June 26, 1863).

U. S. Signal Corps: National Archives (Brady Collection)

Naval reformer and Civil War leader, Connecticut-born Foote spent six months at the U.S. Military Academy in 1822 before his appointment in December of that year as acting midshipman. His first duty was against West Indian pirates on the schooner *Grampus* (1822–23) and the sloop *Peacock.* He served on the frigate *United States* in the Pacific (1824–27) and then went back to the Indies on the sloops *Natchez* and *Hornet* (1827–28). Sailing master of the new sloop *St. Louis* in the Pacific (1829–32), he was promoted to lieutenant in 1830. Following leave, he operated with the ship-of-the-line *Delaware,* flagship of the Mediterranean Squadron (1833–36), and was in the commissioning crew of the sidewheel steamer *Fulton* in the Atlantic (1837). He then circumnavigated the globe aboard the frigate *John Adams* (1838–40), going eastward and bombarding Sumatran forts to protect American merchant ships from being harassed there. After duty at the New York Navy Yard (1841) and teaching midshipmen at the Philadelphia Naval Asylum (1841–43), Lieutenant Foote had a memorable tour as first lieutenant of the new frigate *Cumberland,* the Mediterranean flagship (1843–45). Strongly religious and committed to temperance, he made the *Cumberland* the Navy's first "dry" ship, setting in train the sequence of events which would lead to the elimination of the liquor ration (1862) and ultimately all alcohol (1914) from U.S. warships. Following time at the Boston Navy Yard (1846-48), he put his religious energies to work combating the slave trade off the West African coast as captain of the brig *Perry* (1849–51), taking as prize the slaver *Martha.* He was promoted to commander in 1852, stationed again at the Philadelphia Naval Asylum (1854–55), and placed on the Efficiency Board (1855).

Commander Foote in April 1856 took command of the sloop *Portsmouth,* sailing to the Far East where he attacked the Chinese barrier forts at Canton in November, personally leading a naval brigade in the assault which took the four bastions that had provoked his action by firing upon his vessel during the course of the Anglo-Chinese Arrow War. Foote remained in the Pacific, returning home with his ship in 1858. He then commanded the Brooklyn Navy Yard until promoted to captain in June 1861 and given command two months later of naval operations in the Western theater of war, headquarters at St. Louis. As Flag Officer as of November, Foote provided naval support for the Army's operations against Confederate fortifications on the Upper Mississippi, Ohio, Cumberland, and Tennessee rivers during the autumn and winter of 1861-62. With seven gunboats he bombarded and forced the surrender of Fort Henry, Tennessee, in February, then shifted to Fort Donelson, his flag aboard the sternwheeler *St. Louis,* supporting Gen. U.S. Grant in the capture of that strategic post. He was wounded in the latter action, which impaired his health sufficiently to force his relief following the taking of Island No. 10 on the Mississippi during the spring. Foote was promoted to rear admiral in July 1862 and made Chief of the Bureau of Equipment and Recruiting, which post he held until selected in June 1863 to command the South Atlantic Blockading Squadron. He died, however, en route to assuming this duty.

Admiral Foote wrote *Africa and the American Flag* (1854) on the slave trade. His great-grandson was Vice Adm. Lawrence F. Reifsnider (1887–1956), who commanded amphibious units in the Pacific during World War II.

Forrest, French

(October 4, 1796—November 22, 1866).

A United States and Confederate flag officer, Marylander Forrest received his midshipman's appointment in 1811 and spent six weeks with the frigate *Constitution* before joining the brig *Hornet* in June 1812, on which he spent most of the War of 1812, including the victory over and capture of *H.M.S. Peacock* off British Guiana in February 1813. Ordered in mid-August 1814 to the sloop *Argus* then building at the Washington Navy Yard, his orders were nullified by the burning of that vessel during the evacuation of that city later in the month. After shore duty at Norfolk, he was promoted to lieutenant in 1817 and sent to Baltimore, returning to Norfolk in October 1818 to command the small schooner *Despatch*. Forrest reported to the new ship-of-the-line *Columbus* at the end of 1819 for Mediterranean service until 1821, when he transferred to the Pacific ship-of-the-line *Franklin* (1822-23). He fought West Indian pirates in the brig *Spark* and patrolled the Mediterranean aboard the sloop *Lexington* (1827-30). First lieutenant at Norfolk in 1832, he had little active duty until 1837 at which time he was promoted to commander, helping to recruit men for the South Seas Exploring Expedition.

Commander Forrest excelled as one of the Navy's leading ship captains at mid-century: the sloops *Vandalia* (1838-39), *Warren*, and *St. Louis* (1839-42), which in 1839 he led to the Pacific as the first American warship to enter San Francisco Bay, where he assisted foreigners who had been arrested. He commanded the frigates *Cumberland* and *Raritan*, successive flagships of the Home Squadron in the Mexican War, during which in October 1846 and June 1847 he led landing parties to take Tabasco and directed the embarkation of Gen. Winfield Scott's troops for the Vera Cruz landing in

March 1847. He was also Inspector of Provisions (1843–45) prior to his promotion to captain in June 1845 but had little postwar duty until he was given command of the Washington Navy Yard (1855–56). Forrest commanded the Brazil Squadron as commodore and then as flag officer from September 1856 until May 1859, flagship the frigate *St. Lawrence,* during which in 1858 he led one division of the naval demonstration against Paraguay over its firing on the survey vessel *Water Witch.* Flag Officer Forrest had no further regular assignment; in April 1861 he resigned from the U.S. Navy to join the Southern cause.

Enrolled in the Virginia state navy in April and the Confederate States Navy in June, Forrest received his antedated captain's commission the following October, commanding the Norfolk Navy Yard from April 1861 as flag officer in charge of converting the steam frigate *Merrimack* into the ironclad *Virginia.* During that vessel's battle with the *Monitor* in March 1862 he offered assistance to the former in the small steam tug *Harmony* but was relieved later in the month for his failure to repair the damaged *Merrimack* expeditiously. Placed in charge of the Office of Orders and Detail in May 1862, Flag Officer Forrest subsequently commanded the James River Squadron, flagship the ironclad ram *Richmond,* from March 1863 to May 1864, his last active service. His father-in-law was John D. Simms, Chief Clerk of the U.S. Navy (1840–43), while his son, Assistant Paymaster Douglas F. Forrest, was volunteer aide to Flag Off. Buchanan on the *Merrimack's* sortie and was aboard the *C.S.S. Rappahannock* blockaded at Calais during 1864.

Gallery, Daniel Vincent, Jr.

(July 10, 1901–January 19, 1977).
USNA (Ill.) 1921A (47/285).

Navy Department: National Archives

Skipper of the escort carrier *Guadalcanal* which captured the *U-505* on the surface in the Battle of the Atlantic, engineer expert Gallery went to the 1920 Antwerp Olympic games as a wrestler after his class's early graduation. He was attached to the armored cruiser *Frederick* (ACR-8) for the summer, then began regular service in the Atlantic battleship *Delaware* (BB-28). Following brief engineering instruction on the destroyer *Herndon* (DD-198), he became chief engineer on the *Stevens* (DD-86) in the Atlantic (1921–22), transferring to the engineering department of the *Pittsburgh* (ACR-4) in European waters (1922–24) and returning on the *Colorado* (BB-45). Lieutenant (j.g.) Gallery sailed on the transport *Rappahannock* (AF-6) before a long Pacific tour as a turret officer on the *Idaho* (BB-42) (1924–27). After flight training at Pensacola throughout most of 1927, he flew with Torpedo Squadron Nine out of Norfolk, then (1930–32) taught flying at Pensacola and (1932–35) studied aviation ordnance engineering at Annapolis and the Washington Navy Yard. Reporting to Scouting Four on the carrier *Langley* (CV-1) in mid-1935, one year later he became its commanding officer in the rank of lieutenant commander. Skipper of Observation Three with the U.S. Fleet's battleships (1937–38), he then headed the Aviation Ordnance Section of the Bureau of Aeronautics and in January 1941 reported to the American embassy in London as assistant naval attaché for air.

Commander Gallery shifted to the Support Force staff in London in May 1941 and in October back to the embassy as special naval air observer, three months later assuming command of the Patrol Plane Base Detachment in Iceland, directing his planes throughout the crucial period of the U-boat war. Promoted captain in September 1942, he was detached in May 1943 and in July reported to the *Guadalcanal* (CVE-60), bringing her into commission in September. As the nucleus of a hunter-killer task group, which he commanded, Captain Gallery's carrier planes sank *U-544* in January and *U-515* and *U-68* in April 1944 and in June captured the *U-505* by forcing her to be abandoned on the surface; the *Guadalcanal* towed the boat to Bermuda. In September he reported as assistant director, Plans Division, under the Deputy Chief of Naval Operations (Air), and in August 1945 took command of the fast carrier *Hancock* (CV-19) off the Japanese coast. Promoted rear admiral in December, he became Commander (escort) Carrier Division 15, flagship *Rendova* (CVE-114), anchored at San Diego, until November 1946 when he became Assistant for Guided Missiles in the Office of the CNO. Embroiled in the unification quarrels and in subsequent related controversies, Admiral Gallery in November 1949 was assigned to be Deputy Commander of the Atlantic Fleet's Operational Development Force. After commanding fleet air at Quonset Point, Rhode Island (1950–51), he commanded CarDiv Six, flagship *Coral Sea* (CVB-43), in the Mediterranean and throughout most of 1952 the Atlantic Fleet's Hunter-Killer Force.

Admiral Gallery, an accomplished raconteur, had begun to publish autobiographical books with *Clear the Decks!* (1951), and his subsequent commands gave him more time to write: from late 1952 as Commander Naval Air Reserve Training Command, headquarters Glenview, Illinois, as well as Commandant Ninth Naval District at Great Lakes, Illinois; and from the end of 1956 as Commander Caribbean Sea Frontier and Commandant Tenth Naval District at San Juan, Puerto Rico, and additionally in mid-1957 as Commandant Fifteenth Naval District, and from October 1957 as Commander Antilles Defense Command. Detached in July 1960, he retired in October as rear admiral. His other books, some a mixture of fact and fiction, were *Twenty Million Tons Under the Sea* (1956), *Eight Bells and All's Well* (1965), *Now Hear This!* (1965), *Stand By-y-y to Start Engines* (1966), *The Brink* (1968), *Cap'n Fatso* (1969), *The Pueblo Incident* (1970) and *"Away Boarders"* (1971). Two of his brothers also retired as rear admirals: William D. Gallery (1904–   ), who commanded the *Princeton* (CV-37) in the Korean War, and Philip D. Gallery (1907–73), skipper of the *Jenkins* (DD-477) in New Guinea and the Philippines (1944–45) and of the cruiser *Pittsburgh* (CA-72) in the Mediterranean in the early 1950's.

Gayler, Noel Arthur Meredyth

(December 25, 1914——). USNA (At Large) 1935 (44/442).

World War II fighter ace and Pacific area commander during the mid-1970's, the son of Capt. Ernest R. Gayler began his career in naval aviation in 1940 after being a gunnery and engineering officer on the battleship *Maryland* (BB-46), assistant engineer on the new destroyer *Maury* (DD-401) (1938–39), and gunnery officer of the *Craven* (DD-382), all of these generally in the Pacific. After Pensacola flight training, he joined Fighting Squadron Three in November 1940 on the carrier *Saratoga* (CV-3) and in early 1942 transferred to Fighting Two on the *Lexington* (CV-2). Between February and the Battle of the Coral Sea in May, he became an ace by shooting down five Japanese planes. Lieutenant Gayler in June became a fighter test pilot at Anacostia and Patuxent River air stations and was promoted to lieutenant commander in May 1943 and commander the following March. In June 1944 he assumed command of Fighting 12, which joined the *Randolph* (CV-15) at the beginning of the new year. In February 1945 he joined the Pacific Fleet Air Force staff and in May that of Commander Task Force 38, first Adm. J. S. McCain then Adm. J. H. Towers, flagship *Shangri-La* (CV-38), operating off Okinawa and Japan. Briefly on the staff of Carrier Group 61 in the Atlantic, he was Deputy Director of the Special Devices Center at Port Washington, New York (1946–48); operations officer of the escort carrier *Bairoko* (CVE-115) in the Pacific; and head of the Fighter Design Branch of the Bureau of Aeronautics (1949–51), reporting thereafter as Commander Air Development Squadron Three at Atlantic City.

Promoted to captain in November 1953, Gayler three months later took over the Air Warfare Division of the Office of the Chief of Naval Operations and commanded the seaplane tender *Greenwich Bay* (AVP-41) in the

Persian Gulf (1956–57) and the *Ranger* (CVA-61) in the Pacific (1959–60). Staff duties included his being operations officer to Pacific Fleet commander Adm. F. B. Stump (early 1957) and naval aide to Secretary of the Navy Thomas S. Gates, Jr. (1957–59), reporting as U.S. Naval Attaché at London in August 1960, during which, in July 1961, he was promoted to rear admiral. After a year (1962–63) as Commander Carrier Division 20, flagships *Lake Champlain* (CVS-39) and *Intrepid* (CVS-11), in the Cuba missile crisis and general Atlantic operations, Admiral Gayler served in the Office of the CNO as Director of Development Programs (1963–65) and Assistant Deputy CNO (Development) (1965–67). Promoted vice admiral in September 1967, he reported to Offutt Air Force Base, Nebraska, as Deputy Director, Joint Strategic Target Planning Staff for America's nuclear missile and bomber forces, a post he held until July 1969 when he became Director of the National Security Agency. In September 1972 Admiral Gayler became Commander-in-Chief Pacific Command in the rank of admiral for the final stages of the Vietnam War and as U.S. Military Adviser to the Southeast Asia Treaty Organization (SEATO), U.S. Military Representative to the Australia-New Zealand-United States Council (ANZUS), and Military Adviser to the U.S.-Japanese Security Consultative Committee. He maintained these responsibilities until September 1976 when he retired from the Navy.

Ghormley, Robert Lee

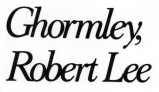

(October 15, 1883–June 21, 1958).
USNA (Idaho) 1906 (12/116).

Navy Department: National Archives

Guadalcanal commander Ghormley's earliest sea duties were aboard the cruisers *West Virginia* (ACR-5), *Buffalo*, *Charleston* (C-22) and *Maryland* (ACR-8), mostly across the Pacific in his first five years. His subsequent ship assignments were as first lieutenant and then gunnery officer of the new battleship *Nevada* (BB-36) in the Atlantic (1916-18); aboard the patrol yacht *Niagara* (SP-136/PY-9) in the West Indies (1920); commanding officer of the destroyer *Sands* (DD-243) in the Eastern Mediterranean during the Greco-Turkish war (1920–22); executive officer of the *Oklahoma* (BB-37) (1925–27) and skipper of the *Nevada* (1935–36), both with the U.S. Fleet in the Pacific. Along with assignments at the Naval Academy (1913–16) and as Assistant Director of Overseas Division, Naval Overseas Transportation Service (1918–20), Ghormley became a much sought-after officer for his keen mind as a staff person: flag lieutenant to Pacific Fleet commander Adm. W. H. H. Southerland, flagship *California* (ACR-6), at the Nicaraguan intervention of 1912; flag lieutenant to Adm. Albert W. Grant, Commander Battleship Force and Squadron Two while on the *Nevada* (1917–18); aide to Adm. H. T. Mayo studying conditions in Haiti (1920); aide to Assistant Secretaries of the Navy Theodore Roosevelt, Jr. (1923-24), and T. Douglas Robinson (1924–25); Secretary of the General Board (1927–30); assistant chief of staff to Adm. Frank H. Schofield, Commander Battle Force (1930–31), flagship *California* (BB-44), and Commander-in-Chief U.S. Fleet (1931–32) in the *Texas* (BB-25); and operations officer to U.S. Fleet commander Adm. Arthur J. Hepburn (1936–37), flagship *Pennsylvania* (BB-38).

Captain Ghormley headed the Tactical Section of the Training Division in the Office of the Chief of Naval Operations (1932–35), completed the senior Naval War College course (1937–38), directed the CNO's War Plans Division (1938–39) and was Assistant CNO (1939–40). Promoted rear admiral in mid-1938, he reported to London in August 1940 to initiate secret Anglo-American naval discussions and in September 1941 was advanced to vice admiral. He returned to Washington the next April for immediate assignment to the Pacific theater. Establishing his headquarters at Auckland, New Zealand, flagship the destroyer tender *Rigel* (AD-13), Admiral Ghormley became Commander South Pacific Area and Force in June, and he successfully organized the amphibious operation which established the beachhead at Guadalcanal in August 1942. The strain of the ensuing arduous campaign and probably also his abscessed teeth hampered his command effectiveness, however, and in October, with the Guadalcanal toehold in critical danger, he was replaced by Adm. W. F. Halsey, Jr. After several months at the Navy Department, he returned to the Pacific in February 1943 as Commandant Fourteenth Naval District and Commander Hawaiian Sea Frontier at Pearl Harbor, where his intellectual abilities were available to Pacific Fleet commander Adm. C. W. Nimitz until October 1944. From December 1944 to December 1945 Admiral Ghormley was Commander U.S. Naval Forces in Germany (Task Force 124). After service as chairman of the General Board from January to April 1946, he retired in August in the rank of vice admiral.

Gleaves, Albert

(January 1, 1858–January 6, 1937).
USNA (Tenn.) 1877 (18/45).

Convoy organizer and transport commander during World War I, Gleaves had extensive sea duty in his early years while writing articles on naval reform for the U.S. Naval Institute *Proceedings*: in the Atlantic aboard the screw sloops *Hartford* (1877–79) and *Plymouth* (1879), in Europe and the Mediterranean with the gunboat *Nipsic* (1879–83), in the Far East with the steam frigate *Trenton* (1883–86) and with the unarmored cruiser *Dolphin* (1889–91), and the protected cruiser *Boston* (1891–93) in the Squadron of Evolution, followed by promotion to lieutenant. He had ordnance duty at the Washington Navy Yard (1886–87, 1893–95) and the Proving Ground (1887–89) before operating in the Atlantic aboard the new battleship *Texas* (1895–96) and along the West coast with the monitor *Monadnock* (1896). Taking command of the torpedo boat *Cushing* (TB-1) in 1897, Gleaves became a close friend of then Assistant Secretary of the Navy Theodore Roosevelt, invented a device which improved the accuracy of torpedoes and then patrolled the Cays during the war with Spain. He had brief battleship service with the *Alabama* (BB-8) and *Indiana* (BB-1) in the Atlantic before commanding Presidential yachts *Dolphin* (PG-24) (1901–02) and *Mayflower* (PY-1) (1902–04). He commanded the Newport torpedo station (1904–08) and went to Europe to study methods of governmental torpedo manufacture, which were then initiated in 1909 at Newport.

After commanding the cruiser *St. Louis* (C-20) in the Pacific (1908–09), Gleaves was advanced to the rank of captain (July 1910) and given command of the *North Dakota* (BB-29) for a cruise to Europe. He commanded in succession the Newport Naval Station and Second Naval District (1911–12) and New York Navy Yard (1912–14) and Third Naval

District (1912–13), and in September 1914 he became skipper of the *Utah* (BB-31) and temporary commander of the Atlantic Fleet's Second Division. Promotion to rear admiral in July 1915 led to a November appointment to command that Fleet's Torpedo Flotilla (later Destroyer Force), with which he devised methods of underway refueling. Following America's entry into World War I, Admiral Gleaves in July 1917 took command of the fleet's Cruiser and Transport Force, flagship *Seattle* (ACR-11), and quickly developed antisubmarine convoys and techniques by which American supply ships and troop transports crossed the Atlantic in relative safety. Promoted to vice admiral in December 1918 and to admiral the following September, he assumed command of the Asiatic Fleet, flagship *South Dakota* (ACR-9), renamed *Huron* (CA-9), during which duty he became alarmed over Japanese naval expansion. Stepping down in February 1921, Gleaves reverted to rear admiral in command of the Boston Navy Yard until his retirement in this rank on the first day of 1922. He authored several biographies, notably a life of Adm. S. B. Luce (1925) and *A History of the Cruiser and Transport Force* (1921), and in retirement (1928–31) served as governor of the Naval Home at Philadelphia, during which (1930) he was restored to the full rank of admiral. A son-in-law was Commo. T. L. Van Metre (1887–1973).

Goldsborough, Louis Malesherbes

(February 18, 1805—February 20, 1877).

Bureau of Ships: National Archives

A major Union commander early in the Civil War, Goldsborough provides an interesting comparison with fellow officer French Forrest *(q.v.)* in being from Maryland, and in that his father Charles W. Goldsborough (1779–1843) was for many years (1798–1813) chief clerk of the Navy Department.

Though his midshipman's warrant is dated June 1812, he did not report for duty at Boston until 1816. He joined the ship-of-the-line *Franklin* at Chester, Pennsylvania, in September 1817, for her first three-year tour as flagship of the Mediterranean Squadron and then her second and final tour (1821–24) as flagship in the Pacific. Acting lieutenant during his last year on this vessel, he was promoted fully to lieutenant at Washington early in 1825. Given leave to study in Europe, in 1827 he joined the schooner *Porpoise* to fight Eastern Mediterranean pirates, and that September he led a four-boat night expedition which recovered the British merchantman *Comet* from pirate hands. Detached two years later, Goldsborough recommended to the Secretary of the Navy the creation of the Depot of Charts and Instruments, done in December 1830 with him in charge. Taking leave in 1833 he led a group of German immigrants to the Florida estate of his father-in-law, the eminent statesman William Wirt, then commanded a steamboat expedition and a mounted volunteer company in the Seminole War.

Goldsborough returned to the Navy in September 1839 for Pacific duty with the frigate *United States,* at the end of which, in September 1841, he was promoted to master commandant. He was with the sloop *Marion* when that unfortunate vessel sank at Rio de Janeiro in 1842, transferred to the Portsmouth Navy Yard (1843-45), and wrote a tract refuting criticism of the Navy (1845). In November 1846 he reported to the recommissioned ship-of-the-line *Ohio,* on which he participated in the bombardment of Vera Cruz the following March and led a landing at Tuxpan in April. Detached in June, he briefly commanded the Naval Rendezvous at Baltimore and had detached duty as senior naval member of a commission which explored newly acquired California and Oregon (1849–50). Commander Goldsborough waited a year and a half before taking command, in April 1852, of the frigate *Cumberland,* flagship in the Mediterranean, shifting in November to command of the sloop *Levant,* whose skipper had suddenly died. He was detached in April 1853 and six months later became Superintendent of the Naval Academy, a post he held for four years and during which—in September 1857—he was promoted to captain. After several months at the Washington Navy Yard, in June 1859 he took command of the frigate *Congress,* flagship of the Brazil Station.

With the outbreak of the Civil War, the Navy ignored the regulation requiring Captain Goldsborough's retirement after 45 years' active service and in August 1861 appointed him flag officer and in September commander of the Atlantic Blockading Squadron, flagship the steam frigate *Minnesota.* After this unit's reorganization late in October, Goldsborough retained command of the North Atlantic Blockading Squadron and led it against the North Carolina coast early in 1862, his flag aboard the sidewheel steamer *Philadelphia.* In these operations he assisted the Army in the capture of Roanoke Island in February, for which achievement his retirement was postponed another ten years. Again in the *Minnesota,* Flag Officer Goldsborough rendered support to Gen. George B. McClellan in the Peninsular Campaign during the spring, but was deterred from sending the James River Flotilla upriver against Richmond until after the scuttling of the ironclad *Merrimack (Virginia)* in May; even then, this sortie failed. Although promoted to rear admiral in July 1862, he asked to be relieved following public criticism over his failure to accomplish what in fact had been McClellan's task on land; it was granted in September. Subsequent administrative duties included writing a regulations code for the Navy and throughout most of 1863 the presidency of the Naval Academy's Board of Visitors, though he contributed little else to the war effort. In April 1865 Admiral Goldsborough began two and a half years as commander of the European Squadron, flagship the screw frigate *Colorado*. The Navy resisted efforts to retire him and in March 1869 made him head of a board which examined steam engines on active warships. In October he became Port Admiral of Washington, D.C., and Inspector of Hulls in Ordinary. One year later Goldsborough transferred to command of the Washington Navy Yard, a post he held four years. Designated in August 1873 to command the Asiatic Station, he instead was finally retired in October.

Goodrich, Caspar Frederick

(January 7, 1847—December 26, 1925).
USNA (Conn.) 1865 (1/31).

U. S. Navy Photograph

Naval intellectual Goodrich operated initially in European waters aboard the screw frigate *Colorado* (1865-66) and the sidewheel steamer *Frolic* (1866-68), later shifting to the South Atlantic with the sloop *Portsmouth* (1868-71). His superior talents accounted for his rise from ensign in 1866 to lieutenant commander three years later and his appointment in 1871 to teach physics and chemistry at the Naval Academy. During his three years there he was instrumental in the founding of the U.S. Naval Institute. With Luce and Sampson he became one of the three key leaders of the Institute in its early years and a prolific writer in its *Proceedings,* serving eventually (1904–09) as its president. Goodrich spent his Asiatic Station tour aboard the flagship steam frigate *Tennessee* and screw sloop *Kearsarge* (1875–77), going hence to the Newport torpedo station (1878–80). After a year's leave abroad, he was made executive officer of the steam sloop *Lancaster* for European and Mediterranean cruising (1881–84), during which in 1882 he was naval attaché to Gen. Sir Garnet Wolsley during the British bombardment of Egyptian Alexandria and was also an assault commander. In the rank of commander he brought the Greely relief ship *Alert* to New York (1884), then inspected ordnance at Washington and Newport, at the latter as chief inspector (1886–89).

A member of the Endicott Board on coastal fortifications (1885), Commander Goodrich helped found the Naval War College (1884), of which he served as president (1889, 1897–98) and for the rest of his career as a lecturer there on naval history, twice for regular tours of duty (1895–97, 1900–01). Following an extended leave, he commanded the training sloops *Jamestown* on the Eastern seaboard (1891–92) and *Constellation* for a special visit to Europe in connection with the Columbian Exposition (1892–93). He returned to the Orient to command the gunboat *Concord* (PG-3) (1893–94), was promoted to captain in 1897, and early the next year founded the Coast Signal Service. In April 1898 Captain Goodrich brought the auxiliary cruiser *St. Louis* into commission in time for war; the ship cut several underwater Spanish cables, captured a merchantman, engaged Cuban shore batteries, landed troops and fought at Santiago Bay. In August he transferred to command of the protected cruiser *Newark* (C-1) and shelled Manzanillo, Cuba, in the last naval action of the war. His remaining sea commands were the battleship *Iowa* (BB-4) in the Pacific (1899–1900) and the Pacific Squadron itself (1904–05), flagship the armored cruiser *New York* (ACR-2), he having been advanced to rear admiral in February 1904. His shore commands were the League Island Navy Yard, including Philadelphia's receiving ships *Richmond* (1901–02), *Minneapolis* (1902–03) and *Puritan* (1903–04), and the navy yards at Portsmouth (1905–07) and New York (1907–09). Although he retired in January 1909, in wartime Admiral Goodrich commanded the Naval Training Unit (1918) and Pay Officers Material School (1918–19), both at Princeton University. A writer of many historical and doctrinal essays, he was president of the Naval History Society (1914–16).

Grenfell, Elton Watters "Jumping Joe"

(November 6, 1903——). USNA
(Mass.) 1926 (93/456).

Naval Photographic Center

Submariner Grenfell took instruction in aviation at Annapolis (1926) and in torpedoes at Newport (1927) and served in the battleship *Florida* (BB-30) (1926–27), the carrier *Lexington* (CV-2) (1927–28) and the destroyer *Childs* (DD-241) all in the Atlantic before sub training at New London (1928) and duty on the sub *R-4* (SS-81) in both oceans (1929–33). Postgraduate work in mechanical engineering at Annapolis and the University of California (M.S. 1936) preceded his fitting out and serving in the *Pickerel* (SS-177) in the Pacific and Bureau of Engineering (later of Ships) duty developing landing craft (1939–41). In February 1941 Lieutenant Commander Grenfell reported to the *Gudgeon* (SS-211) which he brought into commission in April, took into the Pacific and, from December 1941 to June 1942, led on two war patrols to sink the Japanese sub *I-173* and two cargo ships. A plane crash injury in Hawaii disabled him until August when he commissioned and took command of the *Tunny* (SS-282) for four months. In December he became strategic planning officer for Pacific submarine commander Adm. C. A. Lockwood in Hawaii—with advancement to captain in mid-1943—and held this key post until August 1944, the next month taking command of Submarine Division 44 in Hawaii. In June 1945 Captain Grenfell took over Submarine Squadron 34, flagship *Moray* (SS-300), in the western Pacific and in September SubRon Five, flagship *Chub* (SS-329), with which he operated out of Subic Bay and Pearl Harbor until August 1946.

Assistant Deputy for Undersea Warfare, Submarines as well as Submarine Member of the Ship Characteristics Board, Grenfell returned (1948–49) to the Pacific submarine command as assistant chief of staff for plans to Adm. John H. Brown. He attended the Industrial College of the Armed

142

Forces (1951–52) and commanded Submarine Flotilla One (1952–53), flagships the sub tenders *Nereus* (AS-17) and *Sperry* (AS-12) at San Diego, leading to his assignment to the Bureau of Naval Personnel in connection with military personnel security and with promotion to rear admiral. In 1955 his title became Assistant Chief of Personnel for Personnel Control. Admiral Grenfell commanded the Submarine Force both of the Pacific Fleet (1956–59) and the Atlantic Fleet (1960–64), including NATO's subs, in the latter capacity advising the Atlantic Fleet commander on the deployment of the first Polaris nuclear guided missile-armed boats. Assistant Chief of Naval Operations (Logistics) between his two oceanic submarine commands, he became vice admiral in February 1960 and retired in October 1964. His second wife (1944) was the widow of Lt. Cdr. Eugene E. Lindsey, skipper of Torpedo Squadron Six, lost off the *Enterprise* (CV-6) during the Battle of Midway.

Navy Department: National Archives

Halsey, William Frederick, Jr. "Bull"

(October 30, 1882—August 16, 1959).
USNA (At Large) 1904 (43/62).

Hero of the South Pacific and Third Fleet commander in World War II (nicknamed by the press), this descendant of seafarers and son of a Navy captain (1853–1920) who commanded the cruiser *Des Moines* (C-15) in the Atlantic (1905–06) first cruised to the Mediterranean aboard the battleship *Missouri* (BB-11) in the rank of passed midshipman (1904–05) and was commissioned ensign in February 1906 while operating in the Caribbean Sea on the former Spanish gunboat *Don Juan de Austria.* In the commissioning crew of the *Kansas* (BB-21) in April 1907, he circumnavigated the globe with the "Great White Fleet," returning in February 1909 with concurrent promotion that month to both grades of lieutenant. His career thereafter was generally divided into three parts: torpedo warfare (1909–34), naval aviation (1934–42), and theater and fleet command (1942–45).

Lieutenant Halsey took torpedo instruction at Charleston, South Carolina, before commanding the torpedo boat *DuPont* (TB-7) in the Atlantic (1909), and then helped to outfit the destroyer *Lamson* (DD-18) and briefly served on board. He directed training at Norfolk aboard the receiving ship *Franklin* (1910–12) and commanded the *Flusser* (DD-20) from August 1912 and additionally the Atlantic Torpedo Flotilla's First Group from the following February. He transferred to command of the *Jarvis* (DD-38) (1913–15) where he participated in the Mexican intervention. While assigned to the Executive Department at the Naval Academy, Halsey in August 1916 was promoted to lieutenant commander. Leaving there in December 1917, he reported to the *Duncan* (DD-46) at Queenstown, Ireland, then commanded the *Benham* (DD-49) early in 1918 and the *Shaw* (DD-68) from May to August, both on antisubmarine patrol, promotion to commander occurring in February. He brought the *Yarnall* (DD-143) into commission as her skipper in November 1918 for European cruising, and commanded Destroyer Division 32, plus the *Chauncey* (DD-296) and then the *John F. Burns* (DD-299) in the Pacific (1920); DesDiv 15 and the *Wickes* (DD-75), also in that ocean (1920–21); the *Dale* (DD-290) (1924–25); and the *Osborne* (DD-295) (1925), the latter two tours in European waters. Commander Halsey, in the Office of Naval Intelligence (1921–22), was naval attaché in Germany (1922–24) as well as Norway, Denmark, and Sweden (1923–24), returning to the Pacific as executive officer of the *Wyoming* (BB-32) (1926–27). Promoted to captain in February 1927, he commanded the Naval Academy station ship *Reina Mercedes* (IX-25) (1927–30) and Destroyer Squadron 14 (changed to DesRon Three in 1931) of the Atlantic Scouting Force in the *Hopkins* (DD-249). He then attended the war colleges of the Navy (1932–33) and the Army (1933–34).

Captain Halsey entered flight training at Pensacola in July 1934 and was designated naval aviator the following May at the rather advanced age of 52 years! Two months after that he assumed command of the aircraft carrier *Saratoga* (CV-3) for a full two-year tour in the Pacific, followed by command of the air station at Pensacola (1937–38) and promotion to rear admiral in March 1938. He commanded Carrier Division Two, flagship *Yorktown* (CV-5), and (1939–40) CarDiv One on the *Saratoga*. Advanced to vice admiral in June 1940, he became Commander Aircraft Battle Force as well as ComCarDiv Two, rotating his flag in the *Yorktown* and *Enterprise* (CV-6). The Pearl Harbor attack found him at sea with the latter vessel, with which he led a two-carrier task force in attacking the Marshall and Gilbert islands, Wake and Marcus early in 1942. That April Admiral Halsey's main title was changed to Commander Carriers Pacific, and at the head of Task Force 16 he delivered Lt. Col. J. H. Doolittle's Army bombers to their launch point from the *Hornet* (CV-7) against Tokyo, Halsey remaining aboard the *Enterprise*. Late in May a skin rash forced him into the hopsital, but he turned over his staff to Adm. R. A. Spruance who then defeated the Japanese fleet at the Battle of Midway in June. Preparing to resume his carrier command in mid-October, he was instead called upon to rally the sagging American forces at Guadalcanal.

Admiral Halsey became Commander South Pacific Force and Area, headquarters Nouméa, New Caledonia, and succeeded in directing his units to victories off the Santa Cruz Islands and Guadalcanal in October and November 1942, leading to his promotion to admiral in the latter month. After the Japanese quit Guadalcanal early in 1943 the admiral organized and directed the offensive up the Solomon Islands throughout the rest of that year and into 1944, through attrition operations and landings at New Georgia, Vella Lavella and Bougainville. Islands not taken were bypassed and kept neutralized by air power, including the great Japanese base at Rabaul in the Bismarcks. Appointed Commander Third Fleet in June 1944, Halsey two months later hoisted his flag in the *New Jersey* (BB-62) to begin carrier support for the Philippines campaign, the timetable for which he had dramatically and suddenly moved up after probing weak enemy defenses. Following the October assault on Leyte Island, however, Halsey began to have troubles, failing to cover the offshore shipping from an enemy fleet attack, although his forces did sink many enemy heavy fleet units in the Battle of Leyte Gulf. Then, in December, he took the Fleet into a typhoon and lost three destroyer escorts which foundered. The Philippines, however, were finally secured, and in January 1945 Halsey passed command to Spruance in order to plan the next operation. He resumed command, flag aboard the *Missouri* (BB-63), late in May to provide air cover for the final stages of the Okinawa campaign, only to take the Third Fleet into another typhoon in early June. During July and August his ships and planes attacked the Japanese home islands, the surrender of Japan taking place on his flagship in September. Thereafter shifting his flag to the *South Dakota* (BB-57), he brought much of the fleet home and relinquished command in November 1945. Promoted to fleet admiral the next month, Halsey made public appearances throughout 1946 and retired at his own request in March 1947. He then wrote his memoirs, *Admiral Halsey's Story* (1947).

Hart, Thomas Charles "Tommy"

(June 12, 1877–July 4, 1971). USNA (Mich.) 1897 (13/47).

Navy Department: National Archives

Asiatic Fleet commander at the outbreak of World War II, submariner Hart had sea duty which antedated the Spanish-American War, in the Atlantic training wooden sail gunboat *Alliance* (1897) and the battleship *Massachusetts* (BB-2), on which latter vessel he entered the war, going to the blockade of Cuba and the converted yacht *Vixen* in which he fought in the Battle of Santiago in July 1898. In September he went to the armed steamer *Hist* off Cuba, then the *Indiana* (BB-1) and the Atlantic training sloop *Hartford* (1899–1902), with promotions to ensign in 1899 and lieutenant (j.g.) in 1902. After teaching gunnery at the Naval Academy, he sailed to the Mediterranean as a division officer on the *Missouri* (BB-11) as lieutenant (1904–05) and commanded the training torpedo boat destroyer *Lawrence* (DD-8), taking her out of commission late in 1906 and bringing the *Hull* (DD-7) back into commission, all in the Atlantic. Hart had Bureau of Ordnance duty (1907–09) before six months (January to June) as aide to Assistant Secretaries of the Navy Herbert L. Satterlee and Beekman Winthrop and his promotion to lieutenant commander. Briefly ordnance officer on the *Virginia* (BB-13), he assisted in fitting out the *North Dakota* (BB-29) as her gunnery officer and in the Atlantic (1910–11). Torpedo instruction at Newport followed, then service as executive officer of the *Minnesota* (BB-22) on board which he patrolled off Mexico (1914–16). He commanded the Pacific Torpedo Flotilla's Third Submarine Division, tended by the sub tender *Alert* (AS-4) and old cruiser *St. Louis* (C-20), at Hawaii from February 1916 to May 1917; the New London sub base and the *Chicago* (CA-14) in the rank of commander; and from August 1917 to June 1918 commanded both Submarine Divisions Four and Five, flagship

146

Bushnell (AS-2), operating against German U-boats in the waters between northern Ireland and the Azores.

Captain (since April 1918) Hart became Director of Submarines at the Navy Department in July 1918 and exactly two years later Commander Submarine Flotilla Three, its tender *Beaver* (AS-5), and briefly during 1921 also SubDiv 18, at Portsmouth, New Hampshire, and in the Far East. He graduated from the Navy (1923) and Army (1924) war colleges before serving on the staff of the latter. Commanding officer of the *Mississippi* (BB-41) in the Pacific (1925-27), he went to New York as Assistant Commandant Third Naval District and then Harbor Supervisor and afterward (1927-29) to Newport as chief ordnance inspector in charge of the torpedo station. In September 1929 he became rear admiral while in his second month as Commander Submarine Divisions Battle Fleet, flagship *Holland* (AS-3). In May 1930 Admiral Hart shifted his flag to the *Camden* (AS-6) as Commander Control (redesignated Submarine eight months later) Force, U.S. Fleet, then served as Superintendent of the Naval Academy (1931-34). Commander Cruiser Division Six, flagship *Louisville* (CL-28), in both oceans, he transferred to CruDiv Five and command of all Scouting Force cruisers in April 1935, flagship *Chicago* (CA-29), then joined the General Board in June 1936, becoming its chairman in December. Elevation to the rank of admiral occurred in July 1939 when Hart became Commander-in-Chief Asiatic Fleet, flagships *Augusta* (CA-31) and *Houston* (CA-30). The tense Far Eastern diplomatic situation finally degenerated into war, and in January 1942—although past retirement age—Admiral Hart became Allied naval commander in the Far East. After fighting a desperate defensive withdrawal, he was replaced by Adm. C. E. L. Helfrich of the Dutch navy for a political reason, that is, the allowing of that navy to direct the vain defense of the Netherlands East Indies. His command being obliterated in subsequent operations, in June he was detached and retired in the rank of admiral the next month.

Admiral Hart immediately returned to active duty as chairman of the Board of Awards until October 1942, in August of that year returning also to the General Board. Early in 1944 he also assisted in the study of the Pearl Harbor disaster and in February 1945 left all active duty to fulfill a vacated Senatorial seat from Connecticut which expired two years later. His father-in-law, Adm. Willard H. Brownson (1845-1935), preceded him as Asiatic commander in 1906-07. One son, Lt. Cdr. Thomas Comins Hart (1917-45), commanded the *Bullard* (DD-660) in the Pacific war.

Heineman, Paul Ralph

(December 7, 1897——   ). USNA
(Pa.) 1920 (195/460).

Courtesy of Admiral Heineman

U-boat killer in the Battle of the Atlantic, Heineman had World War I summer cruises in the training battleships *New Jersey* (BB-16) (1917), *Oklahoma* (BB-37) and *Vermont* (BB-20) (1918) before graduating early with this class in June 1919 and receiving assignment to the *Utah* (BB-31). In destroyers for most of his subsequent sea duty, he served aboard the *Worden* (DD-288) (1923–24); with Destroyer Squadron 11 of the Battle Fleet (1926–29); as executive officer of the *Perry* (DD-340) in the Pacific (1931–33); as commanding officer of the minesweeping *Robin* (AM-3) (1933–34); aboard the destroyer tender *Rigel* (AD-13) (1936); as navigator of the light cruiser *Detroit* (CL-8) (1936–39), the latter three based at San Diego; skipper of the *Moffett* (DD-362) in the Atlantic quasi-war with Germany from April 1941; and as skipper of Destroyer Division 13 for a month early in 1942. Heineman's shore assignments were postgraduate study in electrical engineering at Annapolis and Columbia University (M.S. 1926) and at three industrial firms the ensuing summer; inspection and survey duty at San Francisco (1929–31); and the Bureau of Engineering (1939–1941, the latter year known as the Bureau of Ships).

Commander Heineman in February 1942 reported to Task Force 24 and command of American-Canadian North Atlantic convoy escorts, broad pennant in the *Benson* (DD-421) in March and April and the Coast Guard cutters *Campbell* and *Spencer* thereafter. Promoted captain in June 1942, he commanded several units, culminating with Ocean Escort Unit A-3, "Heineman's Harriers," an Anglo-American-Canadian-Polish force which escorted large convoys west and east in February and March 1943, heavily engaging U-boats with much success due to Heineman's tactical skills, though also suffering heavy merchant losses in these dark days of the Battle of the Atlantic. His tactics laid the foundation for future operations against sub wolf packs, and in May 1943 he was made the Atlantic Fleet's Anti-Submarine Warfare Officer and commander of that Fleet's Anti-Submarine Warfare Unit, and in July changed to Coordinator of that Fleet's ASW Training Command, centered near Norfolk. As such he contributed importantly to turning the tide against the German U-boat arm until detached in August 1944. Two months later Captain Heineman assumed command of the *Biloxi* (CL-80), leading her in carrier and amphibious support units of the Leyte, Luzon, Iwo Jima and Okinawa operations, and attacking Wake Island in July 1945. Relieved the next month, he served as chief of staff to Adms. Herbert F. Leary and T. C. Kinkaid, commanders of the Atlantic Reserve Fleet (1945–48), and in the Office of the Chief of Naval Operations until he retired in June 1949 in the rank of rear admiral.

Hewitt, Henry Kent

(February 11, 1887–September 15, 1972). USNA (N.J.) 1907 (30/209).

Senior American naval commander in the Mediterranean during World War II, Hewitt graduated in September 1906 to the battleship *Missouri* (BB-11), her Jamaica earthquake relief mission, and the global voyage of the "Great White Fleet" (1907–09). Commissioned ensign 24 months after graduation, he became lieutenant (j.g.) exactly three years after that following a year in the Atlantic with the *Connecticut* (BB-18) and upon joining the destroyer *Flusser* (DD-20) as navigator and executive officer. A watch officer aboard the *Florida* (BB-30) still in the Atlantic (1912–13), he taught mathematics at the Naval Academy before taking command of the converted yacht *Eagle* in July 1916 for survey and patrol work in the Caribbean, promotions to lieutenant and lieutenant commander taking place in December 1913 and July 1917 respectively. Hewitt transferred his entire crew to the converted yacht *Dorothea* in December 1917 in the same waters. In June 1918 he prepared for destroyer command by cruising out of Brest in the *Conner* (DD-72) then escorted convoys as commander of the *Cummings* (DD-44) in the same area. He became commander in July 1918, brought his vessel back to the East coast and the following spring briefly commanded the *Ludlow* (DD-112) on the West coast. Instructing in electrical engineering and physics again at the Academy (1919–23), he was gunnery officer of the *Pennsylvania* (BB-38) in the Pacific, head of the Gunnery Section in the Division of Fleet Training (1923–26), and gunnery officer to Adm. Louis R. de Steiguer, first Battleship Divisions commander in the Battle Fleet, flagship *West Virginia* (BB-48), and then (1927–28) Commander Battle Fleet, flagship *California* (BB-44).

Commander Hewitt completed the senior Naval War College course (1928–29), served two years there on the staff, and commanded Destroyer Division 12, flagship *Chandler* (DD-206), in the Battle Force. Promoted to captain in June 1932, he reported as assistant chief of staff and operations officer to Battle Force commander Adm. Luke McNamee and went on to head the Academy's mathematics department (1935–36) before commanding the cruiser *Indianapolis* (CA-35) which took President F. D. Roosevelt to Buenos Aires late in 1936. He was chief of staff to Adm. J. K. Taussig, cruiser commander in the Scouting Force, flagship *Chicago* (CA-29) (1937–38), and commander of the ammunition depot at Puget Sound, becoming rear admiral in December 1939. The following August he became Commander Special Service Squadron, flagship the gunboat *Erie* (PG-50), in the Caribbean until its dissolution in November. Admiral Hewitt commanded Cruiser Division Eight, flagship *Philadelphia* (CL-41), in both oceans and in June 1941 took over all Atlantic Fleet cruisers, escorting convoys and patrolling until early 1942. In April he took command of that Fleet's Amphibious Force and from the flagship *Augusta* (CA-31) directed the North African landings in November, the same month he was advanced to vice admiral. He established his next command, U.S. Naval Forces in Northwest African Waters—the Eighth Fleet, in Algiers in February 1943 and led it in the Sicily and Salerno landings in July and September, flagships the attack transport *Monrovia* (APA-31) and command ship *Ancon* (AGC-4) respectively and the *Catoctin* (AGC-5) thereafter. Headquartered at Naples from July 1944, he commanded Allied naval forces in the southern France invasion the next month. Hewitt was promoted to admiral in April 1945 and shortly returned home for the Pearl Harbor investigation but in August 1945 became Commander U.S. Naval Forces in Europe—the Twelfth Fleet. Special duty at the Naval War College (1946–47) preceded United Nations duty with the Security Council's Military Staff Committee and his retirement in March 1949.

Hill, Harry Wilbur

(April 7, 1890–July 19, 1971). USNA (Calif.) 1911 (24/193).

Naval Photographic Center

Amphibious leader in the Pacific war, Hill spent his career in the surface line, before World War I in the armored cruiser *Maryland* (ACR-8), the torpedo boat tender *Iris,* and the destroyer *Perry* (DD-11), all in the Pacific; in the cruiser *Albany* (CL-23) as engineer officer, both oceans; during that war in the battleships *Texas* (BB-35) and *Wyoming* (BB-32), navigator of the latter, both attached to the British Grand Fleet; and immediately after the war as navigator of the *Arkansas* (BB-33) and flag lieutenant to Adm. R. E. Coontz, commander of the Atlantic Fleet's Division Seven, flagship *Arizona* (BB-39), and then of the Pacific Fleet's Division Six, flagship *Wyoming.* Continuing as aide to Coontz as Chief of Naval Operations (1919–23), Hill studied chemical warfare before joining the *Concord* (CL-10) as gunnery officer in the Pacific (1923–25) and of the *Memphis* (CL-13) in the Caribbean (1925–26); between the latter two assignments he was again aide to Coontz, then commanding the U.S. Fleet, flagship *Seattle* (CA-11). After duty as executive officer of the receiving barracks at Hampton Roads, he was gunnery officer of the *Maryland* (BB-46) (1928–31) and in the Executive Department at the Naval Academy. A number of his ships having won gunnery awards under his direction, he was (1933–34) made Battle Force gunnery officer to Adm. Walton R. Sexton, flagship *California* (BB-44). Commander Hill commissioned and commanded the *Dewey* (DD-349) in the Caribbean and California, served in the Office of the CNO (1935–37), and attended the senior course at the Naval War College, becoming captain in May 1938.

War plans officer to U.S. Fleet commander Adm. Claude C. Bloch (1938–

151

40) and in the Office of the CNO, Captain Hill took command of the *Wichita* (CA-45) early in 1942 and escorted Murmansk convoys until September when he was promoted to rear admiral and made Commander Battleship Division Four, flagship *Maryland,* in the South Pacific, where however his force saw no action. In September 1943 this inaction changed with his appointment as Commander Amphibious Group Two for the Central Pacific offensive, commanding the Southern Attack Force (Task Force 53) from the *Maryland* in the Gilberts operation late in the year; the Majuro and Eniwetok Attack Group (Task Group 51.2) from the attack transport *Cambria* (APA-36) early in 1944; second-in-command of the Northern Attack Force at Saipan but commander of the Tinian assault during the summer also in the *Cambria;* and Task Force 53 at Iwo Jima in the new command ship *Auburn* (AGC-10) in February 1945. Admiral Hill was promoted to vice admiral in April 1945 and in May became Commander Fifth Amphibious Force and CTF 51/31 for the second half of the Okinawa campaign, flagship *Eldorado* (AGC-11). In late August his ships landed occupation troops in southwestern Japan, and in November he began the first of several postwar administrative assignments: Commandant Army-Navy Staff College, first Commandant of the National War College (1946–49), Chairman of the General Board, and Superintendent of the Naval Academy and Severn River Naval Commander (1950–52). Although he retired in the rank of admiral in May 1952, he was not detached from his final assignment until the following August. Admiral Hill then reported as governor of the Naval Home at Philadelphia (1952–54).

Hollins, George Nichols

(September 20, 1799–January 18, 1878).

One of the Confederacy's senior flag officers, Midshipman Hollins spent his initial tour of duty in the U.S. Navy blockaded at his native Baltimore aboard the sloops *Erie* and *Ontario* (1814), was captured with the frigate *President* trying to break out in January 1815, and later that year fought actively against Algiers aboard the frigate *Guerriére.* He returned to the Mediterranean aboard that squadron's three successive flagships-of-the-line *Washington* (1815–19), *Franklin* and *Columbus* (1819–21). Following a long furlough during which he commanded an East Indiaman, he was promoted to lieutenant in 1825 and ordered to the schooner *Grampus* in the Atlantic, transferring two years later to the brig *Hornet* in the West Indies for one year. He returned to the *Ontario* for a Mediterranean cruise (1829–32), went thereafter to leave status, and sailed on America's first formal Far Eastern diplomatic mission aboard the sloop *Peacock* (1835–36) before operating off the west coast of Central and South America as an officer of the schooner *Enterprise* (1836–38). At the conclusion of further leave, Lieutenant Hollins helped bring the new sloop *Decatur* into service and went with her to the Brazil Station (1840–41). Shortly after joining the brig *Pioneer* at Baltimore in 1841, he was promoted to commander and sent to the navy yard at Pensacola.

Commander Hollins reported aboard the new frigate *Savannah* in July 1843 for passage to the Pacific where he was to assume command of the vessel, only to have his orders revoked in November. New ones moved him to the sloop *Cyane,* with which he returned to Norfolk the next year. After duty at Pensacola (1845–46), in May 1846 he accepted the transfer of the Republic of Texas flagship, the sloop *Austin,* into the U.S. Navy at

Galveston as her commanding officer, only to move the worn-out vessel back to Pensacola, where he served ashore for the remainder of the Mexican War and doing a report on lighthouses. Hollins commanded the *Cyane* (1852–54) along the Atlantic coast and in the Caribbean, obliterating Greytown, Nicaragua, by naval bombardment in July 1854 as retaliation for the poor treatment of American citizens there. He commanded the naval rendezvous at New York (1854) and at Philadelphia (1854–55) and the station of Sackett's Harbor (1858–60), being promoted to captain in 1855. Mediterranean command of the sidewheel steamer *Susquehanna* (1860–61) ended with his appointment in June 1861 as captain in the Confederate Navy and concurrent dismissal from the U.S. Navy.

Captain Hollins assisted in the seizure of the passenger steamer *St. Nicholas* near the end of June 1861, assumed command of her and immediately seized three prizes in the Chesapeake Bay. He then directed the naval defenses of the James River from the end of the month and through July before taking command of the naval station at New Orleans and the defenses afloat of the lower Mississippi and Louisiana coast in the rank of flag officer, flagship the steam sloop *McRae*. With a small squadron built around the ironclad ram *Manassas,* of which he was captain, in October Hollins successfully attacked and drove off the Union blockading vessels from Head of Passes on the Mississippi. Early in 1862 he transferred upriver in the *McRae* to command the South's naval defenses on the Upper Mississippi. With seven ironplated gunboats, he planned to contest the Union advance on Island No. 10 in April but withdrew before superior forces and to assist in the defense of New Orleans. He was criticized by his government for this move as his squadron in fact was rendered useless and some of its ships had to be broken up. Flag Officer Hollins then commanded the naval stations at Richmond (1862–63, 1864), Charlotte (1863) and finally Wilmington from July 1864 until its capture early in 1865.

Hopkins, Esek

(April 26, 1718–February 26, 1802).

By Thomas Hart: Anne S. K. Brown Military Collection, Providence, R.I.
Naval Photographic Center

The only commander-in-chief in the Continental Navy, Rhode Islander
Hopkins was a merchant sailor and captain for most of his life and a
successful privateer captain for the British side in the Seven Years (French
and Indian) War before retiring to farming in 1772. Appointed a battery
commander in April 1775 and then brigadier general and commander of his
state's military defenses in October, Hopkins the next month was given
command of the colonial fleet being assembled by the Marine Committee—
of which his brother Stephen was a member—of the Continental Congress.
His final appointment as its commander-in-chief came late in December at
Providence, and in January 1776 he took command of his eight-vessel fleet
at Philadelphia, flagship the converted 24-gun warship *Alfred.* Setting sail
for the Bahamas in February, Commodore Hopkins directed his force in the
attack on and capture of New Providence, Nassau the next month. The little
fleet captured three small warships on the return voyage in April but failed
to prevent the escape of the larger *Glasgow* following a long engagement in
Long Island Sound during which much damage was sustained by the
American vessels. Commodore Hopkins was censured for inaction by
Congress in June but restored to fleet command in October, then failed to
sail or break out of the British blockade of Narragansett Bay. Criticized
from all sides, he was suspended from command in March 1777 and
formally dismissed from the Navy the following January. His son, Commo.
John B. Hopkins (1742–96), commanded a three-vessel squadron, flagship
his own frigate *Warren,* and captured seven British merchant ships and one
warship during 1779.

Hughes, Charles Frederick "Handle Bars"

(October 14, 1866—May 28, 1934).
USNA (Me.) 1888 (20/35).

Inter-world war leader Hughes—nicknamed for his mustache—served most of his early years at sea: the screw steamers *Omaha* (1888–90) and *Marion* (1890) in the Far East, the new protected cruiser *Boston* (1890–92) on both coasts, the steam gunboat *Thetis* (1892–93), the gunboat *Albatross* patrolling sealing grounds of the Bering Sea (1893–94, 1895–96), and the screw sloop *Mohican* on the West coast (1894–95). After very brief shore duty inspecting steel, he returned to sea on the monitor *Monterey* (BM-6), based at Mare Island, in October 1896—duty interrupted by a cruise on the gunboat *Wheeling* (PG-14) during the late summer of 1897—and journeyed to Manila for the final bombardment in August 1898 and where the following March he joined the utility ship *Iris* and in May the *Concord* (PG-3) for operations against the Filipino insurrectionists. During the autumn Lieutenant Hughes helped to outfit the training bark *Chesapeake* and in December took charge of the Hydrographic Office's Philadelphia branch, at the end of which tour twelve months later he shifted to the battleship *Massachusetts* (BB-2) as gunnery officer for North Atlantic cruising (1900–04) and a short torpedo course at Newport. During a tour at the Bureau of Equipment (1904–06) he was promoted to lieutenant commander and appointed navigator then executive officer of the new armored cruiser *Washington* (ACR-11) for voyages to Panama and France before her assignment to the Pacific Fleet. Recorder of the Board of Inspection and Survey (1908–10) and promoted commander, he commanded the scout cruiser *Birmingham* (CL-2) for early aviation experiments and the first post-*Titanic* ice patrol in the spring of 1912 and later that year commanded the cruiser *Des Moines* (C-15) off politically-tumultuous Mexico.

156

Commander Hughes was chief of staff to Atlantic Fleet commander Adm. C. J. Badger, flagship *Wyoming* (BB-32) (1913–14), for the Vera Cruz affair, became captain in July 1914, and then joined the General Board. He commanded the *New York* (BB-34) from October 1916 till October 1918 in the Atlantic, the vessel from December 1917 serving as flagship of Battleship Division Nine and the Sixth Battle Squadron of the British Grand Fleet, being rammed by one U-boat and avoiding the torpedoes of another. Promoted to rear admiral, Hughes commanded the Fourth Naval District and Philadelphia Navy Yard (1918–20) before progressing up the ladder to the top sea-going fleet commands: Battleship Division Four, Atlantic Fleet (1920–21); Division Three and Battleship Squadron Two Atlantic (1921); BatDiv Seven Pacific Fleet (changed to BatDiv Four, Battle Fleet) (1921–23); the Battle Fleet (1925–26); and the entire United States Fleet (1926–27), the latter two billets in the rank of admiral. Admiral Hughes also attended the Naval War College (1923–24) and as Director of the Division of Fleet Training (1924–25) coordinated the sinking of the *Washington* (BB-47) in accordance with the arms limitation treaty. He became Chief of Naval Operations in November 1927 and continued in that capacity until he resigned the post in September 1930. He thus reverted in rank to rear admiral, retiring as such two months later. Hughes was son-in-law of Adm. C. E. Clark *(q.v.)*.

Hull, Isaac

(March 9, 1773–February 13, 1843).

By L. Pellegrin: Navy Department

Victor as skipper of the *Constitution* over the *Guerrière* in the War of 1812, Hull entered the Navy as fourth lieutenant in the first crew of the frigate *Constitution* in 1798 after twelve years as a merchant seaman and master. Patrolling in the Atlantic and West Indies, he participated in this vessel's several captures of French warships, personally leading an expedition at Santo Domingo near the end of the quasi-war in 1800 and remaining as senior officer of the ship while it was laid up in ordinary (1801–02). After brief duty on the frigate *John Adams,* Hull took command of the schooner *Enterprise* for operations against the shipping and coasts of Tripoli during 1803, shifting to command of the brig *Argus* later in the year for the same work throughout 1804, during which he was promoted to master commandant. With the *Argus* he cooperated with the Army in the capture of Derne, Libya, in April 1805, and one year later received his promotion to captain, returning home with his ship in July 1806. He reported to Connecticut to superintend the construction of four gunboats, going to Norfolk the next year to serve on courts of inquiry. After three weeks with the laid-up *John Adams* early in 1809, he served ten weeks with the frigate *Chesapeake* at Norfolk, going hence to command Portland Station.

Captain Hull took command of the *Constitution* in 1810, cruised to France and England the next year and returned home early in 1812. After avoiding several British warships off the East coast in a long nip-and-tuck chase, in August the *Constitution* captured several merchantmen and soundly defeated and captured the frigate *Guerrière* whose shot had bounced off the vessel to be henceforth known as "Old Ironsides." In rapid succession (1812–14) Hull commanded the navy yards at New York, Boston and

158

Portsmouth, New Hampshire, and reported to Charleston, South Carolina early in 1814. Although appointed to the Board of Commissioners in February 1815, he soon resigned in order to resume command at Boston, where he remained until 1822, successfully resisting charges of fiscal mismanagement. Assigned command of the Pacific Squadron, flagship the frigate *United States,* in August 1823 Commodore Hull arrived off South America early the next year to protect his nation's interests during the Latin American revolutions, usually from Callao, Peru. Relieved at the beginning of 1827, he again had to defend himself against claims of financial irresponsibility and remained on leave until obtaining command of the Washington Navy Yard (1829–35), followed by more leave time. In 1838 he chaired a board revising ships' allowances, afterwhich (1838–41) he commanded the Mediterranean Squadron, flagship the ship-of-the-line *Ohio,* operating against African slavers and supporting other American policies in these waters, among them preparing for a war against Great Britain in 1841 but which never materialized. He took several leaves soon after this, and died while on leave in early 1843.

Ingersoll, Royal Eason

(June 30, 1883–May 20, 1976). USNA (Ind.) 1905 (4/114).

Naval Photographic Center

World War II Atlantic Fleet commander, this son of Adm. Royal Rodney Ingersoll (1847–1931), who was chief of staff to Adm. "Fighting Bob" Evans in the "Great White Fleet," began his career in the Fleet he would eventually command, that is, aboard the battleship *Missouri* (BB-11) (1905–06), the gunboat *Marietta* (PG-15), the New York receiving ship transport *Hancock* (AP-3), and the new *Connecticut* (BB-18) (1906–07, 1908–11), in which he circumnavigated the globe. Commissioned ensign in January 1907 and promoted lieutenant (both grades) in January 1910, he received instruction at the Bureau of Ordnance (1907–08), attended a Naval War College conference (1911), taught seamanship, international law, and English at the Naval Academy (1911–13), and joined the Asiatic Fleet flagship armored cruiser *Saratoga* (ACR-2) as her first lieutenant, then as flag lieutenant to Fleet commanders Adms. Walter C. Cowles and Albert G. Winterhalter. He finally transferred to the *Cincinnati* (C-7) as executive officer. In June 1916, two months before his promotion to lieutenant commander, Ingersoll became Assistant for Communications in the Office of the Chief of Naval Operations and developed the Navy's Communications Office during World War I, for which he became a commander and was selected to establish the communications office at the Versailles Conference. He returned to the *Connecticut* in the Atlantic as exec (1919–20), moved to the *Arizona* (BB-39) in the same post, and had a lengthy tour in the Office of Naval Intelligence (1921-24) prior to commanding the survey gunboat *Nokomis* (PY-6) in the Caribbean. At the end of his year's study at the Naval War College, June 1927, he was promoted to captain and retained on the staff.

His organizational talents now well known and admired, Captain Ingersoll served as assistant chief of staff to Adm. W. V. Pratt, Commander Battle Fleet, flagship *California* (BB-44), and then (1929–30) U. S. Fleet commander in the *Texas* (BB-35). He went on to direct Fleet Training for CNO Pratt (1930–33), briefly commanded the cruiser *Augusta* (CA-31) and fitted out and commanded the *San Francisco* (CA-38), both for Pacific cruising (1933–35), and returned to the CNO's office to direct the War Plans Division and participate in the London Naval Conference of 1935–36. Promoted to rear admiral in May 1938, he took command of Cruiser Division Six in the Pacific, flagship *Minneapolis* (CA-36), for a two-year tour before becoming Assistant to CNO Adm. H. R. Stark. On New Year's Day of 1942 Ingersoll became vice admiral and Commander-in-Chief Atlantic Fleet, flagship *Augusta,* with promotion to admiral the following July. In June his son Lt. R. R. Ingersoll II was killed on board the carrier *Hornet* (CV-8) at the Battle of Midway. Admiral Ingersoll superintended the North African invasion of November and oversaw the antisubmarine effort in the Battle of the Atlantic as well as the defense of the Eastern seaboard of the Americas during the war against Germany and Italy. In November 1944, these nations beaten at sea, he lent his organizational and logistical talents to the war against Japan by becoming Commander Western Sea Frontier at San Francisco, the post carrying the additional titles of Deputy Commander-in-Chief U. S. Fleet and Deputy CNO. With the end of the war, Admiral Ingersoll shed the latter two titles in October 1945 but continued in the former post until the following April for the demobilization. He retired in August 1946.

Ingraham, Duncan Nathaniel

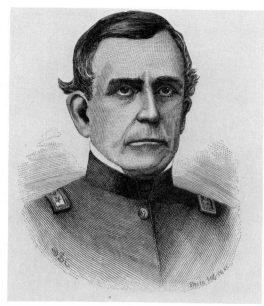

(December 6, 1802—October 16, 1891).

Principal naval officer in the Koszta affair of 1853, South Carolinian Ingraham followed his family to the sea by accepting a midshipman's appointment from his state in June 1812, shipping out in the frigate *Congress* raiding British commerce in the Atlantic (1813–14) and a few months in the schooner *Madison* on Lake Ontario. After a merchant cruise to Europe (1815), he operated against slavers in the Gulf of Mexico aboard the brigs *Boxer,* until her loss (1817), and *Hornet,* in which he also visited Europe (1817–20). His health poor, Ingraham was stationed ashore at Charleston and New York and on the receiving ship *Columbus* at Boston before returning to sporadic duty aboard the frigate *Macedonian* (1822–23), his health again forcing his return to Boston, then Charleston. He sailed in the survey sloop *Florida* (1824–25), during which he was promoted to lieutenant, and joined the sloop *Lexington* in May 1826, just prior to her commissioning, for a Mediterranean cruise which ended for him in September 1828 when illness again forced him ashore, this time for seven years. An attempt to return to sea duty aboard the sloop *St. Louis* (1835–36) in the West Indies proved premature for the same reasons, but he did lighthouse service and participated in the first cruise of the new sloop *Marion* to Brazil late in 1839, only to be sent home early in the new year. A lengthy period of standby status followed (1840–45).

Commander Ingraham assumed command of the brig *Somers* in August 1845 at Pensacola, stood blockade duty with her early in the Mexican War, and joined in the capture of Tampico as flag captain to Commo. David Conner just prior to his relief again for reasons of health in November 1846. After a few days aboard the Home Squadron flagship *Cumberland,* he took communications to the Navy Department and again had no active duty until he commanded the Philadelphia Navy Yard (1850–52). He returned to the *St. Louis* as her commanding officer in June 1852, sailing for Mediterranean patrol two months later. In June and July 1853 he confronted the Austrian brig *Hussar* and three smaller consorts at Smyrna, Turkey, demanding the release from the vessel of the former Hungarian revolutionary Martin Koszta, who had emigrated to the United States and on a visit to Smyrna had been seized by Austrian agents. The *St. Louis* cleared for action following an ultimatum by Ingraham, leading quickly to a diplomatic settlement at the last moment which resolved the crisis, Koszta eventually obtaining his freedom and Ingraham receiving a medal from Congress for his actions. Relieved in May 1855, he was immediately promoted to captain and soon made Chief of the Bureau of Ordnance and Hydrography (1856–60). He brought the steam sloop *Richmond* into commission as her skipper in September 1860 and departed with her the next month for the Mediterranean. Because of the secession crisis in his native state, he was detached from his command at his own request on New Year's Eve.

Captain Ingraham resigned his commission in February 1861 and the next month entered the Confederate States Navy in the same rank, briefly commanding at Pensacola before taking charge of the Bureau of Ordnance and Hydrography. In November he transferred to command of the naval defenses of South Carolina as flag officer, headquarters at Charleston, where he directed the construction of ironclads from January 1862. The following January Flag Officer Ingraham used two of these vessels and three tenders to attack and defeat Union blockading forces off Charleston, his flagship the ram *Palmetto State*. In March he gave up command of the local flotilla but continued to command the Charleston naval station until its evacuation in February 1865. With him at the end was his son-in-law, Lt. Wilburn B. Hall, top man in the U. S. Naval Academy class of 1859 (in which A. T. Mahan was second), a prominent Confederate ship captain in the defense of South Carolina and Georgia, commandant of midshipmen at the Confederate States Naval Academy (1863–64), and finally an officer of the ironclad ram *Chicora* at Charleston.

Ingram, Jonas Howard

(October 15, 1886–September 10, 1952).
USNA (Ind.) 1907 (187/209).

World War II commander in the South Atlantic and football coach, Ingram circled the globe while attached to the new battleship *Nebraska* (BB-14) as part of the "Great White Fleet" (1907–10), served with the Atlantic training ships *Hartford* (1910–11) and *Iowa* (BB-4) (1911), taught at the Culver Summer Naval School in Indiana (whose military course he had attended in 1902–03) and commanded the steam tug *Tacoma,* all the while spending each football season at Annapolis where he had starred as a midshipman player. He joined the precommissioning detail of the *Arkansas* (BB-33) in mid-1912, setting gunnery records while commanding one of her twelve-inch gun turrets and distinguishing himself in a landing party at Vera Cruz in April 1914. After quick successive Atlantic tours on the reserve pre-dread-noughts *Wisconsin* (BB-9), *Kearsarge* (BB-5), *Kentucky* (BB-6) and *Alabama* (BB-8), he was head football coach at the Naval Academy (1915–17), later directing football and all athletics there (1926–30). World War I found him as flag lieutenant to Adm. Hugh Rodman, Atlantic Battleship Division Three and American battle squadron commander with the British Grand Fleet, flagship *New York* (BB-34), remaining as flag lieutenant to that officer as commander of the Pacific Fleet (1919–21) on the *New Mexico* (BB-40). Commander Ingram was chief of staff to Capts. Daniel W. Wurtsbaugh and Waldo Evans, successive commanders of the Ninth Naval District at Great Lakes (1921–24), and skipper of the destroyer *Stoddert* (DD-302) and acting destroyer division commander throughout the Pacific. Executive officer and temporary captain of the *Pennsylvania* (BB-38), which was undergoing modernization and then was U. S. Fleet flagship (1930–32), he afterward directed the Navy's Public Relations Branch. He also briefly served (1935) as

163

aide to Secretary of the Navy Claude A. Swanson before commanding Destroyer Squadron Six, flagship *Litchfield* (DD-336), in the Pacific (1935–37), and then becoming Captain of the New York Navy Yard. Although he unofficially became a naval aviator early in his career, he never occupied an air billet.

Captain Ingram, after taking the senior course at the Naval War College, commanded the *Tennessee* (BB-43) in the Pacific from July to December 1940, being promoted the next month to rear admiral as Commander Cruiser Division Two, flagship *Memphis* (CL-13), and moving into the South Atlantic for patrols during the quasi-war with Germany. Remaining there for most of World War II, he became Commander Task Force 3 (later CTF 23) in February 1942 in the rank of vice admiral and key diplomat in cementing American-Brazilian relations and in defending the seaward approaches to Brazil. His flag aboard the oiler *Patoka* (AO-9) at Recife, Admiral Ingram in September 1943 had his post upgraded to be Commander South Atlantic Force, the following March redesignated the Fourth Fleet, flagships the destroyer tender *Melville* (AD-2) and converted yacht *Perseverance* (PYc-44), at Recife, all the while countering the U-boat menace in the South Atlantic until detached in November 1944. That month he was appointed Commander-in-Chief Atlantic Fleet in the rank of admiral, continuing in the post until September 1946. Retiring the following April after several months of inactivity, he served as commissioner of the All-American Football Conference (1947–49) and was succeeded by his deputy, Adm. O. O. "Scrappy" Kessing (1890–1963), another Navy football great who had commanded forward bases in the war against Japan. Navy relatives included two brothers who starred in football and crew as did Ingram and his son Capt. William T. Ingram II who commanded the minelayer *Shannon* (DM-25) at Okinawa.

Jones, Jacob

(March 1768—August 3, 1850).

Naval Photographic Center

Although originally a Delaware physician by profession, Jones began his Navy career at age 31 in April 1799 as midshipman first aboard the frigate *United States,* which took emissaries to enemy France, and then as second lieutenant on the armed merchantman *Ganges* against the French in the West Indies. Advanced to lieutenant early in 1801, he sailed in the frigate *Philadelphia* during the summer of 1803 against Tripoli, the harbor in which he was taken prisoner with Bainbridge when the vessel ran aground in October. Not released for nearly two years, Jones then operated off the East coast on the frigate *Adams* (1805–06), and was stationed ashore at New Orleans and again off the Southern coast on the brig *Argus* as skipper. He was promoted to master commandant in 1810 and given command of the 18-gun sloop *Wasp* in June 1812. Putting to sea that October, the *Wasp* attacked and took the 22-gun British brig *Frolic,* which was escorting a convoy, but both vessels had to be surrendered later the same day to the vastly superior 74 *Poictiers.* Paroled at Bermuda and exchanged at New York, Jones received his promotion to captain in March 1813 and command of the newly captured frigate *Macedonian,* blockaded at New York, then New London. Transferred with his officers and crew to Lake Ontario in April 1814, he brought the frigate *Mohawk* into service two months later and participated in the blockade of Kingston and the naval support of army operations around Niagara. Resuming command of the *Macedonian* in February 1815 for the brief war against Algiers, Captain Jones took shore leave late in that year and commanded the frigates *Guerrière* (1816–18) and *Constitution* (1818–21), both in ordinary at Boston. He assumed command of the Mediterranean Squadron, his flag in the *Constitution,* in 1821 for two patrols until 1824, was a Navy Commissioner and then transferred to command of the Pacific Squadron, flagship the frigate *Brandywine* (1826–29). Commodore Jones commanded the Baltimore station (1829–42), the vessels afloat at New York as port captain (1842–45), the receiving ship *North Carolina* there (1845–46), and the Naval Asylum at Philadelphia (1847–50).

Jones, John Paul

(July 6, 1747–July 18, 1792).

By Noah Saunders: Navy Department

The nation's first great naval figure and the greatest of the Revolutionary War, especially for his victory in the *Bonhomme Richard* over the *Serapis,* this native Scot first shipped out as an apprentice in an English merchantman at the age of twelve, served as mate on slaving vessels and commanded the West Indian merchant ship *John* (1769–70), being then imprisoned for apparently mortally injuring one of his sailors by flogging. Cleared and freed, he served as master of the merchantman *Betsey* in the West Indies (1773), but crushed a mutiny resulting in another death and in his own quiet departure for Virginia. With the outbreak of the Revolution, he helped to outfit the converted armed merchantman *Alfred* and secured a lieutenant's commission in December 1775 with the billet of first lieutenant on the *Alfred.* Jones participated in the expedition which captured New Providence, Nassau, and ensuing engagements in March and April 1776, and in May took command of the sloop *Providence* with the temporary rank of captain. He supported Gen. George Washington's army at New York as convoy escort and received his permanent captain's commission in August. The *Providence* took three brigantines individually off the Middle Atlantic coast before sinking and capturing several fishing vessels off Nova Scotia during September and October.

Captain Jones transferred to command of the *Alfred* and in company with the *Providence* successfully plundered more British shipping in Nova Scotian waters, taking many prizes during the last two months of 1776. He brought the new 18-gun sloop *Ranger* into service in the summer of 1777 and sailed with despatches for France, taking two prizes en route and arriving in December. Although frustrated from receiving the promised command of the new frigate *Indien* in Holland, he sortied in 1778 into English waters in the *Ranger,* took several prizes, raided the English coast, convoyed merchant vessels, and defeated and captured the 20-gun sloop *Drake*—the first victory of an American warship over an Englishman in British waters. The allied French navy, impressed by his successes, in February 1779 gave Jones command of the 42-gun converted frigate *Duc de Duras,* renamed *Bonhomme Richard,* in which he based at L'Orient and cruised the Bay of Biscay at the head of a small Franco-American squadron during the summer. After a second sortie in August, this force took 16 merchant prizes in British waters, and late in September Jones in the *Bonhomme Richard* encountered, engaged in a furious night battle, and took the larger frigate *Serapis* off Flamborough Head on the east coast of England. Switching to the captured ship as the battered *Bonhomme Richard* sank, Jones sailed for neutral Holland where he transferred his flag to the frigate *Alliance* in February 1780. Another vessel was also taken by his squadron in the action. The former skipper of the *Alliance,* Capt. Pierre Landais, seized the *Alliance* in June and sailed for America, Commodore Jones having little choice but to transfer to the sloop *Ariel.* He sailed her home, capturing a British vessel en route, during the winter of 1780–81. (Landais [1731–1820] was expelled from the Navy but in 1792 became a rear admiral in the French Navy.)

Charged with completing the young republic's first ship-of-the-line, the *America,* Jones reported to Portsmouth, New Hampshire, in August 1781 but was instead frustrated by her slow building progress and then with her being given to the French Navy as a gift in November 1782. He then embarked as an observer aboard the French flagship *Triomphante* for an uneventful West Indian cruise. With the dissolution of the Continental Navy at the end of the war, Commodore Jones' American naval career came to an end. He had lent much naval expertise to his government in the form of essays and letters and had received many honors and much praise, but had also been controversial and envied by rivals—conditions which were repeated upon his appointment as rear admiral in the Russian navy early in 1788. Hoisting his flag in the 66-gun ship-of-the-line *Vladimir* in June in the Black Sea for the Russo-Turkish War, Admiral Jones commanded the Ship Fleet of 14 sailing men-of-war in a successful naval battle before Ochakov in the Liman late in June and an additional flotilla of 26 gunboats and bomb vessels with which he blockaded Ochakov in July and August. Relieved and furloughed in October because of disputes with rival officers, Jones left naval service permanently.

Jones, Thomas ap Catesby

(April 24, 1790–May 30, 1858).

Navy Department

Twice commander of the Pacific Squadron during the mid-nineteenth century, Virginian Jones received his midshipman's appointment in 1805 but did not report for regular duty until the summer of 1807 at Norfolk and early the following year at New Orleans for an extended period. Going to Washington early in 1812, where he was promoted to lieutenant, Jones returned to New Orleans in September to command *Gunboat No. 156,* his first regular sea duty. He distinguished himself fighting Gulf pirates, particularly in one boarding action at Barataria in September 1814, and three months later commanded a small squadron of five gunboats and two schooners which cooperated with Gen. Andrew Jackson's army in defending New Orleans against the British amphibious assault. Though the squadron was taken in a prolonged engagement, and Jones himself was seriously wounded and captured, his performance had contributed importantly to the general victory. After recuperating from his wounds, he served on board the ship-of-the-line *Washington* in the Mediterranean (1816–18), at Norfolk, then at Washington (1819–25), where in 1822 he became Inspector and Superintendent of Ordnance.

Master Commandant Jones returned to sea as captain of the sloop *Peacock* (1825–27), which he took to the Pacific where he negotiated a treaty of friendship with the Hawaiian islanders and denied British claims to the same islands. The *Peacock* being irreparably damaged in an encounter with a whale, Jones was given command of the new sloop *Peacock,* bringing her into service in November 1828 to prepare for an exploring expedition to the South Pacific. Instead, he was appointed Inspector of Ordnance with the rank of captain the following June, a post he held until resigning it in 1834.

168

After more ordnance work at the Washington Navy Yard (1835–36), Jones brought the new frigate *Macedonian* into service in November 1836 and also assumed command of the other vessels gathering for the South Sea Exploring Expedition. On board the *Macedonian* also was his nephew, Midshipman Catesby ap Roger Jones (1821–77), who in the 1850's would figure importantly in the development of the Dahlgren gun. Captain Jones fell ill over disputes with his superiors in raising the necessary ships and personnel for the Expedition and was obliged to resign his command in December 1837. Several successive leaves of absence ensued.

Selected to command the Pacific Squadron in April 1841, Commodore Jones took charge in September, hoisting his flag in the frigate *United States.* Wrongly suspecting that war had broken out with Mexico, in October 1842 he brazenly seized possession of the Mexican port of Monterey, Upper California, with two vessels, his error resulting in his relief in 1843. Returning home aboard the frigate *Constellation* the next year, he served as Inspector of Ordnance during the early hostilities with Mexico, May 1846 to October 1847, departing then for the Pacific to resume command of the Squadron. He hoisted his flag aboard the ship-of-the-line *Ohio* early in 1848 and arrived off the Mexican Pacific coast just weeks before the war ended. The next year he shifted his flag to the frigate *Savannah* and returned home in the summer of 1850. For misusing funds solely appropriated for transporting Mexican refugees, he was court-martialed and suspended from active duty in February 1851.

Restored to active duty in 1853 and ordered to take command of the Mare Island Navy Yard, Commodore Jones then had his orders revoked. He was placed on the retired list in 1855. His nephew Catesby became a lieutenant in the Confederate Navy and executive officer of the ironclad *Virginia (Merrimack),* commanding her in the famous battle with the *Monitor* in March 1862, and spent most of the rest of the Civil War as an ordnance manufacturer at Selma in the rank of commander.

Jouett, James Edward

(February 7, 1826–September 30, 1902).
USNA (Ky.) 1847.

Naval Historical Center

A leader of the post-Civil War "dead period" Navy, Jouett became midshipman in 1841 and operated with the razee *Independence* (1841–43) in the Home Squadron and off Liberia aboard the sloop *Decatur* (1843–45), returning home on the eve of the Mexican War, in which he participated in east Mexican coast blockading operations aboard the frigate *John Adams* and completed his training at Annapolis. In the commissioning crew of the new frigate *St. Lawrence* in 1848, Passed Midshipman Jouett cruised in European and Mediterranean waters for two years. He participated in Commo. M. C. Perry's famous cruise to the Far East aboard the storeship *Lexington* (1853–55), after the end of which he received a promotion to lieutenant. Remaining in the Eastern Pacific, he patrolled the Central American coast with the sloop *St. Mary's* and shifted to the South Atlantic aboard the chartered screw steamer *M. W. Chapin* for the Paraguay demonstration (1858–59). Returning to the Home Squadron in 1860, Jouett was captured the next year at Pensacola by the seceding Floridians, rejected the parole offered him and escaped. Assigned to the blockade of Galveston aboard the frigate *Santee,* he led her boats into the harbor early in November 1861 and overpowered the crew of the armed schooner *Royal Yacht,* which was then burnt, Jouett having sustained several severe wounds in the hand-to-hand struggle.

Given command of the new screw steamer *Montgomery* in December 1861 and promoted to lieutenant commander the following July, Jouett continued his blockade duties between Mobile and Texas, the *Montgomery* capturing several blockade runners. In April 1863 he moved to command of the screw gunboat *R. R. Cuyler,* took eight more prizes off Mobile and while

170

hunting for the Confederate raider *Tallahassee* in September was ordered to New York to bring into commission the new fast sidewheel gunboat *Metacomet,* which he did in January 1864. Returning to the Gulf, Jouett chased down more blockade runners, then participated in the Battle of Mobile Bay in August, the *Metacomet* lashed to Adm. D. G. Farragut's flagship *Hartford* for the charge past the rebel torpedoes (mines). The vessel then disabled the gunboat *Gaines* and pursued, engaged and captured the gunboat *Selma.* It thereafter blockaded Galveston and cleared torpedoes from Mobile until the end of the war. After a year at the Philadelphia Naval Rendezvous, Commander Jouett was stationed at the Brooklyn, New York Navy Yard (1867–68) and commanded the sidewheel steamer *Michigan* on the Great Lakes (1868–70), on which he had served two previous tours (1858, 1861). On ordnance duty at the Gosport Navy Yard (1871–73) and the Board of Inspection, during which he briefly commanded the recommissioning monitor *Dictator,* he was promoted to captain in January 1874 and given command of the sidewheel steam frigate *Powhatan* (1874–76). Following more duty with the Board of Inspection (1876, 1877–80), he commanded the Port Royal Naval Station and its station ship *Wyoming.* Promoted to commodore in January 1883, Jouett had board chores at New York, then as acting rear admiral commanded the North Atlantic Squadron (1884–86), flagship the screw frigate *Tennessee,* during which—in the spring of 1885—he led eight vessels to Panamanian waters and used landing parties to keep open isthmian traffic during a revolt against Colombia. Permanently promoted to rear admiral in February 1886, Admiral Jouett was president of the Board of Inspection (1886–89) and retired in February 1890.

Joy, Charles Turner

(February 17, 1895–June 13, 1956).
USNA (Ill.) 1916 (84/177).

Navy Department: National Archives

Korean War leader Joy spent his first four and a half years aboard the new battleship *Pennsylvania* (BB-38), flagship of the Atlantic Fleet during World War I, and early in 1921 began ordnance engineering study at Annapolis which took him elsewhere, including the University of Michigan (M.S. 1923). Flag lieutenant to Yangtze Patrol commander Adm. Charles B. McVay, Jr., flagship gunboat *Isabel* (PY-10), he remained in the Far East (1925–26) to be executive officer of the destroyer *Pope* (DD-225) then returned stateside for duty in the aviation ordnance section of the Bureau of Ordnance. Back in battleships as assistant gunnery officer of the *California* (BB-44) in the Pacific (1928–31), Lieutenant Commander Joy was thereafter ordnance officer at the Yorktown mine depot, skipper of the *Litchfield* (DD-336) with the Battle Force (1933–35), gunnery and operations officer to Battle Force destroyer commander Adm. Clark H. Woodward in the cruiser *Detroit* (CL-8), and exec then head of the Department of Gunnery and Ordnance at the Naval Academy (1937–40). He joined the cruiser *Indianapolis* (CA-35) as exec and in February 1941 changed his billet on the ship to be operations officer to Commander Scouting Force, Adm. Wilson Brown. The flag shifted to the aircraft carrier *Lexington* (CV-2) for engaging the enemy Japanese off Bougainville, Lae, and Salamaua early in 1942.

Captain Joy commanded the *Louisville* (CL-28) from September 1942 to the following June, fighting off the Rennell Islands in the South Pacific in January and towing the stricken *Chicago* (CA-39) until she was sunk, and participating in the occupation of Attu in the spring. In August 1943 he became head of the Pacific Plans Division at Fleet headquarters in Washington, receiving promotion to rear admiral in April 1944. The next month he took over Cruiser Division Six, flagship *Wichita* (CA-45), supporting fast carrier and amphibious forces in the Marianas and Philippines operations in the summer and fall, and in the *San Francisco* (CA-38) at Iwo Jima and Okinawa during the first half of 1945. That June he took command of Amphibious Group Two at Coronado; in September of the Yangtze Patrol Force (Task Force 73), flagship *Nashville* (CL-43), for minesweeping duties; and in January 1946 (until April of that year) Task Force 74, flagship *Los Angeles* (CA-135), off the Chinese coast. After a lengthy tour as commanding officer of the Naval Proving Ground at Dahlgren, Virginia, in August 1949 Admiral Joy became Commander Naval Forces Far East in the rank of vice admiral, headquarters Tokyo. With the outbreak of war in Korea in June 1950, his command was expanded to include all United Nations naval forces there which he directed against the North Korean and Chinese enemy until June 1952, serving additionally during the last year as senior United Nations delegate in the armistice talks, which he recorded in a book, *How Communists Negotiate* (1955). Admiral Joy concluded his naval career as Superintendent of the Naval Academy and Severn River naval commander, retiring in June 1954 in the full rank of admiral.

Naval Historical Center

Kimball, William Wirt

(January 9, 1848–January 26, 1930).
USNA (At Large) 1869 (7/74).

Ordnance and submarine pioneer, strategist, and commander of the Nicaraguan expedition, this native of Maine and son of Col. William K. Kimball of the 12th Maine Infantry (1862–64) served in the training frigate *Sabine* at New London before beginning his career in torpedoes in the first torpedo class at Newport (1870–71). Assigned to the Atlantic screw gunboat *Shawmut,* he participated in the seizure of American vessels in the Orinoco River in 1872, then joined the experimental battery at Annapolis (1873–75), a tour interrupted by his help in commissioning the Navy's first two torpedo boats, the *Alarm* and *Intrepid,* and operating with them in the North Atlantic during the latter half of 1874; his duty station on both vessels was torpedo officer. Lieutenant Kimball had Asiatic service on the gunboat *Alert* (1875–79), helped develop machine guns and armed railroad cars and inspected ordnance at Washington, Springfield, Hartford, and elsewhere throughout the 1880's, and while assigned to the screw frigate *Tennessee* (1882–86) used his armed cars in the 1885 occupation of the Isthmus of Panama. Before duty with the apprentice training ship *Monongahela* (1891–93), he made several important contributions, political and technical, to the completion of the early Holland submarines, transferring next to the protected cruiser *San Francisco* (C-5) for cruises in the North and South Atlantic.

Still a lieutenant, Kimball became executive officer of the new *Detroit* (C-10) early in 1894 and thereon participated in the American naval demonstration off revolution-torn Brazil before transferring to the Office of Naval Intelligence in October where he developed the final draft of the basic war plans for the Asiatic and North Atlantic squadrons against the Spanish Philippines and Cuba respectively. Promoted to lieutenant commander late in 1896, he joined the torpedo boat *Rodgers* (TB-4) the following June to assist her completion. In September 1897 he assumed command of the Navy's first torpedo boat flotilla, organized it, flagship the new *Foote* (TB-3), and led it as the Atlantic Torpedo Boat Flotilla, although not into battle. Instead, he was with the *DuPont* (TB-7) off Cuba during the war with Spain. He then commanded several more warships, some for only a few days, the others being the collier *Caesar* (AC-16) (late 1898) and the supply steamer *Supply* (early 1899), both in the Caribbean; the yacht *Vixen* (1899); the *Abarenda* (AC-13) in the Pacific (1902); the *Alert* on West coast training service (1902–04); and the battleship *New Jersey* (BB-16), which he brought into commission in May 1906 and led during the Cuban insurrection the next year.

Promoted commander in 1899 and captain in 1905, Kimball served on a labor board and had equipment duty at Washington (1900–01), and was a lighthouse inspector at New Orleans (1904–05) and a member of the Examining and Retiring boards (1905–06, 1907–09). He was promoted to rear admiral in December 1908 and twelve months later assumed command of the Nicaragua Expeditionary Squadron, flagship the cruiser *Albany* (CL-23). Protecting American interests there during an internal struggle until April 1910, Admiral Kimball was however placed on the retired list in January 1910, ceased active service in June, then returned later to duty in World War I as a naval examiner (1917–18) and officer in charge of the historical section in the Navy Department (1918–19). He became and remained an advocate of aviation as well as of submarines.

174

Kimmel, Husband Edward

(February 26, 1882–May 14, 1968).
USNA (Ky.) 1904 (13/62).

Office of War Information: National Archives

Pacific Fleet commander during the Pearl Harbor attack, this son of a Confederate Army major and son-in-law of Adm. Thomas W. Kinkaid (1860–1920)—after short precommissioning tours in the Annapolis school ship *Santee,* battleship *Kentucky* (BB-6) and destroyer *Lawrence* (DD-8) along the Atlantic coast, and the Norfolk receiving ship *Franklin*—spent much of his career in battleships: in the new *Virginia* (BB-13) (1906); in the "Great White Fleet's" *Georgia* (BB-15) from Hampton Roads to San Francisco (1907–08), thereafter on the *Wisconsin* (BB-9) and *Louisiana* (BB-19) as aide to Fourth then the Third Division commander Adm. Seaton Schroeder; in the ship's company of the latter vessel in the Atlantic (1909–11); in the *New York* (BB-34) as gunnery officer to Adm. Hugh Rodman, Sixth Battle Squadron commander in the British Grand Fleet (1917–18); in the *Arkansas* (BB-33), in the same force as her executive officer (1918–20); in the *New York* as her captain in the Pacific (1933–34); and in the *West Virginia* (BB-48) as chief of staff to Adms. Walton R. Sexton and Thomas T. Craven, Commanders Battleships Battle Force (1934–35). Other sea assignments were the armored cruiser *California* (ACR-6) (1913–14) which became the *San Diego,* flagship of Pacific Fleet commanders Adms. Thomas B. Howard and C. McR. Winslow, to whom he was fleet gunnery officer (1914–16); with the British fleet as an instructor in modern American gunnery techniques during the autumn of 1917, once in action at Heligoland; as commander at Cavite and of two Asiatic Fleet destroyer divisions (1923–25), 45 aboard the *Preble* (DD-345) and 38 aboard the *Tracy* (DD-214); and as Commander Destroyer Squadron 12, flagship *Litchfield* (DD-336), in the Battle Fleet (1928–30).

175

Kimmel became captain in July 1926 also because of his superior gunnery and staff achievements ashore: instruction in ordnance engineering (1907), twice assistant director of target practice and engineering performances (1911–13, 1916–17), aide to Assistant Secretary of the Navy Franklin D. Roosevelt (1915), diplomatic services (1917), production officer at the Naval Gun Factory in Washington (1920–23), and instruction in the senior course at the Naval War College (1925–26). He served in the Policy and Liaison Division (with the State Department) of the Office of the Chief of Naval Operations and headed its activities during the Nicaraguan intervention (1926–28), as director of ships movements in the same office (1930–33), and as Navy Budget Officer (1935–38). In November 1937 he became rear admiral, the following July Commander Cruiser Division Seven, flagship *San Francisco* (CA-38), in the Pacific and Caribbean for a goodwill tour of South American ports, and in June 1939 Commander Cruisers Battle Force and ComCruDiv Nine, flagship *Honolulu* (CL-48). In February 1941 Admiral Kimmel was jumped over 46 more senior officers to become Commander-in-Chief U. S. Fleet and Pacific Fleet, flagship *Pennsylvania* (BB-38), in the rank of admiral, and was ashore when the Japanese carrier planes struck his anchorage at Pearl Harbor on December 7. With Gen. Walter C. Short, Army commander in Hawaii, he was charged with the major responsibility for the disaster and relieved from command ten days afterward. In his defense he later wrote *Admiral Kimmel's Story* (1955). After brief duty involving the post-attack investigation at the Fourteenth and Twelfth Naval District headquarters at Pearl Harbor and San Francisco respectively, Kimmel was retired as rear admiral in March 1942. Later in a civilian capacity he designed a drydock which was used in the Pacific war.

In the summer of 1944 Admiral Kimmel's son, Lt. Cdr. Manning M. Kimmel, was captured and murdered by the Japanese after the submarine under his command, the *Robalo* (SS-273), had sunk after striking a mine in the South China Sea. Another son, Capt. Thomas Kinkaid Kimmel, was exec of the *S-40* (SS-145) on five war patrols (1941–42) and commanded *Bergall* (SS-320) at the end of the war.

King, Ernest Joseph

(November 23, 1878–June 25, 1956).
USNA (Ohio) 1901 (4/67).

Navy Department: National Archives

Commander-in-Chief United States Fleet, Chief of Naval Operations and the principal American naval strategic leader of World War II, King went to war first as a naval cadet on the protected cruiser *San Francisco* (C-5) for anti-Spanish shipping patrols off the coasts of Florida and Cuba during the summer of 1898. Three summers later he received torpedo instruction at Newport then became navigator of the survey yacht *Eagle* in the Caribbean. He soon transferred to the Atlantic Fleet battleship *Illinois* (BB-7) for cruises to European waters and the Caribbean (1902–03) and went on to the Asiatic Fleet and the Mediterranean with the *Cincinnati* (C-7), from which he observed the Russo-Japanese War. Commissioned ensign in June 1903, King returned to Atlantic battleship duty in the *Alabama* (BB-8) (1905–06) with promotion to lieutenant (both grades) in June 1906 and assignment to teach ordnance at the Naval Academy. After his final year there on the Executive Staff, he was back in the Atlantic Fleet's battleships: as aide to Third Division commander (and his former skipper on the *Cincinnati)* Adm. Hugo Osterhaus, flagship *Minnesota* (BB-22) (1909–10); as assistant and then senior engineer of the *New Hampshire* (BB-35) in Europe and the Caribbean; and as flag secretary to Adm. Osterhaus, now (1911–12) Atlantic Fleet commander, flagships *Connecticut* (BB-18), *Nebraska* (BB-14) and armored cruiser *Washington* (ACR-11).

Promoted to lieutenant commander in July 1913, King served at the Engineering Experimental Station at Annapolis (1912–14), where he additionally edited several numbers of the U.S. Naval Institute *Proceedings,* in which he also published, and briefly commanded the destroyer *Terry* (DD-25) during the spring 1914 Mexican crisis, the *Cassin* (DD-43) while aide to

Atlantic Fleet Torpedo Flotilla Commander Cdr. W. S. Sims (1914–15), and the Sixth Division of that Flotilla, flagship *Cassin.* In December 1915 King became engineering officer and then assistant chief of staff to Adm. H. T. Mayo, Atlantic Fleet second-in-command, flagship *Arkansas* (BB-33), who fleeted up the next year to be Commander-in-Chief and who eventually wore his flag in the *Wyoming* (BB-32) and *Pennsylvania* (BB-38). He continued in this capacity during America's involvement in World War I, being promoted to commander in 1917 and not detached until early 1919. A temporary captain from September 1918 to June 1921 when he received his permanent promotion, he also reverted briefly to commander from December 1921 to June 1922; during these postwar fluctuations he headed the Postgraduate Department at the Naval Academy (1919–21) and commanded the refrigerator ship *Bridge* (AF-1) along the Eastern seaboard. These tours, in effect, ended his close involvement with the surface line—unofficially, the "Gun Club" or "black shoes"—for his career henceforth branched out into submarines and aviation.

Captain King took submarine training at New London (1922) prior to commanding Submarine Division 11, initial flagship the *S-20* (SS-125) in the Atlantic (1922–23), also serving the final months as commander of SubDiv Nine. He then (1923–26) commanded the Submarine Base, subs and Mine Depot at New London and distinguished himself in directing the salvage operations of the sunken *S-51* (SS-162) off Block Island during the summer of 1926, giving him an expertise for the salvage of the *S-4* (SS-109) off Provincetown, Massachusetts, in the spring of 1928. His first real association with naval aviation came with his command of the aircraft tender *Wright* (AV-1), additionally being senior aide to Capt. H. E. Yarnell, Commander Aircraft Squadrons Scouting Fleet (1926–27). He took flight training at Pensacola (wings May 1927 at age 48!) and returned to the *Wright* (1927–28), remaining on board with his flag briefly as Atlantic Fleet aircraft squadrons commander. Captain King locked into aviation—unofficially, "brown shoe"—billets thereafter: Assistant Chief, Bureau of Aeronautics (1928–29); commanding officer, Naval Air Base Hampton Roads; skipper of the aircraft carrier *Lexington* (CV-2) in the Pacific (1930–32); in the rank of rear admiral (April 1933) Chief of BuAer (1933–36); Commander Aircraft Base (later Scouting) Force, flagship *Wright,* in the Pacific and Caribbean (1936–37), additionally commanding Patrol Wing One toward the end; and as vice admiral (January 1938) Commander Aircraft [Carriers] Battle Force, flagship *Saratoga* (CV-3), in the Pacific and Caribbean, until June 1939.

Already a keen strategic thinker about the Pacific, especially from his lifelong study of military history and his senior course at the Naval War College (1932–33), Admiral King henceforth served in the highest policy-making echelons of the Navy. Reverting in rank to rear admiral, in August 1939 he joined the General Board and in December 1940 assumed command of the Fleet's Patrol Force, flagship *Texas* (BB-35), in the Atlantic. This billet was upgraded in February 1941 to be Commander-in-Chief Atlantic Fleet, in the rank of admiral, with King shifting his flag in April to the heavy cruiser *Augusta* (CA-31) to direct the undeclared antisubmarine quasi-war against Germany. From this time—off Argentia in August—he also participated in virtually every major Allied strategic planning conference, being elevated late in December to be Commander-in-Chief United States Fleet based in Washington and in March 1942 to be in addition Chief of Naval Operations. His resolute leadership enabled him to fashion the basic strategy against Japan in the Pacific and to prosecute the Battle of the Atlantic against Germany, notably by the creation of the Tenth Fleet in May 1943 with King in direct command and Adm. Francis S. Low as operational commander. King was a forceful figure on the Allied Combined Chiefs of Staff and the U.S. Joint Chiefs of Staff, bypassing the mandatory retirement age of 64 in 1942 and being promoted to fleet admiral in December 1944. The Tenth Fleet was dissolved in the summer of 1945, and the following October King's dual post of Cominch-CNO was reorganized into CNO only. Admiral King retired in December 1945 in the rank of fleet admiral and subsequently published his memoirs, *Fleet Admiral King* (1952).

Navy Department: National Archives

Kinkaid, Thomas Cassin

(April 3, 1888–November 17, 1972).
USNA (At Large) 1908 (136/201).

Seventh Fleet commander against Japan, Kinkaid joined the new battleship *Nebraska* (BB-14) as passed midshipman for the Pacific leg of the voyage of the "Great White Fleet" at the time that his father, Cdr. Thomas W. Kinkaid (1860–1920), headed the steam engineering department at the Norfolk Navy Yard. He transferred in the rank of ensign to the *Minnesota* (BB-22) in the Atlantic (1911–13) and patrolled off revolution-wracked Cuba, his father, now a captain, heading the engineering department at the

Annapolis Experimental Station. Young Kinkaid reported to the latter place to study ordnance engineering, moving subsequently to several other locations, government and private, on the Eastern seaboard, his studies interrupted by deployment (1914) in troubled Caribbean waters aboard the gunboat *Machias* (PG-5). In June 1916, a lieutenant (j.g.), he reported to the new *Pennsylvania* (BB-38) for maneuvers off the East coast before and during America's participation in World War I. Late in 1917, after promotion to lieutenant (and his father to rear admiral), he transferred to duty with the British Admiralty, going on in April 1918 to the *Arizona* (BB-39) as gunnery officer, this vessel escorting President Woodrow Wilson to Europe at the end of the year and cruising off embattled Smyrna, Turkey, early in 1919.

After a tour at the Bureau of Ordnance, Kinkaid became lieutenant commander and (1922–24) assistant chief of staff to Adm. M. L. Bristol, commanding American naval forces in Turkish waters, flagship the gunboat *Scorpion* (PY-3). He commanded the destroyer *Isherwood* (DD-284) on the East coast; served at the Naval Gun Factory in Washington (1925–27); in the rank of commander was U.S. Fleet gunnery officer to its Commander-in-Chief Adm. Henry A. Wiley, flagship *Texas* (BB-35); had duty as a senior student at the Naval War College (1929–30); and during as well as after his tenure as secretary of the General Board participated in the Geneva disarmament conference. Commander Kinkaid became executive officer of the *Colorado* (BB-45) in the Battle Force (1933–34); headed the Bureau of Navigation's Officer Detail Section; in the rank of captain commanded the cruiser *Indianapolis* (CA-35) in the Fleet (1937–38); and late in 1938 reported as naval attaché at Rome, in March 1939 additionally in the same post at Belgrade, Yugoslavia, billets he occupied until March 1941. Captain Kinkaid took command of Destroyer Squadron Eight, flagship *Wainwright* (DD-419), in June for escorting transatlantic convoys through the war zone, but was detached in November upon his promotion to rear admiral and appointment to command Cruiser Division Six, flagship *Minneapolis* (CA-36), in the Pacific.

Admiral Kinkaid led his division as part of the screen in the early 1942 carrier raids on Rabaul, Lae and Salamaua, and at the battles of the Coral Sea and Midway in May and June, then shifted his flag as Commander Task Force 16 to the carrier *Enterprise* (CV-6) for the Guadalcanal campaign and the naval battles of the Eastern Solomons (August), Santa Cruz (October), and Guadalcanal (November). Briefly commanding a large cruiser force, late in November he was detached and the following January made Commander North Pacific Force. Throughout most of 1943 he successfully directed the Aleutians campaign, notably the recapture of Attu and Kiska, from his headquarters at Kodiak, Alaska. Promoted vice admiral in June and detached in October, he assumed command of Allied Naval Forces Southwest Pacific and the U. S. Seventh Fleet in late November 1943 and supported the Army's operations under Gen. Douglas MacArthur in New Guinea and the Philippines. He was shorebased at Brisbane for the former campaign in the spring of 1944 and afloat on the amphibious command ship *Wasatch* (AGC-9) for the landings at and Battle of Leyte Gulf in the fall and the Luzon operations early in 1945. His forces mopped-up in the Southern Philippines thereafter, with Kinkaid being promoted to admiral in April 1945, and in the Central Pacific landed Marine occupation forces in China following the Japanese surrender. Detached from the Seventh Fleet in November, Admiral Kinkaid commanded the Eastern Sea Frontier at New York from January to June 1946, when he took command of the Sixteenth Fleet, which was redesignated the Atlantic Reserve Fleet the following January. He occupied this post until his retirement in May 1950.

Kinney, Sheldon Hoard

(August 27, 1918——). USNA (Calif.) 1941 (87/399).

Naval Photographic Center

World War II and Cold War sub hunter-killer, Kinney deployed in the cruiser *Omaha* (CL-4) in Central American waters following his enlistment as a seaman late in 1935, in 1937 going to the Academy preparatory school and a summer cruise to England in the battleship *New York* (BB-34). Commissioned ensign in February 1941, he the next month became gunnery officer of the destroyer *Sturtevant* (DD-240), escorting convoys in the North Atlantic and Caribbean against U-boats until she was sunk by a mine off Key West in April 1942. In the meantime his brother Gilbert L. Kinney had gone down with the *Arizona* (BB-39) at Pearl Harbor. He taught gunnery at the sub chaser school at Miami during the second half of 1942, after which he joined the destroyer escort *Edsall* (DE-129), becoming her executive officer and navigator upon commissioning in April 1943 and her commanding officer from July through November again at the Miami training center.

In December Lieutenant Kinney assumed command of the *Bronstein* (DE-189), which participated in the sinking of the *U-709* and *U-801* and alone sank the *U-603* the following March along with transferring Polish gold from French West Africa to New York (!). After patrolling off the Eastern seaboard and Gulf coast in the *Bronstein,* he was detached in December 1944 to become antisubmarine warfare and planning officer to Commander Destroyers Atlantic Fleet, Adms. Oliver M. Read and later Frank E. Beatty, until September 1946. The next two years were spent at the Judge Advocate General's office and studying law at George Washington University (J.D. 1960).

After brief duty on the staff of Cruiser Division Four, Kinney served as aide to the Commandant of the Sixth Naval District, Adm. Robert W. Hayler (1948–50); navigator of the cruiser *Columbus* (CA-74) in European waters; recommissioning skipper of the *Taylor* (DDE-468) in the Korean War throughout 1952; at the Bureau of Naval Personnel (Current Plans); and as antisubmarine and naval gunfire support instructor at the Naval Academy (1954–56), where he was also active in the U.S. Naval Institute as its secretary-treasurer and *Proceedings* editor. Commander Kinney commanded the frigate *Mitscher* (DL-2) in Atlantic hunter-killer operations before duty with the Anti-Submarine Warfare Readiness section at the Navy Department (1958–59). After instruction at the National War College, he was assistant chief of staff (logistics) for American naval forces in Europe (1960–62) and skipper of the oiler *Mississinewa* (AO-144) in the Mediterranean. Captain Kinney commanded Amphibious Squadron 12 and the Amphibious Force of the Sixth Fleet, flagships the attack transport *Francis Marion* (APA-249) and the amphibious command ship *Taconic* (AGC-17), briefly before serving as commandant of midshipmen at the Naval Academy (1964–67) and studying international affairs at George Washington (M.A. 1966).

As rear admiral (July 1967), Kinney spent a tour as Commander Cruiser-Destroyer Flotilla 11, Commander Cruiser-Destroyer Group Seventh Fleet, and Commander Task Group 70.8, flagships *Chicago* (CG-11) and *Newport News* (CA-148), in the Vietnam War. He was then Assistant Chief of Naval Personnel for Education and Training (1969–70), Deputy Chief of Naval Personnel (1970–71), and briefly Commander Cruiser-Destroyer Force Pacific Fleet before retiring in September 1972 to become Superintendent of the State University of New York Maritime Academy at Fort Schuyler the same month.

Kirk, Alan Goodrich

(*October 30, 1888–October 15, 1963*).
USNA (N.J.) 1909 (45/174).

Navy Department: National Archives

American naval commander at the D-Day, Normandy, landings, Pennsylvanian Kirk, nephew of Adm. C. F. Goodrich (*q.v.*), spent his entire career in the surface line aboard many ships: the Atlantic Fleet battleship *Kansas* (BB-21) (1909–11); the Asiatic gunboat *Wilmington* (PG-8) and as gunnery officer off revolution-torn China on the armored cruiser *Saratoga* (ACR-2) there (1911–14); the *Utah* (BB-31) in the Atlantic (1914–16); the *Connecticut* (BB-18) as gunnery officer returning troops from Europe (1919–20); the Atlantic's *Arizona* (BB-39) as assistant gunnery officer (1920–21); the Presidential yacht *Mayflower* (PY-1) as executive officer (1921); the *North Dakota* (BB-29) as gunnery officer for Pacific cruising (1921–22); the *Maryland* (BB-46) in the same billet and ocean (1924–26); the *Arkansas* (BB-33) in the Atlantic as navigator (1926); the *Wyoming* (BB-32) as gunnery officer to Commander Scouting Fleet, Adm. Ashley H. Robertson (1926–28), in the Atlantic; the destroyer *Schenck* (DD-159) in both oceans as commanding officer (1931–32); the *West Virginia* (BB-48), Pacific, as exec (1932–33); the cruiser *Milwaukee* (CL-5) as skipper (1936–37); the *California* (BB-44) as operations officer to Adm. Claude C. Bloch, Battle Force commander (1937–38); and the *Pennsylvania* (BB-38) in the same post to the same officer who had "fleeted up" to be U.S. Fleet commander (1938–39). Kirk's shore billets were by contrast relatively few but longer: proof and experimental officer at the Dahlgren ordnance proving ground during World War I (1916–19); centralizing records at the Bureau of Ordnance as well as aide to Presidents Warren G. Harding and Calvin Coolidge (1922–24); a student (1928–29) then operations staff member (1929–31) at the

Naval War College; and assistant director of the ships movements division at the Navy Department (1933–36).

Captain Kirk spent World War II in close liaison with the Royal Navy. Having served as a special aide to Adm. Sir Walter Cowan RN during a British naval visit to Philadelphia in the late 1920s, Kirk became U.S. naval attaché in Britain in June 1939 and remained in England throughout the early stages of the Anglo-German fighting until March 1941. Following several months as Director of Naval Intelligence, he was advanced to rear admiral in November while in the midst of a short assignment as Commander Destroyer Squadron Seven, flagship *Plunkett* (DD-431), in Atlantic antisubmarine convoy work. In December he was made a transport division commander with the Atlantic Fleet's amphibious forces. In May 1942 Admiral Kirk again became naval attaché but also chief of staff to Adm. H. R. Stark, U.S. Naval commander in Europe, headquarters London, transferring the following February to be Commander Amphibious Force Atlantic Fleet. His flag in the amphibious command ship *Ancon* (AGC-4) he led Task Force 85 in delivering and supporting the Army in its assault at Scoglitti, Sicily in the summer of 1943. The next November he became senior American naval commander under supreme British naval command planning the Normandy landings, which began on June 6, 1944, his flag in the *Augusta* (CA-31) as Commander TF 122 (Western Naval Task Force). In July, following the capture of Cherbourg, he was relieved, two months later becoming Commander U.S. Naval Forces France and naval commander to Gen. Dwight D. Eisenhower and commanding naval units in the advance into Germany. Detached and promoted vice admiral in July 1945, Admiral Kirk served on the General Board until his resignation and retirement in the full rank of admiral the following March in order to enter diplomatic service. Already skilled and experienced in this work, he was then American ambassador to Belgium and Luxembourg (1946–47), the Soviet Union (1949–52), and Nationalist China (1962–63).

Knight, Austin Melvin

(December 16, 1854–February 26, 1927). USNA (Fla.) 1873 (6/29).

Naval intellectual and Asiatic Fleet commander during World War I, Massachusetts native Knight began his career on the Asiatic Station with four vessels: the steam sloop *Tuscarora* for deep-sea soundings (1873–74), the screw sloop *Kearsarge,* and gunboats *Palos* and *Saco* (1874–75). He then served the first of several tours at the Naval Academy, where he taught in the English, history, and law department (1876–78) and later in physics and chemistry (1892–95), and finally headed the seamanship department (1898–1901), commanding the training vessel *Newport* (PG-12) (1900) and writing the textbook *Modern Seamanship* (1901). Promoted master in 1879, lieutenant (j.g.) in 1883 and lieutenant in 1885, Knight contributed many articles to the U.S. Naval Institute *Proceedings* during its important formative years, served in the European Squadron aboard the new screw corvette *Quinnebaug* (1878–79) and there and in the South Atlantic with the equally new wooden steamer *Galena* (1880–83), giving earthquake relief at Chios, Greece in 1881 and observing the British attack on Alexandria in 1882. He studied ordnance before and while at the ordnance proving ground at Annapolis (1883–85), which he then commanded (1885–89). In the commissioning crew of the cruiser *Chicago,* flagship of the Squadron of Evolution in the Atlantic, as ordnance officer (1889–92), he served with the steam sloop *Lancaster* and the gunboat *Castine* in the South Atlantic (1895–97) and transferred to the new monitor *Puritan* as navigator and on which he participated in the blockade of Cuba and taking of Puerto Rico (1898).

Lieutenant Commander Knight briefly attended the Naval War College (1901), surveyed the Cuban coast while commanding the armed yacht *Yankton* (1901–03), and cruised in the Atlantic as skipper of the *Castine*

(1903–04). He presided over an ordnance board and a joint Army-Navy board on smokeless powder (1904–07) and profitted from the Navy's rapid expansion by being promoted to captain (1907) and given command of the armored cruiser *Washington* (ACR-11) in the Pacific (1907–09), however then returned again to head the smokeless powder board. Appointed to command of the Narragansett Bay Naval Station, Knight became rear admiral in 1911 and the next year took command of the Reserve Fleet, except for temporary duty at the head of a special service squadron to patrol the Eastern Mediterranean during the Balkan War. In December 1913 he assumed the presidency of the Naval War College, a post he held until February 1917. Two months later he hoisted his flag in the *Brooklyn* (ACR-3) as Commander-in-Chief Asiatic Fleet in the rank of admiral. As such, he directed American naval operations during the Allied intervention in the Russian Civil War at Vladivostok and the Russian Far East and was chairman over the ten-nation international council attempting to maintain order there. Admiral Knight relinquished his command and retired as rear admiral in December 1918 but remained in service for another two months to head a war decorations board. Admiral Knight's son-in-law was Adm. Forrest B. Royal (1893–1945), secretary of the Combined and Joint Chiefs of Staff (1942–44) and an amphibious group commander in the Philippines and at Borneo (1944–45).

Land, Emory Scott "Jerry"

(January 9, 1879–November 27, 1971).
USNA (Wyo.) 1902 (6/59).

World War II merchant shipping administrator, Land served only two-plus years in the line—on the battleships *Oregon* (BB-3) (1902–04) and *Kentucky* (BB-6) on the Asiatic Station—before beginning his career in the Construction Corps as assistant naval constructor in October 1904, a career which included many inspection and ship-testing boards and related duties. During his first tour at the Boston Navy Yard, he studied naval architecture at the Massachusetts Institute of Technology (M.S. 1907), then transferred to construction and repair duty at the New York Navy Yard, during which he helped to revise the Navy's mess system. After service at the Bureau of Construction and Repair and as recorder of two boards, one on tool steel specifications, the other on fuel oils (1911–14), he was fleet constructor on the staff of the Atlantic Fleet commander, Adm. F. F. Fletcher, flagship *Wyoming* (BB-32), and then aide to that Fleet's submarine commander Adm. Albert W. Grant, flagship the cruiser *Columbia* (C-12) (1916). Stints at New York and the Bureau in Washington preceded his World War I work in the design and construction of submarines, with temporary attachment to Adm. W. S. Sims' staff in London in mid-1918. He remained in Europe on the Allied naval armistice commission and then as assistant naval attaché in London (1919–21).

Captain Land moved into aviation in November 1921, about the same time as did his cousin Charles A. Lindbergh, reporting to the Bureau of Aeronautics and in July 1922 qualifying as a naval aviation observer. A close confidant of Bureau Chief Adm. W. A. Moffett, he, in 1926, became Assistant Chief of Bureau, and two years after that took leave to promote aviation and earn his private pilot's license. Land then joined the staff of Adm. W. V. Pratt, U.S. Fleet commander, flagship *Texas* (BB-35) (summer

187

1930), and Chief of Naval Operations (1930–32), following which in October 1932 he was promoted rear admiral and appointed Chief, Bureau of Construction and Repair. A key figure in the drafting of the Vinson-Trammell naval legislation (1934) of the New Deal, he retired early from the Navy as rear admiral in April 1937 in order to be appointed that same month to the newly-created U.S. Maritime Commission. The following February he replaced Joseph P. Kennedy as Chairman of the Commission, charged with mobilizing the American merchant marine prior to and during World War II. In July 1940 he also became coordinator of shipping activities for the National Defense Commission and the following March head of the Division of Emergency Shipping. In February 1942 Admiral Land was in addition appointed Administrator of the War Shipping Administration, giving him a multiple role for the monumental tasks of coordinating the design, construction, and maintenance of over fifty million deadweight tons of American merchant shipping for supporting all the war fronts of the world extending from Northern Russia via the North Atlantic to Australia via the South Pacific. For his efforts in creating the largest merchant fleet in the world, he was specially promoted to vice admiral in the Construction Corps in July 1944. He resigned as Maritime Chairman in January 1946 and later wrote *Winning the War with Ships: Land, Sea and Air—Mostly Land* (1958).

Leahy,William Daniel

(May 6, 1875–July 20, 1959). USNA (Wisc.) 1897 (35/47).

Navy Department: National Archives

Chairman of the Joint Chiefs of Staff during World War II but also the only officer to hold that post as well as those of Chief of Naval Operations and Chief of the Bureaus of Ordnance and of Navigation (Personnel), native Iowan Leahy began his extraordinarily long career of public service as a naval cadet on the battleship *Oregon* (BB-3) in the Pacific, rounded the Horn with her, and fought at the Battle of Santiago in July 1898. He transferred to the second-class battleship *Texas* in October but went to the Far East the next year to see action in the Philippine Insurrection and Boxer Rebellion aboard the gunboat *Castine,* the supply ship *Glacier* (AF-4) and the gunboat *Mariveles* as the latter's commanding officer until 1902. After helping to train the crew for the new cruiser *Tacoma* (C-18), Lieutenant Leahy served aboard the protected cruiser *Boston* (1904–07) patrolling off the Panama Canal during its construction and participating in the relief of victims of the 1906 San Francisco earthquake and fire. Following a science teaching assignment at the Naval Academy, he returned to the Pacific as navigator of the armored cruiser *California* (ACR-6) (1909-11), as staff ordnance officer to Fleet commander Adm. Chauncey Thomas on the same ship (1911–12), and as chief of staff to Adm. W. H. H. Southerland, flagship *West Virginia* (ACR-5), during the Nicaraguan intervention of 1912. Assistant Director of Target Practice and Engineering Competitions at the Navy Department (1912–13) and detail officer at BuNav (1913–15), he commanded the despatch gunboat *Dolphin* (PG-24) in the West Indies, helping to occupy Santo Domingo in 1916, demonstrating off Mexico, and searching in vain for enemy German supply craft during the spring of 1917.

Commander Leahy became executive officer of the *Nevada* (BB-36) for wartime training patrols out of Norfolk and in April 1918 took command of the troop transport *Princess Matoika* which ferried elements of the American Expeditionary Force to Europe. Promoted to captain that July he returned to Washington as Director of Gunnery Exercises and Engineering Performances before commanding the *St. Louis* (CA-18), flagship of the naval forces off tumultuous Turkey (1921), and then the Atlantic Fleet's Mine Squadron One, its flagship minelayer *Shawmut* (CM-4) and in 1922 also the Control Force of submarines and smaller craft. Captain Leahy directed the Officer Personnel Division of BuNav (1923–26) and commanded the *New Mexico* (BB-40) in the Pacific before his advancement to rear admiral and assignment as Chief of BuOrd in October 1927. He held this key post—head of the "Gun Club" of the surface line—for four years and then took command of the destroyers of the Scouting Force and the U.S. Fleet, flagship *Raleigh* (CL-7), operating out of Boston. Top posts and commands then followed in rapid succession: Chief of BuNav (1933–35); Commander Battleships Battle Force, flagship *West Virginia* (BB-48), as vice admiral; Commander Battle Force in the *California* (BB-44) in the rank of admiral (1936–37); and Chief of Naval Operations, virtually running the Navy because the Secretary, Claude A. Swanson, was ill. He retired as CNO in July 1939 and from the Navy the next month in the rank of admiral at the mandatory age of 64.

With the approach of World War II, however, Admiral Leahy's administrative skills could not be allowed to go unutilized, and although he never again served directly in the Navy chain of command, his roles bore closely on national and thus naval policy. He became governor of Puerto Rico in September 1939 and American ambassador to Vichy France in November

1940, a post which required the utmost delicacy, given the German control over French foreign policy. With America's entry into the war, he was restored to active duty in July 1942 as Chief of Staff to President Franklin D. Roosevelt and Chairman of the Joint Chiefs of Staff. As such he participated in all Allied strategic conferences, being senior American member of the Combined Chiefs of Staff. Promoted to fleet admiral in December 1944, Admiral Leahy continued in his advisory role to President Harry S. Truman during the early years of the Cold War. He resigned this post in March 1949, two months before his 74th birthday, and then published his wartime memoirs, *I Was There* (1950). His son William H. Leahy retired in the rank of rear admiral.

Lee, Samuel Phillips

(February 13, 1812–June 5, 1897).

Naval Photographic Center

The only prominent member of the Lees of Virginia to remain loyal to the Union and as an important naval commander at that, this grandson of the Revolutionary War statesman Richard Henry Lee became midshipman late in 1825. He sailed briefly in the West Indies on the brig *Hornet* and the newly-activated ship-of-the-line *Delaware* (1828–29), received schooling at Norfolk and went to the frigate *Java* (1830–31), the latter two vessels being flagships of the Mediterranean Squadron. Promoted to passed midshipman in 1833, he operated in the Pacific aboard the frigate *Brandywine* but soon shifted to the sloop *Vincennes* (1834–36). He reported to Capt. Charles Wilkes as lieutenant on the brig *Pioneer* (1837–39) between the East coast and West Indies. Aside from a tour of duty at Pensacola (1844–46), Lee spent most of the next several years with the U.S. Coast Survey at

Washington and Philadelphia but notably as commander of its brig *Washington* during the Mexican War, especially in the second expedition which took Tabasco in June 1847. He later commanded the Survey screw steamer *Legare* and the brig *Dolphin,* with which he cruised about the Atlantic (1852–53) assisting Lt. Matthew Fontaine Maury's oceanographic research and making a report thereafter. Hydrographic duty with the U.S. Naval Observatory in Washington followed, during which (1855) he was promoted to commander. He then awaited orders and examined midshipmen (1858).

The sloop *Vandalia* was placed under Commander Lee's command in October 1860 and sailed for the East Indies, only to turn around on the captain's initiative at the Cape of Good Hope upon receiving news of the outbreak of the Civil War. The *Vandalia* blockaded Charleston, with Lee being relieved in September 1861 and assigned to command the fitting-out screw sloop *Oneida* in January 1862. Upon her commissioning the next month, he took her to the Gulf where in April she participated in the attack on New Orleans, disabling the rebel gunboat *Governor Moore* and taking its crewmen after they had fired their vessel. The *Oneida* pressed upriver with the fleet, twice passing Vicksburg in June and July, Lee's reward being promotion to captain. Two months later he assumed command of the North Atlantic Blockading Squadron as acting rear admiral, flagships the sidewheel steamer *Philadelphia* until January 1863, then the steam frigate *Minnesota.* Charged with blockading Virginia and North Carolina, Admiral Lee developed a distant line of vessels to overhaul blockade runners out of Wilmington and garnered a rich sum of prize money in the process. In May and June 1864 he flew his flag from the new sidewheel gunboat *Agawam,* then shifted to the captured steamer *Malvern* during the summer to support Grant's army in the Wilderness Campaign.

Not considered aggressive enough to command the amphibious attack then planned for Wilmington, Admiral Lee switched jobs in October 1864 with Adm. D. D. Porter, commanding the Mississippi Squadron, flagship the sidewheel river steamer *Black Hawk.* He immediately supported Gen. George H. Thomas in meeting the Confederate invasion of Tennessee by keeping open Union supply routes and cutting off the retreat of Gen. John B. Hood's army from Nashville at the Tennessee River in December. After his flagship burned and sank near Cairo, Illinois, in April 1865, he shifted to the sidewheeler *Tempest,* receiving the last rebel naval surrenders in the West, with his command being dissolved in August. Promoted to the permanent rank of commodore in July 1866, Lee served at Washington as head of the signal service for one year and on several boards, notably as president of the Examining Board. In April 1870 he was promoted to rear admiral and in August given command of the North Atlantic Squadron, flagship the screw sloop *Severn.* Admiral Lee cruised with his Squadron in the West Indies, flying his flag during 1872 in the steam sloop *Worcester.* Relieved in August, he retired the next year.

Among his distant cousins on the rebel side were the brothers Gen.

Robert E. Lee, commander of the coast defenses of South Carolina, Georgia and East Florida (1861–62), the Army of Northern Virginia (1862–65) and of all Confederate forces in the field (1865), and Capt. S. Smith Lee, flag officer commanding Confederate naval forces in Virginia during the Peninsular Campaign (1862) and chief of the Office of Orders and Detail (1864–65). Admiral Lee's son F. P. Blair Lee in 1913–17 was U.S. Senator from Maryland.

Lee, Willis Augustus, Jr. "Ching"

(May 11, 1888–August 25, 1945).
USNA (Ky.) 1908 (106/201).

National Archives

Senior battleship commander afloat in the war against Japan and victor at the Naval Battle of Guadalcanal, Lee—a direct descendant of Charles Lee, Attorney General under Washington and Adams—went straight into battleships, the new *Idaho* (BB-24) in the Caribbean (1908–09) and was in the recommissioning crew of the protected cruiser *New Orleans* for a voyage to the Far East where he joined the gunboat *Helena* on the Yangtze and South China patrols (1910–13). An expert marksman in many competitions throughout his early years, including the 1920 Olympic Games (winning five team gold medals!), he transferred these skills to naval guns, returning to the *Idaho* (1913) and moving to the *New Hampshire* (BB-25) in which he participated in the Vera Cruz affair in the spring of 1914 in the midst of general Atlantic operations. After inspecting ordnance in Illinois from the end of 1915 until November 1918, Lieutenant Commander Lee served a month on the destroyer *O'Brien* (DD-51) out of Ireland, then commanded the *Lea* (DD-118) out of Brest and was briefly a port officer at Rotterdam, Holland. He was executive officer of the submarine tender *Bushnell* (AS-2) returning to operate with captured U-boats in North America (1919–20) and skipper of the *Fairfax* (DD-93) in the Atlantic (1920–21) and the *William B. Preston* (DD-344) which he took to the Orient via Suez. After service at the New York Navy Yard (1924–26), he became exec of the target repair ship *Antares* (AG-10) on the East coast and then captain of the *Lardner* (DD-286) in the same waters (1927–28).

Following instruction at the Naval War College (1928–29) and ordnance inspection duty on Long Island (1929–30), Commander Lee became navigator then exec of the *Pennsylvania* (BB-38) in the Pacific (1931–33), and had five tours with the Division of Fleet Training in Washington (first, 1930–31), heading its gunnery section (1933–35) and tactical section (1935–36), as well as being Assistant Director (1939–41) and Director (1941–42). Promoted captain in 1936, he commanded the light cruiser *Concord* (CL-10) in the Battle Force, Pacific (1936–38), remaining on that vessel (1938) on the staff of the Commander Cruiser Divisions, Adm. H. R. Stark, and going with him to the *Honolulu* (CL-48) as chief of staff (1938–39). Promoted to rear admiral in January 1942, Lee, in addition to his headship of Fleet Training which early in 1942 became the Readiness Division, in December 1941 became assistant chief of staff to Adm. E. J. King, U.S. Fleet commander-in-chief in Washington, for six months. In August, he took command of Battleship Division Six, flagship *Washington* (BB-56), for operations in the Pacific. While commanding Task Force 64, Admiral Lee defeated Japanese heavy fleet units at the Naval Battle of Guadalcanal in mid-November 1942, his greatest achievement. Given the position of Commander Battleships Pacific Fleet in April 1943 in addition, in September he occupied Baker Island, flagship the cargo ship *Hercules* (AK-41), and throughout the rest of the war commanded Task Force 54/34 usually in the *Washington* and later the *South Dakota* (BB-57), providing cover for the Fast Carrier Task Force. Promoted to vice admiral in March 1944 and made Commander Battleship Squadron Two in December, he participated in the taking of the Gilberts, Marshalls, Marianas, Philippines, Iwo Jima and Okinawa until mid-June 1945. Still ComBatron Two, he went home to develop anti-kamikaze tactics at Casco Bay, Maine, flagship the training ship *Wyoming* (AG-17), as Commander Composite Task Force, Atlantic Fleet (CTF 69), where he died on a launch.

Levy, Uriah Phillips

(April 22, 1792—March 22, 1862).

Navy Department

The first Jewish officer to achieve flag rank in the Navy, the controversial Levy served as a merchant seaman apprentice (1802–04, 1806–10), and attended naval school in his native Philadelphia (1808). He was first mate (1810–11) and then part owner and master of the merchant schooner *George Washington* from its purchase in October 1811 until its loss to mutineers in the West Indies in January 1812. Warranted a sailing master in the Navy the following October, he joined the storeship *Alert* at New York and transferred in June 1813 to the brig *Argus* as acting lieutenant for a voyage to France. When the *Argus* took the prize *Betty,* he was placed in the prize crew for the trip to France, only to be captured in August and imprisoned in England until the end of 1814. After duty at the Philadelphia Naval Station (1815–16), Levy reported aboard the ship-of-the-line *Franklin,* then under construction, as second master, becoming lieutenant in March 1817 and sailing aboard her in October to the Mediterranean, where he transferred to the frigate *United States* in February 1818. Detached in June 1819, he was court-martialed and dismissed from the service due to his constant quarrels, petty arrogance and lack of popularity stemming in no small measure from anti-Semitic prejudice against him. His career was thereafter checkered with similar recurrences and court-martials, in addition to problems of health.

Reinstated by action of President James Monroe, Lieutenant Levy took passage in the frigate *Constitution* during the summer of 1821 to the Mediterranean and the brig *Spark,* cruising aboard her to the West Indies where a pirate vessel was taken. Going ashore at Charleston the following March, he went on to command *Gunboat No. 158* on anti-pirate and anti-slaving patrol in the West Indies (1822–23), then studied in France before

194

joining the frigate *Cyane* on the Brazil Station (1825–27). Ill health confined him during another visit to France, but he reported on European naval developments to the Navy Department. His extended leaves led to outright inaction "waiting orders" (1834–37), but he was promoted to master commandant early in 1837 and commanded the sloop *Vandalia* in the Caribbean (1838–39). After injuries sustained from a runaway horse, Levy in 1842 was court-martialed and cashiered for administering unusual punishment to one of his men. Reinstated by President John Tyler, he was promoted to captain in May 1844 only to be thwarted from further duty for the next decade. His great energy thus idled, he turned to enhancing his private fortune through business ventures, but contributed to the naval reform movement which led to the abolition of flogging in the Navy. In the streamlining of the Navy in 1855, he was dropped from the rolls. Captain Levy campaigned for reinstatement, was granted a court of inquiry and obtained his goal early in 1858. In April of that year he assumed command of the razeed sloop *Macedonian*, which he took to the Mediterranean during the summer. In October 1859 he was ordered to take command of the Mediterranean Squadron, and did so in January 1860 in the rank of flag officer, his flag on the *Macedonian*. He returned home with his flagship during the summer and assumed court-martial duty in Washington late in 1861, his last active service. A dedicated patriot, Flag Officer Levy had purchased and preserved Thomas Jefferson's home "Monticello" and offered his considerable personal fortune to the government at the outbreak of the Civil War. Of his three merchant captain brothers, one, Jonas P. Levy (1807–1883), was master of the transport *American* which delivered the Army's surfboats for the assault on Vera Cruz early in 1847.

Lockwood, Charles Andrews, Jr.

(May 6, 1890–June 6, 1967). USNA (Mo.) 1912 (136/156).

Navy Department: National Archives

Top submarine leader in the war against Japan, Lockwood alternated between subs and the surface line throughout his career. In the latter, he served in the Atlantic battleships *Mississippi* (BB-23) and *Arkansas* (BB-33) (1912–13); on the Yangtze Patrol gunboats *Quiros* (PG-40) (1922–23) and *Isabel* (PY-10), on the latter as flag lieutenant to Patrol commander Adm. William W. Phelps (1923); for the ensuing year on that station successively as commanding officer of the *Elcano* (PG-38), executive officer of the destroyer *Perry* (DD-226), and skipper of the *Smith Thompson* (DD-212); as first lieutenant of the *California* (BB-44) in the Pacific (1931–32); and as navigator then exec of the cruiser *Concord* (CL-10) there (1932–33). His shore billets were at the Great Lakes Training Station (1913–14); at the Tokyo embassy as inspector of purchased ships (1918); at the Portsmouth Navy Yard as repair officer (1924–25); at the Naval Academy teaching seamanship (1933–35); and as naval attaché in London from January to March 1942. Lockwood trained in submarines aboard the sub tender *Mohican* at Cavite, Philippines in the autumn of 1914 and there commanded the sub *A-2* (SS-3) (1915–17) as well as the *B-1* (SS-10) (1916–17). In July 1917 he assumed command of the Asiatic Fleet's First Submarine Division, flagship the monitor *Monadnock,* which he also commanded from September 1917 until detached the following April.

After commanding in quick succession the *G-1* (SS-19½) at New London and the *N-5* (SS-57) at New York (1918–19) and the captured German minelaying sub *UC-97* in England (1919), Lieutenant Commander Lockwood outfitted, commissioned, and commanded three new subs; the *R-25* (SS-102) in the Atlantic and Caribbean (1919–20); the *S-14* (SS-119), which he commanded Submarine Division 13, flagship *Cuttlefish* (SS-171), on the Eastern Pacific (1925–28). Advising the Brazilian Navy on subs (1929–31), he commanded Submarine Division 13, flagship *Cuttlefish* (SS-171), on the West coast (1935–37); worked on sub matters at the Office of the Chief of Naval Operations (1937–39); and was chief of staff to U. S. Fleet Submarine Commander Adm. Wilhelm L. Friedell, flagship *Richmond* (CL-9), in the Pacific (1939–41). In May 1942, the month after he became Commander Submarines Southwest Pacific (Task Force 51), Lockwood was promoted to rear admiral. From Fremantle in western Australia he directed the underwater war against Japanese shipping in those waters in the dark days of 1942, and then in February 1943 he moved to Pearl Harbor as Commander Submarines Pacific Fleet. From there he coordinated the destruction of the enemy's merchant marine and much of his fleet during the American counteroffensive. Promoted to vice admiral in October 1943, Admiral Lockwood moved with Pacific Fleet headquarters to Guam early in 1945 until relieved that December. He served as Naval Inspector General in Washington (1946–47) and retired as vice admiral in September 1947. He wrote his autobiography *Down to the Sea in Subs* (1967) and co-authored a number of war histories.

Luce, Stephen Bleecker

(March 25, 1827–July 28, 1917). USNA (N.Y.) 1847.

Naval Photographic Center

A major naval intellectual and founder of the Naval War College, Luce became midshipman late in 1841 and went to the frigate *Congress*—via the New York receiving ship *North Carolina*—for her maiden cruise in the Mediterranean and the South Atlantic (1842–45), then journeyed to China and Japan and operated in the Eastern Pacific during the Mexican War with the *Columbus,* 74 (1845–48). After a year studying for his examinations for passed midshipman at the Naval Academy, he returned to Pacific patrol aboard the sloop *Vandalia* (1849–52), then worked briefly with Lt. James M. Gilliss in Washington on astronomical observations. After a year on the sidewheel steamer *Vixen* in the Home Squadron, he served with the U.S. Coast Survey (1854–57) aboard its vessels *Madison, Crawford,* and *Bibb.* Promoted to lieutenant in 1855, Luce rejoined the Home Squadron in the West Indies as an officer of the sloop *Jamestown* (1857–60). He reported to the Naval Academy in March 1860 to teach seamanship and transferred one year later to the steam frigate *Wabash,* which blockaded the Carolina coasts from May 1861 to January 1862 and participated in the captures of Hatteras and Port Royal. He returned to the Academy, located at wartime Newport, as head of the Department of Seamanship, in which capacity he wrote the textbook *Seamanship* (1863) and commanded the training sloop *Macedonian* in the 1863 summer cruise to Europe.

Lieutenant Commander Luce took command of the monitor *Nantucket* off Charleston in October 1863, then of the double-ender gunboat *Pontiac* the following September on the same station, engaging Confederate shore batteries. In January 1865 the *Pontiac* supported Gen. William T. Sherman's crossing of the Savannah River from Georgia into South Carolina and the capture of Charleston and in March took the rebel steamer *Amazon* in the same waters. Being intensely interested in naval education as well as having principles of naval warfare awakened in him late in the war, he served as commandant of midshipmen at the Academy (1865–68), including promotion to commander in 1866 and command of three successive annual summer squadron practice cruises. Luce commanded the double-ender *Mohongo* in the Eastern Pacific (1868–69); the screw sloop *Juniata* in European waters, observing naval operations in the Franco-Prussian War (1869–72); then, as captain, the screw sloop *Hartford,* flagship of the North Atlantic Squadron but cruising the Pacific (1875–77); the old training frigate *Minnesota* at New York (1878–81); the Naval Training Squadron at Newport (1881–84), flagship the ship-of-the-line *New Hampshire,* in the rank of commodore; and temporarily the North Atlantic Squadron as temporary rear admiral (1884).

An innovator in all aspects of the naval profession, Commodore Luce, reporting as equipment officer at the Boston Navy Yard in 1872, was instrumental in the founding of the U. S. Naval Institute in 1873, publishing the first paper in the initial number of its *Proceedings* that year and many thereafter as well as in *The United Service* and other journals, and serving later for many years as Naval Institute president (1887–98). He was appointed first president of the newly-established Naval War College at Newport, the creation of which he had recommended, in October 1884 and set it on its progressive course in many ways, not least by appointing Capt. A. T. Mahan *(q.v.)* to the faculty. In June 1886 he hoisted his flag in the screw sloop *Lancaster* as commander of the North Atlantic Squadron, having been promoted to rear admiral the previous October. He held this post until February 1889, his last flagship being the steamer *Galena,* retiring from active duty the next month. Admiral Luce remained an active proponent of American naval power, writing many articles and advising governmental leaders. He was attached to the Naval War College on special active duty during the rise of the modern battleship navy of the Theodore Roosevelt period (1901–10), including service on the Board of Naval Reorganization in 1909. He also compiled *Naval Songs* (1883).

Lynch, William Francis

(April 1, 1801—October 17, 1865).

Middle Eastern explorer and Confederate flag officer, Virginian Lynch shipped out as midshipman in 1819 in the frigate *Congress* to the Far East via Brazil and transferred to the new schooner *Shark* on anti-slave patrol off Africa (1821–22). Following a year's merchant voyage to China on furlough, he spent several weeks at New York (1823) with the in ordinary ship-of-the-line *Washington* and the frigate *Cyane* before joining the "Mosquito Fleet" suppressing piracy in the West Indies, principally aboard the schooner *Beagle* and the brig *Hornet* (1823–25). He sailed to the Mediterranean late in 1825 with the frigate *Brandywine,* transferring ashore at year's end, disabled from a lingering ankle injury sustained while on the *Congress.* Incapacitated for two years, Lynch served early in 1828 as sailing master of the new sloop *Falmouth,* spent another year ashore, was promoted to lieutenant in March 1829, and the following October joined the sloop *Erie* for several months' service in the West Indies. Laid up again with his malady, he spent a year (1830–31) on the receiving ship at Norfolk, only to contract cholera while there. His attempt to return to active duty with the *Brandywine* early in 1834 was aborted by his health. However, he finally managed two brief tours to the middle sea, with the frigate *John Adams* (1834–35) and the ship-of-the-line *Delaware* (1835–36), although he still had intermittent sick leaves ashore.

Lieutenant Lynch was in the commissioning crew of the sidewheel steamer *Fulton* for Atlantic service (1837–40), except for a voyage to Europe in 1838 aboard the British steamer *Great Western* as part of the latter vessel's unsuccessful speed competition with the *Fulton.* Eye trouble further interrupted his *Fulton* service (1838–39). After briefly commanding the fitting-out sidewheel gunboat *Poinsett* (1840), he served in the sloop *Fairfield,* flagship of the Mediterranean Squadron (1841–42), part of the time as her skipper; at the New York naval rendezvous a few weeks; and as commanding officer of the sidewheel steamer *Colonel Harney* between Norfolk and New Orleans (1844–45). Mexican War service was confined to Pensacola (1845–46). Lynch went to New York in the summer of 1847 to prepare for an exploring expedition to the Dead Sea and took command of the storeship *Supply* in September. He then sailed to the Middle East and explored extensively around the Dead Sea region. After the *Supply* decommissioned at the end of 1848 Lynch took several months to prepare his long and still invaluable report, published unofficially in 1849 and officially in 1852 along with his autobiographical *Naval Life* in 1851. He was promoted to commander in 1849 and reconnoitered the West African coast with the *John Adams* (1852–53), partly in conjunction with a scheme of his to colonize the interior. After commanding the screw steamer *Alleghany* at Norfolk briefly (1853), he commanded the sloop *Germantown* on the Brazil Station (1853–57), landing Marines and sailors twice in 1855 to protect American interests in revolutionary Uruguay and collecting sugar cane plants. Made captain in 1856, he was waiting orders until the outbreak of the Civil War.

Lynch became captain in the Virginia then Confederate navies in April and June 1861 respectively and commanded the naval batteries at Aquia Creek, Virginia, which engaged Union gunboats on the Potomac. As commander of Virginia's and North Carolina's naval defenses, flagship the sidewheeler *Sea Bird,* Flag Officer Lynch used his small "Mosquito Fleet" to harass Union blockaders until it was destroyed while opposing the Union advance on Roanoke Island and Elizabeth City, North Carolina, in February 1862. The next month he assumed command of Vicksburg's naval defenses and the Mississippi River Squadron, returning in October to his North Carolina command. In May 1864, his flag aboard the new ironclad ram *Raleigh* and accompanied by two smaller vessels, he sortied from the Cape Fear River and engaged Union blockading vessels off New Inlet, only to then retire and run aground, requiring scuttling. Lynch shifted his flag to the steam gunboat *Yadkin* and commanded at Smithville, North Carolina, during the Union attacks on Fort Fisher in December 1864 and January 1865, his last active service.

Macdonough, Thomas

(December 31, 1783—November 10, 1825).

Victor at the Battle of Lake Champlain during the War of 1812, Macdonough left his native Delaware as midshipman aboard the armed converted merchantman *Ganges* in 1800 for a war cruise to the West Indies during which four French vessels were taken. Transferring to the frigate *Constellation* in October 1801, he sailed to the Mediterranean for the blockade of Tripoli the next year and in May 1803 joined the frigate *Philadelphia* to operate against the same enemy. When the *Philadelphia* captured the Moroccan warship *Mirboka* in late August, Macdonough helped take her into Gibraltar as second officer. He then joined the schooner *Enterprise,* Capt. Stephen Decatur, and with the latter helped to destroy the captured *Philadelphia* in February 1804 and thereafter to attack the port of Tripoli and its defending gunboats. The next year he was promoted to lieutenant, made first lieutenant of the *Enterprise,* then transferred to the brig *Syren* also as first lieutenant for another year of cruising in the middle sea. After several weeks late in 1806 constructing gunboats in Connecticut, he was first lieutenant of the sloop *Wasp* (1807–09) on a trip to England and coastal embargo-policing patrol, followed by a few months in the latter work aboard the frigate *Essex.* A year commanding the gunboats of Rhode Island and Connecticut (1809–10) was followed by furlough for merchant service to the Orient.

Lieutenant Macdonough returned to duty for one month each on the *Constellation* and at Portland, Maine, commanding gunboats before his appointment in September 1812 to command the small squadron forming on Lake Champlain. Promoted to master commandant the next summer, he suffered an early reverse but by mid-1814 had 14 vessels ready with which to defend Plattsburg, flagship the new 26-gun corvette *Saratoga,* which he also commanded. In September 1814 he met and defeated the British squadron of Commo. George Downie in the Battle of Lake Champlain, the *Saratoga* alone overpowering the British flagship *Confiance,* 36, and sinking the brig *Linnet,* while the squadron took the two other larger enemy vessels; Downie was mortally wounded. The victory saved Plattsburg, for now the British army retreated into Canada, and earned Macdonough promotion to captain in November. Given command of the Portsmouth, New Hampshire, Navy Yard (1815–18) with his health impaired by the rigors of his war service, he there equipped the ship-of-the-line *Washington* and later returned to sea commanding the frigate *Guerrière* (1818–20) for a lengthy cruise to the Mediterranean via the Baltic. Commodore Macdonough commanded the ship-of-the-line *Ohio,* in ordinary at New York (1820–24), and the Mediterranean Squadron and its flagship the frigate *Constitution* (1824–25). Returning home on the merchantman *Edwin,* he died at sea. His son, Capt. Charles S. Macdonough, served in the Union navy during the Civil War.

Mahan, Alfred Thayer

(September 27, 1840–December 1, 1914). USNA (N.Y.) 1859 (2/20).

Naval Photographic Center

America's most influential naval historian and naval philosopher, Mahan (rhymes with "the man") grew up in an Army environment, inasmuch as his father Dennis Hart Mahan (1802–71) taught at the U.S. Military Academy and there educated the entire generation of Civil War leaders in the art of war. Mahan sailed on the frigate *Congress,* flagship of the Brazil Squadron

(1859–61), before promotion to lieutenant and Civil War assignment on the screw steamer *Pocahontas* in the Port Royal, South Carolina, expedition of November 1861. During 1862–63 he served at the wartime Naval Academy in Newport, including the '63 summer cruise to Europe in the razeed sloop *Macedonian*. He had blockade duty off Sabine Pass, Texas, aboard the screw sloop *Seminole* (1863–64) and in the South Atlantic Squadron with the *Adger* (1864) and on its admiral's staff, J. A. B. Dahlgren, flagship the sidewheel steamer *Philadelphia,* off Charleston. In the late spring of 1865 Mahan transferred back to the *Adger* then to the monitor *Muscoota* in the rank of lieutenant commander to observe the French in Mexico and on to the steam sloop *Iroquois* on the Asiatic Squadron (1867–69) which ship he briefly commanded. After a tour of Europe, he served aboard the chartered relief ship steam frigate *Worcester* for French victims of the Franco-Prussian War (1871).

Promoted to commander in November 1872 Mahan the next month assumed command of the sidewheeler *Wasp* in which he cruised the South Atlantic until relieved in January 1875. He then reported to the Naval Academy on the Board of Examiners (1876–80) and thereafter to the Navigation Department of the New York Navy Yard (1880–83). Following command of the steam sloop *Wachusett* in the Southeast Pacific, Mahan reported in October 1885, in the rank of captain, to the Naval War College as lecturer on naval tactics and history, being elevated to the presidency the next year. His lectures resulted in his magnum opus, *The Influence of Sea Power upon History, 1660–1783* (1890). In 1889–90 he helped to select the site for the naval station at Bremerton, then returned to the Naval War College to complete his sequel, *The Influence of Sea Power upon the French Revolution and Empire, 1793–1812* (1892), again to serve as College president (1892–93) and to assert his now considerable influence on the development of the "new" United States Navy. Captain Mahan commanded the protected cruiser *Chicago,* flagship of a special squadron which visited European ports (1893–95), and returned briefly to the College before voluntarily retiring in November 1896 to devote full time to writing. He lectured thereafter at the College and wrote many books and articles, most notably *Sea Power and Its Relations to the War of 1812* (1905) and *Naval Strategy* (1911). Recalled to active duty on the Naval Board of Strategy for the war with Spain (1898), he also was an American delegate to the first Hague Peace Conference (1899). Mahan was promoted to rear admiral on the retired list in June 1906 and was a member of the commission on naval reorganization three years later.

There can be no doubt that Admiral Mahan's writings provided a powerful stimulus not only to American overseas expansion and battleship construction but to the similar activities of Great Britain, Germany, Japan and many lesser countries and to the naval arms race that helped to bring on World War I. Also, his work in naval history raised that discipline to an unprecedented level of respectability and ranked with that of his British counterpart, Sir Julian Corbett. Between his historical impact and his reputation, he has been canonized by the U.S. Navy, though it must also be said that those who have honored him have generally done so uncritically and without real understanding of his tenets and their limitations. His brother, Commo. Dennis Hart Mahan (1849–1925), at one time commanded the battleship *Indiana* (BB-1).

Mayo, Henry Thomas

(December 8, 1856–February 23, 1937).
USNA (Vt.) 1876 (14/42).

Naval Photographic Center

Atlantic Fleet commander during World War I, this son of a Lake Champlain steamboat captain, after a tour of duty with the Asiatic Squadron aboard the steam frigate *Tennessee* (1876–78), spent a great deal of time surveying Puget Sound in the Coast Survey vessels *Earnest* and *Eagre* (1879–82, 1886–89, 1892–95), the final period as branch commander of the Hydrographic Office at Port Townsend, Washington. As ensign he participated in the 1883 Greely Relief Expedition to the Arctic while assigned to the screw sloop *Yantic* (1882–85), and then had a year at the Naval Observatory. As lieutenant (j.g.) he joined the apprentice training sloop *Jamestown* for voyages to Europe and the Caribbean (1889–92) and attended the Naval War College (1892). As lieutenant he surveyed Pearl Harbor while navigator of the gunboat *Bennington* (PG-4) (1895–98), on which he cruised in uneventful Spanish-American War duty, finishing it as her executive officer. He also had brief duty on the gunboat *Thetis* (1896) and the receiving ship *Independence* at Mare Island (1898). As lieutenant commander Mayo reported to Union Iron Works at San Francisco in October 1898 to inspect the battleship *Wisconsin* (BB-9) under construction there, joining the ship's company in 1900 and becoming navigator (1901), then exec (1902). He transferred ashore to the Boston Navy Yard (1904–05) and as commander inspected lighthouses at San Francisco (1905–07) and commanded the protected cruiser *Albany* (CL-23) along the West coast and off Central America (1907–08). As captain he was secretary to the Lighthouse Board (1908–09) and skipper of the armored cruiser *California* (ACR-6) on the California coast (1909–10), remaining there to command the navy yard at Mare Island (1911–13).

Appointed Aid for Personnel at the Navy Department in April 1913, Captain Mayo was promoted to rear admiral two months later and soon afterward billeted briefly at the Naval War College. In December he broke his flag in the *Connecticut* (BB-18) as Commander Fourth Division Atlantic Fleet, operating in the Caribbean. When some of his sailors were arrested by Mexican authorities while taking on gasoline at Tampico in April 1914 he demanded and received their release and a public apology. This resolute action led to his promotion in June to vice admiral, the nation's first three-star naval officer since S. C. Rowan a generation before, and additional posting as second-in-command of the Atlantic Fleet, flagships successively *Minnesota* (BB-22), *Kansas* (BB-21) and *Vermont* (BB-20), operating in the same waters. In October Admiral Mayo transferred to command of the First Division, flagships *Arkansas* (BB-33) and *New York* (BB-34), serving primarily in the North Atlantic. In June 1916 he became Atlantic Fleet commander, flagships *Wyoming* (BB-32) and from October the new *Pennsylvania* (BB-38), in the rank of admiral. Between January and April 1917 the Fleet maneuvered in the Caribbean but then returned to the Chesapeake Bay to begin wartime operations against Germany. Mayo controlled all American warships in Atlantic and European waters during World War I, during which he twice journeyed abroad. In January 1919 his command became the United States Fleet (Atlantic, Pacific, Asiatic), which he held until June, he reverting then to rear admiral for General Board duty. Also head of an examining board late in 1919, Admiral Mayo retired in December 1920 in the rank of rear admiral and ended all active duty two months later. He was governor of the Philadelphia Naval Home (1924–28) and then was advanced to admiral on the retired list (1930).

McCain, John Sidney "Slew"

(August 9, 1884–September 6, 1945).
USNA (Miss.) 1906 (80/116).

Navy Department: National Archives

A World War II naval aviation leader, McCain had over four years of initial duty on the Asiatic Station with the battleship *Ohio* (BB-12), cruiser *Baltimore* (C-3), gunboat *Panay,* and destroyer *Chauncey* (DD-3), and as assistant to the captain of the Cavite Yard where at the end of 1908 he joined the *Connecticut* (BB-18), flagship of the "Great White Fleet," en route home. Once there he briefly saw West coast duty on the armored cruiser *Pennsylvania* (ACR-4), then returned to the Atlantic while assigned to the *Washington* (ACR-11). After directing the machinist mates' school at Charleston (1912–14), he was executive and engineer officer of the *Colorado* (ACR-7) patrolling the Pacific side of politically-troubled Mexico until September 1915 when he joined the Pacific Fleet flagship *San Diego* (ACR-6). In her, McCain escorted Atlantic wartime convoys until assigned to the Bureau of Navigation in May 1918, to which he returned three times, in charge of the Officers Records Section (1923–26), the Recruiting Section (1929–31), and the Planning Section (1933–35). Helping to outfit the *Maryland* (BB-46) as her navigator in the Atlantic (1921–23), he briefly (1926) commanded the cargo ship *Sirius* (AK-15) in that ocean before becoming exec of the *New Mexico* (BB-40) in the Pacific. Duty as Naval War College student (1928–29) and skipper of the ammunition ship *Nitro* (AE-2) cruising between oceans (1931–33) preceded his enrollment for flight training at Pensacola in June 1935 after nine years of trying for the assignment.

Captain McCain became a naval aviator in August 1936 at the advanced age of 52 and was assigned to command Coco Solo air base and its squadrons in the Panama Canal Zone. He then commanded the aircraft carrier *Ranger* (CV-4) in the Pacific and Caribbean (1937–39) and Naval Air Station San Diego until February 1941 when he was promoted rear admiral and given command of the Scouting Force's aircraft and U.S. Fleet patrol wings on the West coast. His planes, which included all aircraft of the Western Sea Frontier, patrolled coastal waters during the first six months of the Pacific war, and in May 1942 he transferred to command of all Navy land-based aircraft in the South Pacific, flagship the seaplane tender *Curtiss* (AV-4) at Nouméa, New Caledonia, from which base he participated in the Guadalcanal campaign until late September. The next month Admiral McCain became Chief of the Bureau of Aeronautics and in August 1943 was upgraded to be the first Deputy Chief of Naval Operations (Air) in the rank of vice admiral. Twelve months after that he was designated Commander Second Fast Carrier Force Pacific and led Task Group 38.1, flagship *Wasp* (CV-18), in the Philippines for three months, then Task Force 38, flagships *Lexington* (CV-16) and *Hancock* (CV-19), in Southeast Asia air strikes until late January 1945. After leave, from late May through August he again commanded TF 38, flagship *Shangri-La* (CV-38), in the final attacks on the Japanese home islands. Relieved at the beginning of September, Admiral McCain died en route to becoming Deputy Director of the Veteran's Administration and was advanced posthumously to admiral. His uncle, Henry P. McCain, and his brother, William A. McCain, retired from the Army as general officers, and his son *(q.v.)* achieved prominence in the Cold War Navy.

McCain, John Sidney, Jr. "Junior"

(January 17, 1911--   ). USNA (At Large) 1931 (424/441).

Naval Photographic Center

Pacific Area commander during the latter half of the Vietnam War, Iowa-born submariner McCain followed his father (*q.v.*) into the Navy, operating with the Battle Force battleship *Oklahoma* (BB-37) in the Pacific before undergoing sub training at New London in 1933. He returned to the Pacific with the sub *S-45* (SS-156) out of Pearl Harbor and then to New London and the training sub *R-13* (SS-90). After teaching electrical engineering at the Naval Academy (1938–40), he cruised in the *Skipjack* (SS-184) between Hawaii and California until April 1941 when he, as skipper, recommissioned the *O-8* (SS-69) for New London training. In May 1942 Lieutenant Commander McCain reported to Groton to fit out the *Gunnel* (SS-253), commissioned in August, and commanded her during the North African landings in November and off the Japanese coast for two war patrols during 1943 and early 1944, sinking three Japanese cargo ships. Detached in July 1944 for a brief stay at New London, he joined the *Dentuda* (SS-335) in October, commissioned her in December, and took her on one patrol in the East China Sea, sinking two patrol craft, during mid-1945. Detached in August, he became Director of Records at the Bureau of Naval Personnel in November, where he remained until early 1949 when he took over Submarine Division 71, flagship *Carp* (SS-338), exploring far northern Pacific depths, and briefly at year's end took over SubDiv 51 also in the *Carp*.

After a year as executive officer of the cruiser *St. Paul* (CA-73), including Formosa patrolling early in the Korean War, Captain McCain held the first of several senior posts at the Navy Department: Director of Undersea Warfare Research and Development (1950–53), Director of the Progress

Analysis Group (1955–57), Chief Legislative Liaison (lobbyist!) for the Office of the Secretary of the Navy (1958–60), and Chief of Information (1962–63). Commanding officer of Submarine Squadron Six, flagship *Sea Leopard* (SS-483), in the Atlantic (1953–54); the attack transport *Monrovia* (APA-31) supplying the Sixth Fleet in the Mediterranean (1954–55); and the Atlantic Fleet's *Albany* (CA-123) as she began conversion into a guided missile cruiser (1957–58), he was promoted to rear admiral in November 1958 and then held three Atlantic Fleet amphibious commands: Group Two, flagships the amphibious command ships *Taconic* (AGC-17) and *Mt. McKinley* (AGC-7), in the Med (1960–61); the Training Command (1961–62); and the entire Amphibious Force (1963–65), in the latter post as vice admiral and during which tour in April 1965 he led the intervention into the Dominican Republic as Commander Task Force 124. Admiral McCain then (1965–67) wore three "hats": vice chairman of the delegation to the United Nations Military Staff Committee, Commander Eastern Sea Frontier, and Commander Atlantic Reserve Fleet (this last until 1966). Advanced to admiral in May 1967, he became Commander-in-Chief U.S. Naval Forces Europe and fourteen months later Commander-in-Chief Pacific, in which capacity he directed American forces during the gradual disengagement from the Vietnam War (1968–72). From September to November 1972, when he retired, Admiral McCain was special assistant to Chief of Naval Operations Adm. E. R. Zumwalt, Jr. His son, Lt. Cdr. J. S. McCain III, while operating his plane off the carrier *Oriskany* (CVA-34), was shot down over Hanoi, badly wounded, captured and imprisoned by the North Vietnamese for over five years (1967–73).

McCalla, Bowman Hendry

(June 19, 1844–May 6, 1910). USNA (N.J.) 1865 (4/31).

American commander during the Boxer Rebellion relief expedition, Mc-Calla hunted rebel cruisers in the yacht *America* (1864) and had training on the screw gunboat *Marblehead* (1864–65), then cruised off Brazil on the steam sloops *Susquehanna* (1865–66) and *Brooklyn* (1866–67), trained apprentices at New London on the frigate *Sabine* (1867–68), operated in the steamers sloop *Tuscarora* (1868–71), frigate *Wabash* (1871–74), and sloop *Wachusett* before seeing his first shore duty at the Naval Academy (1874–78). Made lieutenant commander in 1869 and commander in 1884, he was executive officer of the sidewheeler *Powhatan* in home and Caribbean waters (1878–81) and assistant to the Chief of the Bureau of Navigation (1882–87) before commanding the screw sloop *Enterprise* in European and African waters (1887–90). Court-martialed and briefly suspended for harsh treatment of one of his men, Commander McCalla served at Mare Island (1893–97) and the Naval War College (1897), commanded the cruiser *Marblehead* (C-11) in the North Atlantic and during bombardments of Cuban installations and the capture of Guantanamo Bay (1897–98), was skipper of the Navy's first repair ship, *Vulcan,* there, and went to Norfolk as equipment officer (1898–99). He was promoted to captain early in 1899 and given command of the *Newark* (C-1) which sailed to Chinese waters via the Philippines, where Luzon insurrectionists surrendered to him. During the Boxer Rebellion (1900), Captain McCalla as second-in-command of the American squadron left his ship to lead the first landing party and the international relief expedition to the foreign legations at Peking, receiving three wounds during the heavy fighting. He transferred from the *Newark* the next year to command the battleship *Kearsarge* (BB-5) in the North Atlantic and then the San Francisco training station (1902–03). Following promotion to rear admiral in 1903 he commanded the Mare Island Navy Yard until his retirement in 1906. Admiral McCalla's son-in-law was Commo. Dudley W. Knox (1877–1960), official Navy historian during World War II.

Library of Congress

McDougal, David Stockton

(September 27, 1809–August 7, 1882).

Commander in the Shimonoseki incident of 1863, Ohioan McDougal took instruction at New York's Naval School as midshipman (1828–29), went to the Mediterranean in the sloop *Boston* (1830–31) and the frigate *Brandywine* (1831–33), and received additional naval schooling at Brooklyn. Following leaves at New York, he operated in the West Indies aboard the sloop *Natchez* (1836–38) and the schooner *Grampus* (1838–39), then did survey work of Southern ports in the brig *Consort* for a year, then ashore. Upon advancement to lieutenant in 1841, McDougal served briefly in the sidewheel steamer *Fulton* before joining the sloop *Falmouth* in the new Home Squadron (1841–44), including a brief interruption due to illness. Part of the commissioning crew of the lake sidewheeler *Michigan,* he cruised the Great Lakes in her for two tours (1844–47, 1851–54), with his only Mexican War duty being the Vera Cruz landings in March 1847 aboard the sidewheeler *Mississippi,* his detachment occurring in July following an ankle injury. On the African Station with the brig *Bainbridge* (1848–50), he commanded the storeship *Warren* at Mare Island (1854–57) except for six months during 1856 when he commanded the screw steamer *John Hancock* in supporting the Army and driving off Indian attacks at Puget Sound.

A commander from January 1857, McDougal remained in California following his relief in October, and at the request of the Navy Yard commander, Capt. D. G. Farragut, he returned to duty at Mare Island early in 1858 where he remained until the outbreak of the Civil War. Given command of the screw sloop *Wyoming* on the Pacific Station in May 1861, he cruised off the South American coast until sent to Chinese waters early in 1862 to protect Union shipping from Confederate commerce raiders. The *Wyoming* cruised the East Indies during 1863 in a futile search for the cruiser *Alabama* and replied to Japanese shore batteries and vessels which fired upon her at Shimonoseki in July by sinking a brig and a steamer. During the spring of 1864 McDougal was promoted to captain, and he searched for the raider *Florida* on the homeward voyage, but in vain. Later in the year he became commander of Mare Island, until July 1865. Briefly skipper of the screw steamer *Pensacola* in the North Pacific during the spring of 1867, he commanded the sidewheeler *Powhatan,* flagship of the South Pacific Squadron (1868–69), when, in June 1869, he was promoted to commodore. Detached from the *Powhatan* in December, Commodore McDougal commanded the South Atlantic Squadron, flagship the screw sloop *Ossipee* (1870–72). Retired in 1873, he was advanced to rear admiral two years later. His son, Cdr. Charles J. McDougal, drowned in 1881 while inspecting California lighthouses. His grandsons included Adm. David McDougal LeBreton (1884–1973), top man at the Naval Academy in 1904 and commander of the naval force which landed the Marines in Iceland during the summer of 1941, and Gen. Douglas C. McDougal (1876–1964), commanding general of the Fleet Marine Force in 1935–37. A great-grandson was Lt. Col. David S. McDougal, USMC, killed in action at Okinawa in 1945.

McMorris, Charles Horatio "Soc"

(August 31, 1890–February 11, 1954).
USNA (Ala.) 1912 (6/156).

A leading staff officer in the war against Japan, McMorris utilized his intellectual talents (as did SOCrates) teaching at the Naval Academy, in seamanship (1925–27), and English and history (1930–33), simultaneously serving the U.S. Naval Institute *Proceedings* as assistant editor during the first tour and as editor during most of the second; he also attended the senior Naval War College course (1937–38). His career however began in the surface line—the battleship *Delaware* (BB-28), armored cruiser *Montana* (ACR-13), and the *New Hampshire* (BB-25) for two years in the Atlantic, culminating aboard the latter off Vera Cruz in April 1914. After briefly attending torpedo classes on the *Montana,* he joined the *Maryland* (ACR-8), in which he helped to salvage the submarine *F-4* (SS-23) off Pearl Harbor. Serving in the destroyer *Shaw* (DD-68) from the precommissioning detail in January 1917 through convoying out of Irish Queenstown to July 1918, he then fit out and was executive officer of the *Meredith* (DD-165) until mid-1919, helping to guide the NC flying boats. Commanding officer of the *Walke* (DD-34) for a month and a recruiter in Pittsburgh for three months, McMorris served as detailing officer twice at the Bureau of Navigation (1919–22, 1935–37), as navigator of the decommissioning minelayer *Baltimore* (C-3) at Pearl, exec of the layer *Burns* (DM-11) in Hawaiian waters (1922–24), and then ashore with Mine Squadron Two briefly. He commanded the *Shirk* (DD-318) in the Pacific and during the Nicaraguan crisis (1927–30) and then the *Elliott* (DD-146) for a few subsequent months in the same waters.

Commander McMorris was navigator of the *California* (BB-44) with the Battle Force in the Pacific (1933–35) and operations officer to Commander

Scouting Force (and from October 1939, Commander Hawaiian Detachment as well), Adm. Adolphus Andrews, flagship the heavy cruiser *Indianapolis* (CA-35), from mid-1938 to January 1941. In the rank of captain he became war plans officer to Pacific Fleet commander Adm. H. E. Kimmel in February 1941, in which capacity he was present during the Japanese attack on Pearl Harbor in December, continuing his assignment under the new Fleet commander, Adm. C. W. Nimitz, until April 1942. Captain McMorris took command of the *San Francisco* (CA-38) the next month, supported the Guadalcanal landings in August, fought in the battle of Cape Esperance in October, and was detached early in November upon his promotion to rear admiral. Made Commander Task Force Eight the next month and hoisting his flag aboard the *Richmond* (CL-9), he bombarded Attu in the Aleutians in February 1943 and fought to a draw with a Japanese surface force in the battle of the Komandorski Islands in March. In June he became chief of the Joint Staff to Admiral Nimitz and as such supervised the planning and execution of the Central Pacific counteroffensive from then until the defeat of Japan, playing an obviously key role. A temporary vice admiral from September 1944 to July 1948, he commanded the Fourth Fleet in the Atlantic from February to September 1946 and then served on the General Board, also as its president from December 1947 to August 1948. Admiral McMorris spent his final tour of duty in Hawaii commanding the Fourteenth Naval District and Hawaiian Sea Frontier and also, from June 1951, commanding the Pearl Harbor Naval Base, retiring in the rank of vice admiral in September 1952.

McNulty, Richard Robert

(April 20, 1899——).

Leader in developing federal training for merchant marine officers, McNulty graduated in 1919 from the wartime Massachusetts (his home state) Nautical School and its schoolship, *Ranger,* later *Nantucket* (PG-23), on which he had had wartime East coast patrols, and spent two years (1920-22) in the Navy's Hydrographic Office, concurrently attending the School of Foreign Service at Georgetown University (B.S. 1922). He was then employed as a shipping executive in New York with Mallory Transport Lines and C. D. Mallory and Company (1922-26, 1929-36) except for an interval at the U.S. Shipping Board's Bureau of Research (1927-29). An early proponent of the view that merchant deck and engineering officers deserved a proper professional education matching that of Navy officers and that this therefore was the responsibility of the federal government, he wrote many articles during 1929-34 supporting his position, an effort which resulted in his appointment in August 1937 to the new Maritime Commission, specifically to head its Division of Cadet Training (and Assistant Director, Division of Training, to Adm. Henry A. Wiley, USN [Ret.]). Working with the new U. S. Maritime Service through the U. S. Coast Guard, Mr. McNulty administered the equally new U. S. Merchant Marine Cadet Corps, its shore schools and training ships from Washington as the prewar and wartime merchant fleet expanded. Pressing for a permanent home for one federal academy, he led the movement which culminated in the December 1941 establishment of the U. S. Merchant Marine Academy at King's Point on Long Island, New York, an achievement which earned him the sobriquet "Father of the Merchant Marine Academy." (His old schoolship *Nantucket* also went to the Academy, there renamed *Emery Rice).*

215

In July 1942 McNulty supervised the shift of the actual training from Coast Guard management to that of the War Shipping Administration, the cadet midshipmen from King's Point as well as from the San Mateo Cadet School in California and the Pass Christian Cadet School in Mississippi henceforth being hurried through training and into merchant billets before and after graduation, some to perish in action particularly in North Atlantic convoys. McNulty remained at his post for the duration, in July 1945 being appointed commodore and later rear admiral in the U. S. Naval Reserve, and in April 1946 to the additional position of Superintendent of the Merchant Marine Academy. Three months later he was appointed rear admiral in the U. S. Maritime Service, remaining at the Academy until April 1948 when he returned full-time to his other WSA post, which in May 1950 was transferred to the direct jurisdiction of the Maritime Administration under the Department of Commerce. That September Admiral McNulty retired. In 1952 he returned to his alma mater, the Georgetown Foreign Service program, as Director of Shipping Research and subsequently as Head of the Department of International Transportation, where he remained until he retired as professor emeritus in 1970. In March 1975 he was promoted to vice admiral, USMS, retired.

Merrill, Aaron Stanton "Tip"

(March 26, 1890—February 28, 1961).
USNA (Miss.) 1912 (142/156).

National Archives

Victor at the Battle of Empress Augusta Bay in the Pacific war, Merrill started his career in the line with the battleship *Louisiana* (BB-19) and armored cruiser *Tennessee* (ACR-10) in the Atlantic but then (1913–14) operated out of Constantinople as engineer of the gunboat *Scorpion* (PY-3), the vessel to which he returned subsequently as aide to Adm. M. L. Bristol, U.S. High Commissioner to Turkey during that country's postwar time of troubles (1919–23). After some months with the Naval Academy's practice squadron, he cruised off the Eastern seaboard with the destroyers *Roe* (DD-24) (1914–16) and *Conyngham* (DD-58), on which he sailed out of Queenstown, Ireland, in World War I. After training chores at San Francisco and Detroit, he completed the war patrolling from Plymouth in the *Aylwin* (DD-47), followed by a few months (1919) in Northern European waters with the yacht *Harvard* (SP-209) and the Lafayette Radio Station at French Croix D'hins. Lieutenant Commander Merrill served on the New York receiving ship (1923–24), on the *Nevada* (BB-36) in the Pacific as communications officer, the *McCormick* (DD-223) as skipper in the Asiatic Fleet, and aboard the gunboat *Elcano* (PG-38) on the Yangtze Patrol, ending this tour as Destroyer Squadron engineer of that Fleet (1926–27). Captain of the *Williamson* (DD-244) (1929–32), he was in Washington with Naval Intelligence (1927–29, 1932–33) and as aide to Assistant Secretary of the Navy Henry L. Roosevelt (1933–34).

First lieutenant of the cruiser *Pensacola* (CA-24) in both oceans (1934–35), Commander Merrill commanded Destroyer Division Eight, flagship *Childs* (DD-241), and was naval attaché at Santiago, Chile (1936–38), and senior student at the Naval War College. He commanded DesDiv 17, flagship *Somers* (DD-381) (1939–40), and then Destroyer Squadron Eight, flagship *Winslow* (DD-358), both on Atlantic neutrality patrol, before becoming professor of naval science and tactics for the Naval Reserve Officers Training Corps unit at Tulane University early in 1941. In April 1942 Captain Merrill brought the new *Indiana* (BB-58) into commission and took her to the South Pacific in November to screen aircraft carriers. Designated Commander Cruiser Division 12, flag in the new *Montpelier* (CL-57), in the rank of rear admiral in February 1943, Merrill became a leading surface commander during the Solomons campaign. His Task Force 68 sank two Japanese destroyers off Vila in March; his TF 39 sank the cruiser *Sendai* and drove the enemy navy away from Bougainville in the Battle of Empress Augusta Bay in November; and his vessels continually bombarded Japanese coastal positions until his relief in March 1944. Admiral Merrill directed the Navy's public relations office from June 1944 to April 1945 and took command of the Eighth Naval District in January 1946 and in June additionally the Gulf Sea Frontier, headquarters New Orleans. He retired as vice admiral in November 1947.

Mitchell, John Kirkwood

(January 1, 1811—December 5, 1889).

Naval Photographic Center

One of the Confederacy's most active flag officers, North Carolinian Mitchell became acting midshipman in the U.S. Navy in 1825 and received his regular warrant two years later when he shipped out aboard the ship-of-the-line *Delaware* (1827–30), flagship of the Mediterranean Squadron. After a stint at Norfolk he went to the West Indies and in 1832 was made acting master of the sloop *Vandalia* for two years. Promoted lieutenant in 1836 after several leaves, he returned to the Caribbean aboard the sloop *Boston* (1836–38), had shore duty at the New York Navy Yard, and was loaned to the Coast Survey at Washington (1840–42). After duty afloat with the sloop *Vincennes* (1842–44), Lieutenant Mitchell was hospitalized at New York then stationed at the Philadelphia naval rendezvous, followed by brief duty with the anchored frigate *Savannah* at the end of 1848. In November 1849 he assumed command of the sloop *Lexington* in California and sailed to the East coast, being detached early in 1851. After some months at the Norfolk receiving ship, he commanded the sidewheel steamer *Fulton* in the western Atlantic and Caribbean (1854–56), spending early 1855 in a vain search for the disappeared sloop *Albany*. Promoted to commander in 1855, he was stationed at Pensacola Navy Yard (1856–59) before commanding the steam sloop *Wyoming* in the Pacific.

Appointed commander in the Confederate Navy in November 1861, Mitchell was immediately frustrated from raising a squadron at Columbus, Kentucky, by Union advances but transferred that same month to command of the small squadron at New Orleans with a subsequent promotion to captain and status as flag officer. Greatly understrength, his force failed to arrest Farragut's attack on New Orleans in April 1862, and in August he was

218

ordered to take over the Office of Orders and Detail at Richmond. In the spring of 1864 Flag Officer Mitchell assumed command of the James River Squadron, flagship the ironclad steam sloop *Virginia II,* and in June engaged Union forces at long range at Trent's and Varina reaches and thereafter supported Gen. Robert E. Lee's army in the defense of Richmond. With twelve vessels at his disposal, he sortied against Grant's base at City Point late in January 1865, only to be forced back by Union artillery when two of his vessels ran aground. The next month he was replaced by Adm. Raphael Semmes and his active naval service came to an end.

Navy Department: National Archives

Mitscher, Marc Andrew "Pete"

(January 26, 1887—February 3, 1947).
USNA (Okla.) 1910 (108/131).

Premier fast carrier leader during World War II as Commander Task Force 58, born in Wisconsin and raised in Washington, D.C., Mitscher became a pioneer in aviation as Naval Aviator No. 33 in 1916 following initial tours of duty aboard the armored cruiser *Colorado* (ACR-7) in the Pacific (1910–12); briefly the *South Dakota* (ACR-9), gunboats *Vicksburg* (PG-11) and *Annapolis* (PG-10) in the Caribbean; then (1913–15) the *California* (ACR-6), renamed *San Diego* just after the Vera Cruz affair of 1914; and briefly the destroyers *Whipple* (DD-15) and *Stewart* (DD-13) and the *North Carolina* (ACR-12) in the Atlantic. Reporting to Pensacola for flight training in October 1915, he won his wings the following June and remained at Pensacola for advanced training. In April 1917 Lieutenant (j.g.) Mitscher joined the *Huntington* (ACR-5) for balloon and catapult experiments at Pensacola, then convoy escort until October, when he moved to Long Island,

New York, first Naval Air Station Montauk Point and in February 1918 NAS Rockaway as commanding officer. Several weeks later he assumed command of NAS Miami and in February 1919 transferred to the Aviation Section in the Office of the Chief of Naval Operations. As pilot of the NC-1 flying boat in his intended transatlantic flight of May 1919 he fell just short of the Azores (but Lt. Cdr. Albert C. Read in the NC-4 made it across). Four months later he left his Navy Department post to report to the minelayer *Aroostook* (CM-3) in California, the vessel converting to an aviation tender the next summer and Mitscher in December 1920 assuming the additional role of commander of the Pacific Fleet's air detachment at San Diego.

In Washington during the latter part of 1922 in command of NAS Anacostia and then at the Plans Division of the Bureau of Aeronautics, Lieutenant Commander Mitscher also led Navy teams in the International Air Races of 1922 and 1923 at Detroit and St. Louis respectively. He served in the Pacific aboard the Navy's first aircraft carrier, the *Langley* (CV-1), during the second half of 1926 before reporting to the precommissioning detail of the *Saratoga* (CV-3), of which he became air officer when she entered the Fleet in November 1927. After participating aboard her in Fleet Problem IX off Panama which demonstrated offensive carrier air power, he was detached in June for a year back on the *Langley* as executive officer. He served at BuAer in the rank of commander (1930–33) and as chief of staff to Base Force air commander Adm. Alfred W. Johnson, flagship the seaplane tender *Wright* (AV-1), in the Pacific. Commander Mitscher returned successively to the *Saratoga* as exec (1934–35), to BuAer in charge of the Flight Division (1935–37), and the *Wright* as skipper (1937–38). Promoted to captain, he commanded Patrol Wing One at San Diego and in June 1939 became Assistant Chief of BuAer, a post he held until July 1941. Captain Mitscher brought the *Hornet* (CV-8) into commission the following October and launched Col. Jimmy Doolittle's Army bombers from her deck to bomb Tokyo in April 1942. Two months later he led the *Hornet* into the Battle of Midway and was detached in July upon his promotion to rear admiral and assignment to command Patwing Two at NAS Kaneohe in Hawaii.

Shifting to the South Pacific and the Guadalcanal and Solomons campaign, Admiral Mitscher became Commander Fleet Air at Nouméa in December 1942 and the following April Commander Air Solomon Islands, rotating home in August to command fleet air units on the West coast. In January 1944 he assumed command of Carrier Division Three and the Fast Carrier Task Force or TF 58 in the Central Pacific, flagship *Yorktown* (CV-10), and led the fast carriers against the Marshalls, Truk, New Guinea and the Marianas, culminating in his victory over the Japanese Fleet in the Battle of the Philippine Sea in June, his flag then in the *Lexington* (CV-16). Dropping his CarDiv Three title in March, he was promoted to vice admiral that month and the next August redesignated Commander First Fast Carrier Force Pacific and CTF 38, in which capacity he fought in the Battle of Leyte Gulf, flag still aboard the *Lexington,* and in Philippines operations until late November 1944. Admiral Mitscher returned from leave at the end of

January 1945 to command the fast carriers, again TF 58, in the strikes on Iwo Jima, Okinawa and the Japanese home islands through May, although severe damage by kamikaze attacks forced him to change flagships the last month from the *Bunker Hill* (CV-17) to *Enterprise* (CV-6) and then *Randolph* (CV-15). In July 1945 he went to Washington as Deputy Chief of Naval Operations (Air) and in March 1946 reported as Commander Eighth Fleet in the Atlantic, flagships *Lake Champlain* (CV-39), *Franklin D. Roosevelt* (CVB-42) and *Leyte* (CV-32), in the full rank of admiral. Admiral Mitscher assumed the post of Commander-in-Chief Atlantic Fleet in September 1946 and died while serving therein.

Moffett, William Adger "Billy"

(October 31, 1869—April 4, 1933).
USNA (S.C.) 1890 (31/34).

The Father of Naval Aviation, Moffett first shipped out in the screw steamer *Pensacola* for a Pacific cruise (1890–91), there transferring to the cruiser *Baltimore* (C-3) from which he witnessed the naval battles of the Chilean revolution. He trained apprentices in the Atlantic on the sloop *Portsmouth* (1892–93) before operating in European waters on the protected cruiser *Chicago* (1893–95). After a year in South Carolina waters with the new monitor *Amphitrite* (BM-2), Ensign Moffett attended the Naval War College during the summer of 1896, then spent six weeks on the training sloop *Constellation* also at Newport, over a year aboard the Massachusetts maritime schoolship *Enterprise* at Boston, and early 1898 in Hawaiian waters on the steam sloop *Mohican*. In May he reported to the *Charleston* (C-2) and took part in the capture of Guam and the final bombardment of Manila, of which he then became port captain to salvage the sunken Spanish warships. While there he also saw duty on the supply ship *Culgoa* and again the *Charleston,* his promotion to lieutenant (j.g.) and lieutenant occurring in March and July 1899 respectively. Brief service at San Francisco on the practice ship *Monongahela* preceded his assignment to the new battleship *Kentucky* (BB-6) in May 1900 for Asiatic duty, the maiden voyage going via Turkey, where he declined the offer of an admiralcy in the Ottoman navy.

Lieutenant Moffett had several successive short sea-going billets: the gunboat *Marietta* (PG-15) in the Pacific (1901); the training sloop *St. Mary's* in both oceans (1901–02), and the *Minneapolis* (C-13), the training steam sloop *Lancaster* and the *Maine* (BB-10) on the East coast. Early in 1904 he rejoined the *Amphitrite* as executive officer at Guantanamo Bay, Cuba, where in March he became commandant of the station and was then promoted to lieutenant commander. Detached in 1906, he had shore duty at the Bureau of Equipment and the Naval War College before reporting as navigator then exec of the armored cruiser *Maryland* (ACR-8) which he molded into an award-winning ship in the Pacific (1908–10). Remaining at San Francisco as lighthouse inspector (1910–12), Moffett helped commission the *Arkansas* (BB-33) as exec, cruising to Panama, and in November 1913 took command of the scout cruiser *Chester* (CL-1). He participated in the Tampico incident, personally delivering Adm. Mayo's ultimatum to the Mexicans, and in the Vera Cruz occupation, both in April 1914. Promoted commander the previous month, Moffett in August became commandant of the Great Lakes Naval Training Station and supervisor of the Ninth, Tenth and Eleventh Naval Districts, revolutionizing naval training throughout the expansion period of World War I. He became captain in 1916 and did not leave this vital post until victory had been achieved. In December 1918 he became skipper of the *Mississippi* (BB-41) in the Pacific, improving her gunnery through the use of aircraft, and in September 1919 he led a large party ashore at Seattle which deterred a radical labor demonstration against visiting President Woodrow Wilson. He relinquished command in December 1920.

Captain Moffett was appointed Director of Naval Aviation in March 1921, the post becoming Chief of the newly-created Bureau of Aeronautics in July with Moffett as rear admiral. Immediately taking to the air as a passenger, within a year he had accumulated the necessary one hundred hours of flight time for designation as a naval aviation observer. More importantly, he fashioned his agency into a virtual superbureau, withstanding Navy critics and Army Air opponents led by Gen. Billy Mitchell to create the nucleus of the Navy's air arm of aircraft carriers, seaplanes, air stations and rigid dirigibles. His success was recognized by three successive four-year tours of duty in the job, with Moffett shunning higher commands in order to see naval aviation firmly established. Admiral Moffett attended the London naval conference of 1930 and perished in the crash of the Navy's airship *Akron* (ZRS-4) out of Lakehurst, New Jersey, the fifth American flag officer and the first since H. H. Bell over six decades before to die in the line of duty. Of his three naval aviator sons, two commanded squadrons during the Guadalcanal campaign; Charles S. Moffett led fighters from the carrier *Wasp* (CV-7) and W. A. Moffett, Jr., directed heavy bombers (PB4Ys) from Henderson Field,, the former retiring as captain, the latter as rear admiral.

Montgomery, Alfred Eugene

(June 12, 1891–December 15, 1961).
USNA (Neb.) 1912 (29/156).

Navy Department: National Archives

Naval aviator Montgomery had brief careers in the surface line and submarines before achieving flight status in 1922. Atlantic Fleet duty in the battleship *Virginia* (BB-13) (1912–13) and the Newport training sloop *Constellation* preceded several short assignments (1914–15) to the cruisers *Tacoma* (C-18) and *Chester* (CL-1) and the *Connecticut* (BB-18) in the Atlantic. Trained in subs aboard the monitor *Tonopah* (BM-8), he was executive officer of the sub *E-1* (SS-24) in the Atlantic (1915–16), and then reported to Mare Island to help refit the *F-1* (SS-20) and *F-2* (SS-21), recommissioning the former in June 1917 and commanding her until December when she was lost in a collision with the *F-3* while on maneuvers. Fitting out the *R-20* (SS-97) at San Francisco, Lieutenant Commander Montgomery commissioned her in October 1918 as skipper for two years of Pacific cruising during which he received elementary seaplane training at his Pearl Harbor base. After helping to outfit the *S-32* (SS-137) at San Francisco, he superintended new machinery at Mare Island (1921), earned his wings at Pensacola, and served in three observation squadrons in the Pacific, as exec of VO-2 on the aviation tender *Aroostook* (CM-3) (1922–23) and skipper of VO-1 and then (1923–24) of VO-6. Senior aide to Capt. Walter R. Gherardi, commanding the Scouting Fleet's aircraft squadrons from the tender *Wright* (AV-1), he then commanded Torpedo Bombing Squadron One in that force (1924–25). At Naval Air Station San Diego as assembly and repair officer (1925–26) and exec (1926–28, 1938–39), he was air officer of the aircraft carrier *Langley* (CV-1) in the Pacific and skipper of Bombing Torpedo Wing and Torpedo 2-B on the *Saratoga* (CV-3) in the same ocean (1929–30).

Commander Montgomery commanded NAS Seattle (1930–32); fitted out squadrons for the *Langley;* had staff duty as aviation officer to Adm. W. H. Standley, Scouting Force cruiser commander in the *Chicago* (CA-29) (1932–33); headed the air section of the Navy's Ship Movements Division; commanded NAS Anacostia (1934–36); and was operations and plans officer to Adms. Henry V. Butler and Frederick J. Horne, Battle Force air commanders on the *Saratoga.* He also served in the Pacific as exec of the *Ranger* (CV-4) (1936–38) and in the Atlantic later as her skipper (1940–41), remaining on board as chief of staff to Atlantic air commander Adm. Arthur B. Cook hunting German U-boats from July 1941 until April 1942. Head of the Flight Division of the Bureau of Aeronautics (1939–40), he went to Corpus Christi in June 1942 in the rank of rear admiral as air station commander, then in October as Chief of Air Intermediate Training and in November as commander of the Naval Air Training Center there until June 1943. Two months later Admiral Montgomery took administrative command of Carrier Division 12 and from March to December 1944 of CarDiv Three, leading fast carrier task groups in the Pacific counteroffensive: Task Force 14 at Wake (October 1943) and Task Group 50.3 at Rabaul and the Gilberts and Kwajalein (November–December), flagship *Bunker Hill* (CV-17); TG 58.2 in the Marshalls and at Truk (January–February 1944) and Marcus (May), flagship *Essex* (CV-9), and the Palaus, New Guinea (April) and Marianas (June), flagship *Bunker Hill;* and TG 38.1 in the Philippines (November–December) from the *Yorktown* (CV-10). He commanded West coast fleet air from January to July 1945 and as vice admiral Pacific Fleet Air Forces (1945–46); the Fifth Fleet, flagship the amphibious command ship *Appalachian* (AGC-1); and the First Task Fleet, flagship *Iowa* (BB-61), in the Pacific (1947). Reverting to rear admiral, Montgomery commanded the Northern Pacific Area, Alaskan Sea Frontier and Seventeenth Naval District, headquarters Kodiak (1947–49); U.S. Naval Operating Base Bermuda (1949–50); and fleet air at Jacksonville before retiring in the rank of vice admiral in July 1951.

Montgomery, John Berrien

(November 17, 1794—March 25, 1873).

National Archives

A major figure in the conquest of California, Montgomery received his midshipman's warrant at the outbreak of the War of 1812 (along with his younger brother Nathaniel L. Montgomery who was severely wounded on the frigate *President* in 1812) and his first assignments with the schooners *Hamilton, Madison* and *General Pike* on Lake Ontario, fighting in several engagements with the British squadron and covering American landings through August 1813 when he transferred to the brig *Niagara* and fought in the Battle of Lake Erie the next month and in the attack on Mackinac one year later. He followed his last skipper, Capt. J. D. Elliott, to the new sloop *Ontario* for operations against Algiers in 1815 and was promoted to lieutenant in 1818. After two years operating on the African coast (1818–20), he joined the laid-up sloop *Erie* at New York and later cruised the Mediterranean in her (1823–26). Following duty at the Carlisle naval rendezvous, Montgomery was executive officer of the new sloop *Peacock* (1830–31) and had recruiting duty at Philadelphia and New York prior to brief service as exec of the frigate *Constitution* in 1835. He was then based at Boston, commanding first the receiving ship (1837–39) then the rendezvous (1841–44), promotion to commander occurring in 1840.

Commander Montgomery commissioned the sloop *Portsmouth* late in 1844, cruised the Mexican coasts, occupied San Francisco at the outbreak of war in July 1846, and operated in the Gulf of California through 1847, climaxed by the bombardment and capture of Guaymas in October; he was relieved in May 1848. After the war, during which he had lost two sons in an incident at San Francisco, Montgomery had duty as exec of the Washington Navy Yard (1849–51), an ordnance assignment (1853–54) and membership on examining boards for midshipmen (1855, 1857). Promoted to captain in 1853, in May 1857 he brought into commission the screw frigate *Roanoke*, flagship of the Home Squadron, and transported back to the States William Walker's Nicaraguan filibusters during the summer. Remaining in the West Indies with the *Roanoke* for two years, he then commanded the Pacific Squadron, flagship the new screw sloop *Lancaster* (1859–61). New Jersey-born Flag Officer Montgomery officially retired in December 1861 but ably served the Union during the Civil War as commandant of the navy yards at Charlestown, Massachusetts (1862–63) and Washington (1863–65). He was promoted on the retired list to commodore in 1862 and rear admiral four years later, ending his naval career in command of Sackett's Harbor (1866–69). His brother Alexander M. Montgomery was an assistant surgeon in the Navy, 1814–38.

Moore, Edwin Ward

(June 1810—October 5, 1865).

Navy Department

Commodore of the Texas Navy, Virginia-born Moore had a short career in the U.S. Navy punctuated by a delicate physical constitution. Appointed midshipman in 1825, he operated in the West Indies aboard the brig *Horne* (1825–27) and in the Mediterranean with the new sloop *Fairfield* (1828–29), returned home in the ship-of-the-line *Delaware* (1829–30), and rejoined the *Fairfield* in the West Indies (1831–32), becoming acting lieutenant then acting sailing master. Following promotion to lieutenant in 1835, he served in the Indies aboard the sloop *Boston* (1836–39), which he deserted early in 1839 to become senior captain in the Republic of Texas Navy, resigning his

U.S. Navy commission in July. Moore raised a small squadron over the ensuing year, hoisted his flag as commodore in the sloop *Austin* in 1840 to demonstrate off the Mexican coast, and the next year drove Mexican shipping from the sea, captured Tabasco and concluded an alliance with rebellious Yucatan. He refitted his vessels at New Orleans throughout 1842, the year he received the formal rank of post captain commanding. In April 1843, with two Texas and six Yucatan vessels, Commodore Moore broke the Mexican blockade of Yucatan and in May defeated the Mexican squadron at the battle of Campeche. Despite his victory, political infighting led to his relief in June, and his repeated efforts for reinstatement into the U.S. Navy failed.

Naval Photographic Center

Moorer, Thomas Hinman

(February 9, 1912–—   ). USNA (Ala.) 1933 (182/432).

Highest-ranking Naval officer of the Vietnam era, Moorer became a naval aviator in 1936 after gunnery duty in the cruisers *Salt Lake City* (CL-25) in the Pacific (1933) and the new *New Orleans* (CA-35) in the Atlantic (1934–35). Flying first with Fighting Squadron 1-B from the Pacific aircraft carriers *Langley* (CV-1) and *Lexington* (CV-2), he moved (1937–39) to Fighting Six and the *Enterprise* (CV-6) before going into patrol planes. With Patrol Squadron 22 from August 1939 through the battles at Pearl Harbor in December 1941 and the Dutch East Indies, he was shot down and wounded in his PBY north of Darwin, Australia, in February 1942, and picked up by a freighter which was immediately bombed and sunk; he navigated the life boats to an island where he and his crew were rescued. Continuing to fly in this theater with Patron 101 during the spring, Lieutenant Moorer went to

England to observe British aerial mining techniques from August till the following March when he commissioned and took command of Bombing 132 at Key West, operating for twelve months from Cuba to Africa in the Battle of the Atlantic. Remaining in that theater as gunnery and tactical officer to Adm. P. N. L. Bellinger, commander of that Fleet's air forces, until July 1945, he reported in the rank of commander the next month to the U.S. Strategic Bombing Survey interrogating Japanese officials in Japan, and continued in this activity until the following May. Postwar assignments included executive officer of the Naval Ordnance Test Station at Chincoteague, Virginia, and operations officer first of the *Midway* (CVB-42) in the Mediterranean (1948–49) and then to Adm. J. J. Clark, Commander Carrier Division Four, in the same flagship with the Sixth Fleet. Detached in July 1950, Moorer became captain while assigned to NOTS Inyokern, California, studied at the Naval War College, and returned to the staff of ComAirLant, Adms. John J. Ballentine and Frederick G. McMahon, as plans officer (1953–55).

Captain Moorer was aide to Assistant Secretary of the Navy (Air) James H. Smith and skipper of the seaplane tender *Salisbury Sound* (AV-13) in the Western Pacific (1956–57) prior to his selection for rear admiral in July 1957 and Washington assignments as special assistant in the Navy's Strategic Plans Division; Assistant Chief of Naval Operations (War Gaming Matters) (1958–59); and director of the Long Range Objectives Group (1960–62). Admiral Moorer then progressed rapidly up the ladder of key fleet assignments and promotions. He commanded CarDiv Six, flagship *Saratoga* (CVA-60), in the Atlantic and Med (1959–60) and in October 1962 was advanced to vice admiral and given command of the Seventh Fleet, flagship the guided missile cruiser *Providence* (CLG-6), which he led for two years as the nation became gradually involved in Vietnam. In June 1964 he achieved the rank of admiral as Commander-in-Chief Pacific Fleet during the first year of official American participation in the Vietnam War but in April 1965 switched theaters to become Allied NATO commander in the Atlantic, commander of the U.S. Atlantic Command, and Commander-in-Chief Atlantic Fleet, in which capacity he conducted the intervention into the Dominican Republic. Admiral Moorer served as Chief of Naval Operations (1967–70) and as the third Naval officer (after Leahy and Radford) to be chairman of the Joint Chiefs of Staff (1970–74). He retired from the Navy in July 1974. His brother, Vice Adm. Joseph P. Moorer (1922–   ), became Commander-in-Chief, U.S. Naval Forces in Europe in the mid-1970's.

Moosbrugger, Frederick

(October 9, 1900–October 1, 1974).
USNA (Pa.) 1923 (172/413).

National Archives

World War II Pacific destroyerman Moosbrugger had prewar duty with the Battle Fleet, battleship *Nevada* (BB-36); the Yangtze Patrol, destroyer *Truxtun* (DD-229) (1924–27); the Seattle headquarters of the Thirteenth Naval District; the Scouting Fleet, oiler *Brazos* (AO-4) (1927–29); at New London for submarine instruction; the sub *S-6* (SS-111) in the Atlantic (1929–31); at the Naval Academy teaching electrical engineering and physics (1931–34) and ordnance (1937–39); again with the Scouting Force, cruiser *Houston* (CA-30), in both oceans (1934–37); and in the Battle Force with the *Tennessee* (BB-43) as gunnery officer (1939–41). Lieutenant Commander Moosbrugger took command of the *McCall* (DD-400) in April 1941 out of Pearl Harbor and was at sea escorting the carrier *Enterprise* during the Japanese attack in December but participated in the early 1942 carrier strikes on the Gilberts, Marshalls, Wake, and Marcus. In May 1942 he took command of Destroyer Division 11, flagship *Gridley* (DD-380), for operations in the Aleutians from June to October and then in the Solomons usually as convoy escort. Transferring to command of DesDiv 12, flagship *Dunlap* (DD-384), at Tulagi in May 1943, he supported the landings at New Georgia and Rendova during the summer and in August directed the sinking of three Japanese destroyers in the battle of Vella Gulf. Duty at Twelfth Naval District headquarters at San Francisco followed in September.

Captain Moosbrugger served at the Pacific Operational Training Center from November 1943 to June 1944 and as chief training officer with the San Diego Shakedown Group before returning to sea commanding Destroyer Squadron 63 and DesDiv 125 in August. His flag in the seaplane tender

Biscayne (AVP-11), he directed the transport screen in the Iwo Jima operation in February and March 1945 and at Okinawa the following month. In May he was elevated to the rank of commodore as Commander Task Flotilla Five and directed all radar picket destroyers, destroyer escorts and auxiliary craft fending off kamikazes from attacking Okinawa shipping; the flag remained in the *Biscayne* and briefly the command ship *Panamint* (AGC-13). Detached the following December, he served at the Bureau of Naval Personnel until April 1946 when he reverted to captain and assumed command of the General Line Naval School at Newport. Skipper of the *Springfield* (CL-66) on the West coast (1949–50), Captain Moosbrugger commanded Destroyer Flotilla One, flagship the destroyer tender *Prairie* (AD-15) at San Diego, then the Fleet Training Group and Underway Training Element there (1950–51). Promoted rear admiral in mid-1951, he commanded Cruiser Division Five, flagship *Rochester* (CA-124), bombarding the Korean coastline and (1952) the Military Sea Transportation Service at San Francisco. Superintendent of the U.S. Naval Postgraduate School at Monterey (1952–55), Admiral Moosbrugger commanded the Pacific Fleet's Training Command from the end of 1955 until his retirement in the rank of vice admiral the following October.

Moreell, Ben

(September 14, 1892——July 30, 1978).

Navy Department: National Archives

"King Bee of the Seabees," Utah-born but St. Louis-raised Moreell graduated from Washington University in 1913 in civil engineering and was appointed lieutenant (j.g.) in the Civil Engineer Corps in 1917, had indoctrination at Annapolis and spent World War I in the public works office at Ponta Delgada Naval Base in the Azores. Plant engineer at the Destroyer and Submarine Base at Squantum, Massachusetts (1919–20), he was executive officer of public works in Haiti, assistant and then public works officer at Norfolk (1924–26) and Bremerton and the Thirteenth Naval District (1930–32), and assistant design manager in the Bureau of Yards and Docks (1926–30) and of the Ship Model Testing Basin (1933–35) later named for Adm. D. W. Taylor. After studying in France (1932–33), Commander Moreell served as project manager of shipbuilding and repair facilities in the storage and sub base section of the Bureau (1935–37) and as public works officer at Pearl Harbor Naval Base and the Fourteenth Naval District before being appointed Chief of Bureau and Chief of Civil Engineers in December 1937 in the rank of rear admiral. He remained at that post throughout World War II until November 1945. Late in December 1941 he founded the Naval Construction Battalions ("Seabees") of engineers and trained construction crews able to defend themselves unlike the contracted civilian workers taken at Guam and Wake that month. From 3300 men initially, the Seabees—"Can-do boys" he called them—expanded eventually to 250,000, laying down roads during assaults and building base facilities and airstrips on captured territory, often fighting the enemy in the process. Developing the wartime Naval Shore Establishment to over 900 installations around the world, Admiral Moreell was promoted to vice admiral in February 1944—the first officer in the CEC to hold this rank. In October 1945, the month before his assignment as Chief of the Material Division in the Office of the Assistant Secretary, he took charge of the nation's oil refineries and pipe lines seized by the government during a labor dispute (which he helped materially in resolving), held control until April 1946, and in May became Deputy Coal Mines Administrator then Administrator under the Secretary of the Interior when the government seized the bituminous coal mines. Promoted to admiral in June, the first staff corps officer to attain that rank, he retired in October. He wrote *Standards of Design of Concrete* (1922), a major engineering treatise.

Morison, Samuel Eliot

(July 9, 1887—May 15, 1976).

Navy Department

Maritime and naval historian and author of the semi-official history of the Navy in World War II, New Englander Morison received his degrees in history at Harvard University (B.A. 1908, M.A. 1909, Ph.D. 1912) and spent most of his teaching career there (except for the University of California, 1912–15, and Oxford University in England, 1922–25), retiring in 1955. A prolific and brilliant writer of American history and an inveterate sailor throughout his life, he retraced Christopher Columbus's voyage to America in a bark and ketch (1939–40) which led to his Pulitzer Prize winning biography *Admiral of the Ocean Sea* (1942). With only brief Army service in World War I (1918–19) and postwar diplomatic work at Versailles, he received from President Franklin D. Roosevelt in May 1942 the rank of lieutenant commander in the Naval Reserve in order to obtain first-hand experience in writing the Navy's operational history of World War II. He sailed in eight major warships: the destroyer *Buck* (DD-420) in the summer of 1942 and the Coast Guard cutter *Campbell* late in 1944, both on North Atlantic convoys; the cruiser *Brooklyn* (CL-40) during the invasion of North Africa in November 1942; the battleship *Washington* (BB-56) in the South Pacific during the spring of 1943; PT boats in New Guinea waters; the *Honolulu* (CL-48) in the Solomons and the battle of Kolombangara in the summer of 1943 and in the Marianas a year later; the *Montpelier* (CL-57) also in the Solomons campaign; the *Baltimore* (CA-68) in the Gilberts in the autumn of 1943; and the *Tennessee* (BB-43) at Okinawa in the spring of 1945. Curiously, he did not serve aboard an aircraft carrier or a submarine, the two major warship types of the conflict. Promoted commander in 1944 and captain at the end of 1945, Morison left active duty the following

232

September but maintained an office and staff of assistants at the Navy Department and had occasional special duty at the Naval War College for the research and writing of the 15-volume *History of U.S. Naval Operations in World War II* (1947–62), abridged as the one-volume *The Two-Ocean War* (1963). (Regrettably, its companion administrative history by Robert Greenhalgh Albion of Harvard was not published until over three decades after the war. Retired in the rank of rear admiral in the Reserve in August 1951, Morison continued to produce outstanding oceanic history, including a second Pulitzer Prize winner, *John Paul Jones* (1959).

Morris, Charles

(July 26, 1784—January 27, 1856).

Navy Department

A major figure in the Navy for over half a century, Midshipman Morris—son of a merchant captain and Navy purser—sailed on the first cruise of the frigate *Congress,* against the French, late in 1799, only to suffer severe injuries when the vessel's mainmast gave way. Following recovery, he sailed in the frigate *Constitution* against Tripoli (1803–05) and played a key role in Decatur's burning of the *Philadelphia,* and then joined the new brig *Hornet* for a voyage to the Mediterranean (1806–07), during which he was promoted to lieutenant. He was stationed in Maine with some of Jefferson's gunboats before cruising the East coast in the frigate *President* (1809–10). Morris continued to operate in the Atlantic as first lieutenant of the *Constitution,* Capt. Isaac Hull, whom he advised and helped to outrun a British squadron led by the frigate *Guerrière* in July 1812. One month later the *Constitution* pounded the latter vessel into submission, Morris receiving more wounds in the act of unsuccessfully trying to secure the two vessels together for boarding. Promoted to captain in 1813, he commanded the converted sloop *Adams* (1813–14) and took ten prizes off the coast before being chased up the Penobscot River in Maine by a superior British force in September 1814; he landed his guns for a stand but had to set fire to his ship and retire when the local American militia abandoned him. He returned to the *Congress* as her skipper for the war against Algiers in 1815 through the Latin American revolts of 1817 when he also commanded naval forces in the Caribbean.

A tireless leader in the growth of the peacetime Navy, Commodore Morris made his most direct contribution during several tours of duty on the three-man Board of Navy Commissioners (1823–25, 1827, 1832–41). He commanded the naval stations at Portsmouth (1818, 1820) and Boston (1827–32), led a squadron to Buenos Aires in the frigate *Constellation* (1819–20) and took Lafayette home to France in the new frigate *Brandywine* (1825–26), followed by inspections of naval installations in that country and England. Hoisting his flag in the ship-of-the-line *Delaware* late in 1841 as commander of the Brazil Squadron, Morris cruised off politically-disturbed Brazil, Argentina and Uruguay until February 1843 when he sailed in his flagship to the Mediterranean to command that squadron until returning home one year later to help establish the Naval Academy. Chief of the Bureau of Construction, Equipment and Repair during the Mexican War (1844–47), he suffered the loss of his son Lt. Charles W. Morris at Tabasco, Mexico, in 1846, the latter's son Charles (1844–1912) eventually rising to the rank of brigadier general in the regular Army. After a tour as Inspector of Ordnance (1847–50), Commodore Morris served his final duty as Chief of that Bureau (1851–56). Another son, Lt. George U. Morris, commanded the frigate *Cumberland* when she was sunk by the Confederate ironclad *Merrimack* in March 1862. The commodore's posthumous *Autobiography* (1880) covers only part of his career.

Mumma, Morton Claire, Jr.

(August 24, 1904–August 14, 1968).
USNA (Iowa) 1925 (106/448).

PT boat leader Mumma became an expert rifle marksman and coach at the Academy throughout his career, which began in the Pacific with the battleship *Colorado* (BB-45) and destroyer *Marcus* (DD-321) (1926) and in the Atlantic with the *Dale* (DD-290) and the *Dallas* (DD-199) (1927). A career in submarines followed: training at New London (1927–28); based there on the subs *O-6* (SS-67) (1928–30) and *S-9* (SS-114); in both oceans with the *S-23* (SS-128) (1930–32); in command of the *S-43* (SS-154) out of Pearl Harbor (1935–38), a tour bracketed by teaching gunnery at the Academy; and fitting out and commanding the *Sailfish* (SS-192) from early 1940 to her first war patrol out of Manila in December 1941 in which she battled a Japanese convoy escort. After six months on the Asiatic Fleet submarine staff under Capt. John Wilkes, Commander Mumma was naval liaison officer with the Fifth Air Force at Port Moresby, New Guinea, until February 1943 when he was appointed Commander Motor Torpedo Boat Squadrons Seventh Fleet (originally Task Group 50.1) in the same Southwest Pacific theater. He not only directed the PT boats administratively but also patrolled with them fighting enemy planes and ships, and in November hoisted his broad pennant in the tender *Portunus* (AGP-4) at Milne Bay for intensified operations against Japanese-held New Guinea points and New Britain. Detached in February 1944, he was briefly aide to Under Secretary of the Navy James V. Forrestal and in June was promoted to captain and assigned to the Planning and Control Division in the Bureau of Naval Personnel, where he remained until relieved of all active duty in August 1946. Retired in the rank of rear admiral in December, Mumma

235

returned to active duty in the Korean War as captain (1951–53) and assistant chief planning officer at the National Headquarters of the Selective Service System in Washington. Admiral Mumma again retired in rear admiral's rank but for physical disability in April 1953.

Niblack, Albert Parker

(July 25, 1859—August 20, 1929).
USNA (Ind.) 1880 (11/62).

Convoy coordinator at Gibraltar during World War I, Niblack first served in the South Pacific aboard the screw sloop *Lackawanna* and screw gunboat *Adams* (1880–82), and then received instruction at the Smithsonian Institution to survey and explore Alaska with the Coast Survey (1884–88), during which (1887) he saved the crew of the foundered merchantman *Ocean King*. He published anthropological findings on Alaskan Indians in 1890, beginning a lifelong writing activity, especially of essays for the U.S. Naval Institute *Proceedings* during this decade. With the Squadron of Evolution aboard the protected cruiser *Chicago* (CA-14) (1889–92), he was flag lieutenant to Adm. Oscar F. Stanton, North Atlantic Squadron commander (1893–94). During the latter duty and as inspector of naval militia (1895–96), Niblack lectured on naval tactics and signaling at the Naval War College, after which (1896–98) he was American naval attaché to Germany, Italy, and Austria. During the war with Spain he participated in the Cuban blockade and action at Nipe Bay aboard the gunboat *Topeka* (PG-35), May to August 1898, and on the torpedo boat *Winslow* until November, then aboard the cruiser *Olympia* (C-6). His service in the Philippine Insurrection included action at Manila and Ilo Ilo in February 1899 aboard the protected cruiser *Boston,* in Lingayen Gulf at Vigan and Subic Bay during November

236

and December with the battleship *Oregon* (BB-3), and the punitive expedition to the Marinduque Islands in October 1900 aboard the gunboat *Castine,* having taken part with that vessel between February and August in the North China Expeditionary Force in connection with the Boxer Rebellion.

Lieutenant Commander Niblack went ashore in the Philippines in July 1901 to be secretary to the naval commission and director of naval base hydrographic surveys, and then was inspector of target practice (1902), stationed ashore at Pearl Harbor (1903), and commanding officer of the steam tug *Iroquois* (AT-46) in the Hawaiian Islands and at Midway, where he was also customs inspector (1904–06). After another year in the Pacific as executive officer of that Fleet's flagship, the *Chicago,* he was promoted to commander and given command of the Naval Academy training vessels (1907–09) and the *Tacoma* (C-18) (1909–10). Again a naval attaché—to Argentina, Brazil and Chile (1910–11), and Germany (1911–13)—Captain Niblack took command of the *Michigan* (BB-27) in 1913 off the Mexican coast, leading the third seaman regiment ashore at Vera Cruz in April 1914 and operating the next two years along the Eastern seaboard. A student at the Naval War College (1916), he next went to the General Board but with the outbreak of war commanded the First Division, then the First Squadron of Atlantic Fleet battleships, flagship *Alabama* (BB-8), his promotion to rear admiral occurring in August 1917. Three months later Admiral Niblack transferred to command of that Fleet's Second Squadron, Patrol Force, based at Gibraltar, as well as of all U. S. Naval forces there, with the responsibility of controlling all Allied convoys passing between Great Britain and the Mediterranean and into that Sea, the escort vessels being mostly American. He also successfully directed all U. S. Naval forces in the Western Mediterranean until after the end of hostilities.

Admiral Niblack commanded American naval forces in the Eastern Mediterranean and Adriatic where he was a naval commissioner during the tumultuous postwar adjustments of the winter of 1919. In April he became Director of Naval Intelligence, serving until September 1920, and spent most of the next four months as naval attaché to Britain. Promoted to vice admiral in January 1921, he assumed command over all U.S. Navy forces in European waters and finished his active duty as commander of the Sixth Naval District and the Charleston Navy Yard (1922–23). Admiral Niblack retired in July 1923 in the rank of rear admiral. The following February he became a director, and in March 1927 president, of the International Hydrographic Bureau at Monaco, the agency for which he published a book on coast signals in 1926. He also wrote *Why Wars Come* (1922) and was promoted posthumously to vice admiral on the retired list (1930).

Nimitz, Chester William

(February 24, 1885—February 20, 1966).
USNA (Tex.) 1905 (7/114).

Navy Department: National Archives

Commander-in-Chief of the Pacific Fleet during the Pacific war, the victory to which he contributed significantly as the principal Allied naval administrator, submariner Nimitz was first a naval cadet then midshipman before his January 1905 graduation, upon which as a passed midshipman he joined the new battleship *Ohio* (BB-12) on the Asiatic Station. There, 20 months later, he transferred to the cruiser *Baltimore* (C-3) and in January 1907 was commissioned ensign and given command of the recommissioned gunboat *Panay* and the naval station at Polloc for Mindanao patrolling. He shifted his crew to the destroyer *Decatur* (DD-5) six months later in the same waters but ran her aground, for which he was court-martialed and reprimanded in mid-1908. Returning home in the gunboat *Ranger,* he received submarine instruction during the first half of 1909 with the First Submarine Flotilla, flagship the sub *Plunger* (SS-2), which he also commanded, in the Atlantic. Nimitz skipped ranks in his promotion to lieutenant (senior grade) early in 1910, shortly after bringing into commission the *Snapper* (SS-16) for East coast operations where in November he took command of the *Narwhal* (SS-17) and in October 1911 additionally the Atlantic Fleet's Third Submarine Division. Detached from the latter two commands the next month, he outfitted and commanded the *E-1* (SS-24) in early 1912, heroically rescuing a drowning crewman, and kept his broad pennant in this boat as Commander Atlantic Submarine Flotilla (1912–13).

Lieutenant Nimitz became involved with the development of diesel engines for subs on trips to Germany and Belgium and for the tanker *Maumee* (AO-2), of which he eventually became her first executive and engineering officer in the Atlantic (1916–17). Promoted to lieutenant commander in August 1917, he was made engineering aide, then the following February chief of staff, to Captain Samuel S. Robison, Atlantic Fleet Submarine Force commander, flagship the cruiser *Chicago* (CA-14) at New London, with a wartime trip to the British Isles early in 1918 before his detachment in September. He later returned to Admiral Robison's staff as assistant chief of staff when that officer commanded the Battle Fleet (1923–25), flagship the battleship *California* (BB-44), and the U.S. Fleet (1925–26), flagship *Seattle* (CA-11). Lieutenant Commander Nimitz served as senior member of the Board of Submarine Design at the Navy Department (1918–19) and as exec of the *South Carolina* (BB-26) returning troops from Europe (1919–20). He then went to Pearl Harbor where he superintended construction of the submarine base and commanded Submarine Division 14 and the tender *Chicago* (1920–22), during which (1921) he was promoted to commander and after which he was stationed briefly at Mare Island aboard the transport *Argonne* (AP-4). A student at the Naval War College (1922–23), he established and commanded the Naval Reserve Officers Training Corps unit at the University of California at Berkeley (1926–29), during which, in September 1927, he was promoted to captain. He then commanded the Battle Fleet's Submarine Divisions as well as SubDiv 20 at San Diego, flagships the tenders *Argonne* (now AS-10) and *Holland* (AS-3), in April 1931 the former post being dissolved and the latter becoming ComSubDiv 12. He commanded the reserve destroyers at San Diego (1931–33) with their tender *Rigel* (AD-13).

Captain Nimitz was skipper of the *Augusta* (CA-31) in the Asiatic Fleet (1933–35); Commander Cruiser Division Two, flagship *Trenton* (CL-11), with the Battle Force (1938); and Commander Battleship Division One, flagship *Arizona* (BB-39), in the same Pacific unit (1938–39). Service with the Bureau of Navigation as Assistant Chief (1935–38) preceded his promotion to rear admiral in July 1938 and followed it when he became Chief of Bureau in June 1939. On the last day of 1941 Admiral Nimitz became Commander-in-Chief Pacific Fleet (Cincpac) in the full rank of admiral and the following April in addition Commander-in-Chief Pacific Ocean Areas (Cincpoa) at Hawaii. He was instrumental in defeating the Japanese fleet at the Battle of Midway in June 1942 and in moulding together the diverse administrative elements of the Pacific Fleet for the war against Japan. He brilliantly directed the limited offensive of 1942–43 in the Solomons and the multi-faceted Central Pacific counteroffensive of 1943–45 which defeated Japan. Promoted to fleet admiral in December 1944, he moved to advanced headquarters at Guam the following month. Admiral Nimitz signed the Japanese instrument of surrender on behalf of the United States aboard the *Missouri* (BB-63) in Tokyo Bay in September 1945 and was detached two months later. He was Chief of Naval Operations (1945–47) and from the beginning of 1948 made himself available to the Secretary of the Navy as a special assistant, serving also specifically as a goodwill ambassador of the United Nations (1949–51).

Admiral Nimitz's son, later Rear Adm. C. W. Nimitz, Jr., commanded the *Haddo* (SS-225) in the Pacific, sinking five vessels totalling over 14,500 tons in mid-1944. His son-in-law, Capt. James T. Lay, commanded the *Orleck* (DD-886) soon after the war.

Ofstie, Ralph Andrew

(November 16, 1897—November 18, 1956). USNA (Wisc.) 1919 (10/199).

Naval Photographic Center

Test pilot and naval air leader, Ofstie spent his graduation month of June 1918 on the Atlantic cruiser *Chattanooga* (C-16) before doing antisubmarine work with the destroyer *Whipple* (DD-15) out of Brest, shifting in mid-1919 to the U.S. West coast for duty in three new "tin cans": the *O'Bannon* (DD-177) as communication officer of Destroyer Squadrons Eleven and Five; the *Edsall* (DD-219); and the *Melvin* (DD-335). Flight training at Pensacola during the first half of 1922 led to service with Fighting Squadron One at San Diego; test pilot status with the Bureau of Aeronautics' Plans Division (1924–27); duty with Observation Three (later Scouting Five) as aviation officer of the *Detroit* (CL-8) in the Atlantic; head of the Flight Test Division of Naval Air Station Anacostia, D.C. (1929–32); skipper of Fighting 6 on the aircraft carrier *Saratoga* (CV-3) in the Pacific (1933–35); and navigator of the *Enterprise* (CV-6) which he helped to fit out (1937–39). Staff duty increased as Ofstie's administrative talents became known. For example, he became assistant naval attaché at Tokyo (1935–37) and London (April 1941–March 1942); flag secretary to Adm. H. E. Yarnell, commanding the Battle Force's aviation in *Saratoga* (1932–33); operations officer to Adm. W. F. Halsey, Jr., in the same flagship commanding Carrier Division One (1939–40) and in the *Yorktown* (CV-5) as Commander Aircraft Battle Force (1940–

41); a member of the U.S. Fleet staff in Washington (spring 1942); and aviation officer to Adm. C. W. Nimitz, Pacific Fleet commander (June 1942–October 1943).

Captain Ofstie took command of the *Essex* (CV-9) in November 1943 for the attack on Rabaul and the seizure of the Gilbert Islands that month, the taking of the Marshalls and the air attacks on Truk and the Carolines early in 1944, and the Marianas campaign and Battle of the Philippine Sea during the summer. Detached in August, he was immediately promoted rear admiral and made Commander [escort] Carrier Division 26; his flag usually aboard the *Kitkun Bay* (CVE-71), he led eleven escort carriers in the western Carolines, a task unit in the Philippines and the Battle for Leyte Gulf during the autumn, and the escort carrier unit at the Lingayen assault in January. ComCarDiv 23 on the West coast in the *Hoggatt Bay* (CVE-75), he then served as chief of staff to Adm. P. N. L. Bellinger, Atlantic Fleet air commander, from April to August 1945, then was senior naval member of the U.S. Strategic Bombing Survey and head of the Naval Analysis Division which early in 1946 included atomic bomb test evaluations. Admiral Ofstie, after a long tour of duty as naval member of the Military Liaison Committee to the Atomic Energy Commission (1946–50), played a major role in the Korean War: as ComCarDiv Five (August 1950–March 1951) and Commander Task Force 77, flagship *Princeton* (CV-37), covering the American withdrawal from Hungnam and interdicting North Korean and Red Chinese rail lines from December 1950 to April 1951; as chief of staff to Far Eastern Naval commander Adm. C. T. Joy (May 1951–May 1952); and as commander of the First Fleet on the U.S. West coast (June 1952–March 1953) in the rank of vice admiral. After serving as Deputy Chief of Naval Operations (Air) (1953–54), he became Commander Sixth Fleet in the Mediterranean (1955–56), flagships the heavy cruisers *Newport News* (CA-148), *Salem* (CA-139) and *Des Moines* (CA-134), only to have his career terminated by cancer. His wife was Capt. Joy Bright Hancock, director of the WAVES (1946–53), and his brother-in-law was Capt. Cooper B. Bright, prominent ship's officer on the new *Yorktown* (CV-10) in the Pacific (1943–45).

O'Kane, Richard Hetherington

(February 2, 1911——). USNA (N.H.) 1934 (264/463).

Top World War II American submarine skipper in terms of numbers of ships sunk, O'Kane did his mandatory surface line duty in the heavy cruiser *Chester* (CA-27) in the Caribbean and Pacific and the destroyer *Pruitt* (DD-347) in the latter ocean before undergoing sub training at New London in 1938. He immediately joined the minelaying sub *Argonaut* (SM-1) at Pearl Harbor but saw no action prior to his detachment in April 1942 to assist in fitting out the sub *Wahoo* (SS-238) as her executive officer from commissioning in May 1942 until July 1943. Principally under Lt. Cdr. D. W. "Mush" Morton, the *Wahoo* with O'Kane as exec sank 16 Japanese vessels totalling over 45,000 tons. In August 1943 O'Kane reported to the outfitting *Tang* (SS-306) which he commissioned in October and from January 1944 led on five brilliantly successful war patrols which performed lifeguard services for downed aviators and sank two dozen vessels for 93,800 tons, the highest of the war; he later recounted the story in *Clear the Bridge!* (1977). While attacking Japanese convoys during the Battle for Leyte Gulf in October 1944, the *Tang* was sunk by one of its own malfunctioning torpedoes, O'Kane being blown free and taken prisoner for the duration. After his release and hospitalization, Commander O'Kane commanded the sub tender *Pelias* (AS-14) and Pacific reserve ships at Mare Island (1946–48); was exec of the *Nereus* (AS-17) at San Diego; commanded Submarine Division 32, flagship *Redfish* (SS-395), in the Pacific (1949–50); was student at the Armed Forces Staff College at Norfolk (1950–51) and at the Naval War College (1955–56); and taught at the New London sub school (1951–53), the latter part of the tour as its officer-in-chief. Promoted in July 1953,

Captain O'Kane commanded the *Sperry* (AS-12) out of San Diego (1953–54) and Submarine Squadron Seven, flagship the sub rescue ship *Greenlet* (ASR-10), at Pearl Harbor and served with the Ship Characteristics Board in Washington (1956–57) prior to his retirement as rear admiral in July 1957.

Navy Department: National Archives

Oldendorf, Jesse Bartlett

(February 16, 1887–April 27, 1974).
USNA (Calif.) 1909 (141/174).

Battleship leader who capped the Japanese "T" at Surigao Strait, Leyte, in 1944, Oldendorf had several pre-World War I cruises mostly in the Pacific: the armored cruiser *California* (ACR-6), the torpedo boat destroyer *Preble* (DD-12), the cruiser *Denver* (C-14), the *Whipple* (DD-15), again on his first ship but renamed *San Diego,* and the Panama Canal hydrographic survey vessel *Hannibal* (AG-1). Following some months recruiting at Philadelphia, he had wartime duty in two ships that sank: June to August 1917 commanding the armed guard on the Army transport *Saratoga,* which suffered a collision at New York, and as gunnery officer of the troop transport *President Lincoln* from then until she was claimed by a U-boat off Ireland in May 1918. Oldendorf returned troops from France as engineering officer of the *Seattle* (ACR-11), August 1918 to March 1919, and as executive officer of the ex-German transport *Patricia* until July. Briefly in charge of the Pittsburgh recruiting station, he moved to Baltimore as an engineering inspector (1919–20) and officer in charge of the branch Hydrographic Office before joining the patrol yacht *Niagara* (PY-9) then the *Birmingham* (CL-2) in the Caribbean as flag secretary to three Special Service Squadron commanders, Adm. Casey B. Morgan, Capt. Austin Kautz

243

and Adm. William C. Cole (1921–22). He was aide to three navy yard commandants: Adm. Josiah S. McKean at Mare Island (1922–24) and Adms. Thomas P. Magruder and Julian L. Latimer at Philadelphia (1927–28), commanding the *Decatur* (DD-341) in the Pacific in the interim.

Commander Oldendorf took instruction at the Naval and Army war colleges (1928–30), navigated the battleship *New York* (BB-34) in the Eastern Pacific, taught navigation at the Naval Academy (1932–35), returned to the West coast as exec of the *West Virginia* (BB-48), and directed the recruiting section of the Bureau of Navigation (1937–39). In the rank of captain he commanded the *Houston* (CA-30) between Mare Island and Chinese waters and in September 1941 reported to the staff of the Naval War College where he remained until February 1942 when he left to command the Aruba-Curaçao defense sector in the Caribbean in the rank of rear admiral between March and July and then Naval Training Base Trinidad and its defense sector until April 1943. Commander Task Force 24—over all Western Atlantic convoy escorts, flagships destroyer tender *Prairie* (AD-15) and fleet tug *Kiowa* (ATF-72) at Argentia, Newfoundland—from May to December 1943, Admiral Oldendorf in January 1944 took command of Cruiser Division Four, flagship *Louisville* (CL-28), leading battleship-cruiser fire support task groups in support of the landings and related carrier operations in the Marshalls, Truk-Palaus, Marianas, Peleliu and Leyte Gulf. In the latter battle in October 1944 he blocked Surigao Strait and at night destroyed the Japanese "Southern" gun force in the last major surface action in history. Promoted vice admiral in December and given command of Battleship Squadron One and Battleship Division Four, flagship *California* (BB-44), Admiral Oldendorf provided fire support at Lingayen Gulf early in 1945 and after recuperating from an injury commanded Task Force 95, a special surface striking force based at Okinawa, flagship *Pennsylvania* (BB-38), during the summer, where he was wounded in a Japanese aerial torpedo attack in August. From November he commanded the Eleventh Naval District and from January 1946 also San Diego naval base and finally (1947–48) the Western Sea Frontier and "mothball" fleet at San Francisco, retirement in the rank of admiral occurring in September 1948.

Parker, Foxhall Alexander, Jr.

(August 5, 1821–June 10, 1879).

A leading tactician and writer of the Civil War and postwar periods, Virginian Parker grew up in a Navy family, the namesake of his father who had reached the rank of captain. Appointed acting midshipman in 1837, he participated in the Second Seminole War aboard three new vessels of the West Indies Squadron, the frigate *Macedonian* (1837–38), the sloop *Levant* (1838–40), and the schooner *Phoenix* (1840–43). Having received his midshipman's warrant in 1839, he reported as passed midshipman four years later to the razee *Independence,* flagship of the Home Squadron, transferring within a few months to the frigate *Potomac* in the West Indies. After duty with the steamer *Michigan* on the Great Lakes (1844–45), he became acting master of the schooner *Onkahye,* a fast converted sailing yacht in the Indies hunting for slavers off Brazil (1846–47). Parker was acting master first of the Coast Survey schooner *Gallatin* (1847–48) then of the new frigate *St. Lawrence* (1848–50), helping with his father to initiate Prussia into naval matters and reinforcing America's naval presence in the Mediterranean during the revolutions of those years. Promoted to lieutenant in 1850, he joined the sidewheel steamer *Susquehanna* on her maiden voyage as flagship of the East India Squadron (1851–52), and then returned to the Coast Survey (1853–55), principally on the steamer *Bibb,* before going onto the reserve list (1855–59).

Lieutenant Parker, after a tour in the Pacific with the sidewheel steam sloop *Saranac* (1859–61), declared his loyalty to the Union, unlike his brother, Lt. William H. Parker (1826–1896), who became eventual Superintendent of the Confederate States Naval Academy in the rank of captain. Reporting as executive officer of the Washington Navy Yard in May 1861,

Parker helped defend the river approaches to the capitol, and with Marines and sailors manned Fort Ellsworth in Alexandria following the Union army's defeat at Bull Run in July. Detached in June 1862, he was promoted to commander in August and given command of the sidewheel gunboat *Mahaska,* cruising the Chesapeake Bay and North Carolina waters, shelling Confederate positions until the following January, at which time he reported to Adm. L. M. Goldsborough in Washington for special duty which lasted until June. During this latter respite, Parker wrote his first book, *Squadron Tactics under Steam* (1864), in the tradition of his rebel brother who had translated a French naval tactical book before the war and during it wrote two basic manuals for the Confederate Navy, one on light naval artillery. Commander Parker took command of the steam frigate *Wabash* before Charleston and in the bombardment during August 1863 went ashore to Morris Island to direct the naval battery there. Detached in September, after three months he became commander of the Potomac Flotilla, flagships the sidewheeler *Ella* and later the screw steamer *Don.* He supported the army in the Wilderness Campaign and siege of Petersburg and Richmond until the end of the war and the dissolution of the Flotilla in July 1865.

After brief command of the training ship *Savannah* and duty at the Bureau of Navigation, Parker was promoted to captain in August 1866 and sent to Hartford, Connecticut, for special board duty with Commo. S. P. Lee, serving on several other boards through 1870 and as second-in-command of the Boston Navy Yard (1869–70). These light duties enabled him to continue writing his tactical treatises: *The Naval Howitzer Ashore* (1865), *The Naval Howitzer Afloat* (1866), and *Fleet Tactics under Steam* (1870), in which he promoted the oblique maneuver for ramming. He commanded the screw frigate *Franklin,* flagship of the European Squadron (1870–71), and served several months (1872) as chief of staff to Admiral Lee, commanding the North Atlantic Squadron, flagship the steam sloop *Worcester.* During the summer of 1872 he returned to the Navy Department where he drew up a new tactical signal code. His brief service on the Lighthouse Board was accompanied by his promotion to commodore early in 1873, and that July he became Chief Signal Officer of the Navy for a three-year term. Parker chaired the committee which organized the United States Naval Institute that year and early the next year served as chief of staff to Adm. A. L. Case, commanding the united squadron off Florida during the *Virginius* affair. Commander of the Boston Navy Yard (1876–78), he published two books on naval history, and in May 1878 he became Superintendent of the Naval Academy and president of the Naval Institute. Commodore Parker died on active duty.

Patterson, Daniel Todd

(March 6, 1786–August 25, 1839).

Naval Historical Foundation: Navy Department

Naval commander at the Battle of New Orleans in the War of 1812, Patterson served against the French in the West Indies aboard the converted merchantman-sloop *Delaware* as acting midshipman (1799–1801), later joining the frigate *Constellation* to blockade Tripoli in the Barbary wars (1802–03), returning hence with the frigate *Philadelphia* only to be taken with that vessel and held prisoner (1803–05). Aside from several months at New York (1807–08), Lieutenant Patterson spent an inordinately long tenure at and around New Orleans (1806–24), where however he thoroughly distinguished himself. He led a squadron of 12 gunboats based at Natchez Island which helped occupy Baton Rouge (1810–11). Following his promotion to master commandant in July 1813, Patterson in December took command of the New Orleans station and the next September used his gunboats to drive Jean Lafitte's pirates from Barataria Bay, Louisiana. As commodore of the flotilla supporting Gen. Andrew Jackson, flagship the schooner *Carolina*, he delayed the British advance on New Orleans in the sacrificial gunboat action on Lake Borgne in December and thus contributed materially to the final victory in January 1815 at which he commanded a naval battery ashore. Promoted to captain the next month, he continued in command there for nearly ten more years. Commodore Patterson became fleet captain to Commo. John Rodgers, commanding the Mediterranean Squadron in the line-of-battle ship *North Carolina*, joining that vessel at Norfolk in 1824 and going to the middle sea in the spring of 1825 where in October he was given command of the frigate *Constitution*. He continued to cruise those waters until returning home and being relieved in July 1828. Appointed a Navy Commissioner in the administration of the now President

247

Jackson in March 1829, he served three years in the post until May 1832 when he received orders to assume command of the Mediterranean Squadron. His flag first in the frigate *United States* and then in the ship-of-the-line *Delaware,* Commodore Patterson protected American interests there until given command of the Washington Navy Yard in March 1836 where he died on active duty. One son, Rear Adm. Thomas Harman Patterson (1820–1889), commanded the Asiatic Squadron (1878–80), while another, Carlile Pollock Patterson (1816–1881), had varied naval, merchant, and survey service before becoming superintendent of the U.S. Coast Survey (1874–81).

Peary, Robert Erwin

(May 6, 1856—February 20, 1920).

Naval Historical Center

Renowned Arctic explorer, Mainer Peary graduated from Bowdoin College in 1877 and served in the U.S. Coast and Geodetic Survey (1879–81) before being commissioned lieutenant in the Navy's corps of civil engineers in October 1881. He first superintended a construction project at Key West (1882–83), then did canal surveys in Nicaragua in the midst of which (1884–85, 1887–88) he took his first leaves to explore the Arctic ice, in this case Greenland, then returned to engineering duties at New York and Philadelphia (1888–91). Again on leave, he dramatically crossed Greenland by dog sledge (1891–92) which established him as a major explorer determined to reach the North Pole—an unprecedented feat. His Greenland explorations continued, thus interrupting his naval career, and the Navy's attempt to restore him to active duty in 1897 was frustrated by political manipulations which succeeded in extending his leave of absence. Commander Peary served briefly with the

248

Bureau of Yards and Docks (1903) before more leave, during which he pressed even closer to the North Pole. He finally succeeded in April 1909, although his claim has been disputed over the years and the credit also claimed by an unconvincing rival. In recognition of his achievement, Congress in March 1911 passed a special act promoting him to the rank of rear admiral on the retired list in the civil engineer corps. From 1913 until the end of his life Admiral Peary devoted himself to the advancement of aviation, and in 1917 he became chairman of the National Committee on Coast Defense by Air. He published a number of works relating to his Arctic activities.

Perry, Matthew Calbraith "Old Bruin"

(April 10, 1794—March 4, 1858).

Navy Department: National Archives

The man who opened Japan and concluded the naval war against Mexico, Perry followed his father, Capt. Christopher R. Perry (1761–1818), and brother, Lt. Oliver Hazard Perry *(q.v.),* into the Navy in 1809 as midshipman on the latter's ship, the schooner *Revenge,* cruising the East coast until October 1810 when he transferred to the frigate *President,* Commo. John Rodgers, soon becoming aide to the latter. Under Rodgers' tutelage, he participated in the incident involving battle with the British sloop *Little Belt* in May 1811, was wounded in the chase of the frigate *Belvidera* in June 1812, cruised the North Atlantic late in that year and to Europe the following spring, was advanced to acting lieutenant in February 1813, and transferred in November to the frigate *United States* blockaded at New London. Perry rejoined the *President* defending New York from April through December 1814, then joined his brother in Rhode Island for service on the brig *Chippewa,* which was fitting out. He sailed in that vessel in Bainbridge's squadron to and from the Mediterranean throughout 1815, followed by a furlough as master of a merchantman (owned by his father) to Holland (1816–17). Ashore at the New York Navy Yard (1817–19), he was executive officer of the frigate *Cyane* convoying the first American Negro colonists to Liberia and operating against slavers and pirates there (1819–21).

Lieutenant Perry brought the schooner *Shark* into service as her skipper in June 1821, took the American Liberia agent Eli Ayers to his post, patrolled the West Indies against slaving and pirate vessels—taking five—during 1822, occupied and claimed Key West for the United States that March, and cruised West African waters late in the year and to Mexico during the first part of 1823. Detached from the *Shark* in August, he spent a year with the receiving ship *Fulton* at New York before joining the new ship-of-the-line *North Carolina* as exec in September 1824. As flagship for Commo. Rodgers of the Mediterranean Squadron (1825–27), this vessel protected American shipping from pirates during the Greek war of independence in which Perry—promoted to master commandant in March 1826—played a key role in helping to quench a devastating fire at Smyrna. Taken ill by this strenuous duty which permanently impaired his health, Perry commanded the naval rendezvous at Boston (1827–30) before assuming command of the fitting-out sloop *Concord* in April 1830. He conveyed envoy John Randolph to Russia and met the czar who offered him a naval commission which he declined. The *Concord* reached the Mediterranean in July 1832, with Perry briefly commanding the frigate *Brandywine* for the 1833 demonstration before Naples over a diplomatic dispute and coming home in December. He was second-in-command at New York (1833–37) where he developed the Navy's apprentice system, initiated and led the U.S. Naval Lyceum at Brooklyn and *Naval Magazine,* and helped to lay the groundwork for the South Seas Exploring Expedition, command of which he declined.

Captain Perry (as he was promoted in February 1837) applied his vigorous mind to modernizing the Navy to steam propulsion, becoming the leader of the effort and organizing the naval engineer corps while bringing into commission the Navy's first sidewheel war steamer *Fulton* during 1837, commanding her until June 1838. Using observations from abroad and at home, he pioneered in the development of American lighthouses and steam warships and of modern ordnance and gunnery practice, the latter work at Sandy Hook and on the *Fulton* (1837–40). He continued in these roles as commandant of the New York Navy Yard (1841–43) and in May 1843 became the first commander of the new African Squadron, flagship the new sloop *Saratoga* until September, then the frigate *Macedonian.* Returning to Liberian waters after an absence of two decades, Commodore Perry punished native African tribes which had been harassing the settlers of Liberia and further discouraged the slave trade. Detached during the spring of 1845, he helped to develop the first curriculum for the new U.S. Naval Academy, serving on its board of examiners. He inspected merchant steamers and docks at New York from December 1845 until May 1846, outfitted and took two vessels to the Gulf of Mexico and in October took command of the sidewheel steam frigate *Mississippi* whose construction (with the *Missouri*) he had superintended over five years before.

Commodore Perry acted as second-in-command and prospective commander of the Home Squadron while captain of the *Mississippi* in the war against Mexico. By his vigorous leadership, he led the expeditions which took Frontera and Tabasco in October and Carman in December 1846 and participated in the capture of Tampico in November. While the *Mississippi* underwent repairs at Norfolk during the winter of 1847, her captain supervised the outfitting of several smaller vessels. Perry assumed command of the Home Squadron, flagship *Mississippi,* at the height of the Vera Cruz landings and siege in March 1847, assisted the Army in taking that port and other positions, took Tuxpan in April and retook Tabasco in June, kept Yucatan neutral, and maintained the blockade until hostilities ended. Shifting his flag to the frigate *Cumberland* during the summer of 1848, he transferred in November to the post of Superintendent of Ocean Mail Steamers under construction, headquarters New York, remaining there until March 1852. Ordered to command the East India Squadron, he delayed this by resuming command of the *Mississippi* in May 1852 and cruising to the Canadian maritime provinces to help soothe Anglo-American relations over the fisheries question during the summer.

In January 1852 Commodore Perry had been selected to lead an imposing naval force to Japan, to initiate discussions with that isolated country, and to open it to normal trade and diplomatic intercourse, building on the foundations laid by Cdr. James Glynn (1801–1871) three years before. Maintaining his flag on the *Mississippi* as commander of the East India Squadron, he departed Norfolk in November 1852 and travelled to China where he shifted his flag to the sidewheeler *Susquehanna.* Perry entered Tokyo Bay in July 1853, delivered his diplomatic notes and departed for China, returning to Japan the following February to consummate the treaty at Yokohama in March. This done, Perry sailed to Hong Kong, where he was relieved in September 1854. He returned home on a British steamer to complete his lengthy report (1856) and to serve on the Efficiency Board. His active service ended in 1855. Through his sister he was related by marriage to the Rodgers naval family *(q.v.).*

Perry, Oliver Hazard

(August 20, 1785—August 23, 1819).

By J. W. Jarvis: U. S. Naval Academy Museum: Naval Photographic Center

Victor at the Battle of Lake Erie in the War of 1812, Perry went to sea as midshipman on the new frigate *General Greene,* commanded by his father Capt. Christopher R. Perry (1761–1818), a distinguished Revolutionary War veteran, in April 1799, attacked French shipping in the West Indies, and supported the Haitian revolutionaries until the ship was retired in June 1801. He participated in the blockade of Tripoli aboard the frigate *Adams* (1802–03) and in combined operations against that Barbary port, then on subsequent peacetime Mediterranean patrols with the frigates *Constellation,* as acting second lieutenant, and *Constitution* and command of the schooner *Nautilus* (1804–06), returning home as second lieutenant of the frigate *Essex.* Promoted to a permanent lieutenancy in April 1807, he assisted in the construction and then took command of a gunboat flotilla in his native Rhode Island and in Connecticut to enforce Jefferson's embargo (1807–09). Perry assumed command of the schooner *Revenge* in April 1809, its crew including his younger brother Midshipman Matthew C. Perry *(q.v.),* and after the embargo operated along the entire Eastern seaboard. In July 1810 he boldly retook the American vessel *Diana* from her Spanish captors at Amelia Island, Spanish Florida, and brought her home with a prize crew. The *Revenge* surveyed New England and Long Island coastal waters until she ran aground on a reef during a fog and was abandoned in January 1811 (blame for which he was cleared.)

Lieutenant Perry resumed gunboat duty by taking command, headquarters Newport, of those building at Westerly, Rhode Island, and Norwich, Connecticut, in March 1811, during which tour of duty 17 months later he was promoted to master commandant. Chafing for sea duty, he finally received orders to Lake Erie in February 1813, arriving at Erie, Pennsylvania, to begin building and assembling his squadron, save for his participation in the capture of Fort George on Lake Ontario during May. Hoisting his flag on the brig *Lawrence* in August, he sortied with his ten vessels to challenge the British force of six. They met in September in the Battle of Lake Erie, the flagship being so heavily damaged in mid-action that Perry shifted to the brig *Niagara,* from which he received the surrender of the enemy squadron—the only time in history a British fleet was captured by the United States. He supported the army of Gen. William Henry Harrison in the capture of Detroit and was the general's aide at the battle of the Thames. Perry resigned his command in October and the next month received the promotion to captain and command of the Newport Flotilla. Assigned to command of the uncompleted frigate *Java* in July 1814, he remained blockaded at Baltimore but led a battery against the British warships on the Potomac in September. After supervising warship construction in Rhode Island, he demonstrated before the Barbary states and cruised the Mediterranean in the *Java* (1816–17). Commodore Perry commanded at Newport until the spring of 1819 when he hoisted his flag in the frigate *John Adams* and led a small squadron to cement relations with the new nation of Venezuela. Transferred to the schooner *Nonsuch* in July, he carried out diplomatic negotiations, after which he returned to the *Nonsuch* and died on board of yellow fever.

Porter, David

(February 1, 1780—March 3, 1843).

By Thomas Sully: U. S. Naval Academy Museum: Naval Photographic Center

War of 1812 luminary and commander of the early Mexican Navy, Porter was born into a merchant seafaring family and followed his father to sea. The elder David Porter (1754–1808) rose to sailing master in the Navy after privateering during the Revolution and took his son on the first of several West Indian cruises in 1796, both of them under fire by a British warship on one occasion. Young David became midshipman in April 1798 for duty in the same waters on the first voyage of the frigate *Constellation,* during which the next February she engaged and took the French frigate *Insurgente.* Promoted to lieutenant in October 1799 he sailed in the schooner *Experiment* against French West Indian pirates, commanded a prize schooner, and on the first day of 1800 was wounded during the seven-hour battle with and repulse of eleven pirate vessels which had attacked the convoy under *Experiment*'s charge off Santo Domingo. Three of the four merchantmen were captured and two pirate vessels were sunk in the action. In 1801, the war with Barbary Tripoli having begun, he became first lieutenant then captain of the schooner *Enterprise,* later took ashore a raiding party at Tripoli, served as first lieutenant of the frigates *New York* and *Philadelphia,* and was captured when the latter ship ran aground in the harbor of Tripoli in October 1803. He remained imprisoned until June 1805.

Lieutenant Porter acted as captain of the frigate *Constitution* then was captain of the *Enterprise,* both in the middle sea, being promoted to master commandant in 1806. Named commander of the naval forces at New Orleans (1808–10), as successor to his late father, he gained a ward in the young David G. Farragut *(q.v.).* Porter took command of the frigate *Essex* in 1811, became captain the next year and attacked British shipping near

254

Bermuda, taking ten prizes including a troop transport and the sloop *Alert*. The first American Naval vessel to enter the Pacific, the *Essex* ranged an unprecedented distance throughout 1813, its base at the Galápagos Islands, taking two privateer schooners and 13 whalers, one of which Porter converted into a 20-gun warship, *Essex Junior,* under his first lieutenant John Downes. The two vessels, supplied by their captures, refitted in the Marquesas Islands, where they became embroiled in the native wars, then sortied to Chile to give battle to a newly-arrived British squadron. Blockaded on that coast in January 1814 by two enemy frigates, Porter tried to escape in March, only to be damaged in a gale then pounded into surrender by his adversaries during a prolonged engagement. Paroled home on the *Essex Junior,* he joined in the defense of the Potomac River in September by leading a ground force against the retiring British. After briefly commanding the uncompleted experimental steamer *Fulton* during early 1815, in April he became one of the first Navy Commissioners, a post he occupied until December 1822.

Appointed commander of the West Indies Squadron early in 1823, Commodore Porter operated against pirates in his flagship, the sloop *Peacock,* for two years; his brother, later Master Commandant John Porter, commanded the schooner *Greyhound* in this force. For retaliating with a landing force against the Spanish government of Puerto Rico which had harassed his activities, he was recalled and court-martialed, which he accentuated by insubordinate letters and other actions. Though lightly sentenced, he resigned in protest during the summer of 1826 and became commander-in-chief of the Mexican Navy with the rank of general of marine in the struggle for independence from Spain. Late in the year he led a four-ship squadron against Spanish shipping, operating illegally out of neutral Key West. During 1827–28 he used his warships principally as commerce raiders, while he remained at Vera Cruz, his son Midshipman David D. Porter *(q.v.)* seeing considerable action. Compromised by political intrigue, in 1829 he left Mexico and declined offers to return to U.S. Naval duty. Instead he served his country as a diplomat, consul-general at Algiers and chargé d'affaires then minister to Ottoman Turkey. He authored *Journal of a Cruise Made to the Pacific Ocean* (1815). In addition to his famous sons, Adms. David D. Porter and the adopted David G. Farragut, his son Commo. William D. Porter (1809–1864) commanded the ironclad gunboat *Essex* in the operations which led to the destruction of the Confederate ram *Arkansas* during the summer of 1862. Another son, Army Lt. Theodoric Porter, was the first American officer to be killed in the Mexican War (1846), and yet another, Navy Lt. Henry O. Porter, was captured on the blockader *Hatteras* as her executive officer in the engagement with the rebel raider *Alabama* in 1863.

Porter, David Dixon

(June 8, 1813—February 13, 1891).

Bureau of Ships: Navy Department

Civil War hero and the dominant figure of the postwar Navy, this son of David Porter (*q.v.*) accompanied his father to the West Indies Squadron (1823) and served as midshipman in the Mexican warships *Esmeralda* and *Guerrero* (1826–28), the latter under his cousin Lt. David H. Porter, falling prisoner to the Spanish frigate *Lealtad* following a furious battle in which his captain was killed. After his release, early in 1829 he was appointed midshipman in the U.S. Navy for Mediterranean duty aboard the frigate *Constellation* (1829–31). After leave he joined the Mediterranean flagship *United States* (1832–34), where he met and later married the daughter of the squadron commander, Commo. D. T. Patterson. Following promotion to passed midshipman at the Philadelphia receiving ship (1835), he served the next several years (1836–42) with the U.S. Coast Survey, in Washington and aboard the vessel *Jersey* (1836, 1837) where he did important hydrographic work leading to his lieutenancy (1841). Porter helped bring the frigate *Congress* into service from April 1842, splitting a three-year cruise evenly between the Mediterranean and Brazil squadrons. During a tour (1845–46) at the Navy's Hydrographic Office, he spent several months analyzing the political climate in the Dominican Republic for the State Department.

Lieutenant Porter went into Mexican War duty as recruiting officer at New Orleans in November 1846, but the next February he took some of his charges to the Home Squadron off Vera Cruz where he was made first lieutenant of the sidewheel gunboat *Spitfire* in time to participate in the attack on the city and personally lead a dangerous reconnaisance in a ship's boat. After fighting at Alvarado and Tuxpan, he stormed and took the fort at Tabasco with a naval brigade in June 1847. His reward was command of the

256

Spitfire, during the summer, followed by ship purchasing duty and hydrographic work at the Naval Observatory and with the Coast Survey commanding its vessel *Petrel* from August 1848 till October 1849. Porter went on leave to command the merchantman *Panama* in the Pacific (1849–50), the mail steamer *Georgia* in the Atlantic (1850–53), and the fast steamer *Golden Age* on the Australia run (1853–55). He was restored to active duty during the spring of 1855 and given command of the storeship *Supply,* with which he ferried camels from Turkey to Texas for the U.S. Army and during which voyage he observed naval operations of the Crimean War. Detached in February 1857, he reported to the Portsmouth Navy Yard to become a member of the board to examine navy yards until the board was dissolved in mid-1859. He stayed on as first lieutenant at Portsmouth until detached in July 1860 and for a month commanded the frigate *Constitution* training midshipmen at the Naval Academy. On waiting orders and still only a lieutenant, he tired of his plight and planned to return to merchant activity in the Pacific after brief Coast Survey work there, to which he was ordered in September.

On the eve of his planned departure in April 1861 Porter was suddenly given command of the sidewheeler *Powhatan,* with which he helped to relieve Fort Pickens near Pensacola, blockaded Mobile and the Southwest Pass of the Mississippi, and searched the West Indies and South Atlantic for the Confederate raider *Sumter* throughout the spring, summer, and autumn, his promotion to commander coming in August. He left the *Powhatan* in November and the next month took command of the Mortar Flotilla, flagship the sidewheeler *Harriet Lane,* preparing for the attack on New Orleans with the fleet under his adopted brother Flag Off. David G. Farragut. Late in April 1862 the Flotilla engaged Forts Jackson and St. Philip below the city and forced their surrender and two months later covered Farragut's run past Vicksburg. Having bypassed the rank of lieutenant commander he now did the same with those of captain and commodore by being appointed to command the Mississippi Squadron in October 1862 in the rank of acting rear admiral. His flag aboard the newly-commissioned sidewheeler *Black Hawk,* Porter supported Grant's army in the Vicksburg Campaign, playing a conspicuous role in the capture of Arkansas Post in January 1863 and through the siege and capture of Vicksburg in July, at which time he was promoted to rear admiral. In August he took over the entire Mississippi from Cairo to New Orleans, dividing it into naval districts and coordinating the lot with great administrative skill. During the spring of 1864 he led the naval element of the unsuccessful Red River expedition and executed a masterful retreat.

Admiral Porter took command of the North Atlantic Blockading Squadron, flagship the steamer *Malvern,* in October 1864 and was charged with supporting the Army in the capture of Fort Fisher, North Carolina. The initial amphibious effort in December failed but that in January 1865 did not, his fleet of over 60 vessels being the largest to date in American history. Shifting to the James River in his flagship, he was with Grant's army when it took Richmond in April and later that month was detached. After several weeks on the Board of Visitors to the Naval Academy, he spent much of August as ad interim Chief of the Bureau of Navigation, at the end of the month receiving his long-desired appointment as Superintendent of the Naval Academy. He reformed the curriculum and revitalized the entire system there during his tenure, which lasted until late 1869. Porter was promoted to vice admiral in July 1866 and during part of 1866–67 participated in a diplomatic mission to Santo Domingo. Under President Grant in 1869 he became "adviser" to Secretary of the Navy Adolph E. Borie and as such virtually ran the Navy, instituting many general reforms, some of them distinctly unpopular, although his rule waned after 1871. Porter achieved the rank of admiral in August 1870, spent most of his time in Washington from 1870 to 1873 "on special duty," commanded the fleet at Key West during the *Virginius* affair in 1873, and late in 1876 inspected navy yards. In March 1877 he became Head of the Board of Inspection and remained there until his death 14 years later, having little impact during these years on the direction of the Navy.

Founding president of the U.S. Naval Institute in 1873, Admiral Porter wrote a great deal on naval matters, especially in *The United Service,* and autobiographical history (plus some undistinguished novels), notably *Memoir of Commodore David Porter* (1875), *Incidents and Anecdotes of the Civil War* (1885) and *Naval History of the Civil War* (1886). In addition to his distinguished father, father-in-law Patterson and brother-by-adoption Farragut, Porter had other broad Navy family connections, among them his cousin David H. and brother William D. Porter (see above); son Commo. Theodoric Porter (1849–1920) who commanded the armored cruiser *Washington)* (ACR-11) in 1907–08; and grandson Marine Corps Maj. Gen. David D. Porter (1878–1944), who was conspicuous during the Philippine Insurrection. His first cousin was Maj. Gen. Fitz-John Porter of the Second Battle of Bull Run controversy.

Pratt, William Veazie

(February 28, 1869—November 25, 1957). USNA (Me.) 1889 (6/35).

The leading inter-world war admiral, Pratt followed a merchant skipper grandfather and master's mate father to sea, beginning in the new Squadron of Evolution aboard the protected cruiser *Atlanta* (1889–90) and un-protected cruiser *Chicago* (1890–91), and then going to the Far East via the cruiser *Philadelphia* (C-4) (1891), the gunboat *Petrel* (PG-2), and the steam sloop *Lancaster* (1891–95). He taught mathematics at the Naval Academy (1895–97, 1900–02) and cruised to the Caribbean in the new training gunboat *Annapolis* (PG-10) (1897–98) before Spanish-American War duty aboard the converted yacht *Mayflower* (PY-1) and acted as prize master of a captured British blockade runner, being promoted to lieutenant (j.g.) at year's end and lieutenant early the next. Pratt served aboard the protected cruiser *Newark* (C-1) in the Pacific and against the Filipinos (1899–1900), remaining there with the gunboat *Bennington* (PG-4) and then the monitor *Monadnock.* Instructing midshipmen on the battleship *Indiana* (BB-1) (1901), he operated in the North Atlantic as a watch officer of the *Kearsarge* (BB-5) (1902–05) and in the rank of lieutenant commander taught navigation at the Academy (1905–08), navigating one summer on the *Newark.* Executive officer of the cruisers *St. Louis* (C-20) (1908–10) and *California* (ACR-6) in the Pacific, he began the latter tour as commander and ended it with assignment to teach at the Naval War College (1911–13), where he became closely associated with Capt. W. S. Sims. He was thereafter the latter's aide in the Atlantic Torpedo Flotilla, flagships the tender *Dixie* (AD-1) and the cruiser *Birmingham* (CL-2), of which Pratt took command early in 1914 and led during the Mexican crisis of that year.

An occasional lecturer at the Naval War College, Pratt became captain in mid-1915 and spent a year at the Panama Canal Zone (1915–16) and another at the Army War College, toward the end of which he assumed temporary duties on the staff of the Chief of Naval Operations, Adm. W. S. Benson, beginning full-time duties as Assistant CNO in June 1917. In this post he communicated closely with Admiral Sims in Europe and helped importantly to shape American naval policy during World War I, being Acting CNO during Benson's absence in Europe during the autumn of 1918. In January 1919 Captain Pratt transferred to command of the *New York* (BB-34) for operations in both oceans and in November 1920 to the post of Commander Destroyer Force Pacific Fleet, flagship *Charleston* (CA-19). The following June he was promoted to rear admiral and assigned to the General Board. Appointed president of the Naval War College (1925–27), Pratt proved to be a major innovator in its curriculum, but his most notable successes were his successive U.S. Fleet sea-going commands leading to the top: Battleship Division Four, flagship *Pennsylvania* (BB-38) (1923–25); Battleship Divisions Battle Fleet in the *West Virginia* (BB-48) in the rank of vice admiral (1927–28); Commander Battle fleet, flagship *California* (BB-44), in the rank of admiral (1928–29); and Commander-in-Chief United States Fleet, flagship *Texas* (BB-35) (1929–30). Admiral Pratt attended the London Naval Conference of 1930 and in September of that year became Chief of Naval Operations, a post he occupied during the lean Depression years until July 1933, at which time he retired as admiral. A prolific essayist, he returned briefly to active duty to study and recommend antisubmarine measures (1941).

His nephews were Rear Adm. Richard R. Pratt, who commanded the destroyer *Hudson* (DD-475) throughout the Pacific counteroffensive (1943–45), and Capt. W. V. Pratt II, skipper of the *Grayson* (DD-435) in the same campaigns.

By Rembrandt Peale: Navy Department

Preble, Edward

(August 15, 1761—August 25, 1807).

A principal commander during the Barbary wars, Maine-born Preble ran away to sea during the Revolutionary War, sailing to Europe on a privateer in 1777 and returning two years later as midshipman on the Massachusetts state frigate *Protector,* on which he fought several actions until captured in 1781. After imprisonment at New York and his release, he became lieutenant on the Massachusetts sloop *Winthrop,* which took five prizes during 1782, and left the ship with the end of the war the next year. During the years between the Revolution and the quasi-war with France, Preble was a merchant sailor and once a prisoner of pirates. Commissioned lieutenant in the U.S. Navy and given command of the brig *Pickering* in January 1799, he heavily engaged and took the stronger French privateer *L'Egypte Conquise* in the West Indies before relief and promotion to captain in May. He brought frigate *Essex* into service as her first captain later in the year and during 1800 convoyed American merchantmen in the Indian Ocean and East Indies, the first American warship ever to operate in those distant waters. Returning in November, he required an extensive rest to improve his health, being unable to command the frigate *Adams* which was offered him early in 1802.

Assigned command of the Mediterranean Squadron, flagship the frigate *Constitution,* in May 1803, Commodore Preble sailed in August to make war on Barbary Tripoli. He arranged a peace settlement with Morocco under a show of force in November, planned the successful destruction of the captured frigate *Philadelphia* over the winter, and blockaded Tripoli, which port his squadron bombarded and assaulted several times during August 1804. Though the assaults failed, Preble's force sank three and captured three Barbary vessels, but early in September Preble was relieved of command. A stern and respected disciplinarian, the older commodore had welded his younger captains, among them Decatur, Bainbridge, Rodgers, Hull, and Porter, into an effective cadre of excellent naval leaders: "Preble's boys." Although next assigned to construct gunboats, Commodore Preble before long succumbed to his deteriorating health. His nephew was Rear Adm. George H. Preble (1816–1885) who commanded the South Pacific Squadron from 1876 to 1878.

Price, John Dale

(May 18, 1892–December 18, 1957).
USNA (Ark.) 1916 (137/177).

Navy Department: National Archives

Patrol aviation leader before and during World War II, Price did not enter the Navy's air arm until he had served in the line: two flagships of the Pacific Fleet, the armored cruisers *San Diego* (ACR-6) until early 1917 and *Pittsburgh* (ACR-4) the rest of the year; the mine planter *Quinnebaug* (SP-1687) as gunnery and mining officer from the precommissioning detail through the laying of the North Sea Mine Barrage till February 1919; and the battleship *North Dakota* (BB-29) on the East coast. After flight training at Pensacola (1919–20), he operated seaplanes out of Hampton Roads and then (1921–22) inspected naval planes at McCook Field in Dayton, Ohio. Several months at the Naval Aircraft Factory in Philadelphia followed, as well as (1923) duty flying scout planes off the *Maryland* (BB-46) on the West coast. At the end of 1923 Lieutenant Price embarked on nearly a year of setting air records in seaplanes at Anacostia, shifting to experimental night flying from the aircraft carrier *Langley* (CV-1) off the California coast (1924–26). He helped to fit out the *Saratoga* (CV-3) and served aboard her in the

Pacific before commanding Naval Air Reserve Station Sand Point, Seattle (1928–30). While next attached to the seaplane tender *Jason* (AV-2) in the Asiatic Fleet, he briefly, in the summer of 1931, commanded that fleet's aircraft squadrons and the flagship *Jason* in the rank of lieutenant commander.

With the Bureau of Aeronautics in the Plans and Flight divisions (1932–34), Price was operations officer first to Adm. Henry V. Butler, Commander Aircraft Squadrons at Pearl Harbor, then (1935–37) to Adms. Frederick J. Horne and E. J. King, Commanders Aircraft Battle Force, in the Pacific on the *Wright* (AV-1). He was promoted to commander in 1936. He then returned to Anacostia as executive officer and (1938–39) commanding officer, followed by command of Patrol Wing Three at Coco Solo, Panama Canal Zone, until March 1941, when he left to become skipper of the *Pocomoke* (AV-9) during her final weeks of precommissioning. Commander Price assumed command of PatWing Eight from its commissioning at Norfolk in the summer of 1941, transferring with it in December to NAS Alameda where he took on the additional duty of Commander Aircraft Northern Sector, Western Sea Frontier in March 1942. Promoted to captain, he commanded NAS Jacksonville from June to February, then upon his elevation to rear admiral took command of Fleet Air Wing Two in March 1943 at NAS Kaneohe, Hawaii, and spent most of the next 24 months training patrol plane crews in Hawaii for the Central Pacific. During January and February 1944, however, Admiral Price personally led Patrol Bombing Squadron 102 (PB2Y Coronados) in five bombing raids on Wake Island in conjunction with the Marshalls campaign. In April 1945 he took command of Fleet Air Wing One, flagship *Curtiss* (AV-4), in the Okinawa operation and introduced the "Bat" surface-to-air guided missile against enemy targets. Detached in July, after his flagship had been disabled by a kamikaze, he took command of Naval Operating Base Okinawa for the final weeks of the Pacific war.

Admiral Price commanded Alameda's Fleet Air (1946) and the Pacific Fleet's Air Force (1946–48), promotion to vice admiral taking place in August 1946. He was Deputy Chief of Naval Operations (Air) (1948–49) and Vice CNO (1949–50) then Chief of Naval Air Training at Pensacola until his retirement in the full rank of admiral in June 1954.

Pride, Alfred Melville "Mel"

(September 10, 1897–—   ).

The first officer to rise from enlisted rating to vice admiral, Massachusetts-native Pride joined the Navy in March 1917 for World War I service as machinist's mate second class on the armed motorboat *Wild Goose* and from October at the Boston enrolling office where he was promoted to chief quartermaster in March 1918 and allowed to serve with the naval air detachment at the Massachusetts Institute of Technology. Taking flight training at Miami, he was commissioned ensign in the Naval Reserve Flying Corps in September 1918 and assigned to Naval Air Station Montchic-Lacanau in France just before the war ended. Ordnance officer at NAS Chatham, Massachusetts, throughout most of 1919, with promotion to lieutenant (j.g.) in April, he underwent further flight training at Carlstrom Field, Arcadia, Florida, late in the year and at year's end reported to the Atlantic Fleet's Ships Plane Division for testing duties at NAS Hampton Roads, Mitchel Field on Long Island and the battleship *Arizona* (BB-39). Pride, promoted to lieutenant in July 1920, transferred into the regular Navy in that rank in November 1921 and developed the arresting gear for the Navy's first aircraft carrier, *Langley* (CV-1), at Norfolk (1922–24). A student of aeronautical engineering at the Annapolis Postgraduate School (1924–25) and at M.I.T. (1925–26), he participated in the outfitting of the *Saratoga* (CV-3) for a few weeks and of the *Lexington* (CV-2), remaining on board as part of the ship's company and pilot until placed in charge of the experimental detachment at Hampton Roads (1929–32), where in 1931 he landed an autogiro (early helicopter) on the *Langley*.

Promoted lieutenant commander in July 1931, Pride flew off the *Langley* in command of Fighting Squadron Three-B (1932–34) and directed flight testing at Anacostia, going on—despite a serious leg injury suffered in a plane crash—to the Fighter Desk at the Bureau of Aeronautics (1936–37) and then the Pacific as air officer of the seaplane tender *Wright* (AV-1). Four months after his June 1938 promotion to commander he became operations officer to Commander Patrol Wing One, Adm. Charles A. Blakely, flagship *Wright* at San Diego, then returned to BuAer on the Aeronautical Board (1939–41). Commander Price became exec of the *Saratoga* in May 1941 but missed seeing real action because of her torpedoing the following January and his detachment in June. He spent several weeks in the Office of Procurement and Material before going to BuAer in July, with promotion to captain in September 1942. Reporting to the fitting out light carrier *Belleau Wood* (CVL-24) in January 1943, he commissioned her two months later and led her in the early Central Pacific operations at Baker, Tarawa, and Wake (September–October 1943), the Gilberts and Marshalls invasions and related air strikes (November 1943–February 1944), and Task Force 58's western Carolines raids (March–April). Promoted to rear admiral in March 1944, he commanded the Naval Air Center at Pearl Harbor from April to September and then the naval air bases of the Fourteenth Naval District in Hawaii until March 1945.

Admiral Pride took command of the Air Support Control Unit of the Fifth Fleet's amphibious forces in April 1945, flagship the amphibious command ship *Eldorado* (AGC-11), and directed air support at Okinawa through the end of the war and until his detachment in December. In charge of the Material Control Branch at the Navy Department (1946), he successfully commanded, but only briefly, Carrier Divisions Six and Four before his lengthy tenure as Chief of BuAer (1947–51). Commander of CarDiv Two in the Atlantic (1951–52), flagships *Franklin D. Roosevelt* (CVB-42) and *Leyte* (CV-32), he then commanded the naval air test center at Patuxent River and in October 1953 was advanced to the rank of vice admiral and two months later given command of the Seventh Fleet, flagships successively *Wisconsin* (BB-64), *Rochester* (CA-124), *St. Paul* (CA-73), *Helena* (CA-75), and *Eldorado,* for two years protecting Formosa from Communist Chinese threats and in 1955 directing the evacuation of the Tachen Islands. Admiral Pride was Commander Air Force Pacific Fleet (1956–59) and retired in the rank of admiral in October 1959.

Raborn, William Francis, Jr. "Red"

(June 8, 1905——). USNA (Okla.)
1928 (140/173).

Naval Photographic Center

Father of the Polaris strategic missile system, Raborn had mandatory line duty in the battleship *Texas* (BB-35) in the Pacific (1928–32) and the destroyers *Twiggs* (DD-127) and *Dickerson* (DD-157) before receiving training as a naval aviator at Pensacola (1933–34) and assignment to Fighting Squadron Five on the aircraft carrier *Lexington* (CV-2), with a cold weather cruise to Alaska in the *Ranger* (CV-4) early in 1936. With Scouting 11 and 10 on the cruiser *Portland* (CA-33) in the Pacific (1936–37), he returned to Pensacola as pilot instructor with Training Five before going to San Diego for a tour of duty in Patron 11 and in November 1941 to the staff of Patrol Wing One there. This soon moved to Naval Air Station Kaneohe, Hawaii, where he fought attacking Japanese planes in December and where the following March he established the Aviation Free Gunnery School. He remained in charge of it until March 1943 when he became Head of the Aviation Gunnery Training Division in the Navy Department. At the end of November 1944 Commander Raborn reported as executive officer of the *Hancock* (CV-19) and participated in fast carrier operations in the Philippines, at Iwo Jima and Okinawa and against the Japanese homeland. Promoted to captain, he became chief of staff to Adm. Frederick W. McMahon, Commander Carrier Division Two and Commander Task Force 38, flagship *Princeton* (CV-37), in both oceans (1946–47). Duty followed as operations officer to Commander Fleet Air West Coast, Adm. W. Keen Harrill, at San Diego (1947–49).

After a tour at the Bureau of Ordnance developing guided missiles, Captain Raborn commanded the antisubmarine carrier *Bairoko* (CVE-115) in Korean and Formosan waters between November 1950 and August 1951, then attended the Naval War College. In July 1952 he became assistant director of the Navy's Guided Missile Division, working there until April 1954. Skipper of the *Bennington* (CVA-20) in the Atlantic, he left early in 1955 to become assistant chief of staff for operations to Atlantic Fleet commander Adm. Jerauld Wright. Promoted to rear admiral in December, he at that time assumed the directorship of the Navy's Special Projects, the Office which he established, his task being the development of the Fleet Ballistic Missile System for strategic nuclear warheads. Admiral Raborn's technological and organizational genius enabled him to discard the ineffective liquid-fuel Jupiter missile and in early 1957 to shift to the solid-fuel Polaris for underwater-launching from nuclear-powered submarines. He and the Special Projects staff achieved success with the deployment in 1960 of the first Polaris-armed boat, the *George Washington* (SSBN-598). His reward that year was promotion to vice admiral in January and in March 1962 appointment as Deputy Chief of Naval Operations (Development), a post he held until he retired in September 1963. Admiral Raborn returned later to active duty to be Director of the Central Intelligence Agency (1965–66).

Radford, Arthur William

(February 27, 1896–August 18, 1973).
USNA (Iowa) 1916 (59/177).

Navy Department: National Archives

Pacific Fleet commander during the Korean War, naval aviation leader Radford went directly to the battleship *South Carolina* (BB-26) for East coast cruising and one Atlantic convoy in September 1918. Reassigned in December as flag lieutenant to Atlantic Battleship Division One commanders Adms. Carlo B. Brittain, John A. Hoogewerff, and Roger Welles, flagships *Alabama* (BB-8), *Missouri* (BB-11) and *Wisconsin* (BB-9), he also held that post on the staffs of ComBatDiv One in the Pacific, Adm. Clarence S. Williams, flagships *Virginia* (BB-13), *Rhode Island* (BB-17) and *Vermont* (BB-20) (1919), and of Adm. Spencer S. Wood, flagship cruiser *Minneapolis* (C-13), who commanded the Pacific Fleet's Train (1919–20). Designated a naval aviator following flight training at Pensacola, he remained there another year (1920–21) before serving at the Bureau of Aeronautics (1921–23) and in the air detachment of the aircraft tender *Aroostook* (CM-3) in the Pacific. Lieutenant Radford flew with Observation Squadron One on the *Colorado* (BB-45) and *Pennsylvania* (BB-38) in the same waters (1925–27) and in the rank of lieutenant commander at Naval Air Station San Diego and (1929) in charge of the Alaskan Aerial Survey of forest and mineral resources. He joined the aircraft carrier *Saratoga* (CV-3) in November 1929, took command of its crack precision-flying "High Hat" squadron—Fighting One-B—the next July, and shifted thereon to the staff of Adm. H.E. Yarnell, commanding the Battle Force's carriers (1931–32). After another tour at BuAer he was navigator of the tender *Wright* (AV-1) and, after promotion to commander, was again (1936–37) on the carrier staff under Adm. Frederick J. Horne, also on the "Sister Sara."

Commander Radford commanded NAS Seattle prior to assignment to the *Yorktown* (CV-5) as executive officer in May 1940 for twelve months then several weeks in the Office of the Chief of Naval Operations. In August 1941 he began the establishment of NAS Trinidad in the British West Indies, commanding it until November. The next month he became Director of Aviation Training at BuAer—a captain from the second day of 1942—and provided the Navy's pilots for the global war until detached in April 1943 for a brief assignment with Carrier Division Two. In spite of the fact that he had never commanded a ship, Radford achieved the rank of rear admiral in July 1943 as ComCarDiv 11, training the new light carriers at Pearl Harbor and using them to cover the occupation of Baker Island in September. His flag in the heavy carrier *Lexington* (CV-16), he led a task unit against Wake in October, and in the *Enterprise* (CV-6) a task group in the Gilberts in November. The following two months were spent as chief of staff to Adm. J. H. Towers, Pacific Fleet Air Force commander, and most of 1944 as Assistant CNO (Air) in Washington. Admiral Radford became ComCarDiv 6 in November of that year and with his flag aboard the new *Yorktown* (CV-10) led Task Group 58.1 in the Iwo Jima and Okinawa campaigns the first half of 1945 and TG 38.4 against Japan during the summer. Detached in August following the Japanese capitulation, he reported the next month as Fleet Air commander at Seattle and the following January became Deputy CNO (Air) in the rank of vice admiral.

Admiral Radford commanded the Second Task Fleet in the Atlantic from March to December 1947 and was Vice CNO from January 1948 to April 1949 in the rank of admiral. In May 1949 he became Commander-in-Chief Pacific Fleet and High Commissioner of the Trust Territory of the Pacific Islands, in which capacity he administered the Navy's operations during the

Korean War. Although briefly embroiled in the unification crisis ("revolt of the admirals") of 1949, he commanded such political respect that President Dwight D. Eisenhower selected him to become Chairman of the Joint Chiefs of Staff in June 1953 and reappointed him in August 1955—the second Naval officer to occupy the post, after Leahy. Radford remained a strong advocate of nuclear weapons during the Cold War and was a powerful force on the JCS until his retirement in August 1957.

Ramage, Lawson Paterson "Red"

(January 19, 1909——   ). USNA (Vt.)
1931 (107/441).

Medal of Honor submariner Ramage preceded his sub service in the destroyers *Dickerson* (DD-157) in the Atlantic (1931–32) and *Lawrence* (DD-250) in the Pacific (1932–33) and the light cruiser *Louisville* (CL-28) in both oceans (1933–35), on the latter ship being promoted to lieutenant (j.g.) in June 1934. He attended the sub school at New London (1935) and the postgraduate school at Annapolis (1938–39), in the interim operating out of Pearl Harbor on the sub *S-29* (SS-134). Promoted lieutenant in January 1939, he reported in September to the recommissioned *Sands* (DD-243) for East coast and Caribbean neutrality patrols until February 1941. The next month Lieutenant Ramage became radio and sound officer to the Pacific Fleet submarine commander, Adm. Thomas Withers, Jr., stationed at Pearl Harbor until April 1942 when he joined the *Grenadier* (SS-210) as navigator on a war patrol during which it sank the Japanese transport *Taiyo Maru,* which carried scientists and engineers. After this action in Chinese coastal waters, the boat participated in the Midway operation. Detached and promoted to lieutenant commander in June, he took command of the *Trout*

(SS-202) with which he sank three enemy vessels totalling some 5500 tons off Truk and Borneo between August 1942 and February 1943. His promotion to commander occurred in November 1942, detachment in May 1943 and assignment to command the *Parche* (SS-384) in July, bringing her into commission in November.

Commander Ramage began wolf pack operations with the *Parche* in Formosa waters in the spring of 1944, sinking two transports in one convoy on her first war patrol and on her second a patrol boat in June. Then, one late July night, *Parche* and *Steelhead* brazenly attacked a Japanese convoy on the surface in these waters, Ramage maneuvering brilliantly to sink two vessels and assist in dispatching another to the deep—exploits that earned him the Medal of Honor. *Parche*'s third war patrol yielded no kills, but by the time of Ramage's relief in December 1944 he and the *Parche* had been credited with eliminating over 26,000 tons of enemy shipping. The next month he became personnel officer to Adm. C. A. Lockwood, Pacific Fleet sub commander at Pearl, and remained in the job during early 1946 under Adm. Allan R. McCann. He then commanded Submarine Division Two, flagship *Sea Devil* (SS-400), in the Western Pacific and Hawaii; served at the Guided Missile desk at the Navy Department (1947–50); and attended the Armed Forces Staff College at Norfolk, culminating in his promotion to captain in July 1950. Captain Ramage spent the ensuing year as readiness and new developments officer to Adm. Stuart S. Murray, Commander Submarines Atlantic Fleet, then commanded Submarine Squadron Six, flagship *Sea Leopard* (SS-483) in the Atlantic and Caribbean, and the attack cargo ship *Rankin* (AKA-103) during amphibious exercises in the same ocean (1953–54). After instruction at the Naval War College, he spent three months (1955) as chief of staff to Atlantic sub force commander Adm. Frank T. Watkins and 14 months as special assistant to Chief of Naval Operations Adm. A. A. Burke, during which, in July 1956, he was promoted to rear admiral.

Admiral Ramage directed the Surface Type Warfare Division in the Office of the CNO (1956–58) and that office's Anti-Submarine/Submarine Warfare Division (1959–60), and was Assistant CNO (Fleet Operations and Readiness) (1961–62). He commanded Cruiser Division Two, flagship *Newport News* (CA-148), which patrolled the troubled Mediterranean (1958–59), and was deputy commander of Atlantic Fleet submarines (1962–63), with his promotion to vice admiral occurring in July 1963. After a year as Deputy CNO (Fleet Operations and Readiness), Admiral Ramage commanded the First Fleet (1964–66) training naval forces for service in the Vietnam War and then returned to Pearl Harbor as Deputy Commander-in-Chief of the Pacific Fleet. In 1967 he became Commander Military Sea Transportation Service in Washington, continuing in this command until his retirement from the Navy in April 1970. His father-in-law, Vice Adm. James Pine, U.S. Coast Guard (1885–1953), was Superintendent of the U.S. Coast Guard Academy during World War II.

270

Ramsey, DeWitt Clinton "Duke"

(October 2, 1888–September 7, 1961).
USNA (N.Y.) 1912 (125/156).

World War II naval aviation leader Ramsey, born in Arizona into an Army family, took flight training very early with a May 1917 designation as Naval Aviator No. 45 after four years at sea aboard the battleship *New Jersey* (BB-16), the armored cruiser *Montana* (ACR-13), the gunboat *Nashville* (PG-7) and the torpedo boat *Tingey* (TB-34), generally in Latin American and Atlantic waters. During World War I he inspected U.S. naval air stations in France and afterwards served with the Inter-Allied Armistice Commission and as assistant naval attaché for air and Board of Claims member in London. He had three tours of duty as fleet aviation officer to various Commanders-in-Chief U.S. Fleet: Adm. Hilary P. Jones (1921–23), flagships *Pennsylvania* (BB-38), transport *Columbia* (AG-9), *Maryland* (BB-46) and 'cruiser *Seattle* (CA-11); Adm. Henry A. Wiley (1927–29), flagship *Texas* (BB-35); and Adm. Arthur J. Hepburn (1937–38) in the *Pennsylvania.* After refresher training at Pensacola (1923), Ramsey remained there as Superintendent of Training, followed by duty afloat as a pilot of Torpedo Squadron One tended by the *Wright* (AV-1) and as navigator of the aircraft carrier *Langley* (CV-1) at San Diego (1927). At the Naval Academy in command of Training Squadron VN8D5 and a member of the Maryland State Aviation Commission (1929–32), he returned to the *Wright* as executive officer, served in the aviation section of the Ships' Movements Division at the Navy Department (1934–36), and studied at the Naval War College (1936–37).

Commander Ramsey served briefly (1938) as aviation officer to Adm. Edward C. Kalbfus, Battle Force commander on the *California* (BB-44), then went to the *Saratoga* (CV-3) as exec (1938–39) and to the Bureau of

271

Aeronautics—first as head of the Plans Division and then, from July 1941 to May 1942, as Assistant Chief of Bureau in the rank of captain. The latter month he took command of the *Saratoga* and led that vessel in the Guadalcanal landings and campaign, including the battle of the Eastern Solomons, until transferred in October to the staff of Pacific Fleet commander Adm. C. W. Nimitz in the rank of rear admiral. From November 1942 to July 1943 he commanded Carrier Division One again on the "Sara" in the South Pacific, and from August 1943 until June 1945 he was Chief of BuAer. In July and August 1945 Admiral Ramsey served as chief of staff to Adm. R. A. Spruance, Fifth Fleet commander planning the invasion of Japan at Guam, and from November 1945 to January 1946 he was Deputy Pacific Fleet commander in the rank of vice admiral. The latter month he was promoted to admiral and made Vice Chief of Naval Operations, a post he occupied for two years. When the office of CNO was given to Adm. Louis E. Denfeld instead of Ramsey in 1948, the latter became Commander-in-Chief Pacific Fleet. In May 1949 he retired from the Navy and entered the aviation industry.

Read, George Campbell

(1787—August 22, 1862).

Navy Department

Remembered chiefly for his protection of American shipping in the East Indies during the 1830's, the Irish-born Read entered the Navy in 1804 as a midshipman from Pennsylvania but immediately went into merchant service on furlough, being promoted to lieutenant in 1810. He participated in the frigate *Constitution*'s victory over the *Guerrière* and in that of the frigate *United States* over the *Macedonian* (both in 1812) and commanded the schooner *Vixen* during the summer of 1813 before Great Lakes duty. In April 1814 he reported to Baltimore as first lieutenant of the uncompleted frigate *Java* and 14 months later brought the brig *Chippewa* into service in mid-1815 for Decatur's Mediterranean cruise. Inactive while waiting orders, Lieutenant Read next commanded the brig *Hornet* (1818-21) in the West Indies, North Atlantic and Mediterranean, followed by more inactivity. He was promoted to master commandant in 1816 and to captain in 1825 and after a short assignment on the new frigate *Brandywine* commanded the *Constitution* on the Mediterranean station (1826). Board duties, leaves, and continued inaction during the Navy's lean years followed.

Captain Read achieved some notoriety as skipper of the frigate *Constellation* in the middle sea (1832-34) when he was given a year's suspension for his severe treatment of junior officers. In the spring of 1838 he sailed as commodore of a two-ship squadron, flag in the frigate *Columbia,* of which he was also captain, sailing to the East Indies via Africa. After his arrival he learned of the seizure of an American merchantman by Sumatran pirates, whereupon he bombarded one native village and landed a force at another at the end of the year and the beginning of the next. In April 1839 he protected Westerners at Canton during the opium troubles in China and the following year returned home via Hawaii, having circled the globe. Commodore Read commanded the Philadelphia Navy Yard (1840-45, 1849-53), the African and Mediterranean squadrons (1846-47 and 1847-49 respectively) in the *United States,* and was president of the examining board which approved the establishment of the Naval Academy in 1845. Although placed on the reserve list in 1855, in May 1861 he became governor of the Naval Asylum at Philadelphia and was advanced to rear admiral on the retired list in July 1862.

Reeves, Joseph Mason "Bull"

*(November 20, 1872—March 25, 1948).
USNA (Ill.) 1894 (38/47).*

Navy Department: National Archives

Pioneer in naval aviation and major fleet commander during the interwar period, Reeves spent several weeks on the new cruiser *Cincinnati* (C-7) on the East coast before shipping out in the *San Francisco* (C-5) for Atlantic and Mediterranean patrols (1894–96). In the commissioning crew of the battleship *Oregon* (BB-3) in July 1896 and in the rank of assistant engineer, he operated in the Pacific and had charge of her main engines for the famous voyage around Cape Horn in the war against Spain and during the Battle of Santiago, July 1898. Reeves shortly thereafter joined the newly-purchased converted yacht *Sylph* for a short tour at the Washington Navy Yard and in February 1899 became a line officer, ensign, aboard the despatch ship *Dolphin* there and for a South American cruise. As lieutenant (j.g.) he served on board the new *Kearsarge* (BB-5) in the North Atlantic (1900–01), thereafter receiving instruction in torpedoes at Newport. He returned to the *San Francisco* for extended operations to Europe, the Caribbean, the Med and the Far East, where in 1903 he became gunnery officer to the Fleet commander, first Adm. Yates Stirling, then Adm. Charles J. Train, flagships *Wisconsin* (BB-9) and *Ohio* (BB-12).

Lieutenant Reeves taught physics and chemistry and was head football coach at the Naval Academy (1906–08) before reporting as ordnance officer of the *New Hampshire* (BB-25) at her commissioning in mid-1908 for operations between Canadian and Caribbean ports. So superior was his performance that the next year he fleeted up to be gunnery officer to Adm. Seaton Schroeder, Commander Atlantic Fleet, flagship *Connecticut* (BB-18), and was then promoted to commander. After a tour commanding the naval coal depot at Tiburon near San Francisco as a member of the Board of

Inspection and Survey (1910–13), he brought the collier *Jupiter* (AC-3) into commission as her skipper in April 1913 and cruised to the Pacific where the next year he commanded the *St. Louis* (C-20) and other vessels at San Francisco, and then the *Oregon* (1915–16) in that ocean. Stationed at the Office of the Chief of Naval Operations when the U.S. entered World War I, following a brief tour at the Mare Island Navy Yard, Reeves became captain in October 1917 and commanded the *Maine* (BB-10) and *Kansas* (BB-21), both East coast training vessels, before being naval attaché at Rome (1919–21). Briefly skipper of the armored cruiser *Pittsburgh* (ACR-4) in the Atlantic (1921) and Captain of the Mare Island yard, he was also commanding officer of the *North Dakota* (BB-29) in the Atlantic (1922–23). After a year as a student at the Naval War College, he joined its faculty and then in 1925 reported to Pensacola where he qualified—at age 53!—as a naval aviation observer, the minimum prerequisite for holding aviation commands. During the autumn he hoisted his broad pennant on his new flagship, the aircraft carrier *Langley* (CV-1, formerly his old ship *Jupiter*), as Commander Aircraft Squadrons Battle Fleet, in which capacity he hammered out the U.S. Fleet's first real air tactical doctrines.

Entitled to be addressed as commodore in this billet, Reeves interrupted his duties to attend the naval conference at Geneva during the summer of 1927, during which he was promoted to rear admiral. His pioneering efforts in carrier doctrine were crowned by Fleet Problem IX early in 1929—a successful mock carrier attack on the Panama Canal by the *Saratoga* (CV-3). A General Board tour of duty (1929–30) was followed by his return to the same command, now upgraded to Commander Carriers Battle Fleet, flag in the *Saratoga*, wherein he continued his tactical innovations. Admiral Reeves was senior member of the Pacific coast section of the Board of Inspection and Survey (1931–32) and again commandant at Mare Island, but then in 1933 he jumped two stars to admiral as Commander Battle Force, flagship *California* (BB-44), and finally Commander-in-Chief United States Fleet, flagship *Pennsylvania* (BB-38), from June 1934 to June 1936, twice the normal time for this billet. On the General Board for six months in his permanent rank of rear admiral, the final two as chairman, Reeves retired in this rank in December 1936. He was recalled in May 1940 to serve at the Office of the Secretary of the Navy and the following March became the Navy's Lend-Lease Liaison Officer and later also served as senior military member on the Munitions Assignment Board (1945) as well as chairman of the Navy's board of the same title (1945) and of the Joint Munitions Allocation Committee (1944–45). Promoted vice admiral and admiral on the retired list in February and July 1942 respectively, Admiral Reeves also served with the Roberts Pearl Harbor investigation. He ended his Lend-Lease duties in December 1945 and was released from active service twelve months later at age 74.

Richardson, James Otto "Joe"

(September 18, 1878–May 2, 1974).
USNA (Tex.) 1902 (5/59).

U.S. Fleet commander in the Pacific on the eve of World War II, Richardson reported to the Asiatic Station gunboat *Quiros* (PG-40), transferred there to the armored cruiser *New Orleans* (1903–04) and then to the monitor *Monadnock* (BM-3). Next in the Atlantic with the *Nashville* (PG-7) (1905–06) and the new armored cruiser *Tennessee* (ACR-10), he commanded the torpedo boats *Tingey* (TB-34) (1907–09) and *Stockton* (TB-32) as well as the Atlantic Torpedo Boat Flotilla's Third Division. His first shore duty was for postgraduate instruction at Annapolis (1909–11), followed by brief machinery inspection work then return to sea and the new Atlantic battleship *Delaware* (BB-28) as assistant then senior engineering officer (1911–14). Lieutenant Commander Richardson served at the Bureau of Steam Engineering where he helped to create the Navy's petroleum reserve at Teapot Dome, Wyoming, and in June 1917 became navigator of the *Nevada* (BB-36), fleeting up to executive officer the following April for convoy escort work in British waters from August to November. He headed the steam engineering department at the Naval Academy (1919–22); took the *Asheville* (PG-21) to the Orient where he also assumed command of the South China Patrol (1923); was Assistant Chief of the Bureau of Ordnance (1924–27); and commanded U.S. destroyers in Europe as well as Destroyer Division 38, flagship *Whipple* (DD-217), which force was soon ordered back to the Caribbean.

Captain Richardson directed Officer Personnel at the Bureau of Navigation (1928–30) before fitting out the heavy cruiser *Augusta* (CA-31) and commanding her from commissioning through operations in both oceans with the Scouting Force (1931–33). After a year at the Naval War College, he became Budget Officer of the Navy, with promotion to rear admiral in

December 1934 and command of Cruiser Division six on the West coast one month in mid-1935. He was chief of staff to Adm. J. M. Reeves, U.S. Fleet commander on the *Pennsylvania* (BB-38), and afterward (1936–37) Commander Destroyers Scouting Force, flagship *Richmond* (CL-9). Assistant to Chief of Naval Operations Adm. W. D. Leahy, he remained in Washington as Chief of BuNav (1938–39). In June 1939 Admiral Richardson took command of the Battle Force, flagship *California* (BB-44), in the full rank of admiral and the following January became Commander-in-Chief U.S. Fleet, flagship *Pennsylvania*. During this tour of duty the Fleet base was moved from California to Pearl Harbor to deter the Japanese but which action Richardson told President Franklin D. Roosevelt in the fall of 1940 was dangerous. This and other differences of opinion between the two men led to the Admiral's untimely relief in February 1941. In the rank of rear admiral he served on the General Board from March 1941 to May 1942 then as executive vice president of the Navy Relief Society, where he remained until May 1945 in spite of his retirement in October 1942 in the rank of admiral. Admiral Richardson also, from June 1944 to April 1945, headed a joint service committee to study the possibility of unifying the armed forces and ceased all active duty in March 1946. His memoirs were published in 1973: *On the Treadmill to Pearl Harbor.*

Rickover, Hyman George

(January 27, 1900——   ). USNA (Ill.) 1922 (107/539).

Founder and virtual czar of the Navy's nuclear power program for more than three decades, Russian-born Rickover battled a vicious anti-Semitism from his earliest Academy days which contributed to an abrupt, uningratiating, and even obnoxious manner throughout his career. His earlier assignments were checkered: the surface line in the destroyer *LaVallette* (DD-315) and battleship *Nevada* (BB-36) primarily in the Pacific until 1927; postgraduate school in electrical engineering at Annapolis and Columbia University (M.S. 1929); in submarines, training at New London early in 1930 and then spending several months with the sub *S-9* (SS-114) there and two years (1931–33) operating in Panamanian waters with the *S-48* (SS-159), eventually as her executive officer; inspector of naval material at Philadelphia (1933–35); engineer of the *New Mexico* (BB-40) in the Pacific; commanding officer of the minesweeper *Finch* (AM-9) as part of the Asiatic Fleet (1937); and, following his designation late in 1937 as an "engineering duty only" (E.D.O.) officer, service as assistant planning officer at the Cavite Navy Yard, Philippines, until the summer of 1939. Commander Rickover reported to the Bureau of Ships as head of its Electrical Section and proceeded to outfit the Navy's ships with the electrical systems necessary for waging World War II. He continued in this vital role until April 1945 when he joined the staff of Adm. William W. Smith, Commander Service Force Pacific, for two months, and then went ashore at Okinawa as its Industrial Manager and commander of the Naval Repair Base there from July to November.

Captain Rickover had developed a pragmatic, demanding, personalized successful style of technological management which he continued and enlarged upon as he entered the field of nuclear energy. Inspector general of the Nineteenth ("mothball") Fleet at San Francisco from December 1945 to May 1946, he spent the balance of that year as assistant director of operations of the Manhattan District atomic bomb project and of its successor agency, the Atomic Energy Commission, until September 1947. By now a strong advocate of developing a nuclear-powered submarine, he reported to BuShips to promote the idea and in the summer of 1948 became head of its new Nuclear Power Division with additional assignment to the AEC as head of its Naval Reactors Branch. The result was the construction of the nuclear-propelled attack sub *Nautilus* (SSN-571), commissioned in September 1954, and its many successors. Promoted rear admiral in July 1953 and vice admiral in October 1958, Rickover also superintended the creation of the first peaceful nuclear-powered electrical utility central station at Shippingport, Pennsylvania (1953–57); cooperated with Adm. W. F. Raborn, Jr. *(q.v.)* to help fashion the Polaris-missile sub system; and brought nuclear power to surface ships with the first nuclear task force of the aircraft carrier *Enterprise* (CVAN-65), guided missile cruiser *Long Beach* (CGN-9) and frigate *Bainbridge* (DLGN-25), which deployed during Admiral Rickover's tenure as Assistant Chief of BuShips (Nuclear Propulsion) as well as his AEC post (1961–64).

Admiral Rickover reached the mandatory retirement age of 62 years in 1962 but was retained on active duty by Presidents John F. Kennedy and Lyndon B. Johnson until the absolute retirement age of 64. Then, in January 1964, Johnson ruled that he be retained in active duty status in the rank of vice admiral on the retired list. Indeed, political intervention had saved the unorthodox and unpopular officer from being summarily retired by the Navy in 1953 and had also been necessary to force his promotion to vice admiral five years after that. During the 1960's and 1970's Admiral Rickover continued to run his super-agency as Director, Division of Naval Reactors, AEC (later the Energy Research and Development Administration ultimately in the Department of Energy), and Deputy Commander for Nuclear Propulsion, Naval Sea Systems Command. He was promoted to admiral on the retired list in December 1973 to rank from November. In spite of his controversial habits, which included several books and essays on the weaknesses in the American educational system, Rickover stands as the major force in creating the Navy's nuclear-powered naval deterrent for the second half of the twentieth century. He also wrote a historical piece, *How the Battleship* Maine *Was Destroyed* (1976).

The Rodgers Family

The most distinguished and largest of American flag officer families, the Rodgers clan descended from Revolutionary War militia Colonel John Rodgers and Elizabeth Reynolds Rodgers and remained home-based at Havre de Grace, Maryland. Of the original eight children, two sons established the two main Navy lines—John Rodgers and George Washington Rodgers.

Commo. John Rodgers (1772–1838) *(q.v.)* in turn produced two lines. One son, Rear Adm. John Rodgers (1812–1882) *(q.v.)*, gave the Navy Vice Adm. William Ledyard Rodgers (1860–1944), president of the Naval War College (1911–13) and of the Naval Institute (1923–24), commander-in-chief of the Asiatic Fleet (1918–19), member of the General Board (1915–16, 1920–24), and author of several articles in the Institute's *Proceedings* and of the books *Greek and Roman Naval Warfare* (1937) and *Naval Warfare Under Oars* (1939). Another son, Civil War Col. Robert Smith Rodgers, married Sarah Perry, daughter of Matthew C. Perry *(q.v.)*; their sons included Rear Adm. Frederick Rodgers (1842–1917), Commander-in-Chief Asiatic Squadron in 1902, and Rear Adm. John Augustus Rodgers (1848–1933), executive officer of the battleship *Indiana* (BB-1) at the Battle of Santiago in 1898. The latter's son was pioneer naval aviator Cdr. John Rodgers who commanded the naval air station at Pearl Harbor from 1922 to 1925 before perishing in a plane crash the next year.

Commo. George Washington Rodgers (1787–1832) married Ann Maria Perry, sister of Oliver Hazard and Matthew C. Perry *(q.v.)*, rose from midshipman in 1804 to captain in 1825 and commanded the Brazil Squadron in the sloop *Warren* from November 1831 until his untimely death the following May. Two of his sons fell in battle: Alexander P. Rodgers in the attack on Chapultepec in 1847 and Cdr. George W. Rodgers as skipper of the monitor *Catskill* while bombarding Charleston during August 1863. A third son was Rear Adm. C. R. P. Rodgers (1819–1892) *(q.v.)*, who in turn produced Rear Adm. Raymond Perry Rodgers (1849–1925), chief intelligence officer in the Navy (1906–09) and president of the Naval War College (1909–11), and Rear Adm. Thomas Slidell Rodgers (1858–1931), also director of naval intelligence (1912–13) and a battleship division commander in the Atlantic Fleet during World War I.

As seen in the latter's middle name, a third Navy family was linked to the Rodgers and Perry families when Matthew C. Perry married Jane Slidell, who became the mother of Sarah Perry Rodgers and then grandmother of Admirals Frederick and John A. Rodgers. Jane Slidell Perry was sister of Confederate diplomat John Slidell, who figured prominently in the *Trent* affair with Capt. Charles Wilkes *(q.v.)*, and of Cdr. Alexander Slidell Mackenzie (1803–1848), the prolific writer of naval lore and travels, skipper of the brig *Somers* during its mutiny scandal of 1842, and father of the famous Union general and Indian fighter Ranald S. Mackenzie, of Lt. Cdr. Alexander S. Mackenzie who fell fighting on Formosa in 1867, and of Rear Adm. M. R. Slidell Mackenzie (1848–1915), in 1901–02 captain of the armored cruiser *New York* (ACR-2), flagship of his kinsman Adm. John A. Rodgers.

Rodgers, Christopher Raymond Perry

(November 14, 1819–January 8, 1892).

Combat commander in the Civil War, Rodgers received instruction at the New York naval school after his appointment as midshipman in 1833, sailed in the Pacific aboard the frigate *Brandywine,* served ashore at the New York Navy Yard (1836–37), operated off politically turbulent southern South American ports with the sloop *Fairfield* (1837–39), and joined the schooner *Flirt* to help pacify the Seminole Indians in Florida. After transferring to his brother John's vessel *Wave* in these waters, he finished this war in 1842 as commanding officer of the schooner *Phoenix.* Acting Master Rodgers joined the commissioning crew of the sloop *Saratoga* late in 1842 and sailed in her for anti-slaving work off West Africa the next spring, transferring then to the frigate *Cumberland* for Mediterranean patrol (1843–45), during which (1844) he was promoted to lieutenant. Coast Survey duties were interrupted by Mexican War service with the Home Squadron in which he fought at Vera Cruz, Tabasco, and Tuxpan. He left the Survey for the frigates *Congress* (1850–51) on the Brazil Station and *Constitution* (1852–55) on the African Station as flag lieutenant to Commo. Isaac Mayo, went back to the Survey (1856–58), briefly commanding its schooner *Gallatin* and later the *Bibb,* and then on to the steam frigate *Wabash* (1858–59) in the Mediterranean.

Commandant of Midshipmen at the Naval Academy (1860–61), the classes of which he rigidly separated, Lieutenant Rodgers moved the school from Annapolis to Newport at the outbreak of the Civil War. He resumed command of the *Wabash* in September 1861 and led it, flagship of the South Atlantic Blockading Squadron, during the attack on Port Royal, South Carolina, in November, after which he was promoted to commander. He helped to occupy the several towns taken thereafter along the coasts of

281

Georgia and Florida, received the surrender of St. Augustine in March 1862 and took naval parties ashore with the army at Ft. Pulaski, Georgia, in April. He became fleet captain of the Squadron in August, flagship the ironclad steamer *New Ironsides,* participated in the attack on Charleston in April 1863, and was detached in July. In October Rodgers assumed command of the steam sloop *Iroquois,* decommissioned under repair at Baltimore until the following March when she sortied into the North Atlantic and Mediterranean to protect Union commerce. During 1865 the *Iroquois* roamed the Pacific in the futile search for the rebel raider *Shenandoah.* Her skipper then reported to the Norfolk Navy Yard for a three-year tour of duty, being advanced to captain in July 1866. He took command of the screw frigate *Franklin* in 1868 and cruised with her in her capacity as flagship of the European Squadron (1869–70), at the end of which tour he was promoted to commodore. Commodore Rodgers was on special duty in Europe, Chief of the Bureau of Yards and Docks (1871–74) as well as acting Chief of the Bureau of Equipment for a short time, Superintendent of the Naval Academy (1874–78, 1880), and commander-in-chief of the Pacific Squadron, flagship the screw steamer *Pensacola* (1878–80). Made rear admiral in June 1874, he maintained his service connection after his November 1881 retirement, being president of the Naval Institute (1875–78, 1882–83) and president of the International Meridian Conference (1884).

Rodgers, John

(July 11, 1772–August 1, 1838).

Naval Photographic Center

The first person of the famed Rodgers family *(q.v.)* to enter the Navy and achieve flag rank, this prominent War of 1812 leader rose to master during early merchant service (1787–98) and in the quasi-war with France excelled quickly: he was commissioned lieutenant in March 1798 and assigned as second then first lieutenant (executive officer) of the frigate *Constellation,* displaying great bravery in the victory over the frigate *L'Insurgente* off Nevis in February 1799 for which he was promoted to captain in March. As prize master he commanded the vessel, renamed *Insurgent,* in the West Indies until May. In June he launched the sloop *Maryland,* cruised the Caribbean taking a slaver and retaking a captured brig, escorted home a large Anglo-American convoy during the late summer of 1800, and the next year carried American diplomats to and from France. Discharged in October 1801 he became master of the merchantman *Nelly,* sailing to Santo Domingo where he assisted refugees from the devastating wars in progress there until arrested and deported by French authorities. He was restored to rank in the Navy as skipper of the frigate *John Adams* in August 1802, which he directed brilliantly against Barbary Algiers in 1803, taking two major enemy vessels and driving off many gunboats. During this tour he also acted as chief of staff to the Mediterranean Squadron commander, Commo. Richard V. Morris, relieving him briefly in June 1803 for several months. Chief of staff again, but to Commo. Samuel Barron, he commanded the frigate *Congress* (1804–05) in the same Sea.

Elevated to command of the Squadron, flagship the frigate *Constitution,* in May 1805 Commodore Rodgers took charge of the blockade of Tripoli until peace was restored over the ensuing months. Relieved in May 1806, he

283

then built a gunboat at Havre de Grace, his Maryland home, and in July 1807 took command of the gunboat flotilla at New York, thereby having the unpleasant task of enforcing Jefferson's unpopular embargo over the Northeastern seaboard. In 1810 he hoisted his flag in the frigate *President*, 44, as commander of the northern division, and while searching for American sailors impressed into the Royal Navy engaged the British sloop *Little Belt*, 22, in May 1811 off Cape Henry, Virginia. With the outbreak of war in 1812 he sortied with his squadron into the North Atlantic and in June hotly engaged the frigate *Belvidera*, a fight during which he was injured but went on to take eight prizes. Operating in the North Atlantic and Irish Sea through the end of 1813 and in the West Indies shortly thereafter, Commodore Rodgers took 15 more prizes, among them the schooner *Highflyer*. During the spring of 1814 he took command of the Delaware Flotilla and the frigate *Guerrière*, then fitting out at Philadelphia, and led sailors and Marines ashore against the British along the Potomac and in the defense of Baltimore. He served as first head of the Board of Navy Commissioners from its inception in February 1815 until his retirement in May 1837, save for a short period in 1823 when he was temporary Secretary of the Navy and during another tour (1825–27) as commander in the Mediterranean on the ship-of-the-line *North Carolina*, during which he prepared the way for a trade agreement between the United States and Ottoman Turkey.

Rodgers, John

(August 8, 1812—May 5, 1882).

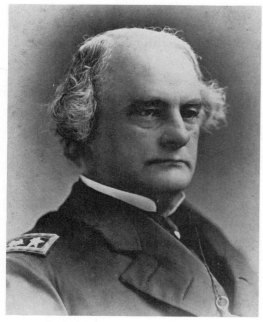

Noted oceanic surveyor and Civil War commander of the monitor *Weehawken,* Rodgers waited a year after his midshipman's appointment to go to sea in the frigate *Constellation* for Mediterranean duty (1829–32) then returned to the naval school at Norfolk (1833–34) and the University of Virginia (1834–35). After several months on the U.S. Coast Survey schooner *Jersey,* he became acting master of the newly commissioned brig *Dolphin* with the Brazil Squadron (1836–39) then commanding officer of the Survey schooners *Wave* and *Jefferson* for Second Seminole War service (1839–42). Lieutenant Rodgers commanded the schooner *Boxer* in the Home Squadron (1842–44) then assisted Lt. William W. Hunter at Pittsburgh in the contruction of the experimental Hunter-wheel steam gunboat *Alleghany* (1844–46). After cruising Mediterranean and African waters in the frigate *United States* (1846–49), he was again ashore and afloat with the Coast Survey, including command of the *Retzel* (1849–50) and *Legare* (1851–52) in Florida coastal waters. He joined the North Pacific Exploring and Surveying Expedition late in 1852, taking command of the screw steamer *John Hancock* the next year. Operating out of Hong Kong, during which time his vessel engaged Chinese pirate shore batteries, Rodgers surveyed the Western Pacific and far north into the Bering Sea. He succeeded to command of the Expedition and of its flagship, the sloop *Vincennes,* in 1854 and visited many islands of the Central and South Pacific. He returned home in 1856 in the rank of commander and spent the years 1857 to 1859 in Washington completing his report, after which he awaited orders.

With the outbreak of war, Commander Rodgers joined Gen. George B. McClellan at Cincinnati in May 1861 and equipped three *Benton*-class ironclad river gunboats, transferring in October to command of the screw steamer *Flag* on the Charleston blockade. Aide to Flag Off. S. F. DuPont during the capture of Port Royal, South Carolina, the next month, he then led a gunboat squadron at the Savannah River and in April 1862 assumed command of the new ironclad *Galena* with which he drove up the James River in May and exchanged heavy fire with Confederate artillery at Fort Darling, then covered McClellan's withdrawal from the vicinity of Richmond at the end of the Peninsular Campaign. Following promotion to captain in July, Rodgers patrolled Hampton Roads until transferred to command of the *Weehawken* in November. He led the futile attack on Fort Sumter in April 1863, and in June in company with the monitor *Nahant* his ship overpowered and took the rebel ironclad ram *Atlanta* in battle at Wassaw Sound, Georgia. Two monitor commands ensued: the *Canonicus* under construction at Boston during the summer and the *Dictator,* which he brought into commission in November and led on the blockade of North Carolina until September 1864. Promoted to commodore in March for his victory over the *Atlanta,* he had also served on the Board of Visitors to the Naval Academy in May. Next skipper of the sidewheel steamer *Vanderbilt,* he made it his flagship in September 1865 when he commanded the squadron which early in 1866 demonstrated off Valparaiso, Chile, during the Spanish bombardment. Detached in June, he went on to command the Boston Navy Yard (1866–69).

Becoming rear admiral in February 1870, Rodgers took command of the Asiatic Squadron in the screw frigate *Colorado* and embarked on a diplomatic mission to Korea with five vessels in April 1871, only to have his force fired upon by two Korean forts at the Han River in June. He replied by landing a naval brigade which destroyed the forts, inflicted heavy casualties and took some 500 guns, the Americans suffering but 13 casualties. Detached the next February, Admiral Rodgers served as president of the Examining and Retiring boards (1872–73), commander of the Mare Island Navy Yard (1873–77), Superintendent of the Naval Observatory (1877–82) and additionally as a member of the Lighthouse Board (1878–82) and president of the first Naval Advisory Board (1881–82). President of the Naval Institute (1879–82), this very active officer died in the midst of these four latter important and several lesser assignments. Among his many achievements was participating in the founding of the National Academy of Sciences in 1863.

Rodman, Hugh

(January 6, 1859–June 7, 1940). USNA (Ky.) 1880 (61/62).

America's World War I battle force commander, Rodman had initial sea tours on three screw sloops—the *Yantic* (1880–82), *Wachusett* (1882–84), and *Hartford* (1884–85)—before a Hydrographic Office assignment (1885–86) and a lengthy Pacific cruise aboard the screw steamer *Essex* (1886–89). An ensign (j.g.) in 1883 and ensign from 1884, he was with the Bureau of Navigation (1889–90) and Naval Observatory (1890–91) before going to the U.S. Coast and Geodetic Survey and work along the Alaskan and British Columbian coasts (1891–95), his promotion to lieutenant (j.g.) occurring in 1893 and lieutenant four years later. He spent one year (1896–97) on its steamer *Patterson*. In the war with Spain Lieutenant Rodman served on board the cruiser *Raleigh* (C-8) in the Philippines from the Battle of Manila Bay through the occupation, returning home in her and transferring to the Fish Commission vessel *Albatross* (1899–1901) and the tug *Iroquois* in the Hawaiian Islands as skipper. Executive officer of the protected cruiser *New Orleans* (1904) and attached to the *Cincinnati* (C-7) (1904–05), both in the Philippines and environs, he operated with the battleship *Wisconsin* (BB-9) before commanding the gunboat *Elcano* (PG-38) on the Yangtze Patrol (1905–07) and transferring stateside to the armored cruiser *West Virginia* (ACR-5). Lighthouse inspection work in the Philippines (1907–08) and general inspection at Mare Island (1910–11) bracketed his tour in command of the *Cleveland* (C-19) in the Far East.

Promoted captain in 1911, Rodman was briefly captain of the Mare Island yard then of the *Connecticut* (BB-18) (1912) and the *Delaware* (BB-28) (1912–13) in the Atlantic Fleet, cruising in the latter to Europe. He superintended the transportation facilities, including the railroad, of the newly-opened Panama Canal (1914–15) prior to commanding the *New York* (BB-34) along the East coast (1915–16). Following a tour on the General Board (1916–17), he took over Battleship Division Three briefly then Battleship Squadron One of the Atlantic Fleet, becoming rear admiral in May 1917. In September Admiral Rodman took command of that Fleet's Division Three of Battleship Force One, shifting two months later to command of Division Nine, BatFor Two. With the latter, flagship *New York*, he deployed in December with the British Grand Fleet, his unit redesignated the 6th Battle Squadron, one of two "fast wings" assigned to engage the German fleet in the van or rear and which nearly did on one occasion. In April 1918 Rodman became Commander U.S. Battleships, returning home at the end of the year to command Division Six of Squadron Three. In July 1919 he reported as Commander-in-Chief Pacific Fleet, flagship *New Mexico* (BB-40), in the rank of admiral, which post he held exactly two years, finishing his career commanding the Fifth Naval District and Norfolk naval operating base, during which tour he performed a diplomatic mission to Peru. Retiring in January 1923 as rear admiral, he spent several subsequent months heading a board on the shore establishment and advising President Warren G. Harding during the latter's fatal trip to Alaska. Admiral Rodman was advanced to admiral on the retired list in June 1930. His autobiography was *Yarns of a Kentucky Admiral* (1928).

Rosendahl, Charles Emery

National Archives

(May 15, 1892– May 14, 1977). USNA (Tex.) 1914 (53/154).

Celebrated lighter-than-air specialist, Rosendahl did not go into rigid airships until the U.S Navy initiated the program which was after he had spent several years in cruisers and destroyers: the *West Virginia* (ACR-5) in the Pacific (1914–15); the *St. Louis* (C-20), battleship *Oregon* (BB-3) and *Cleveland* (C-19) mostly between Bremerton and San Francisco (1915–16); back to his first ship, renamed *Huntington,* there and for operations using shipboard free balloons and wartime Atlantic convoying of troop transports; testing fuel oil at Philadelphia (summer 1918); as engineer officer of the new destroyer *McKean* (DD-90) in the Pacific (1918–19); in rapid succession outfitting and commanding all but the first West coast-built "cans" *Fuller* (DD-297), *William Jones* (DD-308), *Yarborough* (DD-314), *Marcus* (DD-321) and *Melvin* (DD-335); and in West coast operations with the *Claxton* (DD-140) (summer 1921). After teaching electrical engineering and physics at the Naval Academy, Lieutenant Commander Rosendahl underwent lighter-than-aircraft flight training at Lakehurst, New Jersey, naval air station (1923–24) for designation as naval aviator (airship). Reporting as navigator of the dirigible *Shenandoah* (ZR-1) at Lakehurst late in 1924, he survived her crash in a turbulent summer storm near Ava, Ohio, the following September, free-ballooning the forward part of the craft safely to the ground. He remained at Lakehurst and in March 1926 became executive officer and two months later commanding officer of the *Los Angeles* (ZR-3). During this tour of duty, he visited England and Germany, returning on the German dirigible *Graf Zeppelin* during 1928 and circumnavigating the globe as an observer in her during 1929, the same year he assumed collateral duty

289

commanding the Rigid Airship Training and Experimental Squadron attached to the *Los Angeles* at Lakehurst.

After a year (1930–31) at the Plans Division of the Bureau of Aeronautics, Commander Rosendahl outfitted and commanded the *Akron* (ZRS-4) based at Lakehurst. Returning to the line, he became first lieutenant of the Pacific battleship *West Virginia* (BB-48) (1932–33) then navigator of the *Portland* (CA-35) (1933–34) before assuming command of NAS Lakehurst; he flew many times as an observer on the German *Hindenburg* but was not aboard when she crashed at his station in 1937. Exec of the *Milwaukee* (CL-5) in both oceans (1938–40), he served in the Office of the Secretary of the Navy until he undertook lighter-than-air projects from early-1941 in the Office of the Chief of Naval Operations and from April 1942 as Special Assistant (for Lighter-than-Air) at BuAer. That September Captain Rosendahl took command of the *Minneapolis* (CA-36) in the South Pacific and in November took her into the battle of Tassafaronga, in which she was heavily damaged requiring her return to Mare Island for repairs; he was detached in April 1943 and promoted to rear admiral in May. He then became the first Chief of Naval Airship Training, in October changed to Chief of Naval Airship Training and Experimentation and additionally from September as Special Assistant (LTA) in the Office of the Deputy CNO (Air). The dirigibles now gone, he supervised the construction of the Navy's nonrigid blimps and the training of their crews for antisubmarine patrols on both coasts for the duration. Admiral Rosendahl continued at his posts into the postwar period until July 1946. He retired as vice admiral the following November. He authored several essays and books promoting the cause of airships.

Rowan, Stephen Clegg

(December 25, 1808—March 31, 1890).

Navy Department: National Archives

Combat commander in the Mexican and Civil wars, Rowan emigrated from Ireland to Ohio, from which state he was appointed midshipman in 1826. The sloop *Vincennes* was his first assignment (1826–30), going around the world, then he had one tour with the Revenue Cutter Service at New York (1830–32). As passed midshipman on the schooner *Shark*, he operated in the West Indies (1832–33) where he became acting sailing master of the sloop *Vandalia* (1834–36), from which he led landing parties, especially in March 1836, against the Seminole Indians. Promoted to lieutenant aboard the storeship *Relief* for the South Seas Exploring Expedition early in 1837, Rowan instead served with the Coast Survey (1838–41). He cruised in the ship-of-the-line *Delaware* on the Brazil (1841–43) and Mediterranean (1843–44) stations and headed for the Pacific after becoming executive officer, then captain of the sloop *Cyane* in July 1845. When this vessel accepted the surrender of Monterey, California, the next July, Rowan fortified the place and commanded a battalion of sailors and Marines which occupied San Diego, fought alongside the army at San Gabriel and the Mesa, receiving wounds, and joined in the seizure of Los Angeles. When the *Cyane* moved into the Gulf of California in September, he led a party ashore at San Blas and then participated in the blockade and attacks against the Mexicans around Mazatlán and San José in November and December 1847. He was detached the following October.

Lieutenant Rowan inspected ordnance and had other duties at the New York Navy Yard throughout the 1850's, save for a tour of duty commanding the *Relief* on the Brazil Station and then (1855–57) the receiving ship *North Carolina* at New York. He was promoted to commander in 1855. Taking command of the screw sloop *Pawnee* in January 1861, he defended Washington, D.C., virtually alone during President Lincoln's inauguration in March, and arrived too late to help Fort Sumter and nearly too late to assist in the evacuation of Norfolk, both in April. The next month the *Pawnee* engaged Confederate batteries at Aquia Creek and a shore party from her took Alexandria, the vessel thereafter policing the Potomac until August when it played a key role in the capture of Forts Hatteras and Clark, North Carolina. Several prizes were taken in the Hatteras area, afterwhich Commander Rowan took command of a flotilla there, flagship the sidewheel steamer *Delaware*. With this force he joined in the attack on Roanoke Island, North Carolina, in February 1862, and passed up the Pasquotank River to destroy the rebel flotilla and take Elizabeth City. He repeated his successes supporting the army at New Bern in March and remained in the area for a time in command of the sidewheeler *Philadelphia*. In recognition of his exploits, he was advanced to captain and commodore on the same day in July. Given command of the ironclad steamer *New Ironsides,* flagship of the South Atlantic Blockading Squadron, in mid-1863, he was heavily engaged against the coastal fortifications of Charleston throughout the summer, his ship taking many hits and a torpedo (mine) from the Confederate submersible *David* in October. Remaining on the blockade, he temporarily commanded the Squadron early in 1864.

Commodore Rowan commanded the Navy's forces in the North Carolina sounds from August to October 1864 but finished the war waiting orders. Promoted to rear admiral in July 1866, he briefly commanded the uncompleted screw frigate *Madawaska* and then the Norfolk Navy Yard (1866–67) and the Asiatic Squadron (1867–70), flagship the screw steamer *Piscataqua* (renamed *Delaware* in 1869), during which command he protected American interests in the midst of the Japanese civil war. He was promoted to vice admiral in August 1870 in which rank he commanded the squadron which received the Grand Duke Alexis (1871) and then commanded the New York Navy Yard (1872–76). He was also Port Admiral of New York (1872–79), governor of the Philadelphia Naval Asylum (1881–82), and Superintendent of the Naval Observatory (1882–83). Admiral Rowan's numerous board duties included the presidency of the Examining and Retiring boards (1879–81) and the chairmanship of the Lighthouse Board (1883–89), at the culmination of which he retired.

Sampson, William Thomas

(February 9, 1840–May 6, 1902).
USNA (N.Y.) 1861 (1/27).

Navy Department

Fleet commander in the Caribbean during the Spanish-American War, Sampson fought in the Civil War with the Potomac Flotilla briefly, on the frigate *Potomac* (1861), as executive officer on the steam gunboat *Water Witch* in the East Gulf Blockading Squadron (1861–62), as instructor then acting master of the training ship *John Adams* at the Naval Academy at Newport (1862–63), and as exec of the monitor *Patapsco* off Charleston from June 1864 until the following January, when he was blown off that vessel when it struck a torpedo (mine) and sank. A lieutenant since July 1862, he left the blockade in February 1865 and two months later joined the steam frigate *Colorado* at New York, cruising on the European Station until returning home in the summer of 1867. Lieutenant Commander Sampson again taught at the Naval Academy (1867–69) and became head of its science (natural philosophy) department (1869–71), and later of its physics and chemistry department (1876–78), having sea duty as exec aboard the screw sloop *Congress* in the Atlantic and Mediterranean (1871–73). In 1874 he was promoted to commander and the next year brought the iron gunboat *Alert* into commission. He commanded the training ship *Mayflower* at Annapolis (1876) and the screw sloop *Swatara* on the Asiatic Station (1879–82). A student of both science and ordnance, Sampson observed the 1878 solar eclipse from Wyoming, was assistant superintendent of the Naval Observatory (1882–84), including participation in the 1884 international prime meridian and time conference, and with Luce and Goodrich (*q.q.v.*) was one of the principal figures in the early days of the U.S. Naval Institute. He was a major contributor to its *Proceedings* and later (1898–1902) its president.

Commander Sampson commanded the Torpedo Station at Newport and was concurrently a member of the Fortification Board (1884–86) before serving (1886–90) as Superintendent of the Academy, promotion to captain taking place in March 1889 as he was attending the international maritime conference at Washington. In May 1890 he reported for outfitting duty with the protected steel cruiser *San Francisco* (C-5), command of which he assumed upon her commissioning in November, taking her on two years of patrols off politically unstable Chile and Hawaii. His ordnance expertise paid handsome dividends when he was ordnance inspector at the Washington Navy Yard (1892–93) and Chief of the Bureau of Ordnance (1893–97), during which tour he and Lt. (later Adm.) Joseph Strauss (1861–1948) invented superimposed turrets for battleships. Captain Sampson brought the battleship *Iowa* (BB-4) into commission in June 1897 in the North Atlantic. The following February he became president of the board investigating the destruction of the battleship *Maine* and in March commander of the North Atlantic Squadron, flagship the armored cruiser *New York* (ACR-2).

With the outbreak of war in April 1898, Sampson in the rank of acting rear admiral instituted the blockade of Cuba, maintaining it during and after the arrival of the Spanish fleet at Santiago. Off to the eastward when that force sortied on July 3, he rallied to the support of his Flying Squadron commander Commo. W. S. Schley *(q.v.)* for the destruction of the enemy vessels. A bitter controversy ensued between the two men over chief credit for the victory at Santiago, and although Sampson was immediately promoted to commodore his recommended promotion to rear admiral was delayed from August 1898 until April 1899. Had the war not ended, he would have commanded the projected fleet sortie to the coast of Spain. A commissioner to Cuba during the autumn of 1898, Admiral Sampson again commanded the North Atlantic Squadron in the *New York* from December 1898 to October 1899 and from then until October 1901 the Boston Navy Yard. He retired the following February.

Schley, Winfield Scott

(October 9, 1839–October 2, 1911).
USNA (Md.) 1860 (18/25).

Hero of the Spanish-American War, Schley (rhymes with "tie") participated in the homeward voyage of Japan's first diplomatic mission, on the steam frigate *Niagara* (1860–61), the vessel which assumed blockade station off Charleston in May 1861 and immediately captured the blockade runner *General Parkhill,* Schley commanding the latter as prize master, taking her to Philadelphia. There he reported to the sidewheel steamer *Keystone State* for more Atlantic blockade work, became master in August and moved to the Mobile blockade aboard the frigate *Potomac* via Vera Cruz as navigator. He twice distinguished himself near Mobile, especially in January 1862 by assisting the screw gunboat *R. R. Cuyler* during an engagement with a blockade runner. Transferred in the same waters to the screw gunboat *Winona* as executive officer, Schley became lieutenant in July and with his vessel shifted operations to the Mississippi against Port Hudson, during the heavy bombardments of which in March 1863 he temporarily commanded the new screw sloop *Monongahela.* He continued to attack that place as navigator of the steam sloop *Richmond* until it fell in July. Assigned to the steam gunboat *Wateree* as exec, he patrolled in the Pacific (1864–66) and helped to quell rebelling Chinese coolies in the Chincha Islands and landed in strife-torn San Salvador. Between tours on the Naval Academy faculty (1866–69, 1872–76) he operated on the Asiatic Station as exec of the screw sloop *Benicia* and took part in the 1871 attacks on the Korean forts on the Salee River, promotions to lieutenant commander and commander occurring in July 1866 and June 1874 respectively.

A seasoned combat officer, Commander Schley saw no further action for the next quarter of a century: skipper of the screw steamer *Essex* (1876–79), which he brought into commission for Atlantic cruising; lighthouse inspector at Boston (1880–83); commanding officer of the steam whaler *Thetis* and of the three-ship expedition which rescued Army Lt. Adolphus W. Greely and the survivers of his exploring party from the Arctic ice (1884); Chief of the Bureau of Engineering and Recruiting (1884–89); commissioning captain (his rank from April 1888) of the unarmored cruiser *Baltimore* (C-3) for her Pacific duty (1889–92) during which (1891) he diplomatically protected American interests in the midst of the Chilean revolution after two of his sailors had been killed by a Valparaiso mob; lighthouse inspector (1892–95); skipper of the armored cruiser *New York* (ACR-2) in the North Atlantic; member of the Board of Inspection and Survey (1896–97); and chairman of the Lighthouse Board (1897–98). Promoted commodore in February 1898, Schley returned to battery in command of the Flying Squadron, flagship *Brooklyn* (ACR-3), against the Spanish in the Caribbean. After blockading Cuban Cienfuegos and Santiago, he led the battle in July which resulted in the destruction of the Spanish fleet as it sortied from the latter port. Unfortunately, the Navy Department censured him for vacillating in his conduct of the campaign and the Battle of Santiago and tended to side with Commo. W. T. Sampson's claims of credit for the victory in the bitter dispute which followed. His promotion to rear admiral was therefore delayed until August 1899. He served on the Puerto Rico commission in Cuba late in 1898, as president of the retirement board, and as commander-in-chief of the South Atlantic Squadron, flagship the protected cruiser *Chicago* (1899–1901). Admiral Schley, who retired in October 1901, co-authored *The Rescue of Greely* (1885) and wrote *Forty-Five Years Under the Flag* (1904).

Scott, Norman

(August 10, 1889–November 13, 1942).
USNA (Ind.) 1911 (174/193).

Navy Department: National Archives

Victor at Cape Esperance, Scott spent his entire career as a "black shoe" in the "Gun Club": before World War I in the Atlantic battleship *Idaho* (BB-29) (1911–13 and again in 1924); the destroyer *Jenkins* (DD-42) and destroyer tender *Dixie* (AD-1) during the troubles with Mexico, and the *Ammen* (DD-35) in the Atlantic; in the World War as executive officer of the *Jacob Jones* (DD-61) from July 1916 until her sinking by the *U-53* out of Brest in December 1917, and with the *Melville* (AD-2) for the return home; and in the postwar period commanding an Eagle patrol boat division on the *Eagle 3* (PE-3), then commanding the *Eagle 2* (PE-2), both at New York (1919), to the *DuPont* (DD-152) briefly, and skipper of the *Eagle 1* (PE-1) at Constantinople (early 1920). During the 1920's Lieutenant Commander Scott outfitted the *Stoddert* (DD-302) at San Francisco as her skipper (1920); was assistant fire control officer on the *New York* (BB-34) in the Pacific (1920–21); operated with the minelayer *Burns* (DM-11) in Hawaiian waters (1921–22); and was aide and personnel officer to Battle Fleet commanders (1924–27) Adms. Samuel S. Robison, C. F. Hughes, and Richard H. Jackson, flagship *California* (BB-44). In 1930 he went to the aircraft tender *Jason* (AV-2) in the Asiatic Fleet, where he transferred to command of the *MacLeish* (DD-220), then of the *Paul Jones* (DD-230) until 1932, with subsequent duty as exec of the cruiser *Cincinnati* (CL-6) in the Battle Force (1935–37).

Shore billets were at the Office of the Chief of Naval Operations (1918–19), including time as naval aide to President Woodrow Wilson, September 1918 to March 1919; the Office of Naval Communications (1920); the Bureau of Navigation (1920, 1932–34); the Fourteenth Naval District in

Hawaii (1922–24), the second year as aide to commandant Adm. John D. McDaniel; the Naval War College as student (1934–35); and the Naval Mission to Brazil (1937–39). Captain Scott commanded the *Pensacola* (CA-24) out of Pearl Harbor from the end of 1939 until escorting a convoy to Australia from November 1941 to January 1942. At the Office of the CNO the next four months, he was promoted to rear admiral in May and given command of Task Force 18 in the Pacific. His flag in the *San Juan* (CL-54), he helped cover the landings at Guadalcanal in August 1942, patrolled in those waters in the *San Francisco* (CA-38) in September, and while commanding TF 64 defeated a Japanese surface force at the Battle of Cape Esperance in October, sinking a heavy cruiser and a destroyer. Later that month Admiral Scott shifted his flag to the *Atlanta* (CL-51) and under Adm. D. J. Callaghan took part in the Naval Battle of Guadalcanal in mid-November. He was killed in this action by enemy salvos which also caused his flagship to be scuttled.

Selfridge, Thomas Oliver (Jr.)

(February 6, 1836–February 4, 1924).
USNA (Mass.) 1854 (1/6).

Naval Historical Center

Civil War hero and postwar explorer, this first officer to receive a diploma under the permanent Naval Academy system joined the razee *Independence* in the Pacific during the summer of 1854, the year before his father of the same name (1804–1902!), who had commanded the sloop *Dale* in the capture of Guaymas during the Mexican War, was promoted to captain. In January 1857 Passed Midshipman Selfridge received orders to the Coast Survey schooner *Nautilus,* becoming acting master in June before transferring as master to the sloop *Vincennes* in the African Squadron in October. In

298

July 1860 he was promoted to lieutenant and three months later assigned to the frigate *Cumberland,* flagship of the Home Squadron, and with her participated in the evacuation of the Gosport navy base at Norfolk in April 1861. While his father commanded the sidewheel steamer *Mississippi* in the Gulf blockade, he fought at the Hatteras Inlet forts in August and against the ironclad *Merrimack (Virginia)* the following March when that vessel sank his ship. After commanding the ironclad *Monitor* for three days after the famous battle, he became flag lieutenant to the North Atlantic Blockading Squadron commander, Adm. L. M. Goldsborough, flagship the steam frigate *Minnesota.* In July he briefly commanded the experimental submarine battery *Alligator,* followed by promotion to lieutenant commander just as his father became commodore and commandant of the Mare Island Navy Yard (1862–64).

Lieutenant Commander Selfridge commanded the ironclad gunboat *Cairo* on the Mississippi from August 1862, only to lose this vessel when it exploded from a torpedo it was sweeping near Haines Bluff, Mississippi, in December. He shifted to command of the sidewheeler *Manitou* (ex-*Fort Hindman)* but in June commanded a naval battery ashore in the siege against Vicksburg. After the latter place fell in July, Selfridge led a gunboat flotilla in the *Conestoga* up the Little Red and other local rivers, capturing the Confederate steamers *Louisville* and *Elmira.* The squadron proceeded to the same area for the Red River campaign, yet in March 1864 his flagship collided with another vessel and sank, Selfridge's third sinking of his still-young career. He was immediately given command of the ironclad *Osage* in the expedition, led the entire naval force as acting fleet captain around the Red River dam in May, and then commanded the ram *Vindicator* on the Mississippi. A favorite of Adm. D. D. Porter, Selfridge went East with him and in October took command of the screw steamer *Huron* which he directed in both attacks on Fort Fisher, notably in the second, January 1865, in which he personally led one assault column ashore. Late the next month he participated in the capture of Wilmington. During his first postwar tour, at the Naval Academy (1865–68), he commanded the training frigate *Macedonian,* and his father retired as rear admiral. He became skipper of the gunboat *Nipsic* in the West Indies to search for a naval base site in 1868 and late the next year achieved the rank of commander.

Commander Selfridge's career as an explorer began in January 1870 when he took command of a survey expedition south of Panama to establish a transisthmian canal route, completing his work and report in 1874. After a tour at the Boston Navy Yard (1874–77), he surveyed 1300 miles up the Amazon and Madeira rivers in the screw sloop *Enterprise* during the summer of 1878, the next two years commanding this vessel on the European Station and participating in an international interocean canal conference at Paris (1879). Promotion to captain in November 1880 was soon followed by command of the Torpedo Station at Newport at which he conducted many experiments and began the manufacture of gun cotton for the Navy. In March 1885 Captain Selfridge assumed command of the screw sloop *Omaha* on the Asiatic Station, being relieved two years later and court-martialed for holding target practice in Japanese waters. Acquitted, he served on the Board of Inspection and Survey (1888–90) and was its president (1894–95), commanded the Boston Navy Yard (1890–93), headed the commission which selected the navy yard site at Puget Sound, Washington (1890), and was promoted to commodore in April 1894 and temporary rear admiral in November 1895, permanent rank occurring the following February. Admiral Selfridge's last command was the European Squadron, flagship the armored cruiser *New York* (ACR-2) (1895–97), during which in 1896 he was the American naval delegate to the coronation of Czar Nicholas II. He retired in February 1898 and eventually published his *Memoirs* (1924).

Semmes, Raphael

(September 27, 1809–August 30, 1877).

U. S. Signal Corps: National Archives

Celebrated skipper of the Confederate raider *Alabama,* Marylander Semmes first sailed as midshipman on the maiden voyage of the sloop *Lexington* off Labrador, to the West Indies, and in the Mediterranean (1826–28) and on a cruise of the sloop *Erie* to South America (1828–29). Brief assignments to the frigate *Brandywine* (1830) and the schooner *Porpoise* in the West Indies (1830–31) preceded his study at the Norfolk naval school (1831–32) and warranting as passed midshipman in June 1832. He participated in a survey of Narragansett Bay (1832) and took charge of the Navy's chronometers in Washington (1833–34), but then he studied law while awaiting a vacancy in the list of lieutenants. Semmes operated with the frigate *Constellation* as acting master against the Seminole Indians (1835–37), an assignment which culminated in his promotion to lieutenant in February 1837. After shore duty at Norfolk (1838–40), he surveyed the Southern coast, especially Ship Island, on the brig *Consort* (1840–41), and served at the Pensacola Navy Yard (1841–43), followed by a month with the sloop *Warren*. He commanded the sidewheel gunboat *Poinsett* in surveying the waters near Tampa, Florida (1843–45). From the end of 1845 until September 1846 he operated with the brig *Porpoise* in the Home Squadron, transferring to its flagship frigate *Cumberland* for a month of fighting against Mexico.

Lieutenant Semmes took command of the brig *Somers* in October 1846, mistakenly destroyed the American spy ship *Criolla* off Vera Cruz in November, and the following month lost his vessel when it capsized in a sudden storm. Held blameless, he joined the staff of Home Squadron commander Commo. David Conner as flag lieutenant on the frigate *Raritan*, went ashore with the artillery at Vera Cruz in March 1847, participated in the foray to Tuxpan, and accompanied the army overland to Mexico City to arrange for the exchange of naval prisoners and distinguished himself in action as a volunteer aide to Gen. W. J. Worth until November. He commanded the storeship *Electra* supplying the Squadron during the final operations against Mexico, January to July 1848, and cruised the coast of Yucatan with the schooner *Flirt* during duty with the office of the Inspector of Provisions and Clothing at Pensacola (1848–49). While waiting orders during most of the postwar period, Lieutenant Semmes practiced law and utilized his legal talents in several court-martial cases at Pensacola and once (1854) as judge advocate at the Memphis Navy Yard. Promoted commander in September 1855, he was a district lighthouse inspector under the Department of the Treasury (1856–58) and then Secretary of the Lighthouse Board (1858–61). Upon the secession of Alabama, his home state for many years, he left the Navy in February 1861 and that same month began serving the new Confederate government at Montgomery.

Semmes purchased arms and equipment for the Confederate Navy in the weeks prior to Fort Sumter, being commissioned commander in March 1861. For two weeks in April he was chief of the Lighthouse Bureau but then was given command of the converted screw steamer *Sumter*, which he armed at New Orleans and took to sea at the end of June to raid Union commerce. He captured a dozen prizes in the Caribbean area and six more while crossing the Atlantic to Cadiz, then Gibraltar, where he was blockaded and forced to sell the ship in April 1862. During the summer Semmes was promoted to captain and given command of the screw sloop *Alabama* at the Azores. He attacked Yankee shipping along the Atlantic seaboard the rest of the year, sinking the sidewheel steam blockader *Hatteras* off Galveston in January 1863. The *Alabama* operated into the summer in the South Atlantic, Semmes converting one capture into the tender *Tuscaloosa*, and in August cruised into the Indian Ocean, as far as Singapore by December, and then back. Upon reaching Cherbourg, France, in June 1864, the *Alabama* could boast of 82 captured merchantmen, most of them destroyed, but several days later Captain Semmes accepted combat with the Union screw sloop

Kearsarge, only to have his famous vessel sunk in the action off Cherbourg. Rescued by an English yacht, the captain returned home via the circuitous route of Mexico, reached Richmond in January 1865, and was promoted to rear admiral the next month.

Admiral Semmes took command of the James River Squadron, flagship the ironclad steam sloop *Virginia II,* a few days after his promotion, but when his three ironclads and five wooden gunboats were unable to escape the final Union army advance on Richmond at the beginning of April, he had them all put to the torch. Commissioned a brigadier general in the Confederate army, Semmes organized his crews into a brigade of artillery and infantry, with his son Midshipman Raphael Semmes, Jr., on his staff, and commanded the defenses of Danville, Virginia, until several days later when his brigade moved on to Greensboro, North Carolina, to surrender with the Army of Tennessee late in April 1865. He wrote *Service Afloat and Ashore during the Mexican War* (1851); *Campaign of General Scott in the Valley of Mexico* (1852); *The Cruise of the Alabama and Sumter* (1864); and *Memoirs of Service Afloat During the War between the States* (1869). Directly related to Admiral Semmes were Commo. Alexander A. Semmes (1825–1885), commander of the ironclad force supporting Grant's army on the James River during the Wilderness Campaign, and Adm. Benedict J. Semmes, Jr., Commander Second Fleet and NATO's Striking Fleet Atlantic (1968–70), president of the Naval War College (1971–72), and son-in-law of Adm. W. L. Ainsworth *(q.v.).*

302

Naval Photographic Center

Sharp, Ulysses S. Grant, Jr.

(April 2, 1906——   ). USNA (Mont.)
1927 (289/579).

Pacific Commander during the height of the Vietnam War, Sharp had extensive sea duty in the Pacific—the battleship *New Mexico* (BB-40), the transport *Henderson* (AP-1), the destroyers *Sumner* (DD-333) and *Buchanan* (DD-131), and the aircraft carrier *Saratoga* (CV-3)—before receiving postgraduate training in engineering at Annapolis (1934–36) for engineering duty on the cruiser *Richmond* (CL-9) and as engineer of the new *Winslow* (DD-359). As lieutenant commander, he served at the Bureau of Ships (1940–42) and commanded the high-speed destroyer-minesweeper *Hogan* (DMS-6) for Caribbean convoy escort work and the invasion of North Africa. His brother, Lt. Cdr. Thomas F. Sharp, who stood very high at Annapolis in the Class of '35, was lost off Honshu in the spring of 1943 with the submarine *Pickerel* (SS-177) on her seventh war patrol. Reporting in January 1943 to the *Boyd* (DD-544), Sharp brought her into commission in May for carrier support operations at Baker Island (September), Wake (October), the Gilberts and Nauru where the ship was damaged by a shore battery (November-December), Hollandia-Truk (April–May 1944), the Marianas and Battle of the Philippine Sea (June–August), the Palaus (September), and Philippines operations (October). Detached in November 1944, Commander Sharp served as combat information center and tactical radar officer to Pacific Fleet Cruiser-Destroyer Force commanders Adms. W. L. Ainsworth, W. H. P. Blandy, Francis S. Low and Frank G. Fahrion from January 1945 till mid–1948. After commanding the Fleet Sonar School at San Diego (1948–49), he attended the Naval War College and in June 1950 became Commander Destroyer Squadron Five, flagship *Rowan* (DD-782).

Captain Sharp interrupted his Korean escort chores to be Seventh Fleet planning officer to Adm. A. D. Struble for the Inchon landing during the summer of 1950. The following January he became operations officer, then in October chief of staff, to Adms. Matthias B. Gardner and F. B. Stump, Commanders Second Fleet, until the summer of 1953 when he assumed command of the heavy cruiser *Macon* (CA-132) in the Atlantic. In the middle of his next tour (1954–56) as deputy chief of staff (plans and operations) to Pacific Fleet commander Stump, he was promoted to rear admiral, in which rank he commanded Cruiser Division Five in the *Helena* (CA-75) and *Columbus* (CA-74) on the West coast. He served in the Strategic Plans Division in the Office of the Chief of Naval Operations as assistant director (1957–58) then director (1958–59) and was ComCruDesPac (1959–60). Advanced to vice admiral in April 1960, Sharp commanded the First Fleet for fewer than three months and was then made Deputy CNO (Plans and Policy), in which capacity he played a leading role in the Cuban missile blockade of October 1962. He was appointed Commander-in-Chief Pacific Fleet in September 1963 in the rank of admiral and the following June Commander-in-Chief Pacific. In August 1964 he obtained permission from the Department of Defense to launch retaliatory carrier strikes against North Vietnamese PT-boat bases, thus initiating the full American involvement in that war with he directing all American military operations through the gradual buildup of the mid-1960's. Admiral Sharp retired in August 1968.

Shepard, Alan Bartlett, Jr.

(November 18, 1923——). USNA (N.H.) 1945 (463/914).

The first American to fly in space, astronaut Shepard, son of an Army colonel, was commissioned early (June 1944), was briefly stationed at Naval Air Station Jacksonville, and in August 1944 reported to the destroyer *Cogswell* (DD-561) with which he screened fast carriers in the Palaus and Philippines until January 1945, stood on radar picket off Okinawa in May and June, and again screened the carriers attacking Japan in July and August. After flight training at Corpus Christi and Pensacola, October 1945 to March 1947, he instructed at Cecil Field near Jacksonville and at Norfolk, joined Fighting Squadron 4-B briefly, then Fighting 42, both on the carrier *Franklin D. Roosevelt* (CVB-42) on the East coast and in the Mediterranean (1948–50), the last year on the *Midway* (CVB-41). Trained as a test pilot at Patuxent River, Maryland, he remained there (1951–53, 1955–57) to conduct high altitude tests, in-flight refueling techniques, carrier suitability trials for the F2H-3 Banshee, and the first angled deck experiments; to be project test pilot on the F5D Skylancer; and to test the F3H Demon, F8U Crusader, F4D Skyray and F11F Tigercat. These duties were complemented by a tour (1953–55) as operations officer of night Fighting 193 out of Moffett Field, California, and aboard the *Oriskany* (CVA-34) in the Western Pacific. A student at the Naval War College (1957–58), he ended his career as a naval aviator by serving as aviation readiness officer of the Atlantic Fleet.

Upon selection with six others for astronaut training in April 1959, Commander Shepard in May joined the Project Mercury staff, phase one of the National Aeronautics and Space Administration's Manned Satellite Program, at Langley Air Force Base, Virginia, for pre-space flight training. In May 1961—three weeks after Russian cosmonaut Yuri Gagarin had become the first human being to fly in space—Shepard rode the *Freedom 7* Mercury space capsule 115 miles above and 302 miles downrange from Florida's Cape Canaveral in suborbital flight. Subsequently ground-based with NASA during the Gemini and Apollo programs, he became Chief of the Astronaut Office in March 1969 and later commander of the Apollo 14 lunar landing crew. Captain Shepard piloted this space craft to the surface of the Moon and back in January and February 1971, he himself walking on the Moon for some eight hours. The following December he was promoted to rear admiral, the first astronaut to achieve flag rank. Admiral Shepard continued in the space program, retiring from the Navy in August 1974.

Sherman, Forrest Percival

(October 30, 1896—July 22, 1951).
USNA (Mass.) 1918 (2/199).

Navy Department: National Archives

Principal strategic adviser in the Pacific war and architect of the unification Navy, New Hampshire-born Sherman graduated early—in June 1917—for World War I convoy escort in the Mediterranean aboard the gunboat *Nashville* (PG-7) and at the very end of hostilities on the destroyer *Murray* (DD-97) in the Atlantic. Continuing in that ocean aboard the battleship *Utah* (BB-31) (1919–20) and the *Reid* (DD-292), he commanded the understrength *Barry* (DD-248) in reserve (mid-1921) and was flag lieutenant to Adm. Newton A. McCully, Jr., commanding the Control Force of Atlantic escort and underwater warfare vessels, flagship *Florida* (BB-30). Flight training at Pensacola (1922) inaugurated his career in naval aviation, teaching flying there (1924–26) after a year with Fighting Squadron Two in

306

the Battle Fleet. Lieutenant Sherman's intellectual talents began to be manifested during his Naval War College tour (1926–27) and early articles in the U.S. Naval Institute *Proceedings,* but duty involving flying was always paramount: fitting out and service aboard the aircraft carrier *Lexington* (CV-2) (1927–28); Scouting Two on the *Saratoga* (CV-3), briefly as squadron commander; flag secretary to Adm. J. M. Reeves, Aircraft Squadrons commander on the latter ship (1929–30) and to his successor Adm. H. E. Yarnell (1931–32), in the interim teaching flight tactics at the Naval Academy; and skipper of award-winning Fighting One on the *Saratoga* (1932–33).

After a lengthy tour of duty (1933–36) as director of the Aviation Ordnance Section at the Bureau of Aeronautics, Commander Sherman returned to sea for a year as navigator of the *Ranger* (CV-4) and (1937–40) as fleet aviation officer to Adm. Claude C. Bloch, Battle Force and then U.S. Fleet commander, flagships *California* (BB-44) and *Pennsylvania* (BB-38). Assigned to the War Plans Division of the Office of the Chief of Naval Operations early in 1940, he participated importantly in preparing the country for war, additionally as a member of the American-Canadian Joint Board on Defense and as naval aviation adviser at the "Atlantic Charter" conference off Argentia, Newfoundland in August 1941. The following February he moved over to U.S. Fleet headquarters and the Joint Strategic Committee, but was soon promoted to captain and in May given command of the *Wasp* (CV-7). Taking his ship from the Atlantic to the South Pacific, Captain Sherman supported the Guadalcanal landings in August 1942 but lost his ship to a Japanese submarine the next month. In October he became chief of staff to Adm. J. H. Towers, Commander Air Force Pacific Fleet, and transferred in November 1943 to be Assistant then Deputy Chief of Staff (Plans) and head of the staff War Plans Division to Pacific Fleet commander Adm. C. W. Nimitz. In this latter role and in the rank of rear admiral, he became Nimitz's alter ego, key adviser and lieutenant at all major strategic conferences, culminating at the Japanese surrender ceremonies in September 1945.

Admiral Sherman was administratively designated Commander Carrier Division One during the autumn of 1945 and thereafter Deputy CNO (Operations), with promotion to vice admiral in December. During this assignment he hammered out the Navy's position on the unification of the armed services and afterward (1948–49) commanded U.S. Naval Forces in the Mediterranean (changed to Sixth Task Fleet in June 1948). In the wake of the revolt of the admirals against unification, fiscal retrenchment, and sagging Navy morale, Sherman was called upon to restore the leadership lost during the tenure of Adm. Louis E. Denfeld as CNO by assuming that post in November 1949 in the full rank of admiral. The youngest CNO to that time, 53 years, he ran the Navy under the titular Secretaryship of Francis P. Matthews, directed the service in the early months of the Korean War, and became the dominant figure on the Joint Chiefs of Staff, on which he strongly supported President Harry S. Truman's removal of Gen. Douglas MacArthur from command in the Far East. Physically exhausting himself in building up the Navy's fighting posture, Admiral Sherman died in the line of duty while on a diplomatic mission to Spain.

Sherman, Frederick Carl "Ted"

(May 27, 1888–July 27, 1957). USNA (Mich.) 1910 (24/131).

Navy Department: National Archives

Carrier commander Sherman (no relation to F. P. Sherman) spent most of his career in line-of-battle ships and submarines, beginning with pre-World War I duty stations on the armored cruiser *Montana* (ACR-13) and battleship *Ohio* (BB-12) in the Atlantic, the *Maryland* (ACR-8) in the Pacific, and the submarine tender *Cheyenne* (BM-10) for sub training on the West coast (1914–15), where he remained on the subs *H-3* (SS-30) and *H-2* (SS-29), commanding the latter. Reporting to the outfitting *O-7* (SS-68) in December 1917, he commanded her from commissioning in July 1918 through wartime coastal patrols along the Atlantic seaboard until the following spring when he was navigator of the troop-carrying *Minnesota* (BB-22). Lieutenant Commander Sherman served ashore at the Bureaus of Engineering (1919–21) and Navigation (1925–31), as a Naval War College student (1924–25, 1939–40), at the Division of Fleet Training (1926–26, 1931–32), and at San Diego as aide to Adm. William T. Tarrant, commandant of the Eleventh Naval District (1934–35). At sea, he commanded Submarine Division Nine, flagship *R-2* (SS-79), out of San Pedro, California (1921–24); was award-winning gunnery officer of the *West Virginia* (BB-48) in the Pacific (1926–29); was navigator of the Pacific light cruiser *Detroit* (CL-8) (1932–33); and commanded in that ocean Destroyer

308

Divisions Eight, flagships *Lawrence* (DD-250), *Humphreys* (DD-236), and *King* (DD-242) (1933–34), and One for a short time (1934). In spite of his age he undertook flight training at Pensacola (1935–36) and was executive officer first of the aircraft carrier *Saratoga* (CV-3) in the Pacific (1936–37), then of Naval Air Station San Diego.

Captain (from June 1938) Sherman preceded World War II as Commander Patrol Wing Three at Coco Solo, Canal Zone (1938–39), Naval War College student and skipper of the *Lexington* (CV-2) from June 1940, cruising out of Pearl Harbor immediately before and after the attack there. His carrier's planes struck Rabaul in February 1942 and Lae and Salamaua, New Guinea in March, he as Air Commander under Adm. Wilson Brown. They sank the Japanese light carrier *Shoho* in the Battle of the Coral Sea in May, but the *Lexington* herself was sunk in that action by aerial torpedoes and bombs. Advanced immediately to rear admiral, he spent the summer in Washington as assistant chief of staff to Adm. E. J. King, U.S. Fleet commander, then returned to the South Pacific in October as Commander Task Force 16 then of Carrier Division Two, flagship *Enterprise* (CV-6), supporting the Solomons campaign. In July 1943 Admiral Sherman became ComCarDiv One on the *Saratoga* to attack Rabaul and support the Bougainville and Gilberts landings in November, in the first two as CTF 38 and in the third leading Task Group 50.4, late in the operation shifting his flag to the *Bunker Hill* (CV-17). After a rest commanding West coast Fleet Air (March–August 1944), he returned as ComCarDiv One and as CTG 38.3/58.3, flagship *Essex* (CV-9), fought in the Philippines and Battle of Leyte Gulf (August–January 1945) and in the Iwo Jima and Okinawa operations (February–June 1945). In July 1945 he was made vice admiral and given command of the First Fast Carrier Force Pacific and Task Force 58, flagships *Wasp* (CV-18) and the new *Lexington* (CV-16) for the occupation in August, then the *Shangri-La* (CV-38) and *Intrepid* (CV-11). He commanded the Fifth Fleet in the *Iowa* (BB-51) and *Vicksburg* (CL-86) from January to September 1946, and was inactive until his retirement the following March in the rank of admiral. He wrote *Combat Command* (1950).

Shubrick, William Branford

(October 31, 1790–May 27, 1874).

Mexican War leader and commander of the Paraguay expedition of 1859, South Carolinian Shubrick was one of four Navy sons of Continental Army Col. Thomas Shubrick. The others were Capt. Edward R. Shubrick, commander of the frigate *Columbia* before being lost at sea in 1844; Cdr. Irvine Shubrick, skipper of the sloop *Saratoga* in 1846; and Lt. John Templer Shubrick, distinguished officer on the frigates *Constitution* and *President* and sloop *Hornet* during the War of 1812 and on the frigate *Guerrière* against Algiers before disappearing at sea along with his new command, the sloop *Epervier,* in 1815. The latter's son, Lt. Edmund T. Shubrick, fought in the Mexican War. As midshipman in 1806, W. Branford Shubrick joined the sloop *Wasp* in the Mediterranean. While on the brig *Argus* along the Atlantic seaboard later, he befriended shipmate James Fenimore Cooper, the novelist who later dedicated two books to him. After duty on board the *Hornet* (1811–12) and promotion to lieutenant, he went to Hampton Roads with the frigate *Constellation* and commanded a gunboat defending Craney Island and Norfolk (1813). Joining the *Constitution* late in 1813, he operated for the duration in the Atlantic and played a leading part in the battle which resulted in the capture of British frigate *Cyane* and sloop *Levant* in February 1815, completing the cruise as executive officer.

Lieutenant Shubrick cruised to and throughout the Mediterranean in the ship-of-the-line *Washington* (1815–18), commanded the Charleston Navy Yard in the rank of master commandant (1820–23), and following leave brought the sloop *Lexington* into service as her captain in June 1826, protecting American fishing craft off Labrador before going to Trinidad the next year and returning home with the remains of Commo. O. H. Perry.

310

Shubrick commanded the sloop *Natchez* in the Caribbean and Atlantic (1829–30) and reported to the Washington Navy Yard where he was promoted to captain in 1831 and then had ordnance duty (1833–37). He assumed command of the West India Squadron, flagship the frigate *Macedonian,* in 1838 and after two years of pacification operations against the Seminoles took over the Norfolk Navy Yard. Chief of the Bureau of Provisions and Clothing (1844–46), he began his Mexican War sea service by hoisting his flag in the razee *Independence* in January 1847 to take command of the Pacific Squadron, but a confusion in orders led to a postponement during which, in the spring, he directed the blockade of Mazatlán. He took command of the Squadron at California in July, captured Mazatlán with landing forces in November and also seized Guaymas, La Paz, and San Blas before the end of the war and his relief in May 1848. Command of the Philadelphia Navy Yard followed (1849–51), and after brief ordnance duty he became chairman of the Lighthouse Board in 1852, a post he occupied until 1871!

Commodore Shubrick wore his flag on the new screw steamer *Princeton* during the summer of 1853 while commanding the Eastern Squadron protecting American fishing interests off Nova Scotia, negotiating a treaty there with British Admiral Sir George Seymour. After duty as Chief of the Bureau of Construction and Repair (1853–54), he gave full attention to his Lighthouse Board tasks. In 1857 he headed a board to formulate naval regulations. In September 1858, Flag Officer Shubrick raised his flag on the frigate *Sabine* as commander of the Brazil Squadron with orders to obtain retribution for Paraguay's firing on the American Survey steamer *Water Witch.* He led an imposing expedition of 19 vessels to Paraguay, arriving in January 1859, and immediately negotiated a settlement and a new treaty with great success. Returning home in May, Shubrick returned to his lighthouse work for another full decade, which included the Civil War, although he was placed on the retired list in December 1861. He was advanced to rear admiral on that list the following July.

Shufeldt, Robert Wilson

(February 21, 1822–November 7, 1895).

Naval Historical Center

Promoter of American Far Eastern trade, New Yorker Shufeldt became midshipman in 1839 and operated in the Caribbean with the frigate *United States* (1839–40), the Brazil Squadron aboard the frigate *Potomac* (1840–41) and the sloop *Marion* (1841–42), and the Home Squadron in the new brig *Bainbridge* (1842–43) and again the *Potomac* (1843–44). After a year of study at the Philadelphia Naval School, he became passed midshipman and went to the Coast Survey (1845–46) then the African Squadron briefly aboard the *United States* and again (1846–48) the *Marion*, which shifted to the Mediterranean. He left the Navy for several years on the Coast Survey schooner *Morris* (1849), as watch officer of the mail steamers *Atlantic* (1850–51) and *Georgia* (1851), and extended furlough. Although promoted to master in March 1853 and lieutenant a year later, he resigned from the Navy in June 1854 in order to help organize the Steam Commercial Marine of New York. Shufeldt commanded the Collins Line steamer *Liverpool* between Liverpool and New York (1854–56); superintended the construction of the steamers *Black Warrior* and *Catawba*, which he commanded on the New York-to-New Orleans coastal run; and was commanding the steamer *Quaker City* on the New York-Havana route when the Civil War broke out. He turned down a lieutenancy in order to be Consul-General to Cuba (1861–63), during which in 1862 he carried out a special mission to French-occupied Mexico.

Commissioned commander in the Navy in April 1863, Shufeldt commanded the fitting-out sidewheel steamer *Fort Jackson* for three weeks then the sidewheeler *Conemaugh* blockading and bombarding Charleston and capturing Morris Island. He transferred to the screw steamer *Proteus* in

312

October, and outfitted and commissioned her as skipper the next March for blockade patrol around Key West. The *Proteus* captured four blockade runners during 1864–65 and in March 1865 supported the army's operations at St. Mark's River against Tallahassee, where Shufeldt was senior officer present. Detached in May, the next month he assumed command of the screw sloop *Hartford*, flagship of the new Asiatic Squadron, transferring there to command of the screw sloop *Wachusett* (1866–68). After brief command of the naval rendezvous at New York, he was captain of the monitor *Miantonomah* in the North Atlantic (1869–70). During this tour, he was promoted to the rank of captain, and then had brief ordnance duty at Portsmouth. Following up on a project he had begun privately in the late 1850's to survey Mexico's isthmus of Tehuantepec for a possible canal route, Captain Shufeldt in September 1870 was given command of such an official surveying expedition, which he held until the following August. He commanded two vessels of the European Squadron, the flagship steam frigate *Wabash* (1871–72) and the screw sloop *Plymouth* (1871–73). After duty as executive officer of the New York Navy Yard (1873–75), he was Chief of the Bureau of Equipment and Recruiting (1875–78), being promoted to commodore early in 1877. During the latter tour he commanded the naval forces at New Orleans in the midst of disturbances over the Presidential election of 1876, and he modernized the system for naval apprentices.

Because of his strong advocacy of utilizing the Navy to promote American trade with the underdeveloped regions of the world, especially China and Korea, Commodore Shufeldt hoisted his flag in the screw sloop *Ticonderoga* in November 1878 to cruise to the Orient via Liberia, in which place he tried in vain to settle a boundary quarrel. In order to open American trade relations with Korea, during the spring and summer of 1880 he convinced China to agree to aid Korea in return for American assistance in creating a navy for China. He returned home but was back in China the next year as naval attaché in which capacity he helped to finalize the formal treaty as its main architect, completed in May 1882, Korea's first treaty with a Western nation. He then served as president of the Naval Advisory Board (1882–84), being instrumental in the planning of the "New Navy", and was concurrently Superintendent of the Naval Observatory (1883–84). Promoted to rear admiral in February 1884, he was retired several days later. Shufeldt authored *The Relation of the Navy to the Commerce of the United States* (1878).

Sigsbee, Charles Dwight

*(January 16, 1845–July 19, 1923).
USNA (N.Y.) 1863 (19/29).*

Naval Historical Center

Captain of the *Maine* and hydrographer, Sigsbee saw Civil War service on the blockade and at the battles of Mobile Bay and Fort Fisher aboard the screw sloops *Monongahela* and *Brooklyn,* going thereafter to the Far East on the screw sloop *Wyoming* and sidewheel gunboat *Ashuelot* (1865–69). Much of his subsequent career was spent between teaching at the Naval Academy (1869–71, 1882–85, 1887–90) and hydrographic work with the Coast Survey, commanding its steamer *Blake* in the Gulf of Mexico and developing several deep-sea scientific devices (1875–78). Several tours at the Hydrographic Office in Washington (1873–74, 1878–82) culminated in his appointment as its Chief (1893–97). Seagoing duty included the Atlantic steam sloops *Severn, Worcester,* and *Canandaigua* (1871–73) and command of the training sloops *Dale* (1883–84), *Constellation* (1889) and *Portsmouth* (1890–92) and the screw sloop *Kearsarge* (1885–86) in European waters, and he served on the Examining and Retiring boards in Washington (1887). Captain Sigsbee commanded the battleship *Maine* from April 1897 until it exploded and sank off Havana the following February. He then brought the auxiliary cruiser *St. Paul* into commission in April 1898, captured a collier in the West Indies in May, defeated the Spanish cruiser *Isabel II* and destroyer *Terror* off Puerto Rico in June, and transported troops thereafter. He commanded the battleship *Texas,* wrote an account of the *Maine*'s destruction (1899), and served as chief intelligence officer (1900–03) before promotion to rear admiral in August 1903. Admiral Sigsbee commanded the League Island Navy Yard (1902–03); the Caribbean Squadron, flagship cruiser *Olympia* (C-6); the South Atlantic Squadron, flagship armored cruiser *Brooklyn* (ACR-3) (1904–05); and the North Atlantic Fleet's Second

314

Division (1905–06), flagship battleship *Alabama* (BB-8). In the *Brooklyn*, in 1905 he transported the remains of John Paul Jones from France to the United States. After special duty, he retired in January 1907.

Admiral Sigsbee had many Navy and seagoing relatives: his father-in-law was Gen. H. H. Lockwood, for a quarter of a century (1841–76) professor of mathematics at the Naval Academy; his brother-in-law was Arctic explorer James Booth Lockwood; one son-in-law was Rear Admiral S. E. W. Kittelle (1867–1950), Commander Fleet Base Force in 1928–29; another was Rear Adm. C. B. T. Moore (1853–1923), commander of the *Chicago* (ACR-7) in the Far East (1909–10); and his grandson was Rear Adm. Charles J. Moore (1889–   ), chief of staff to Adm. R. A. Spruance, Commander Fifth Fleet, during the Central Pacific offensive of 1943–44.

Simpson, Edward

(March 3, 1824–December 1, 1888). USNA (N.Y.) 1846.

Naval Historical Center

A leader in late 19th century naval ordnance, Simpson served as midshipman (1840) with the razee *Independence* in ordinary at New York (1841–42), on the new frigate *Congress,* sloop *Decatur* and frigate *Potomac* in the Mediterranean and South Atlantic (1842–45), and with the New York receiving ship prior to his year at the new Naval Academy, to which he returned to teach gunnery (1853–54) then direct it (1858–60) and be the first head of the ordnance department there (1860–62) and commandant of midshipmen (1862–63). He fought in the Mexican War on the sidewheel steamer *Vixen* at Tabasco, Tampico, Tuxpan, and Vera Cruz (1846–47), went to the Coast Survey (1848–49, 1855–56), and served as acting master of the *Congress,* flagship of the Brazil Squadron, thwarting the slave traffic

315

(1850–53). As lieutenant, Simpson sailed in the sloop *Portsmouth* to the Far East, where he participated in the battles with the barrier forts near Canton (1855–58). In the Civil War he briefly commanded the screw frigate *Wabash* in the rank of lieutenant commander before leading the monitor *Passaic* during the 1863 attacks on Charleston. He brought the sidewheeler *Isonomia* into commission in July 1864 and operated on the blockade from North Carolina to Key West until the end of the year. Promoted to commander, in March 1865 he became fleet captain to Adm. H. K. Thatcher, West Gulf Blockading Squadron commander, in the sidewheeler *Stockdale* for the final amphibious assault on Mobile in April.

Commander Simpson commanded the steam sloop *Mohican* and sidewheel gunboat *Mohongo* in the Pacific (1866–68), headed the Hydrographic Office, was Assistant Chief of the Bureau of Ordnance (1869–70), became captain in 1870, had special duty in Europe before commanding the torpedo station at Newport (1873) and then the screw frigates *Franklin* (1873–74) and *Wabash* (1874) both in the Atlantic, and was skipper of the screw sloop *Omaha* in the South Pacific (1875–77). In 1878, after a year at the New York Navy Yard, he was promoted to commodore and given command of the naval station at New London for two years, then of the yard at Philadelphia's League Island (1880–83). Between tours as president of the Gun Foundry Board (1883–84) and of the Naval Advisory Board (1884–85) Simpson reached the rank of rear admiral and finished his career as president of the Board of Inspection and Survey (1885–86), retiring in March 1886. In addition to many other books, essays and reports on ordnance Admiral Simpson wrote *Treatise on Ordnance and Naval Gunnery* (1859) and co-authored *Modern Ships of War* (1888). He was president of the Naval Institute (1886–88) and father of Rear Adm. Edward Simpson (1860–1930), in 1920–21 commander of the Atlantic Fleet's Train.

Sims, William Sowden

(October 15, 1858–September 28, 1936).
USNA (Penn.) 1880 (33/62).

Premier World War I U.S. naval commander and leading innovator and reformer throughout his career, Sims began his service in the North Atlantic aboard the screw frigate *Tennessee* (1880–82) and after six months with the receiving ship *Colorado* at New York went to the screw sloops *Swatara* (1883–86) and *Yantic* (1886–88) in the Atlantic and Caribbean, having been promoted successively to midshipman (1882), ensign (j.g.) (1883) and ensign (1884), and then (1893) to lieutenant (j.g.). After a year studying French in that country on leave, he instructed Pennsylvanian maritime students aboard the school ship *Saratoga* (1889–93) at Philadelphia before reporting to the cruiser *Philadelphia* (C-4) for a year on the Pacific Station. He moved to the *Charleston* (C-2) on the Asiatic Station (1894–96) where he observed the First Sino-Japanese War. Lieutenant (j.g.) Sims returned to Philadelphia's station ship, the *Richmond,* before assignment in February 1897 as naval attaché at Madrid, Paris, and St. Petersburg with promotion to lieutenant the next month. Although detached from the Spanish post in August on the eve of war, he studied major foreign navies sufficiently to realize how far his own navy had to progress to catch up. From his French and Russian posts, he directed American wartime secret service operations in Spain, Italy, and Russia. In November 1900 he reported to the new battleship *Kentucky* (BB-6) at Gibraltar for a voyage to the Far East where the following March he joined the monitor *Monterey* (BM-6) at Shanghai.

Lieutenant Sims learned the revolutionary accurate method of "continuous aim" for naval guns from British Captain Percy Scott, skipper of *H.M.S. Terrible* in the Orient, introduced it into the U.S. Asiatic Fleet with much success and promoted its use throughout the Navy, even by addressing

President Theodore Roosevelt directly. Joining the staff of Asiatic Squadron commander Adm. George C. Remey, flagship the armored cruiser *Brooklyn* (ACR-3), in October 1901, he became that force's inspector of target practice the next February but in September was ordered home by the President to be fleet intelligence officer and Inspector of Target Practice. As lieutenant commander (from November 1902), he instructed the Navy in continuous aim, usually operating with the North Atlantic Fleet flagship, and with this and other techniques greatly improved the Navy's firing accuracy. Sims in July 1907 became commander and four months later assumed the additional duty of naval aide to the President, in which role he promoted reforms in naval administration and ship design as well as ordnance until the end of the pro-Navy Roosevelt administration. In March 1909 Commander Sims, in spite of his junior rank, was given command of the *Minnesota* (BB-22) in the Atlantic, taking her on a voyage to England the next year where he made strong pro-British utterances which precipitated an international debate. Promoted captain in May 1911, he reported that same month to the Naval War College, where he remained two years as student then instuctor. Command of the Atlantic Destroyer (or Torpedo) Flotilla followed in May 1913, flagships the tender *Dixie* (AD-1) and *Birmingham* (CL-2), with participation in the Mexican intervention one year later. Captain Sims became prospective commanding officer of the *Nevada* (BB-36) in November 1915 and brought her into commission the following March, operating along the Eastern seaboard until detached in January 1917.

Sims' new duties as president of the Naval War College and commandant of the Second Naval District and of Narragansett Bay (later Newport) Naval Station did not last more than a few weeks, for in March 1917 he received his promotion to rear admiral (to date from the previous August) and special assignment to carry dispatches to England, war with Germany then being imminent. Hostilities commencing, late in April he assumed command of all American destroyers, tenders, and auxiliaries operating from British bases, his flag in the destroyer *Wadsworth* (DD-60) for a month then the tender *Melville* (AD-2). In May 1917 Admiral Sims became a vice admiral, his title being changed in June to Commander U.S. Naval Forces Operating in European Waters, with additional duty from November as naval attaché at London, where he established his headquarters. From his arrival in England he endorsed and promoted the use of convoys in the antisubmarine war, and he was instrumental in the employment of naval aircraft, mine barrages, and an American battle squadron in the war against the Central Powers. In April 1918, just as the Navy began to land the American Expeditionary Force in France, Admiral Sims participated in meetings of the Allied Naval Council in Paris. With the end of the war, late in December he was promoted to admiral for the balance of this tour, which ended in March 1919. The next month he reverted in rank to rear admiral when he resumed his presidency of the Naval War College, where he wrote *The Victory at Sea* (1920) and had additional duty with a naval examining board during 1921. He created another furor by criticizing the wartime naval administration, but the ensuing Congressional investigation revealed little. Sims retired in October 1922 as rear admiral, became an outspoken advocate of naval aviation, had temporary duty relating to it in Washington in 1925, and was promoted to admiral on the retired list in June 1930. His son-in-law was the historian Elting E. Morison, who wrote his biography.

Sloat, John Drake

(July 26, 1781—November 28, 1867).

The man who took California for the United States, Sloat followed his father, Continental Navy Captain John Sloat, into the U.S. Navy with a midshipman's appointment from New York in 1800. He shipped out in the first crew of the frigate *President* in the West Indies against the French that summer through the following February, only to be discharged in the peacetime naval retrenchment. He commanded his own merchant ship between wars and was appointed sailing master in January 1812 for duty on the frigate *United States,* aboard which he participated in the capture of the *Macedonian* in October. Although appointed as acting and then as permanent lieutenant the next year, he remained blockaded in Connecticut's Thames River with the *United States* for the duration. Furloughed as master of the merchant schooner *Transit* (1815–16), Sloat had shore duty at the navy yards of New York (1816–20) and Portsmouth (1820–21). After several weeks with the in-ordinary ship-of-the-line *Washington* at New York, he sailed with its sister ship *Franklin* for the Pacific (1821–22) and transferred to anti-pirate work in the Caribbean as first lieutenant of the frigate *Congress* (1822–23). He took command of the schooner *Grampus* at the end of 1823 and operated two more years against West Indian pirates. In March

1826 he was promoted to master commandant. Briefly at the New York naval rendezvous, he commissioned the sloop *St. Louis* in 1828 as skipper and took her to Peru where she stood by during the revolution, returning home late in 1831.

Master Commandant Sloat commanded the New York naval rendezvous (1832–37) until promoted to captain and detached in March 1837. He commanded the Portsmouth yard (1840–43) and received orders to command the Pacific Squadron, flagship the new frigate *Savannah,* in August 1844, assuming command at Callao, Peru, the following March. Although beset by ill health and a somewhat indecisive nature, he concentrated the squadron at Mazatlán, Mexico, in November, sortied in June 1846 and occupied Monterey bloodlessly in July, another part of his force taking over San Francisco. Claiming California for the Union, he stepped down from his command at the end of July, returning to the East coast via Panama. In November Commodore Sloat reported for four months of duty examining steamers at New York and Philadelphia then examined midshipmen during the summer of 1847. He commanded the Norfolk Navy Yard and Station (1848–50) and was senior member of a commission studying the location for a navy yard in California (1852). While assigned to the Bureau of Construction and Repairs (1852–55), he directed the construction of the Stevens Battery. Placed on the reserve list in September 1855, Sloat transferred to the retired list in December 1861 and was promoted to commodore the next July and to rear admiral in August 1866.

Smoot, Roland Nesbit

(May 7, 1901——) USNA (Utah)
1923 (42/413).

World War II destroyerman Smoot began his career in a destroyer, the *Chase* (DD-323),on the West coast, but then shifted to submarines for nearly a decade: New London instruction (1925); navigator of the *S-7* (SS-112) between California and Panama (1926–27); engineer of the *S-26* (SS-131) in the same areas (1927–28); and on the sub cruiser *V-1* (SC-1) or *Narwhal* (SS-167) in the Atlantic and Pacific (1930–33), with postgraduate schooling (1928–30) in mechanical and diesel engineering at Annapolis and Pennsylvania State University (M.S. 1930), teaching it at the Naval Academy (1933–35). In the Battle Force aboard the battleship *Maryland* (BB-46), he was then Shop Superintendent at Pearl Harbor Navy Yard (1938–39) and commanding officer of the *Aulick* (DD-258) on Caribbean patrol (1939–40). Lieutenant Commander Smoot brought the *Monssen* (DD-436) into commission in March 1941 for antisub patrols between New England and Iceland from June 1941 to February 1942 then Pacific duty: the Halsey-Doolittle raid on Tokyo (April 1942), the Battle of Midway (June), the Guadalcanal landing and Battle of the Eastern Solomons (August), and ASW actions there prior to his detachment in October. Two months later he reported to the West Coast Sound Training Squadron at San Diego and in April 1943 took command of it and of the West Coast Sound School. In the spring of 1944, in the rank of captain, he took command of Destroyer Squadron 14 and Destroyer Division 27, flagship *Frazier* (DD-607), patrolling and bombarding bypassed Japanese-held positions in the Marshall Islands through the summer.

Captain Smoot assumed command of DesRon 56 and DesDiv 11, flagship *Newcomb* (DD-586), in October 1944 and that month launched a night torpedo attack in Surigao Strait during the Battle of Leyte Gulf which helped to sink the battleship *Yamashiro*. His vessels battled kamikazes off Leyte and Lingayen Gulf from November through January 1945 and off Iwo Jima in February as he commanded screens for heavy gun ships. He continued in this role off Okinawa, in April the *Newcomb* being so battered by kamikazes that the flag had to be shifted to the *Richard P. Leary* (DD-664). Promoted that month to commodore, he completed the Okinawa campaign and in July took command of Task Flotilla Four, flagship the cruiser *San Diego* (CL-53), covering the fast carriers attacking Japan and then, flag in the *Oakland* (CL-95), the transports occupying Yokosuka, of which he became Port Director in September and October. Reverting to captain in November, Smoot was Director of Officer Personnel (1945–48); chief of staff to Adm. Heber H. McLean, commanding the Atlantic midshipmen's cruise of 1948 in the *Missouri* (BB-63); the next year commissioning skipper of the *Newport News* (CA-148) in the Atlantic; and (1950) chief of staff to Atlantic cruiser commander Adm. Allan E. Smith, flagship *Albany* (CA-123). After a year at the Office of the Chief of Naval Operations, he became Assistant Chief of Naval Personnel (Personnel Control) in the rank of rear admiral in July 1951 for two years and later (1955–57) was made simply Assistant Chief. Admiral Smoot commanded Cruiser Division Three (later One) (1953–54) in the *Helena* (CA-75) in the Sea of Japan and then (1954–55) the Pacific Fleet's Mine Force. After a year of duty as Deputy CNO (Administration), he was promoted to vice admiral in July 1958 and given command, ashore, of the Taiwan Defense Command from the Matsu crisis of that year until April 1962, retiring two months later.

322

Sprague, Clifton Albert Frederick "Ziggy"

(January 8, 1896–April 11, 1955).
USNA (Vt.) 1918 (43/199).

Defender of the Leyte Gulf beachhead, this native of Massachusetts patrolled the war-torn Mediterranean in the gunboat *Wheeling* (PG-14) from after his June 1917 graduation until October 1919, spent several weeks on the East coast with the destroyer *Manley* (DD-74) and at Hampton Roads, and then went to Newport and New York for preparing the crew for the new battleship *Tennessee* (BB-43), on which he served for the six months after her June 1920 commissioning. Pensacola flight training (1919–20) and flying duty initiated his specialty in naval aviation, first with Scouting and Bombing Squadron One, then Scouting One attached to the airship tender *Wright* (AZ-1) on the West coast (1922–23). Executive officer of Naval Air Station Anacostia, D.C., he returned to NAS Hampton Roads (1926–28) for developing arresting gear for the Navy's new aircraft carriers. Lieutenant Commander Sprague joined one of them, the *Lexington* (CV-2), as assistant air officer (1928–29), then went to command of Training Squadron 8D5 at the Naval Academy. He commanded Patrol Squadron Eight, tender *Wright* (now AV-1), first at San Diego (1931–33), then at Coco Solo, Canal Zone, and finally at Pearl Harbor. After another tour at NAS Hampton Roads as operations officer (1934–36), he helped to outfit the *Yorktown* (CV-5) and became her air officer (1937–39). After brief instruction at the Naval War College, he directed the conversion of the oiler *Patoka* (AV-6) which he commanded in both oceans (1939–40) before commanding the *Tangier* (AV-8) in the Pacific from August 1940.

At the outbreak of war against Japan, Captain Sprague directed the *Tangier* through the air attack on Pearl Harbor and from June 1942 to March 1943 was chief of staff to Gulf Sea Frontier commander Adm. James

L. Kauffman fighting U-boats, headquarters at Miami. Commander Naval Air Center and NAS Seattle from April to October, he brought the *Wasp* (CV-18) into commission in November and commanded her in the Wake and Marcus raids (May 1944), the Saipan operation, and the Battle of the Philippine Sea (June). Already selected for rear admiral, he became Commander Carrier Division 25 in August 1944 and with his flag aboard the escort carrier *Fanshaw Bay* (CVE-70) supported the Morotai landings in September. As Commander Task Unit 77.4.3 ("Taffy 3") he helped cover the Leyte landings in October, during the battle off Samar courageously engaging Japanese battleships in defense of the offshore shipping. In February 1945 Admiral Sprague became ComCarDiv 26 and Commander Support Carrier Units, his flag in the *Natoma Bay* (CVE-62), for the Iwo Jima operation and in the *Fanshaw Bay* for Okinawa. Relieved in mid-May, he became ComCarDiv Two in the *Ticonderoga* (CV-14), but the war ended before he could command a fast carrier task group, and he returned to the West coast in the *Bennington* (CV-20). As commander of Joint Task Group 1.1.2 and the Navy Air Group of JTF One, flagship *Shangri-La* (CV-38), he played a key role in the summer 1946 atomic bomb tests in the Pacific. Departing to Corpus Christi, he was Chief of Naval Air Basic Training (1946–48), redesignated Commander Naval Air Advanced Training (1948), then was ComCarDiv Six, flagship *Kearsarge* (CV-33), in the Mediterranean (1948–49). Admiral Sprague's last duty was Commandant Seventeenth Naval District and Commander Alaskan Sea Frontier at Kodiak until his retirement in November 1951 in the rank of vice admiral.

Sprague, Thomas Lamison

(October 2, 1894–September 17, 1972).
USNA (Ohio) 1918 (19/199).

Naval aviator Sprague (no relation to C. A. F. Sprague) convoyed Atlantic vessels on the protected cruiser *Cleveland* (C-19) from June 1917 until April 1918, had training instruction duties at Charleston for two months, and helped commission the destroyer *Montgomery* (DD-121) in July for antisubmarine patrol out of Hampton Roads and routine operations on both coasts, Sprague commanding her from January to November 1920. He received flight training at Pensacola, served at Naval Air Station Anacostia (1921), on the staff of Pacific Air commander Adm. Henry V. Butler on the tender *Aroostook* (CM-3), and with Aircraft Squadron Spot Four (later Observation Squadron Two) tended by the same vessel on the West coast (1922–23). Twice stationed at Pensacola (1923–26, 1937–40), the second tour as Superintendent of Flight Training, he returned (1926–28) to the Battle Fleet with Observation One on the battleship *Maryland* (BB-46) and spent three years at NAS San Diego before commanding (1931–32) Scouting Six as well as being aide to Cruiser Division Three commander Adm. Clark H. Woodward on the *Concord* (CL-10). Lieutenant Commander Sprague headed the U.S. Fleet's Cruiser Wing and Scouting Ten; superintended the aeronautical engine laboratory at the Philadelphia naval aircraft factory; was assistant then air officer of the carrier *Saratoga* (CV-3) (1935–36) and navigator of the *Langley* (CV-1), both in the Pacific; and was executive officer of the *Ranger* (CV-4) on neutrality patrol in the Atlantic (1940–41). After helping to convert the tender *Pocomoke* (AV-9), he took command of her at Argentia for antisubmarine operations late in 1941 and early the next year brought the escort carrier *Charger* (AVG-30) into commission in the rank of captain for training chores in the Chesapeake Bay until December 1942.

Captain Sprague served as chief of staff to Quonset Point Fleet Air commander Adm. Arthur C. Davis during January and February 1943 and to Atlantic Fleet Air commanders Adms. Alva D. Bernhard and Patrick N. L. Bellinger from February to June, at which time he was assigned as prospective commanding officer of the *Intrepid* (CV-11). After commissioning in August 1943, he led her in the Marshalls-Truk operations the following January and February, being detached in March. Briefly Alameda Fleet Air commander in the rank of rear admiral, in July 1944 he took command of Carrier Division 22, flagship *Sangamon* (CVE-26), for the capture of Guam through August, the Morotai operation in September, and as Commander Task Group 77.4 ("Taffy One"), for the escort carrier support operations and Battle of Leyte Gulf in October. After several weeks commanding the Pacific Fleet's training carriers (CarDiv 11), Admiral Sprague became ComCarDiv Three in March 1945 off Okinawa, flagships *Wasp* (CV-18) and *Bennington* (CV-20), and in July and August commanded TG 38.1 from the *Hancock* (CV-19) in the final air strikes against Japan. Detached in December, he next reported to the Bureau of Naval Personnel, first as Deputy Chief (1946–47) then Chief (1947–49) and directed the team which fashioned the Navy parts of the Officer Personnel Act of 1949. In August 1949 he was promoted to vice admiral and in October made Commander Air Force Pacific Fleet, a post he held until his retirement in the rank of admiral in April 1952. He had also held simultaneous command of the First (Task) Fleet (1950) and later (1956–57) returned to active duty to participate in negotiations with the Philippine government over the status of U.S. military and naval bases in that nation.

Spruance, Raymond Ames

(July 3, 1886–December 13, 1969).
USNA (Ind.) 1907 (25/209).

Navy Department: National Archives

Victor of Midway and Commander Fifth Fleet during the Central Pacific offensive against Japan, Spruance became passed midshipman upon graduation in September 1906 and operated less than a year in the North Atlantic on the battleship *Iowa* (BB-4) before transferring to the new *Minnesota* (BB-22) for the global voyage of the "Great White Fleet" (1907–09), during which—in September 1908—he received his ensign's commission. After instruction in electrical engineering at the General Electric Company in Schenectady, New York, he returned to the Atlantic Fleet on the *Connecticut* (BB-18) for a year (1910–11) and went to the Asiatic Fleet as senior engineer of the cruiser *Cincinnati* (C-7). He remained in those waters to command the destroyer *Bainbridge* (DD-1) in the rank of lieutenant (j.g.) (1913–14), when he was again promoted. Lieutenant Spruance inspected machinery at the Newport News Shipbuilding and Dry Dock Company, and then helped to outfit and serve as electrical officer of the *Pennsylvania* (BB-38) from February 1916 through Chesapeake maneuvers until November 1917. As lieutenant commander he was assistant engineer officer at the New York Navy Yard—making trips to Britain to study fire control—until late in 1918 when he was made executive officer of the troop transport *Agamemnon* for four months and in the rank of commander. In April 1919 he commissioned and commanded the first of two "tin cans": the *Aaron Ward* (DD-132) for station ship duties during the flight of the NC boats and Pacific operations, and the *Percival* (DD-298) in March 1920 out of San Diego until June 1921.

Commander Spruance enjoyed a keen mind which made him desirable both as a ship commander and a naval strategist. After tours of duty as head of the Electrical Division at the Bureau of Engineering (1921–24), twenty days crossing the Atlantic as skipper of the *Dale* (DD-290), and as assistant chief of staff to Adm. Philip Andrews, commanding U.S. Naval forces in European waters (1924–25) on the armored cruiser *Pittsburgh* (ACR-4), his subsequent sea duties included command of the *Osborne* (DD-295) in European and Mediterranean waters (1925–26), exec of the *Mississippi* (BB-41) with the Battle Fleet (1929–31) in both oceans and later (1938–40) her skipper, and chief of staff to Commander Destroyers Scouting Force, Adm. Adolphus E. Watson, flagship light cruiser *Raleigh* (CL-7), along the West coast (1933–35). But his intellectual powers showed forth with his most uncommon three tours of duty at the Naval War College, studying and teaching the art of naval command and the strategic problems of potential war in the Pacific: a senior student during the progressive leadership of Adm. W. V. Pratt (1926–27); officer in charge of the correspondence courses (1931–33); and as head of three departments—the junior course (1935–36), Senior Class Tactics (1936–37), and Operations (1937–38). He also spent a tour (1927–29) at the Office of Naval Intelligence and was promoted captain in June 1932 and rear admiral in December 1939.

As commandant of the new Tenth Naval District at San Juan, Puerto Rico, Admiral Spruance controlled Caribbean waters from February 1940 until July 1941. The next month he took command of Cruiser Division Five, flagship heavy cruiser *Northampton* (CA-26), and operated out of Pearl Harbor, participating in the carrier raids against the Gilbert and Marshall Islands and Wake in February 1942, Marcus in March, and Tokyo in April. In May he relieved the bedridden Adm. W. F. Halsey, Jr., as Commander Task Force 16, flagship the carrier *Enterprise* (CV-6), to be junior admiral under Adm. F. J. Fletcher in contesting the Japanese advance on Midway Island. Having inherited Halsey's carrier staff, however, and with the turn of events, nonaviator Spruance emerged as the major commander in the crushing carrier victory over the Japanese fleet in the Battle of Midway in early June. Two weeks later he reported as chief of staff (and in September also as Deputy) to the other principal figure in the victory, Pacific Fleet commander Adm. C. W. Nimitz, with whom over the ensuing year he mapped out the strategy for the counteroffensive. Promoted to vice admiral in May 1943, Spruance assumed command of that offensive and the Central Pacific Force in August. In this capacity he hoisted his flag in the *Indianapolis* (CA-35) in November for the invasion of the Gilberts, going on to take the Marshalls in January and February, and with his flag in the *New Jersey* (BB-62) raided Truk in the latter month.

Promoted admiral in March 1944 and redesignated Commander Fifth Fleet in April, Admiral Spruance raided the Palaus that month again in the *Indianapolis,* directed the invasion of the Marianas during the summer, and defeated but missed the opportunity of destroying the Japanese fleet in the Battle of the Philippine Sea in June. From August 1944 to January 1945 at Pearl Harbor he planned the Iwo Jima and Okinawa operations, then commanded them during February and March to May respectively, flagship

Indianapolis until she took a kamikaze hit in April, then the *New Mexico* (BB-40). From June until August at Guam Admiral Spruance prepared the invasion plans for Japan and thereafter participated in the occupation, flagship *New Jersey.* Relieved of this Fifth Fleet command in November, he became Commander-in-Chief Pacific Fleet later that month and in February 1946 left this post to become President of the Naval War College. He retired from the Navy in July 1948, his reputation intact as the most brilliant fleet commander in World War II. Admiral Spruance later served as Ambassador to the Philippines (1952–53). His son, Capt. Edward D. Spruance (1915–69), commissioned and commanded the submarine *Lionfish* (SS-298) in the Yellow Sea during the Okinawa campaign.

Standley, William Harrison

(December 18, 1872—October 25, 1963). USNA (Calif.) 1895 (22/41).

Navy Department: National Archives

Interwar administrator and wartime diplomat, Standley first operated on the Asiatic Fleet flagship, the new cruiser *Olympia* (C-6) (1895–97), then went to the monitor *Monterey* (BM-6) on the West coast where he transferred to the iron gunboat *Alert* before the Spanish-American War. During that conflict he moved to the Far East and the gunboat *Yorktown* (PG-1). In the Philippine Insurrection he distinguished himself in a reconnoitering expedition at Baler in April 1899. Returning home two years later on the *Marietta* (PG-15) to be chief branch officer of the Hydrographic Office at San Francisco, he was with the training ship *Pensacola* at the same base (1902–03). Lieutenant Standley reported next to Tutuila, Samoa, where for over three years he served variously as engineer of the station ship gunboat *Adams,* aide to the station commandant, Captain of the Yard, chief customs officer, and commander of the Native Guard. Assigned to the San Francisco receiving ship *Independence* (1907–09) as executive officer, he became exec and navigator of the protected cruiser *Albany* (CL-23) on the West coast especially in the Nicaraguan Expeditionary Squadron (1909–10), as navigator of the armored cruiser *Pennsylvania* (ACR-4) in those waters when the first aircraft trials were held from her decks (1910–11), and as aide to the commandants of the Mare Island Navy Yard, Adm. Hugo Osterhaus and Capt. H. T. Mayo (1911–14), culminating in his promotion to commander.

Exec of the battleship *New Jersey* (BB-16) in the politically disturbed Caribbean, Standley then commanded the *Yorktown* (1915–16) off the Mexican west coast before he took charge of the buildings and grounds at the Naval Academy, and then served briefly as commandant of midshipmen during the extensive wartime expansion (1918–19). His success led to advancement to the rank of captain in January 1918 and command of the *Virginia* (BB-13) (1919–20), then study at the Naval War College. After briefly helping to outfit the Navy's first airship tender *Wright* (AZ-1), in July 1921 he became assistant chief of staff to Adm. E. W. Eberle, Commander-in-Chief Battle Fleet, at the end of 1922, flagship *New Mexico* (BB-40). Captain Standley first assisted then directed the War Plans Division in the Office of the Chief of Naval Operations (1923–26) and headed the Division of Fleet Training (1927–28), commanding in the interim the *California* (BB-44) in the Pacific. Promoted to rear admiral in November 1927, he was Assistant CNO (1928–30) prior to commanding the U.S. Fleet's destroyers (1930–31) and then its cruisers and Cruiser Division Five (1931–32), flagships *Omaha* (CL-4) and *Detroit* (CL-8) in the former command and the *Concord* (CL-10) in the latter. Elevated to vice admiral in January 1932 and to admiral in May 1933, the next month he became Commander Battle Force, U.S. Fleet, in the *California* but remained only three weeks in the post with his advancement to be Chief of Naval Operations as of July 1933.

Admiral Standley superintended the Navy's modest building programs under President Franklin D. Roosevelt's New Deal policies, often as Acting Secretary of the Navy in place of the ailing Claude A. Swanson, and represented the United States at the abortive London Naval Conference of 1934–35. Retiring from the Navy on the first day of 1937 in the rank of rear admiral, he was advanced to admiral on the retired list in 1938. Recalled to active duty in 1939 he served as special naval adviser to President Roosevelt and on the Naval Board for Production Awards and then as Naval Representative on the Priorities Board of the Office of Production Management during 1940–41, and from March 1941 served on the OPM's Production Planning Board. In the autumn of that year Admiral Standley became U.S. Naval Member of the Beaverbrook-Harriman Special War Supply Mission (Lend Lease) to the Soviet Union then in February 1942 was appointed United States Ambassador to that nation until the fall of 1943, a memoir of which he published as *Admiral Ambassador to Russia* (1955). He also served on the Roberts Pearl Harbor Commission (1941–42) and on the Planning Group of the Office of Strategic Services (1944–45) and was relieved of all active duty at the end of August 1945. His son, Rear Adm. W. H. Standley, Jr., commanded the destroyer *Plunkett* (DD-431) in the Salerno landings (1943).

Stark, Harold Raynsford "Betty"

(November 12, 1880–August 20, 1972).
USNA (Pa.) 1903 (30/50).

Chief of Naval Operations during the 1941 quasi-war with Germany, Stark held several key staff posts throughout his career: with Adm. W.S. Sims in World War I London (November 1917–March 1919); aide and later chief of staff to the Battle Fleet's destroyer commander Adm. Thomas J. Senn, flagships the cruiser *Omaha* (CL-4) and destroyer tender *Melville* (AD-2) (1928–30); and aide to Secretaries of the Navy Charles Francis Adams (1930–33) and Claude A. Swanson (1933). His sea assignments were in the surface line: the protected cruiser *Newark* (C-1) (1903–04), the training ship *Hartford,* and the gunboat *Newport* (PG-12) (1904–07), all along the Eastern seaboard and in the West Indies; the new battleship *Minnesota* (BB-22) for the global cruise of the "Great White Fleet" (1907–09); successively commander of the torpedo boats *Porter* (TB-6) and *Stringham* (TB-19) and the destroyers *Lamson* (DD-18) and *Patterson* (DD-36), all along the Atlantic coast, and engineer of the armored cruiser *Brooklyn* (ACR-3) out of Boston (1909–15) and in the Asiatic Fleet, whose torpedo flotilla he commanded in the tender *Monterey* (June to November 1917); executive officer of the *North Dakota* (BB-29) (1919–20) and *West Virginia* (BB-48) (1923) in the Atlantic; skipper of the ammunition ship *Nitro* (AE-2) plying between coasts (1924–25); skipper of the *West Virginia* in the Pacific (1933–34); and commander of Cruiser Division Three in the *Concord* (CL-10) in the Battle Force (1937–38) and of that Force's cruisers (1938–39) in the *Concord* and *Honolulu* (CL-48). Stark had shore billets at the Newport torpedo station (1915–17); the Norfolk training station as exec (1920–22); the Naval War College as student (1922–23); the Dahlgren proving ground and Indian Head powder factory as chief ordnance inspector (1925–28); and Chief of the Bureau of Ordnance (1934–37). Promoted rear admiral in November 1934, he became CNO in the rank of admiral in August 1939 and built up the Navy until hostilities began during 1941 and he was relieved in March 1942. Admiral Stark the next month became Commander U.S. Naval Forces in Europe at London, also Commander Twelfth Fleet in October 1943, occupying both posts during the war against the Axis powers until August 1945, additionally in the last months as U.S. Naval Adviser to the European Advisory Commission. He was attached to the Office of the CNO from the autumn until his retirement in April 1946.

Stewart, Charles "Old Ironsides"

(July 28, 1778–November 6, 1869).

Naval Photographic Center

Prominent for six decades, from the quasi-war with France to the Civil War, Philadelphian Stewart shipped out in a merchantman in 1791, rose to master, and received a lieutenant's commission in 1798. He joined the frigate *United States* which took four French privateers in the West Indies, and became her first lieutenant. In July 1800, after briefly commanding the small schooner *Enterprise*, he took command of the schooner *Experiment* and returned to the Indies to capture several vessels and recover a number of American ships. Back at Norfolk early in 1801 he superintended the frigate *Chesapeake* then in ordinary and the next year became first lieutenant of the frigate *Constellation* blockading Tripoli. As skipper of the brig *Syren* (1803–05), which he brought into service, he participated in the destruction of the captured frigate *Philadelphia,* took two Tripolitan warships, and operated against Barbary Tunis. Stewart, promoted master commandant in the spring of 1804 and to captain two years after that, superintended gunboat construction at Philadelphia (1806–07) before taking furlough as a merchant captain (1807–11), interrupted only for two months in the winter of 1809 to bring the frigate *Essex* back into commission. During the War of 1812 he successively commanded the brigs *Argus* and *Hornet* with only moderate success in the open Atlantic, and protected Norfolk as skipper of the *Constellation* early in 1813. However, in May, he took over the frigate *Constitution,* with which he captured a schooner and three prizes early in 1814, and one year later—during February 1815—took two more prizes before overpowering the British frigate *Cyane* and sloop *Levant* in battle.

Captain Stewart commanded the ship-of-the-line *Franklin* (1816), which became his flagship while he commanded the Mediterranean Squadron (1818–20) and when he shifted to the Pacific Squadron especially to protect American whaling vessels (1821–24), leading to his overinvolvement, court-martial and acquittal. President of the Examining Board (1829), he served as a Navy Commissioner (1830–33) and then awaited orders until appointed to command the navy yard in his native Philadelphia (1837–41). Commodore Stewart returned to sea duty as first commander of the new Home Squadron, flagship the razee *Independence* (1842–43), operating out of New York and Boston. Appointed president of the Board on Rank in 1850, he spent most of his remaining career in command at Philadelphia (1846–49, 1853–60) and although placed on the reserve list in 1855 was accorded the singular honor of being designated Senior Flag Officer by a special act of Congress in April 1859. On leave in Europe during 1858–59, he was consulted by President Abraham Lincoln on the problem of relieving Fort Sumter on the eve of the Civil War. At 83 years of age Flag Officer Stewart declined active duty and finally retired in December 1861 and was the first officer to be promoted to rear admiral on the retired list, in July 1862.

Stirling, Yates, Jr. "Stormy Petrel"

(April 30, 1872–January 28, 1948).
USNA (Mass.) 1892 (22/40).

Naval Historical Center

As Yangtze Patrol commander, controversial naval writer Stirling was following his admiral father (1843–1929) to the Far East, the elder Stirling commanding in succession (1902–05) the Philippine Squadron and Cruiser Squadron of the Asiatic Fleet then that Fleet itself. The son began his career policing the Eastern Pacific aboard the cruiser *San Francisco* (C-5) (1892–93) and the South Atlantic with the *Charleston* (C-2) (1893–94). Briefly attached to the *Detroit* (C-10) on the East coast, he patrolled the Caribbean with the *New York* (ACR-2) (1894–95) before transferring to the gunboat *Thetis* for a year. After Pacific operations aboard the Fisheries Commission vessel *Albatross* (1896–98), Ensign Stirling had Spanish-American War duties as assistant equipment officer at Newport News, on the Cuban blockade with the cruiser *Dolphin*, and aboard the auxiliary cruiser *Badger*, with which he cruised to the Pacific in 1899 where he served briefly on the survey ship *Ranger* and the collier *Scindia* (AC-14). Reporting to the storeship *Celtic* (AF-2) in the Philippines in 1900, he transferred there as lieutenant to command of the gunboat *Paragua* for the fight against the insurrectionists. Remaining in the Pacific, Stirling had service on the hospital ship *Solace* (AH-2) (1901–02), briefly on the *Brooklyn* (ACR-3), and as an equipment officer at Puget Sound (1902–03). He was aide to his father on the Asiatic Station (1903–05), flagships the battleship *Wisconsin* (BB-9), the converted merchantman *Rainbow* and the cruiser *New Orleans*, this tour coincident with the Russo-Japanese War.

Lieutenant Commander (since 1906) Stirling early in his career established himself as a naval writer and reformer, at first with essays in the U.S. Naval Institute *Proceedings* and ultimately in a number of books; the time

334

for his writing was made possible by tours of duty at the Naval Academy (1906–07) and the Naval War College (1911–12, 1912–13). In all his assignments, however, he was outspoken and aggressive. Nevertheless, most of his time was spent in sea-going billets: the *Massachusetts* (BB-2) in the Atlantic (1905–06), the *Indiana* (BB-1) and monitor *Arkansas* (BM-7) at Annapolis, as ordnance and later navigation officer of the *Connecticut* (BB-18) for the "Great White Fleet's" trip around the world (1907–09), as commissioning skipper of the destroyer *Paulding* (DD-22) in the Atlantic (1909–11), as temporary commander of the scout cruiser *Salem* (CL-3) at Boston (1912), and as executive officer of the *Rhode Island* (BB-17) in the Atlantic and during the diplomatic crisis with Mexico (1913–14). Promoted to commander in 1912, Stirling two years later became commander of the Atlantic Fleet's Submarine Flotilla, in addition being flagship skipper of the monitors *Ozark* (ex-*Arkansas)* and *Tonopah* (BM-8). When the post was upgraded in 1915 and given to Adm. Albert W. Grant, Stirling became his chief of staff and captain of the new flagship, the *Columbia* (C-12). Inasmuch as he had helped to formulate the Navy's first submarine policy, he became the first commanding officer of the Submarine Base and School at New London in 1916, the next year taking on the additional duties of chief of staff to Commander Submarine Force Atlantic Fleet, Captain Samuel S. Robison, and skipper of the flagship *Chicago*.

Promoted captain in August 1917, Stirling fitted out and commanded the troop transport *President Lincoln* during 1917, taking troops to Europe, and then the converted auxiliary cruiser *Von Steuben* (1917–18), commanding several troop convoys on it. He was chief of staff to the commandant of the Third Naval District, New York (1918–19) prior to commanding the *Connecticut* (1919–20) and the *New Mexico* (BB-40) (1922–24) in the Atlantic and Pacific respectively. Captain of the Yard at Philadelphia (1920–22) and at Washington (1924–26), he was promoted to rear admiral in 1926. Admiral Stirling was chief of staff to the Commander-in-Chief U.S. Fleet, Adm. C. F. Hughes, flagships *Seattle* (CA-11) and *Texas* (BB-35), transferring late in 1927 to command of the Yangtze Patrol in the converted patrol yacht *Isabel* (PY-10), patrolling that river during the internal struggles in China until 1929 when he went to Washington as president of the Naval Examining Board. He commanded the Fourteenth Naval District and base at Pearl Harbor (1930–33) until retired as rear admiral in May 1936. Among Admiral Stirling's books were *Fundamentals of Naval Service* (1916), the autobiography *Sea Duty: Memoirs of a Fighting Admiral* (1939), *How to be a Naval Officer* (1940), *Warriors of the Sea* (1942), and *Why Seapower Will Win the War* (1944).

Stockton, Robert Field

(August 20, 1795—October 7, 1866).

Pioneer of the steam Navy and Mexican War leader, Stockton checkered his naval career with—and eventually left it for—politics in his native New Jersey and business activities in canals and railroads, although he started as a common midshipman in September 1811 and served on the frigate *President* for four successful cruises against British shipping in the North Atlantic, Irish waters, and West Indies (1812–14). He so impressed his captain, John Rodgers, that he stayed with him as acting master's mate and aide-de-camp during flotilla duty defending Baltimore and aboard the new frigate *Guerriere,* being made lieutenant in December 1814. During the summer of 1815 he was with the schooner *Spitfire* as first lieutenant in operations against Algiers and then spent a few weeks with the brig *Chippewa* in ordinary at Boston. He served most of 1816 aboard the ship-of-the-line *Washington,* flagship of the Mediterranean Squadron, then early in 1817 went to the sloop *Erie* in the same waters as second lieutenant, rising to first lieutenant and in July 1819 to skipper, returning home with her early in 1820. After duty at New York, Stockton broght the schooner *Alligator* into service and with her helped to found Liberia and to suppress the West Indian slave trade, capturing several slaving vessels across the ocean (1821–22). He surveyed the Southern coast (1822–23, 1826–28), tours interrupted and followed by extensive leave to pursue his business activities, with promotion to master commandant in 1830.

An intimate of President Andrew Jackson, Stockton returned to active duty in command of the newly-commissioned ship-of-the-line *Ohio,* flagship in the middle sea (1838–39), but soon left her to visit England where he studied British naval architecture, especially steam propulsion which he wanted for his own navy. After promotion to captain early in 1839, he took leave for political activities which resulted in an offer—which he declined—of the Secretaryship of the Navy. With John Ericcson he supervised construction of the Navy's first screw steamer, *Princeton,* named for his home town, at Philadelphia (1841–43), brought her into commission as captain in September 1843 and took her on several test runs. Captain Stockton also directed the construction of the "Peacemaker," one of the *Princeton*'s two large guns but which exploded in February 1844 killing Secretary Thomas Gilmer, Secretary of State Abel P. Upshur, two Congressmen, and Chief of the Bureau of Construction, Equipment and Repairs Capt. Beverly Kennon and wounding Stockton. In early 1845 he took command of a four-vessel squadron, flagship *Princeton,* which he led to Gulf of Mexico waters to reinforce the Home Squadron, returning with emissaries from Texas. In August he became captain of the frigate *Congress,* transported diplomats to Hawaii, and in July 1846 assumed command of the Pacific Squadron, flag in the *Congress,* at Monterey, California. Commodore Stockton proclaimed himself civil governor and military commander in California and with the army spent the next several months blockading and capturing southern California from the Mexicans; he took Los Angeles and San Diego and assisted in the defeat of the Mexican army at San Gabriel and La Mesa. Relieved in March 1847, he returned to the East overland, saw no further duty, and resigned from the Navy in May 1850. While Senator from New Jersey (1851–53) he opposed flogging in the Navy and promoted coastal defenses.

Stribling, Cornelius Kinchiloe

(September 22, 1790–January 17, 1880).

A major ship captain in the antebellum period, South Carolinian Stribling joined the frigate *Macedonian* at the end of 1812 as midshipman but remained blockaded at New London throughout 1813 until April 1814 when he joined the new frigate *Mohawk* for operations on Lake Ontario. Back on the *Macedonian* for the Algierian campaign of 1815, he remained in the Mediterranean aboard the frigate *Constellation* until 1817. After promotion to lieutenant in 1818, he was stationed at Norfolk (1820–22) and then fought West Indian pirates (1822–25) on the brig *Hornet,* the sloop *Peacock* on which he led barges to capture the schooner *Pilot* in April 1823, the frigate *John Adams,* and the *Constellation.* Stribling went to the middle sea with the frigate *Brandywine* (1826–30), commanded the receiving ship at Norfolk (1831–33), was Assistant Inspector of Ordnance (1833–35), cruised the Far East on the second sloop *Peacock* (1836–37), and in 1839 reported to the Norfolk rendezvous, which he commanded briefly in 1840 in the rank of commander. After a year at the Washington Navy Yard, he commanded the sloop *Cyane* then the frigate *United States* in the Pacific (1841–44) and the receiving ship *Pennsylvania* at Norfolk (1845–47). Commander Stribling's Mexican War duty was as fleet captain to Commo. W. B. Shubrick, commanding the Pacific Squadron in the razee *Independence* in operations in the Californias (1847–48), followed by command of the ship-of-the-line *Ohio* in those waters during the gold rush (1848–50).

In 1853, after three years as Superintendent at the Naval Academy (where the principal walk is named for him), Stribling was promoted to captain, and then was commander of the screw frigate *San Jacinto* in the North Atlantic and Caribbean (1854–55). A member of the Efficiency Board in 1855, he commanded the navy yard at Pensacola (1857–59) before receiving orders to take command of the East India Squadron, flagship the new screw sloop *Hartford,* during the spring of 1859. For two years Flag Officer Stribling cruised primarily in Chinese waters until he was relieved in July 1861. Remaining loyal to the Union, he served on a Senate committee from December to April 1862, on the Lighthouse Board, and as president of a board of examiners for naval students. In August he was promoted to commodore on the retired list but in November given command of the navy yard at Philadelphia. This recall to active duty led to regular promotion to commodore in March 1863 and command of the East Gulf Blockading Squadron in October 1864 as acting rear admiral. Based ashore at Key West, he was chiefly engaged in watching the movements of the Confederate ironclad *Stonewall* until relieved in July 1865. Commissioned rear admiral on the retired list in August 1866, Stribling the next month rejoined the Lighthouse Board and continued board duties until relieved of all active duty in September 1871.

Stringham, Silas Horton

(November 7, 1797–February 7, 1876).

U. S. Navy Photograph

Union blockading commander at the beginning of the Civil War, New Yorker Stringham became midshipman in 1810, reporting immediately to the frigate *President* which engaged the British sloop *Little Belt* the next year and cruised the Atlantic and Caribbean throughout the War of 1812. Promoted to lieutenant late in 1814, he fought the Barbary Algierians in the brig *Spark* in 1815, returned to the Mediterranean with her (1816–18), and transferred to the sloop *Peacock* in the same waters, performing heroic rescue services of French seamen during a storm near Gibraltar. On board the frigate *Cyane* for the Liberian expedition (1819–21) and more Mediterranean cruising (1823–25), he helped capture two slave trade vessels which he then commanded in the taking of two more. Stringham also engaged in anti-pirate activities in the West Indies as executive officer of the brig *Hornet* (1821–22) and assisted in the capture of the infamous slaving schooner *Moscow.* On the receiving ship at New York (1825–26) and at the navy yard there (1826–27, 1828–29), he served in the Caribbean on the second *Peacock* (1829–30) and in March 1831 was promoted commander while on a long leave. He commanded the frigate *John Adams* in the middle sea (1835–37) and returned to the New York yard (1837–40). A captain from September 1841, he briefly commanded the razeed frigate *Independence,* flagship of the Home Squadron (1842–43), and again the New York yard (1843–46). During the Mexican War he commanded the ship-of-the-line *Ohio* at the investment of Vera Cruz and Tuxpan (1846–47) and in the eastern Pacific (1847–48). Midshipman examining duty (1849–50) was followed by command of the Norfolk Navy Yard (1851–52).

Commodore Stringham hoisted his flag on the frigate *Cumberland* in April 1852 as commander of the Mediterranean Squadron and continued in that role until July 1855 when he took command of the navy yard at Boston, a post he held for four years. President of the board of examiners at the Naval Academy (1859) and member of a board examining sailing vessels (1860), he advised Secretary of the Navy Gideon Welles on the Fort Sumter crisis during the spring of 1861 and in May raised his flag on the steam frigate *Minnesota* at Boston as commander of the Atlantic Blockading Squadron. Flag Officer Stringham's ships captured several vessels in Virginia waters and in August supported the army in the capture of the Hatteras Inlet forts of North Carolina. Unfairly criticized by the press and his superiors for lack of aggressiveness, he was relieved at his own request in September and transferred to the retired list in December. Promoted rear admiral on that list the following July, he had board duties until given command of the Boston Navy Yard at the end of 1863, a post he occupied for the duration and until December 1866. Admiral Stringham was president of the Naval Retiring Board (1867, 1868–69) and commanding officer and Port Admiral of the New York Station (1869–72), his final active service.

Struble, Arthur Dewey

(June 28, 1894——). USNA (Ore.) 1915 (12/179).

Navy Department: National Archives

Commander at the Inchon landings, Struble had brief pre-World War I West coast assignments in the cruisers *South Dakota* (ACR-9) and *St. Louis* (C-20) and supply ship *Glacier* (AF-4), then late in 1917 joined the precommissioning detail of the destroyer *Stevens* (DD-86), becoming her engineering officer from her April 1918 commissioning through wartime patrols out of Queenstown, the 1919 flight of the NC boats, and Atlantic cruising. As executive officer of the *Shubrick* (DD-268), he participated in a late 1919 diplomatic mission to Haiti and briefly commanded her before serving as exec of the *Meyer* (DD-279) in the Eastern Pacific (1920–21). After teaching marine engineering and naval construction at the Naval Academy (1921–23), he joined the battleship *California* (BB-44), on which he became flag lieutenant to Adm. Louis R. de Steiguer, Battleship Divisions commander (1925–27). Lieutenant Commander Struble spent three years at the Office of Naval Communications and then two further years as flag secretary to Battleship Division Three commander Adm. J. R. P. Pringle on the *New York* (BB-34) and *Arizona* (BB-39). These Pacific tours continued with the *New York* as gunnery officer (1932–33); at San Francisco as Twelfth Naval District communications officer; with the Scouting Force as first lieutenant of the cruiser *Portland* (CA-33) and then (1936–37) as damage control officer for that Force's cruiser commander Adm. Edward B. Fenner on the *Chicago* (CA-29); as exec of the *Arizona* (1940–41); and in command of the old *Trenton* (CL-11) from January 1941 for operations off Panama through the early days of World War II until he was relieved in May 1942.

Captain Struble, who had served previously (1937–40) with the Central Division of the Office of the Chief of Naval Operations, directed that

Division from May 1942 until October 1943, during which tour he was promoted to rear admiral and after which made chief of staff to Adm. A. G. Kirk, commanding the Western Naval Task Force in the planning and landings at Normandy, June 1944, flagship *Augusta* (CA-31). In August he became Commander Group Two (in October redesignated Amphibious Group Nine) of the Seventh Amphibious Force, directing the initial Philippines landings at Panaon, Leyte and Ormoc during the autumn in the *Hughes* (DD-410); the Mindoro assault in December in the *Nashville* (CL-43) until she was struck by a kamikaze before the actual debarkation and replaced by the *Dashiell* (DD-659); Subic Bay and Zambales, Luzon (January 1945) in the amphibious command ship *Mount McKinley* (AGC-7); Corregidor (February); Negros and Panay in the southern Visayas in the Coast Guard cutter *Ingham* (March); Macajabar, Mindanao (May); and support operations throughout the Philippines until August. The next month Admiral Struble took command of Minecraft Pacific Fleet, flagship *Panamint* (AGC-13), and directed all minesweeping operations in the Western Pacific until June 1946 when he became that Fleet's Amphibious Commander. Promoted vice admiral in April 1948, he was Deputy CNO (Operations) and Naval Deputy on the Joint Chiefs of Staff until May 1950 when he was transferred to command of the Seventh Fleet, flagship *Toledo* (CA-133). Soon after the beginning of hostilities in Korea, he planned and commanded three key operations: the September assault on Inchon as Commander Joint Task Force Seven in the *Mount McKinley;* the landing at Wonsan in October; and the naval backup of the Chosin-Hungnam withdrawal in November and December, thereafter supporting the U.S. Sixth Army. Detached the following March, he commanded the First Fleet (1951–52); served with the JCS; was U.S. Naval Representative on the Military Staff Committee at the United Nations (1952–53); was Chairman of the U.S. Military Delegation to that Committee (1953–55); and finished his career commanding the Eastern Sea Frontier and Atlantic Reserve Fleet. He retired in June 1956 in the rank of admiral.

Stump, Felix Budwell

(December 15, 1894–June 13, 1972). USNA (W.Va.) 1917 (63/182).

Pacific Fleet commander during the height of the Cold War, Stump deployed in the gunboat *Yorktown* (PG-1) for World War I Caribbean patrolling from April to December 1917, there joining the cruiser *Cincinnati* (C-7) and becoming her navigator from May 1918 until she decommissioned eleven months later. After several months with the training battleship *Alabama* (BB-8), he underwent flight training at Pensacola (1919–20), where he remained to train in NC flying boats and with their training destroyer *Harding* (DD-91). He commanded the Experimental and Test Squadron at Naval Air Station Hampton Roads in the rank of lieutenant (1920–22), to which station he later returned for overhaul and repair duties (1927–30). A postgraduate student in aeronautical engineering at Annapolis, the Massachusetts Institute of Technology (M.S. 1923), the Naval Aircraft Factory at Philadelphia and the Bureau of Aeronautics, he flew with experimental Torpedo Squadron Two aboard the aircraft carrier *Langley* (CV-1) with the Battle Fleet (1924–27); commanded Scouting 9-S (1930–31) and Scouting 10-S (1931–32) off the Scouting Fleet's cruisers; and commanded Scouting Two-B on the *Saratoga* (CV-3) (1934–36). Lieutenant Commander Stump served with the maintenance and procurement division of BuAer (1932–34) and with the *Lexington* (CV-2) as navigator (1936–37), returning in the rank of commander to BuAer's maintenance division (1937–40). Executive officer of the *Enterprise* (CV-6) in the Pacific (1940–41), he assumed command of the *Langley,* now a seaplane tender (AV-3), in September 1941 in the Philippines, taking her to Australia after the outbreak of war in December. He was detached there in January 1942 upon his promotion to captain and assignment to be operations and intelligence officer to Asiatic Fleet commander Adm. T. C. Hart and commander of the combined operation center of the Allied American, British, Dutch and Australian (ABDA) high command for the futile defense of the Dutch East Indies until March.

Captain Stump, following several months as air officer to Western Sea Frontier commander Adm. John W. Greenslade, in December 1942 reported to the new *Lexington* (CV-16); he brought her into commission in February 1943 and led her against Tarawa (September), Wake (October), the Gilberts (November), Kwajalein where she was damaged by a torpedo (December), and Mille and the Palaus (March-April 1944). In the rank of rear admiral, he commanded escort Carrier Division 24 for the ensuing year supporting several landings: the Marianas in the summer of 1944, flagship *Corregidor* (CVE-58); Leyte and engaging the Japanese fleet as Commander Task Unit 77.4.2 ("Taffy 2") in October and November, flagship *Natoma Bay* (CVE-62); Mindoro in December and Lingayen in January 1945 in the same ship; and Okinawa from March to May in the *Marcus Island* (CVE-77) and *Saginaw Bay* (CVE-82). Admiral Stump in June 1945 became Chief of Naval Air Technical Training at Chicago then Pensacola and finally Memphis, and in December 1948 he was promoted to vice admiral and designated Commander Air Force Atlantic Fleet, remaining in that ocean to command the Second Fleet (1951–53). In June 1953 he was promoted to admiral and assigned the next month to be Commander-in-Chief of all Army, Navy and Air Force components in the Pacific and of the Pacific Fleet, in which capacity he directed the final weeks of the Korean War, the crisis surrounding the collapse of the French in Indochina, and the strategic realignment under the Southeast Asia Treaty Organization (SEATO), to which he also became U.S. military adviser in March 1955. Given the tension with Red China over Formosa from the latter year, Admiral Stump found his command upgraded in February 1958 and henceforth separated: he relinquished command of the Pacific Fleet and retained that of the overall area Pacific Command. He retired the following August.

Tattnall, Josiah

(November 9, 1795–June 14, 1871).

The most prominent U.S. Naval flag officer to go into Confederate service and a superior combat leader, Georgian Tattnall became midshipman shortly before the outbreak of the War of 1812, attended naval school at Washington, and spent much of the war blockaded at Norfolk aboard the frigate *Constellation,* manning a battery on Craney Island which fought British batteries in June 1813. Detached the following April he took reinforcements to Lake Erie, commanded a force of Washington Navy Yard workers at the battle of Bladensburg in August, and then joined the sloop *Epervier* at Savannah on which he sailed for the attack on Algiers in 1815. Fortunately he was transferred from the *Epervier* shortly before her mysterious disappearance at sea back to the *Constellation* for another year in the Mediterranean. Returning home on the sloop *Ontario* in early 1817, Tattnall was promoted to lieutenant one year later and cruised the Pacific with the frigate *Macedonian* (1818–20), wounding a British officer in a duel over the latter's disparaging remarks about American naval performance during the war. He attended school at Norwich, Vt., before chasing West Indian pirates on the schooner *Jackall* early in 1823.

Lieutenant Tattnall spent a year in the middle sea with the frigate *Constitution* (1824–25), returned home on the frigate *Brandywine,* and again fought pirates in the Caribbean aboard the sloop *Erie* (1828–29), commanding a force of boats which took the pirate vessel *Federal* at St. Bart's. He remained in these waters commanding first a surveying party of the Florida keys and reefs (1829–30), then the schooner *Grampus* (1831–32), with which he captured the Mexican schooner *Montezuma* after it had robbed an American merchantman on the high seas. After conducting experiments in ordnance, he recruited men for the South Seas Exploring Expedition and brought the brig *Pioneer* into service as its captain in 1836, using it the next year to transfer Mexican General Santa Anna, captive of the Texans, to Vera Cruz. As commander (1838), Tattnall commanded the Boston Navy Yard (1838–39), the sloop *Fairfield* in the Mediterranean (1841–42), and the sloop *Saratoga* which he brought into commission and took to the African Squadron as its flagship (1843–44), participating in much activity under Commo. M. C. Perry *(q.v.).* He commissioned the sidewheel gunboat *Spitfire* in August 1846 and took it in November against Tampico and up the Pánuco River to occupy the town of the same name and to seize several Mexican gunboats. The *Spitfire* engaged the fortress of San Juan de Ulloa during the assault on Vera Cruz in March 1847; later in the month Tattnall used the vessel as part of the "Mosquito" gunboat force he commanded in a successful bombardment of the Mexican defenses. The next month he was seriously wounded in the Tuxpan expedition after fighting at Alvarado and was detached from the *Spitfire* in June.

Promoted captain early in 1850, Tattnall served at the Boston Navy Yard (1848–49), commissioned the sidewheel sloop *Saranac* for East coast and Caribbean cruising (1850–51) due to the delicate diplomatic situation caused by the Cuban insurrection, and commanded the Pensacola Navy Yard (1851–54) and the razee *Independence,* flagship in the Pacific (1854–55). After commanding the naval station at Sackett's Harbor, New York, on the Lakes (1855–57), in October 1857 he was appointed commander of the East India Squadron, hoisting his flag three months later aboard the screw frigate *San Jacinto* at Hong Kong to patrol troubled Chinese waters. Shifting to the sidewheeler *Powhatan* in June, Flag Officer Tattnall that month assisted the British squadron against the Chinese forts at the Peiho River in the Arrow War, an unneutral act supported by his superiors. In February 1860 he departed the Far East with Japan's first embassy to the United States. He then returned to command at Sackett's Harbor, but in February 1861, following the secession of his native state, he resigned his commission to accept the appointment of Senior Flag Officer in the Navy of Georgia and command of the state's naval defenses.

Flag Officer Tattnall received his captain's commission in the Confederate Navy in March 1861 and was given command of the naval defenses of Georgia and South Carolina. He raised a small four-vessel flotilla, the Savannah River Squadron, as his command afloat, flag in the sidewheel gunboat *Savannah,* and which helped defend Port Royal, South Carolina, against the Union attack in November but in vain. He assisted the Confederate army at Fort Pulaski, Georgia, until transferred in late March 1862 to command Virginia's naval defenses and the James River Squadron, flagship the ironclad *Virginia* (ex-*Merrimack).* In April he failed to lure the blockading *Monitor* into battle but used other vessels to capture three Union transports in Hampton Roads, then in May had to destroy his flagship in order to prevent its capture by the advancing Union army. In May he returned to command Georgia's naval defenses, flagship the ironclad ram

Atlanta, until March 1863 when he stepped down to command only the shore defenses of Savannah in which capacity he supervised naval construction. Upon the advance of Sherman's army into Savannah in December 1864 he destroyed the property in his charge and withdrew to Augusta and out of the war.

Taussig, Joseph Knefler

(August 30, 1877–October 29, 1947). USNA (At Large) 1899 (17/53).

World War I destroyer commander and naval strategist, the son of Adm. Edward D. Taussig (1847–1921) saw combat as a naval cadet on the armored cruiser *New York* (ACR-2) at the Battle of Santiago in July 1898 and joined the protected cruiser *Newark* (C-1) early the next year just as his father, then a commander in command of the gunboat *Bennington* (PG-4), was taking possession of Wake Island for the United States. Young Taussig was seriously wounded near Tientsin, China, during the Peking Relief Expedition of the Boxer Rebellion in June 1900 and served in the Philippines for seven months from the end of that year aboard the *Nashville* (PG-7) and supply ship *Culgoa,* then for a year in the same waters with the *Yorktown* (PG-1), commanded by his father. He was next on the second-class battleship *Texas* (1902–05) and navigator of the *Topeka* (PG-35), going to Guantanamo Bay's station ship monitor *Amphitrite* (BM-2) (1905–06) and the Atlantic Fleet supply ship *Celtic* (AF-2) (1906–07) as executive officer and navigator. Lieutenant Taussig, after accompanying the new battleship *Kansas* (BB-21) to San Francisco with the "Great White Fleet", was aide (1908–09) to his father, at that time rear admiral and commandant of the Norfolk Navy Yard and Fifth Naval District. He then (1910–11) transferred as flag lieutenant to the staff of his former skipper on the *Kansas,* Adm. Charles B. Vreeland, successively commander of the Atlantic Fleet's Second and Fourth Divisions, flagships *Minnesota* (BB-22) and *Georgia* (BB-15).

Command of the destroyer *Ammen* (DD-35) in the Atlantic followed for Lieutenant Commander Taussig (1911-12), as well as duty at the Bureau of Navigation (1912–15). Bringing the *Wadsworth* (DD-60) into commission in July 1915, he additionally commanded Destroyer Division Six of the Atlantic Fleet until July 1916 when to took command of DesDiv Eight, his broad pennant in the *Wadsworth,* of which he was still skipper. This division was the first U.S. Naval force to arrive in the war zone, May 1917, basing at Queenstown, Ireland. He returned home in November to bring the *Little* (DD-79) into commission in April 1918 and to patrol the French coast with her. In August Captain Taussig became head of the Division of Enlisted Personnel, BuNav, in which capacity he became embroiled in a dispute with Assistant Secretary of the Navy Franklin D. Roosevelt, unsuccessfully opposing the latter's policy of rehabilitating convicted sailors for service in the wartime fleet. He transferred to the Naval War College as a senior student in May 1919 and as a staff member one year later. A keen analyst of matters naval, Taussig was becoming a prolific contributor to the U.S. Naval Institute *Proceedings,* making many valuable suggestions of policy which were adopted in due course. These intellectual talents led to further tours at the College, heading the Department of Strategy (1923–26) and service as chief of staff (1927–30).

Captain Taussig's advice became much sought after during more sea-going commands and several key staff billets. He recommissioned the transport *Great Northern* (AG-9) in August 1921, delivered passengers to the Caribbean and in October had his ship made flagship of the U.S. Fleet, Adm. Hilary P. Jones, the vessel being renamed *Columbia* the next month. In April 1922 he assumed command of the cruiser *Cleveland* (CL-21), provided earthquake and tidal wave relief to Chile in November, and in February began a five-month tour as assistant chief of staff to Admiral Jones, flagships *Seattle* (CA-11), *Maryland* (BB-46), and *Pennsylvania* (BB-38). He commanded the *Trenton* (CL-11) (1926–27) and *Maryland* (1930–31), leading to his selection as rear admiral in January 1932. Early in 1931 Taussig joined the staff of Adm. Richard H. Leigh, Commander Battleship Divisions Battle Fleet (in April 1931 changed to Commander Battleships Battle Force) and from June 1932 U.S. Fleet commander. Transferred in May 1933 to be Assistant Chief of Naval Operations, Admiral Taussig was thereafter frustrated from achieving any major command because of his earlier breach with now, President Roosevelt. He did, however, in June 1936 transfer to command of Battleship Division Three, flagship *Idaho* (BB-42), and one year later to that of Cruisers, Scouting Force, and Cruiser Division Five, flagship *Chicago* (CA-29), until May 1938 when he took up his father's old Norfolk command of three decades before. In September 1941 he retired in the rank of vice admiral.

348

Admiral Taussig's outspokenness typified his career to the end, creating a sensation when he testified before a Congressional committee in April 1940 on the inevitability of war in the Pacific and which led to an official reprimand. On December 7, 1941 his son Ens. J. K. Taussig, Jr. (later Capt.) was badly wounded while commanding an anti-aircraft battery on the *Nevada* (BB-36) at Pearl Harbor. The next day the President rescinded the reprimand. The admiral returned to active duty (1943–46) on the Procurement and Review Board, the Naval Clemency and Prison Inspection Board, and the Naval Discipline Policy Review Board, continuing with the Office of the Secretary of the Navy until relieved of all active duty in June 1947. He co-authored *Our Navy: A Fighting Team* (1943).

Navy Department

Taylor, David Watson

(March 4, 1864–July 28, 1940). USNA (Va.) 1885 (1/36).

Pioneer in modern warship design, Taylor became assistant naval constructor in August 1886 while engaged in advanced instruction in naval construction and marine engineering at the Royal Naval College, completing his studies in 1888. His unprecedentedly high academic performance at both Annapolis and Greenwich was a harbinger of an immense quantity of brilliant and important papers, essays, manuals and books on naval architecture and propulsion in technical and professional forums such as the U.S. Naval Institute *Proceedings* throughout his career. He served at Philadelphia (1888–89, 1891–92), designed battleships at the Bureau of Construction and Repairs (1889–90), was chief constructor at Mare Island (1892–94), and returned to the Bureau in 1894 to increase its design activities. Promoted to the ranks of naval constructor in December 1891 and captain in March 1901, he advocated, designed (1894–99) and directed (1899–1914) the Navy's first experimental ship model basin. In 1914 Captain Taylor became chief naval constructor and Chief of Bureau in which capacity he supervised America's vast prewar and World War I warship, airplane and airship building programs, during which (1916) he was promoted to rear admiral, remaining in that post until 1922, the year before his retirement. Although always active in ship design, notably as president of the Society of Naval Architects and Marine Engineers (1925–27), Admiral Taylor gradually turned more toward aviation; he became a member of the National Advisory Committee for Aeronautics in 1917, was instrumental in developing the NC flying boats (1919), and directed the establishment of NACA's research facilities in Virginia and serving as its vice chairman (1927–30). The Navy's new model basin, named in his honor in 1937, was completed in 1940.

Taylor, Henry Clay

(March 4, 1845–July 26, 1904). USNA (Ohio) 1864 (7/21).

Naval Photographic Center

Naval philosopher and administrative reformer, Taylor saw Civil War action on board the screw sloops *Shenandoah* on the North Carolina blockade (1863–64) and *Iroquois* in the Mediterranean and Indian Ocean searching for Confederate cruisers (1864–65). With the sidewheel steamer *Rhode Island* in the North Atlantic one year (1866), he spent the next in the same waters aboard the sidewheeler *Susquehanna,* both vessels being squadron flagship. Lieutenant Commander Taylor had European duty on the storeship *Guard* (1868–69) before teaching mathematics at the Naval Academy (1869–72) and operating in the North Pacific with the sidewheel

350

sloop *Saranac* (1872–74). He remained on the Pacific coast with the Coast Survey, commanding its steamer *Hassler* (1874–77), and then had two tours in Washington, at the Hydrographic Office (1877–78) and the Navy Yard (1878–80). Promoted commander at the beginning of 1880, he commanded the training ship *Saratoga* until early 1884 and became one of the major contributing writers on naval tactics for the U.S. Naval Institute *Proceedings.* Throughout 1884 he was attached to the New York Navy Yard (1885) while working on its harbor management and the Board of Inspection and Survey (1885–87) and was granted an extended leave to work for a Nicaraguan canal.

Commander Taylor commanded the screw gunboat *Alliance* protecting American interests against the Spanish in the Caroline Islands (1890–91), spent a few weeks at Mare Island and several months (1892–93) on diplomatic duty in Spain, and was president of the Naval War College and head of the Torpedo School (1893–96), during which time he lectured on Greek and Roman naval tactics and (June 1894) was promoted to captain. He assumed command of the battleship *Indiana* (BB-1) in January 1897 for training operations off New England and Spanish-American War duty, bombarding San Juan, Puerto Rico, in May 1898, commanding the convoy of Army forces from Tampa to Santiago, Cuba, in June, and helping to sink two destroyers in the Battle of Santiago in July. Detached in October 1899, Captain Taylor reported the next month to the Naval War College where, in March 1900, he directed the creation of the General Board to advise the Secretary of the Navy. Made a member of that body, he also served as commanding officer of the receiving ship *Vermont* at New York (1900–01) and in March 1901 was promoted to rear admiral for full-time General Board duty. In April 1902 Admiral Taylor became Chief of the Bureau of Navigation, and twice (1902, 1904) served temporarily as chief of staff to Adm. George Dewey, flagship the yacht *Mayflower* (PY-1). He died on active duty. His brother-in-law was Adm. R. D. Evans *(q.v.).*

Thach, John Smith "Jimmy"

(April 19, 1905——). USNA (Ark.)
1927 (494/579).

Naval Photographic Center

World War II fighter pilot and air tactical innovator, Thach followed his brother, Vice Adm. James H. Thach, Jr. (1900–1962), into the Navy, completing his mandatory tours of duty in the line between brief aviation instruction at Annapolis in the summer of 1927 and Pensacola flight school in 1929–30 with year-long battleship assignments in the Pacific aboard the *Mississippi* (BB-41) and the *California* (BB-44). He first flew with the "High Hat" squadron, Fighting One (VF-1), of the aircraft carrier *Saratoga* (CV-3), and became an accomplished aerial gunner (1930–32) which led to his assignment as a test pilot at Hampton Roads (1932–34). While attached to Patrol Squadron Nine, tended by the *Wright* (AV-1) on the West coast, he flew the Navy's largest seaplane, the XP2H, nonstop from Norfolk to Panama in January 1935, and next (1936–37) operated with Scouting 6-B from the cruiser *Cincinnati* (CL-6) off California. After duty with Patrol Squadron 5-F at Coco Solo, Canal Zone, Lieutenant Thach returned to the *Saratoga* as gunnery officer of Fighting Three in the summer of 1939 and developed the two-plane defensive maneuver for fighters known henceforth as the "Thach weave" and which became a standard tactic for American Navy and Army fighter pilots in the Pacific. Succeeding to squadron command, he and VF-3 transferred to the *Lexington* (CV-2) after their parent ship was torpedoed early in 1942. His tactics were first successfully proved by his teammate Lt. E. H. "Butch" O'Hare flying a Grumman F4F Wildcat against Japanese Zeros south of Rabaul in February.

Lieutenant Commander Thach participated in the Lae-Salamaua raids of March 1942 and the Battle of the Coral Sea in May and with the loss of the *Lexington* there shifted with his squadron to the *Yorktown* (CV-5) from which he shot down six Zeros during the Battle of Midway in June, making him an "ace." He reported to Pearl Harbor then the Operational Training Command at Jacksonville to train pilots for the next two years and in the summer of 1944 became air operations officer and principal tactical adviser to Adm. J. S. McCain, Commander Task Group 38.1, flagship *Wasp* (CV-18), in the Philippines and the Battle of Leyte Gulf (August–November 1944). When McCain moved up to command Task Force 38, the staff went with him to the new *Lexington* (CV-16) and the *Hancock* (CV-19) for Southeast Asia strikes (November 1944–January 1945) and in the *Shangri-La* (CV-38) for the last attacks on Japan's home islands (May–August). Promoted to captain in March 1945, Thach in September returned to Pensacola and the Office of the Chief of Naval Air Training as Director of Training and (1947–49) Special Assistant, with another year there. He took command of the *Sicily* (CVE-118) in June 1950 and from August supported ground forces in the Korean War, including the Inchon-Hungnam operations, through January 1951. From August to December he was chief of staff to Carrier Division 17 commander Adm. Herbert E. Regan, flagship *Badoeng Strait* (CVE-116), in antisubmarine patrols off the Korean coast and thereafter was aide to Assistant Secretary of the Navy (Air) John F. Floberg. Skipper of the *Franklin D. Roosevelt* (CVA-42) in the Atlantic (1953–54), he next based at Jax in command of the Sixth Naval District's naval air stations.

Promoted rear admiral in November 1955, Thach served as senior naval member of the Weapon Systems Evaluation Group at the Defense Department (1955–57) and as ComCarDiv 16 which in March 1958 became antisubmarine Task Group Alpha, flagship *Valley Forge* (CVS-45), a permanent ASW task force of his own design. Detached in December 1959, the next month he was promoted to vice admiral and given command of the Pacific Fleet's antisub forces. Admiral Thach was Deputy Chief of Naval Operations (Air) (1963–65) and in March 1965 was promoted to the full rank of admiral to be Commander-in-Chief U.S. Naval Forces in Europe. He retired in May 1967.

Thatcher, Henry Knox

(May 26, 1806–April 5, 1880).

Naval Historical Center

Prominent Union flag officer during the Civil War, this native of Maine and grandson of Revolutionary War General Henry Knox (1750–1806), co-founder of the U.S. Navy, spent several months at West Point before shifting to the Navy as midshipman in 1823. He first briefly served in Porter's "Mosquito Fleet" assembling at Washington (1823) and then on the frigate *United States* in the Pacific (1823–27). After assignment to the ship-of-the-line *Independence,* in ordinary at Boston, he was acting master of the schooner *Porpoise* in the West Indies (1830–32), and after promotion to lieutenant in 1833 at Charleston returned to these waters with the sloop *Falmouth* (1834-35). Leave time was interrupted occasionally during 1838 with duty aboard the sloop *Erie* along the East coast. Lieutenant Thatcher cruised the Mediterranean in the frigate *Brandywine* (1839–41) and served with the receiving ship *Ohio* at Boston and at the navy yard there as inspector. While attached to the sloop *Jamestown* (1847–50) he engaged in food relief to Ireland and protected American interests in the middle sea during Europe's political upheavals. He commanded the storeship *Relief* (1851–52) in supplying the Brazil Squadron and was executive officer of the Philadelphia Naval Asylum (1854–55). After promotion to commander in 1855, he was skipper of the sloop *Decatur* (1857–59) protecting American filibusters in Central America; he thereafter served as exec of the Boston Navy Yard.

Commander Thatcher took command of the sloop *Constellation* in November 1861 and protected Union merchantmen in the Mediterranean against possible Confederate cruisers over the ensuing year and a half. Promoted commodore in July 1862, bypassing the rank of captain, he

354

assumed command of the steam frigate *Colorado* on the Mobile blockade in August 1863. The ship spent most of 1864 at Portsmouth out of commission but from October operated in the North Atlantic Blockading Squadron. Thatcher commanded a division in the 1864–65 attacks on Fort Fisher, North Carolina, and late in January 1865 assumed command of the West Gulf Blockading Squadron as acting rear admiral, flag aboard the receiving ship *Portsmouth* at New Orleans. In March he shifted to the sidewheel steamer *Stockdale* for the final amphibious assault on Mobile and directed the Navy's support of that attack the next month. Admiral Thatcher pursued the rebel flotilla up the Tombigbee River and in May accepted its surrender from the commander, Flag Off. Ebenezer Farrand, CSN. During June he concluded blockading operations against the Texas coast, occupying Galveston, and in July his command was enlarged to be the Gulf Squadron, flagship the sidewheeler *Estrella*. Relieved in December 1865, he left New York in the spring of 1866 to command the North Pacific Squadron in the sidewheeler *Vanderbilt*, a command he held for two years. A rear admiral (since July 1866), he retired in May 1868, but was Port Admiral and station commander at Portsmouth during 1869–70.

Navy Department: National Archives

Towers, John Henry

(January 30, 1885—April 30, 1955).
USNA (Ga.) 1906 (31/116).

The leader of American naval aviation just before and during World War II, Towers circumnavigated the globe while assigned to the battleship *Kentucky* (BB-6) as part of the "Great White Fleet" and helped to outfit the *Michigan* (BB-27) as her first fire control officer (1909–11) for one transatlantic voyage. His career in aviation began during the summer of 1911 when he learned to fly from Glenn H. Curtiss at Hammondsport, New York, in the Navy's first airplane, the Curtiss A-1; he was the second naval officer to earn wings (although in March 1913 he was officially designated Naval Aviator No. 3 after Theodore G. Ellyson, the first, and John Rodgers). In September of 1911 he established the Navy's first air installation at Greenbury Point near Annapolis and in December went to North Island at San Diego to test new aircraft at the Curtiss Flying School. After commanding the first air unit in Fleet maneuvers in the Caribbean in 1913, he survived a disastrous crash which, however, led to the development of safety belts. Executive officer of the first naval air station, Pensacola, part of the time on the training bark *Cumberland* (IX-8), in 1914, Lieutenant Towers that year also commanded the four-plane air unit aboard the *Mississippi* (BB-23) and cruiser *Birmingham* (CL-2) during the Vera Cruz affair. Upon the outbreak of World War I in Europe in August he became assistant naval attaché at London to observe airplane and airship developments overseas, part of the time at the front. Detached in October 1916, he took over Naval Aviation in the Office of the Chief of Naval Operations, later redesignated Supervisor of the Naval Aviation Flying Corps and finally, in 1917, Assistant Director of Naval Aviation; in this role he mobilized America's naval air forces for participation in World War I. In February 1919 as lieutenant commander he took command of Seaplane Division One, the three NC flying boats which tried to fly the Atlantic. As pilot of the NC-3 he came down and had to sail her into port in the Azores Islands, but the NC-4 succeeded.

Exec of the aircraft tender *Aroostook* (CM-3) and senior aide to Pacific Air Detachment commander Capt. Henry C. Mustin at San Diego (1919–20), Commander Towers commanded the tender *Mugford* (DD-105) there before returning to Pensacola as exec (1921–23). He was assistant naval attaché concurrently at London, Paris, Rome, the Hague, and (from 1924) Berlin and served (1925–26) at the Bureau of Aeronautics, returning to it later as Head of the Plans Division (1928–29) and Assistant Chief of Bureau (1929–31). He saw sea duty as exec of the aircraft carrier *Langley* (CV-1) (1926–27) and as chief of staff to Battle Force Aircraft (carrier) commanders Adms. H. E. Yarnell (1931–33) and Frederick J. Horne (1936–37) on the *Saratoga* (CV-3). With a Naval War College and Naval Torpedo Station tour (1933–34), Captain Towers commanded NAS San Diego (1934–36) and the *Saratoga* (1937–38) and was again Assistant Chief of BuAer (1938–39). Promoted rear admiral in June 1939, he assumed the post of Chief of the Bureau and again found himself mobilizing American naval aviation for another world war. Admiral Towers transferred to Hawaii in October 1942 in the rank of vice admiral to be Commander Air Force Pacific Fleet but because of his outspoken crusade for the Navy's air arm was prevented by his superiors from holding a sea command. Nevertheless, he and his staff hammered out naval air policy and logistics for the counteroffensive against Japan.

Admiral Towers became Pacific Fleet commander Adm. C. W. Nimitz's key aviation adviser in his post of ComAirPac and from February 1944 as

Deputy Commander-in-Chief Pacific Fleet and Pacific Ocean Areas. When Nimitz shifted to advanced headquarters on Guam in January 1945, he left Towers in command of the main Fleet headquarters at Pearl Harbor. Detached in July, Towers the next month reported as Commander Second Fast Carrier Force and Commander Task Force 38 off Japan, flagship *Shangri-La* (CV-38), but too late to see action. In November he assumed command of the Fifth Fleet, flagship *New Jersey* (BB-62), in Japanese waters and in the rank of admiral. The following February Admiral Towers took command of the Pacific Fleet for a period of twelve months. He chaired the General Board from March 1947 until his retirement that December.

Triebel, Charles Otto

(November 17, 1907——   ). USNA (Ill.) 1929 (88/240).

Naval Photographic Center

Skipper of the submarine *Snook* against Japan, Triebel operated in the Pacific with the battleship *New York* (BB-34) before undergoing sub training at New London in 1931 and cruising out of Pearl Harbor successively on the subs *S-25* (SS-130), *S-18* (SS-123), and *S-22* (SS-127), and in early 1935 on the decommissioning *S-17* (SS-122) at Philadelphia. After helping to outfit the *Shark* (SS-174) and some maneuvers along the Eastern seaboard, he was assistant superintending constructor with Groton's Electric Boat Company and the New London Ship and Engine works (1936–38). Commanding officer of the *S-41* (SS-146) in Chinese waters (1938–41), he brought the *S-15* (SS-120) back into commission in early 1941 for Atlantic operations until December then Panamanian patrols until relieved in July 1942. Lieutenant Commander Triebel commissioned the *Snook* (SS-279) in October and deployed the following April on the first of five war patrols in the Western

Pacific. Under his command the *Snook* sank 13 cargo vessels and a gunboat totalling nearly 59,000 tons, ninth highest sub score of the war; laid mine fields; and initiated lifeguard services for carrier pilots in the Marcus Island strike of August 1943. Detached upon his return in March 1944 the next month he joined the Bureau of Ordnance, being promoted to captain in March 1945. That July he took over Submarine Division 301 based at Guam, flagship *Boarfish* (SS-327), and in December moved to SubDiv 101 in the *Ray* (SS-271) and *Burrfish* (SS-312). Captain Triebel's postwar assignments were Atlantic sub representative at the Bikini atomic bomb tests of 1946; director of the Special Devices Center on Long Island (1946–47); skipper of the sub tender *Howard W. Gilmore* (AS-16) at Key West; Commander Submarine Squadron Eight in the *Dogfish* (SS-350) in the Atlantic (1948–50); commander of the New London sub base; student at the National War College (1952–53); and inspector general, later assistant chief of staff (strategic plans), to Eastern Atlantic and Mediterranean naval commanders Adms. Jerauld Wright and John H. Cassady at London. In August 1956, after a year as Commander Submarine Flotilla One, flagship *Volador* (SS-490), out of San Diego, Triebel was promoted to rear admiral and later that year made special assistant to the Director of the Strategic Plans Division. He was also a special assistant to the Joint Chiefs of Staff for National Security Council affairs (1957–59). After a year commanding Amphibious Group One, flagship *Eldorado* (AGC-11), in the Pacific, Admiral Triebel directed the Logistic Plans Division until his retirement in August 1962.

Truxtun, Thomas

(February 17, 1755–May 5, 1822).

By Bass Otis: Long Island Historical Society: Naval Photographic Center

The nation's premier sea fighter in the quasi-war with France, Long Islander Truxtun enjoyed a merchant career in the eight years before the American Revolution, interrupted by brief impressed service in the Royal Navy in 1770 aboard H.M. frigate *Prudent* and culminating in a merchant ship command. Captured in 1775 in the West Indies as master of the *Andrew Caldwell* bringing supplies to the Americans and briefly held, he spent the rest of the war in privateers as lieutenant on the *Congress* and master of three vessels successively, the *Independence, Mars* and *St. James.* Most of his great many captures took place in British waters and enhanced his fortune sufficiently for him to enlarge his merchant ship operations after the war, beginning with his voyage in the *Canton* to China in 1786. Appointed captain in the embryonic navy in 1794, Truxtun superintended construction of the frigate *Constellation,* launched in late 1797, and with her convoyed merchantmen during the next summer. At the end of the year the 38-gun ship sailed to the West Indies and in February 1799 engaged and captured the 40-gun French frigate *L'Insurgente* off Nevis. Twelve months later, after some captures of privateers, Truxtun's vessel defeated but was unable to take possession of the 52-gun *La Vengeance* near Curaçao. At this time he was commodore over ten vessels. In August 1800 he brought the frigate *President* into active service for one uneventful war cruise as commodore of the West India Squadron.

Commodore Truxtun in the spring of 1801 took command of the Mediterranean Squadron in the frigate *Chesapeake,* preparing at Norfolk to sortie against the Algierians, but political animosities led to his virtual resignation and the inglorious end of his naval career. Author of several treatises on sailing routes, tactics and other naval matters which reflected his highly-disciplined professionalism and techniques of command, he refused Aaron Burr's offer in 1806 to command naval forces in that person's ill-fated scheme to create an independent state in the West. His grandson was Commo. William Talbot Truxtun (1824–1887), commanding officer of the gunboat *Tacony* in both attacks on Fort Fisher during the Civil War.

Tucker, John Randolph "Handsome Jack"

(January 31, 1812—June 12, 1883).

Naval Historical Center

Flag officer in two navies, the Confederate and Peruvian, Virginian Tucker began his naval career in the U. S. Navy as acting midshipman in 1826, but illness prevented him from going to sea until the next year when he deployed to the Mediterranean aboard the frigate *Java,* transferring to the sloop *Lexington* late in 1829 and back to the *Java* nearly a year later for the return home in 1831. While at the New York receiving ship and naval school in 1833, he passed the examination for passed midshipman, then shipped out to the Brazil Station on the sloop *Erie* (1834–37), becoming her acting master in due course. Early in 1838 he was promoted to lieutenant, spending the ensuing months on the receiving ship *Java* at his home town of Norfolk. Off to the West Indies on the sloop *Warren* early in 1839, he returned home with the sloop *Levant,* remained aboard her at Norfolk, and briefly returned to the *Warren* in 1841. Tucker, between stays at the Norfolk receiving ship (1842–43, 1846–47), patrolled the East Indies with the sloop *St. Louis* and spent 1847 fighting the Mexicans as executive then commanding officer of the bomb brig *Stromboli.* Ill health brought him back to Norfolk. He operated with the Home Squadron in the frigate *Raritan* (1849–50) and in

360

the Mediterranean aboard the frigate *Cumberland* (1852–55), at the end of which cruise he was promoted to commander. In command of the Norfolk receiving ship until 1858, he remained at that port, except for board duty in New York the following spring, until the outbreak of the Civil War.

Appointed commander in the Virginia and Confederate navies in April and June 1861 respectively, Tucker directed the naval defenses of the James River, in which capacity he commanded the sidewheel steamer *Patrick Henry* in operations in the Hampton Roads area from the summer of 1861. He participated in the *Monitor-Merrimack* engagement in March 1862 and the withdrawal of the James River Squadron upriver and in the repulse of its pursuers in May. Transferred in August to command of the ironclad ram *Chicora* at Charleston, which he brought into commission in November, he took part in the attack on the Union blockading forces there the following January. Taking command of the Charleston Squadron in March 1863, the month following his promotion to captain, Flag Officer Tucker continued to defend the city against repeated attacks with his small flotilla and new experimental submarines. With the evacuation of Charleston upon the advance of Sherman's army in February 1865, he scuttled his vessels and took the crews to Richmond as a Naval Brigade to hold Drewry's Bluff, where he assumed command of all naval forces ashore. In April he retreated with Lee's army, led his sailors well at the battle of Sailor's Creek (appropriately named!), but his entire command of some 300 seamen was captured in this action.

Tucker, whose father-in-law Thomas Tarleton Webb had attained the rank of captain in the pre-Mexican War U.S. Navy, returned to sea duty as rear admiral in the navy of Peru during the spring of 1866 for its struggle against Spain. Hoisting his flag aboard the frigate *Independencia* at Valparaiso, he commanded the combined squadrons of Peru and Chile until the threatening Spanish fleet sailed for home. Admiral Tucker then resigned his commission, but remained in South America to survey the Upper Amazon River over the next several years.

Turner, Richmond Kelly

(May 27, 1885–February 12, 1961).
USNA (Calif.) 1908 (5/201).

Navy Department: National Archives

Premier amphibious commander in the Pacific war, in which the Japanese regarded him as "the alligator," Passed Midshipman Turner went first to the Pacific coast for a year on three vessels: the reserve protected cruiser *Milwaukee* (C-21), the San Francisco tug *Active* (YT-14), and the reserve torpedo boat destroyer *Preble* (TBD-12), acting variously as executive officer, engineer and navigator. He then joined the armored cruiser *West Virginia* (ACR-5) for cruises to Japan and throughout the Pacific, with promotion to ensign in June 1910, remaining in that ocean on the *Stewart* (TBD-13) as exec then commanding officer (1912–13). Promoted lieutenant (j.g.) in June 1913, he began postgraduate instruction in ordnance engineering at Annapolis which took him also to Indian Head, Maryland, and the Washington Navy Yard, interrupted by participation in the Dominican Republic intervention during much of 1914 aboard the gunboat *Marietta* (PG-15). He became a turret officer and later assistant gunnery officer of the new *Pennsylvania* (BB-38) in June 1916, the first of three wartime battleship assignments on the Atlantic coast, transferring to the *Michigan* (BB-27) as gunnery officer in September 1917, with promotion to lieutenant that January and to lieutenant commander in December, and in October 1918 to the *Mississippi* (BB-41) for almost a year as gunnery officer. Lieutenant Commander Turner served in the postwar period as ordnance design officer at the Washington Navy Yard (1919–22); gunnery officer of the *California* (BB-44) in the Pacific; Scouting Fleet gunnery officer to Adm. Newton A. McCully on the *Wyoming* (BB-32) in the Atlantic (1923–24); and commander of the destroyer *Mervine* (DD-322) in the Pacific, with promotion to commander in June 1925. After 18 months heading the Design and Turret Mount and Machinery sections at the Bureau of Ordnance, he began a career flirtation with naval aviation.

Commander Turner qualified as a pilot at Pensacola in 1927 at age 42 and early the next year reported to the Asiatic Fleet as commander of its aircraft squadrons and their flagship, the tender *Jason* (AC-12). He then headed the Plans Division of the Bureau of Aeronautics (1929–31); served with the General Board as technical air adviser for the 1932 Geneva disarmament conference; and was exec of the aircraft carrier *Saratoga* (CV-3) in the Pacific (1933–34), remaining on board as chief of staff to the Battle Force carrier commander, Adm. Henry V. Butler. At the beginning of a tour as Naval War College student, July 1935, he was promoted to captain and a year later retained on the staff as Head of the Strategic Section, at the end of which assignment he elected to return to the line as more career-enhancing for him than aviation; he thus commanded the heavy cruiser *Astoria* (CA-34) in both oceans (1938–40). In October 1940 he became Director of the War Plans Division and was promoted to rear admiral the following January. Upon America's entry into World War II in December 1941 he immediately assumed additional duty under U.S. Fleet commander Adm. E. J. King as assistant chief of staff. Admiral Turner thus played a key role in planning the Navy's strategy for the war in the Pacific, particularly the amphibious aspects, leading to his appointment in July 1942 as Commander Amphibious Force in the South Pacific.

Breaking his flag in the transport *McCawley* (AP-10/APA-4), Admiral Turner commanded the landings at Guadalcanal in August 1942 and amphibious support operations there until the island was secured early in 1943. As Commander Task Force 61 he led the assaults on the Russell Islands in February and on New Georgia and Rendova in June and July, transferring his flag to the *Farenholt* (DD-491) when the *McCawley* was mortally stricken by air attack. In mid-July 1943 he transferred to the Central Pacific Force to command its Amphibious Force, numbered the Fifth in August. He led the landings at the Gilbert Islands, flagship *Pennsylvania,* as CTF 52 in November; the Marshalls in January and February 1944 and Marianas in the summer as CTF 51, flagship the amphibious command ship *Rocky Mount* (AGC-3); and Iwo Jima in February 1945 and Okinawa thereafter still as CTF 51, flagship *Eldorado* (AGC-11). He was promoted to vice admiral in March 1944, and his responsibilities were upgraded to be Commander Amphibious Forces Pacific, simultaneously retaining his Fifth Amphibious Force command until April 1945. Detached in mid-May of that year to go to Guam to begin planning for the invasion of Japan, late in the same month he was promoted to admiral. Relieved in October, Admiral Turner spent a month with the General Board and from mid-December was U.S. Naval Representative on the United Nations Military Staff Committee at New York and London, a post he occupied until his retirement from the Navy in July 1947.

Turner, Stansfield

(December 1, 1923––). USNA
(Ill.) 1947 (25/820).

Naval Photographic Center

Naval progressive of the post-Cold War era, Turner graduated in June 1946 for duty on the escort carrier *Palau* (CVE-122) anchored at Norfolk then cruised the Mediterranean (1947) aboard the light cruiser *Dayton* (CL-120) before attending Oxford University in England on a Rhodes Scholarship in foreign affairs (M.A. 1950). He returned to the Med on the destroyer *Stribling* (DD-867), served on the Northeastern Atlantic and Mediterranean command staff at Naples (1951–52), and joined the *Hanson* (DD-832) for carrier screening and shore bombardment in the final months of the Korean War. After a year as flag lieutenant to Adm. Harry H. Henderson, Commander Cruiser Destroyer Flotilla Eight crossing the Atlantic to the Med, he then went to the Policy Division of the Office of the Chief of Naval Operations (1954–56) and to the staff of Pacific Commander Adm. H. D. Felt (1958–60). Afloat, he commanded the ocean-going nonmagnetic mine-sweeper *Conquest* (MSO-488) along the West coast and in the Western Pacific (1956–58) and was executive officer of the *Morton* (DD-948) in the same areas (1960–62) and skipper of the *Rowan* (DD-782) there (1962–63). Systems analyst of Navy force levels in the Office of the Assistant Secretary of Defense (Systems Analysis), Captain Turner became prospective commanding officer of the guided missile frigate *Horne* (DLG-30) in the summer of 1966, commissioned her the following April, and took her into combat escorting the carriers of Task Force 77 off Vietnam.

Then (1968–70) executive assistant and aide to Secretaries of the Navy Paul R. Ignatius and John H. Chafee, Turner was promoted rear admiral in 1970 and given command of CruDesFlot Eight and a carrier task group in the attack carriers *Independence* (CVA-62) and *John F. Kennedy* (CVA-67),

364

keeping watch over the Russian Mediterranean Squadron (1970–71). He returned to the Systems Analysis Division as its director (1971–72). As president of the Naval War College (1972–74) in the rank of vice admiral (since February 1972), he instituted sweeping reforms involving strategy, management, and a new emphasis on military and naval history. Admiral Turner commanded the Second Fleet and then (1975–77) in the full rank of admiral served as Commander-in-Chief of NATO's forces in southern Europe. Early in 1977 his Academy classmate President Jimmy Carter (59th in the class) appointed him to be Director of Central Intelligence and head of the CIA, the fourth naval officer—and a controversial one—to direct American intelligence operations, after Admirals Sidney W. Souers of the Reserve (1946–47), Roscoe H. Hillenkoetter (1947–50), and W. F. Raborn, Jr. (1965–66).

Vosseller, Aurelius Bartlett "Abe"

(January 25, 1903——   ). USNA (Ill.) 1924 (116/523).

Photo courtesy of Admiral Vosseller

U-boat hunter-killer Vosseller went into naval aviation in 1930 after Battle Fleet tours of duty with the battleship *Mississippi* (BB-41), as assistant communications officer to Battleships commander Adm. Louis R. de Steiguer on the *West Virginia* (BB-48) (1926–27), as gunnery officer of the destroyer *Reno* (DD-303), and as assistant gunnery officer to Destroyers commander Adm. Thomas J. Senn on the cruiser *Omaha* (CL-4) (1929–30). After qualifying as a pilot at Pensacola (1931), he served temporarily on the tender *Wright* (AV-1) and with Fighting Squadron Five (VF-5) on the aircraft carrier *Lexington* (CV-2) along the West coast. After a year of postgraduate study in aeronautical engineering at Annapolis, San Diego, and the California Institute of Technology (M.S. 1934), Lieutenant Vosseller flew spotting planes from the *Arizona* (BB-39) in the Pacific (1934–35) and fighters with VF-2 on the *Saratoga* (CV-3) there. Flight deck officer of the *Ranger* (CV-4) in the same waters (1936–37), he helped to develop the high altitude oxygen mask, while at the Aircraft and Equipment desk of the Bureau of Aeronautics' Plans Division, and in mid-1940 reported to Patrol Wing Five to commission and command Patrol Squadron 55 in the West Indies. One year later, in August, this unit, equipped with the first PBM Mariners and redesignated VP-74, flew from Argentia, Newfoundland, to base in Iceland for antisubmarine operations in the Battle of the Atlantic; its skipper was detached in January 1942. Assigned the next month to the Anti-Submarine Warfare Unit of the Atlantic Fleet at Boston, Commander Vosseller utilized his expertise in combating U-boats until December, when he was assigned to help outfit the *Bunker Hill* (CV-17).

But he was brought back to the naval war against Germany in April 1943 to organize and head the Anti-Submarine Warfare Development Detachment of the U.S. Fleet at Quonset Point, Rhode Island, which developed ASW devices, weapons and tactics that helped to turn the tide in favor of the Allies through April 1944. Captain Vosseller assumed command that month of the escort carrier *Bogue* (CVE-9) for Atlantic hunter-killer operations which with the five destroyer escorts also under his tactical command destroyed the *RO-501* and *I-52* in June—both Japanese subs, the only two sunk in the Atlantic!—and the *U-1229* in August, preventing a spy on board from reaching the Maine coast. Detached in November, he transferred to the Pacific as aviation officer to Adm. R. A. Spruance, Commander Fifth Fleet, in which capacity he served in the Iwo Jima and Okinawa campaigns, January to May 1945, in the *Indianapolis* (CA-35) and *New Mexico* (BB-40). He left in July to become aide to Artemis L. Gates, Assistant Secretary of the Navy (Air) and later Under Secretary of the Navy. His postwar billets which led to his rear admiral's promotion in November 1951 were commanding officer of Naval Air Station Patuxent River, Maryland (1946–48), and of the *Coral Sea* (CVB-43) in the Atlantic and Mediterranean, and senior naval representative on the Weapons Systems Evaluation Group (1949–51). Admiral Vosseller commanded Carrier Division 18, flagship *Kula Gulf* (CVE-108), training pilots in the Caribbean and along the East coast before going to Paris as deputy assistant chief of staff for plans at the Supreme Allied Command in Europe and senior U.S. Naval officer at SHAPE (1952–53). Following duty in command of the naval air bases of the Eleventh and Twelfth Naval Districts at San Diego, he retired in September 1956 in the rank of vice admiral.

Waesche, Russell Randolph

(January 6, 1886–October 17, 1946).

World War II Coast Guard commandant Waesche (pronounced Wāy-shē) graduated from the Revenue Cutter Service School of Instruction at Arundel Cove in his native Maryland in October 1906 as third lieutenant (ensign) in that Service (which merged with the Life Saving Service in 1915 to become the U.S. Coast Guard) for cutter patrols in the Atlantic on the *Mohawk,* the Great Lakes on the *Morrill,* and in the Pacific and Alaskan waters on the *Tahoma, Snohomish* and *Rush* (1911–12). Promoted to second lieutenant in 1907 and to first ten years later, he was on the cutter *Pamlico* at New Bern, North Carolina, and in 1915 went to Headquarters where he became first head of the Division of Communications (1916–19). After two months as executive officer of the troop transport *Antigone* in the North Atlantic, he patrolled the Bering Sea on the cutter *Algonquin* (1919–20) and there commanded alternately the *Snohomish* and *Bothwell* (1920–24). Made lieutenant commander in 1923 and commander in 1926, he battled rumrunners violating the Volstead Act on prohibition out of New London as skipper of the destroyer *Beale* (DD-40) (1924–26), outfitter of other destroyers at the Philadelphia Navy Yard, commander of Destroyer Division Four and its flagship *Tucker* (DD-57), and (1927–28) gunnery officer to Destroyer Force commander Cdr. Harry G. Hamlet, USCG, on the flagship *Argus,* an unpropelled "floating base." Commander Waesche then returned to Headquarters as chief ordnance officer, a tour during which he reorganized the service's field forces (1931). After this he served briefly with the War Plans Division in the Navy Department (1932) before becoming aide to Coast Guard Commandant Admiral Hamlet and concurrently budget officer and chief of the Finance Division (1932–36).

In June 1936 President Roosevelt jumped Waesche over many senior officers and the rank of captain to be Commandant in the rank of rear admiral, whereupon he streamlined, modernized, enlarged and generally improved the Coast Guard, bettering its relations with Congress so well that he was reappointed in 1940 and again in 1944. Charged with enforcing the Neutrality Act from 1939 by preventing war material trade to the belligerents in World War II, he also directed Coast Guard participation in the quasi-war of 1941 with Germany and brought the Guard into the Navy from the peacetime Treasury Department in November 1941 for full-fledged participation in the global war. Admiral Waesche became his service's first vice admiral in March 1942 and first admiral in April 1945 while providing Coast Guard vessels for convoy and amphibious operations in all theaters of war. He was retired on the last day of 1945 (the day before the Coast Guard returned to Treasury) because of the cancer which caused his untimely death. One son, R.R. Waesche, Jr., retired as a Coast Guard rear admiral and another, James H. Waesche, was a Coast Guard petty officer during the war.

Wainwright, Richard "Fighting Dick"

(December 17, 1849–March 6, 1926).
USNA (At Large) 1868 (49/81).

Naval Historical Center

Naval progressive and key pre-World War I Navy leader, this great-great-grandson of Benjamin Franklin, grandson of Marine Corps Lt. Col. Robert D. Wainwright (1781–1841) and son of Cdr. Richard Wainwright (1817–1862) (the skipper of Farragut's flagship *Hartford* during the capture of New Orleans) first served in the North Pacific aboard the storeship *Jamestown* (1868–69), and then went ashore to the first of several tours of duty at the

Hydrographic Office (1869–70, 1873–74, 1893–96). Promoted successively to ensign (1869), master (1870) and lieutenant (1873), he cruised the Orient and on the Yangtze River with the screw frigate *Colorado* and sidewheel double-ended gunboat *Ashuelot* (1870–73), engaging the Korean forts in 1871. After duty with the Coast Survey (1874–77) commanding its schooner *Bibb* and steamer *Arago*, Lieutenant Wainwright returned to the Asiatic Station as flag lieutenant to his uncle, Adm. Thomas H. Patterson, flagships the screw frigate *Tennessee*, the sidewheel gunboat *Monocacy*, and the steam sloops *Monongahela* and *Richmond*. While assigned to the Bureau of Navigation in Washington (1880–84), he studied law at Columbia (now George Washington) University (LL.B. 1884). In the North Atlantic with the *Tennessee* (1884–86), part of the time during a demonstration off Panama as secretary to squadron commander Adm. J. E. Jouett, and with the steamer *Galena* (1886–87), he joined the board inspecting steel for the new "ABC" cruisers (1887–88), served at the Naval Academy (1888–90), and cruised the North Pacific and Asiatic waters on the iron gunboat *Alert* (1890–93).

After 21 years (!) in the rank of lieutenant in the dead period of the Navy's history, Wainwright was promoted to lieutenant commander in October 1894, by which time he had become identified with the young naval reformers, publishing essays in the U. S. Naval Institute (of which he was secretary 1888–90) *Proceedings* among other intellectual activities and leading to his appointment as Chief Intelligence Officer of the Navy (1896–97). In December 1897, after lecturing several months at the Naval War College, he became executive officer of the battleship *Maine* and survived her destruction in Havana harbor the following February. After three weeks with the Judge Advocate General's office in May 1898 he assumed command of the newly-commissioned converted yacht *Gloucester*, which he brilliantly led in the Battle of Santiago in July, sinking a Spanish destroyer and chasing another ashore at the cost of no casualties and then took two enemy coastal positions in Puerto Rico. After reporting to the station ship *Santee* at Annapolis in November, Wainwright was promoted to commander in March 1899, commanding the Naval Academy's ships until appointed Superintendent of the Academy to serve from March 1900 to November 1902. Assuming command of the protected cruiser *Newark* (C-1) for a cruise with the South Atlantic Squadron, he temporarily commanded that force during the late summer of 1903, becoming captain in August, and commanding it again early in 1904. In February the *Newark* pacified insurgent-ridden Santo Domingo City with a bombardment and landing. Board duties followed: the General Board from October 1904, the board of engineers to defend coal depots from November, and the Army-Navy Joint Board from March 1905, including a Naval War College conference in 1906, all three posts terminating with his taking command of the battleship *Louisiana* (BB-19) in the Atlantic Fleet in July 1907.

Appointed to command the Second Division, First Squadron of the Atlantic Fleet as rear admiral in May 1908, Wainwright hoisted his flag in the new *Georgia* (BB-15) during the voyage of the "Great White Fleet," his command being redesignated the Third Division, Atlantic Fleet, upon its return from the global cruise in March 1909. In December Admiral Wainwright became the first officer to assume the new and highest post in the Navy, Aid for Operations to the Secretary of the Navy, with additional duty on the Joint Board. Retiring as rear admiral in December 1911, he remained on the latter board and also became a member of the General Board, stepping down from both six months later. He participated then (1912–13) in the preparations for a third Hague conference.

Along with Admiral Patterson (1820–1889), Wainwright's uncles also included Gen. Edward D. Townsend, Adjutant-General of the Union army during the Civil War, and Alexander Dallas Bache, Superintendent of the U. S. Coast Survey from 1843 to 1867. Brothers-in-law were Adm. Seaton Schroeder (1849–1922), Atlantic Fleet commander in 1909–11, and Gen. William W. Wotherspoon, Chief of Staff of the Army in 1914, while his cousin Adm. William H. Emory (1846–1917) commanded a squadron in the Atlantic Fleet (1907–08) and his nephew Alex S. Wotherspoon retired as a rear admiral in 1949. This Wainwright lineage was not related to that of Cdr. Jonathan M. Wainwright (1821–1863), killed in battle at Galveston while commanding the steamer *Harriet Lane,* whose son of the same name (1849–1870) in the rank of master of the screw sloop *Mohican* was mortally wounded fighting the pirate ship *Forward* off San Blas, Mexico, and whose grandson of still the same name rose to general in the Army and defended Corregidor in 1942. The latter's son, J. M. Wainwright IV, served as an officer in the American merchant marine.

Walke, Henry

(December 24, 1808–March 8, 1896).

Best known for his Civil War exploits on the Western rivers, Ohioan Walke reported to the receiving ship *Alert* at Gosport, Virginia, in 1827 and soon deployed on the first voyage of the sloop of war *Natchez* on West Indian patrol (1827–29) then went to the Mediterranean with the sloop *Ontario* (1829–31). At Philadelphia with its receiving ship (1834–36) and navy yard (1836–37), he next policed the troubled Pacific coasts of Latin America aboard the ship-of-the-line *North Carolina,* flagship of the Pacific Station (1837–39). Promoted lieutenant in 1839, Walke circumnavigated the globe on the sloop *Boston* (1840–43) and operated on the Brazil Station with the brig *Bainbridge* (1844–45), accompanying to port the prize Dutch slaving brig *Albert* in September 1845. During the Mexican War, he was at the New York receiving ship before assignment as executive officer of the bomb brig *Vesuvius,* in which he supported the beachhead at Vera Cruz in March 1847 and fought in the Tuxpan foray in April and that before Frontera in June, plus general blockade duty. Detached in October, Walke returned to the New York receiving ship the next year and then sailed with the frigate *Cumberland* for the Mediterranean (1849–51). After two months at the Naval Observatory, he returned again to New York's receiving ship (1851–54) and was moved to the reserved list in 1855 by the Efficiency Board. Campaigning successfully for reinstatement, he was promoted to commander on the active list in 1859 and given command of the storeship *Supply* for African and West Indian cruising.

In January 1861 Commander Walke and the *Supply* evacuated the garrison from Pensacola following that base's seizure by the state of Florida, aspects of which action led to his court-martial, but only slight punishment.

371

In September he obtained command of the gunboat *Tyler* on the Western waters and two months later assisted Gen. U.S. Grant in the capture of Belmont, Kentucky. At the beginning of 1862 he brought into commission the ironclad gunboat *Carondelet* and in February distinguished himself in the investments of Forts Henry and Donelson. Walke's most famous act was running the *Carondelet* past the Confederate batteries at Island No. 10 on the Mississippi during the fighting there in April, followed by the attack against the batteries at New Madrid, the naval battle of Memphis in June and a sharp fight with the ram *Arkansas* on the Yazoo River in July, after which he was promoted to captain. He assumed command of the sidewheel ironclad ram *Lafayette* in February 1863, ran the Vicksburg batteries with her and engaged those at Grand Gulf in April, and then operated on the Mississippi and Red rivers until Vicksburg surrendered in July. Detached in August, the next month Captain Walke took command of the screw sloop *Sacramento* and during 1864–65 cruised off western Europe searching for and blockading Confederate raiders, especially the *Rappahannock* at Calais and Liverpool, the cruise and his command terminating at Boston in August 1865. Advanced to commodore in July 1866, he commanded the Mound City Naval Station, Illinois, on the Ohio River (1868–70) and had duty with Adm. D. D. Porter (1871). Promoted rear admiral in July 1870, Admiral Walke retired the following April but continued to serve as a member of the Lighthouse Board (1871–73).

Ward, Norvelle Gardiner "Bub"

(December 30, 1912——). USNA (Md.) 1935 (185/442).

Naval Photographic Center

Pacific war submariner and Vietnam War leader, Ward went from his first ship, the West coast-based cruiser *Salt Lake City* (CL-25), into New London sub training (1937–38) and the subs *S-26* (SS-131) from Pearl Harbor to New London (1938–39) and the training *R-4* (SS-81) at the latter place. A lieutenant (j.g.) since June 1938, he joined the outfitting *Seadragon* (SS-194) in mid-1939, became her executive officer upon commissioning that October, and cruised with her to the Far East the next year. The *Seadragon* received heavy damage from a Japanese air attack on Cavite in December 1941 and executed four war patrols into Indochinese and Indonesian waters from January to October 1942, all plagued by malfunctioning torpedoes and other poor equipment, for a score of only five cargo vessels amounting to some 24,500 tons. Promoted lieutenant in January 1942, Ward served from November 1942 to January 1943 as assistant personnel officer to submarine Task Force 72 commander Capt. James Fife, Jr., at Brisbane and thereafter as exec of the *Gato* (SS-212) for two war patrols and three sinkings in the Solomons until May. That month he assumed command of the *Guardfish* (SS-217) in the rank of lieutenant commander. His first two war patrols during the rest of 1943 consisted of supporting the landings in the Solomons by putting advance parties ashore, providing aviator rescue services, and making soundings. The next patrol focused on the waters around Truk, including carrier lifeguard duty, in early 1944, and in the fourth the boat operated in Formosa waters as part of the "Mickey Finns" sub group, June and July. Her skipper promoted to commander in March, the *Guardfish* then patrolled in the Sea of Japan as part of a wolf pack. By the time Ward was transferred in October 1944 to be assistant operations officer to Adm. C.A.

Lockwood, ComSubsPac, he had in five war patrols with the *Guardfish* accounted for nine ships sunk with a combined tonnage of nearly 40,000. He remained at Pearl Harbor until November 1945.

Commander Ward served briefly on the staff of Commander Submarine Squadron Two, Capt. Lewis S. Parks, at New London; as skipper of the Navy's first telescopic snorkel-equipped sub *Irex* (SS-482) in the Atlantic (1946–47); as a battalion officer at the Naval Academy; as operations officer to Capts. Willis A. Lent and Stanley P. Moseley, Commanders Submarine Flotilla One, flagship *Volador* (SS-490), in the Pacific (1949–51); as skipper of the destroyer *Yarnall* (DD-541) in Korean War operations, June to December 1951; and was promoted to captain in June 1954. A student at the Armed Forces Staff College at Norfolk (1952–53) and at the National War College in Washington (1957–58), he was antisubmarine warfare officer to Second Fleet commanders Adms. F. B. Stump, Thomas S. Combs and Edmund T. Wooldridge (1953–55) and captain of the oiler *Nantahala* (AO-60) deployed to the Mediterranean (1955–56). Captain Ward commanded SubRons Five, flagships *Volador* and *Diodon* (SS-349), in the Pacific (1956–57) and 14, which he commissioned in July 1958 and worked up as the first Fleet Ballistic Missile (Polaris) Submarine squadron and which based at Scotland's Holy Loch with the tender *Proteus* (AS-19) from March until his relief in August 1961. He then served at the Office of the Chief of Naval Operations as Head of the Navy Plans Branch in the Strategic Plans Division (1961–62) and as assistant for war gaming matters (1962–65), during which—in August 1963—he was promoted to rear admiral. With the escalation of the Vietnam War, Admiral Ward went to Saigon as Chief of the Naval Advisory Group from May 1965 and additionally as Commander Naval Forces Vietnam from April 1966, directing riverine and coastal operations in the Mekong River and Delta areas until May 1967. The following month he transferred to command of Service Group Three, flagship the repair vessel *Ajax* (AR-6), for Seventh Fleet wartime operations until September 1968. Earlier in the latter year his son Marine Capt. Alexander K. Ward died at Danang from wounds received in action. After a tour as Assistant CNO (Safety), Admiral Ward concluded his naval career as commander of the Caribbean Sea Frontier, Tenth Naval District and Antilles Defense Command at San Juan, Puerto Rico (1970–73), retiring in August 1973.

Whipple, Abraham

(September 16, 1733—May 29, 1819).

Daring Revolutionary War leader, Rhode Island merchant seaman Whipple first saw action in the Seven Years (French and Indian) War as captain of the colonial privateer *Gamecock* with which he captured 23 French vessels (1759–60). Then, in June 1772, he led eight launches to destroy the British schooner *Gaspé* off Providence in defiance of the Navigation Acts. Three years later, June 1775, he was given command of two chartered Rhode Island state sloops as commodore and made captain of one, the *Katy,* and immediately succeeded in taking a British tender in the first naval action of the Revolution. Whipple operated in Narragansett Bay the rest of the summer and in December was appointed captain in the Continental Navy, commanding the armed ship *Columbus.* With this vessel he participated in his brother-in-law Commo. Esek Hopkins' raid on the Bahamas early in 1776 and took prizes off New England later in the year. Captain Whipple assumed command of the new frigate *Providence* in 1778, fought his way through the blockade of Rhode Island to sea in April, and cruised to France with dispatches and for naval supplies, returning with another vessel and taking three prizes en route. As commodore of a three-vessel squadron, flagship his own *Providence,* Whipple in July 1779 quietly captured eleven vessels of a large convoy in a fog off Newfoundland and in December took his force to help defend Charleston. He was captured with his ships when the city fell to the British in May 1780 but was paroled for the duration. Commodore Whipple as master sailed the first American flag vessel, the *General Washington,* into the river Thames in 1784.

Whitaker, Reuben Thornton

(September 23, 1911--   ). USNA (Ark.) 1934 (136/463).

Naval Photographic Center

Skipper of the submarine *Flasher* in the Pacific, Whitaker attended the New London sub school after a Pacific Battle Force tour on the cruiser *Concord* (CL-10), graduating at the end of 1936. He operated in Hawaiian waters aboard the sub *Pike* (SS-173) (1937–38) and became engineer and later executive officer in the first crew of the *Sturgeon* (SS-187) between Hawaii and the West coast and from November 1941 in Far Eastern waters for four patrols through August 1942, sinking three vessels and damaging several others. Taking command of the *S-44* (SS-155) in September, he damaged a Japanese destroyer the next month in the Solomons but his own boat suffered so heavily from depth charges it had to return to port, Brisbane. Lieutenant Whitaker was exec of the *Flying Fish* (SS-229) from January to March 1943 under Lt. Cdr. G. R. Donaho *(q.v.)* and in May became prospective commanding officer of the *Flasher* (SS-249), commissioning her in September in the rank of lieutenant commander. On the *Flasher*'s first war patrol, in Philippine waters the first two months of 1944, she sank four vessels; on the second off Indochina during the spring, three more; on the third, in the South China Sea during June and July, four cargo ships and the light cruiser *Oi;* and on the fourth, back in the Philippines in August and September, three more *marus*. Detached from the *Flasher* in November, Whitaker left behind a score of 14 sinkings or nearly 61,000 tons, the sixth highest for a sub skipper in the Pacific war. (Under his relief, Lt. Cdr. George W. Grider, Jr., *Flasher*'s sum total rose to 21 vessels or over 100,000 tons, the highest tonnage sunk by an American sub in World War II.)

    Commander Whitaker spent the remainder of hostilities and all of 1945–46 as prospective commanding officer instructor at New London, returning to the Pacific Fleet and its submarine commander's staff, Adm. James Fife, Jr., as training officer (1947–49). He was occupied during the postwar period studying logistics at the Naval War College (1949–50); commanding Submarine Division 62, flagship *Runner* (SS-476), out of Norfolk; advising Adm. Stuart S. Murray, Atlantic Fleet sub commander, as operations officer (1951–52); heading the submarine branch of the Fleet Maintenance Division of the Office of the Chief of Naval Operations (1952–55); and commanding Submarine Squadron Four, flagship *Clamagore* (SS-343), based at Key West. He was then chief of staff of the Naval group giving military aid to Turkey, headquarters Ankara (1956–58). Captain Whitaker commanded the fleet oiler *Neosho* (AO-143) supplying the Sixth Fleet in the Mediterranean and then the heavy cruiser *Macon* (CA-132) in Atlantic operations (1960) before returning to the Office of the CNO as Deputy Anti-Submarine Warfare Readiness Executive (changed in late 1961 to Special Assistant ASW Projects). In July 1962, shortly after taking command of the Subic Bay Navy Base in the Philippines, he was promoted to rear admiral, going on to command Amphibious Group Four (1964–65), flagship the amphibious command ship *Taconic* (AGC-17), in which he participated in the Dominican Republic intervention. Admiral Whitaker commanded the Military Sea Transportation Service at Brooklyn, New York (1965–68) and also temporarily (summer 1967) the Third Naval District and New York Navy Base. He retired in August 1968.

Wilkes, Charles

(April 3, 1798—February 8, 1877).

Scientist, explorer and the central and controversial figure in the *Trent* affair, New Yorker Wilkes saw merchant service (1815–17) before receiving his midshipman's appointment in 1818 for six months on the ship-of-the-line *Independence* at Boston. He cruised to Russian Baltic waters and in the Mediterranean Sea on the frigate *Guerriére* (1818–21), and after two months with the ship-of-the-line *Washington* in ordinary at New York he operated with her sister ship *Franklin* in the Pacific (1821–23), commanding the merchant ship *O'Cain* on the return to Boston. Furlough followed, during which he studied with F. R. Hassler, founder of the U.S. Coast Survey, but aside from examining and court-martial chores at Washington and Philadelphia (1825) he had no active duty until 1827–29 when as a lieutenant he purchased scientific instruments for the U.S. Exploring Expedition. Wilkes served in the Mediterranean briefly with the sloops *Boston* and *Fairfield* (1830–31) but was thereafter incapacitated by smallpox. He surveyed Narragansett Bay (1832–33) and was Superintendent of the Depot of Charts and Instruments (1833–37), during which (1836–37) he visited Europe to obtain more instruments. After command of the brig *Porpoise* surveying the Southern coast and chasing pirates (1837–38), he commanded the South Seas Exploring Expedition (1838–42), and its flagship, the sloop *Vincennes,* to the South and Western Pacific, the Antarctic (of which he was principal discoverer), Pacific Northwest America and around the world. He recounted his findings in a published narrative (1844) and in scientific accounts the writing of which, with other scientific papers, consumed his energies over the next decade and a half.

Promoted commander in 1843 and captain in 1855, Wilkes in April 1861 received orders to command the screw frigate *Merrimack* at Norfolk but on his arrival found that she had been scuttled to avoid capture by rebel forces, whereupon he assumed command of the screw sloop *Pawnee* and assisted in the further destruction of the navy yard. The next month he sailed for Africa to take command of the screw frigate *San Jacinto,* which he did in August, returning home in search of the Confederate raider *Sumter.* Instead he intercepted the British mail packet *Trent* in the Old Bahama Channel early in November and removed Confederate diplomats John Slidell and James M. Mason, a clear violation of British neutrality, an act which though celebrated in the North was quietly repudiated and the captives released following strong British protests. Detached at the end of November, Captain Wilkes had board duties until July 1862 when he commanded the James River Flotilla, flagship the steam sloop *Wachusett,* supporting the army in Virginia. Promoted commodore in August, he commanded the Potomac Flotilla only a few days in September before transferring to command of the new West India (or "Flying") Squadron, still in the *Wachusett,* to protect American commerce plying between Bermuda, the Bahamas and the West Indies; he held the rank of acting rear admiral. Singularly unsuccessful and further violating neutral rights, he was detached in June 1863. A confusion over his true age had led to the cancellation of his promotion to commodore and reduction to captain on the retired list in November 1862, though he was advanced to commodore on that list the following March.

Ever controversial, hotheaded and outspoken to the point of disobedience, Commodore Wilkes earned the displeasure of Secretary of the Navy Gideon Welles and a court-martial during the spring of 1864, with a suspension from active duty for one year. He was promoted to rear admiral on the retired list in August 1866 and saw only brief special duty in Washington during the summer of 1870 and in 1872–73. His memoirs did not appear until a century after his death: *Autobiography of Rear Admiral Charles Wilkes, U.S. Navy* (1978).

Wilkinson, Theodore Stark "Ping"

(December 22, 1888–February 21, 1946). USNA (La.) 1909 (1/74).

Navy Department: National Archives

Amphibious leader in the Pacific, the erudite Annapolis-born Wilkinson spent much of his early career in battleships: the *Kansas* (BB-21) on the Eastern seaboard (1909–10, 1919–20); the *South Carolina* (BB-26) crossing the Atlantic (1910–11); the *Florida* (BB-30) in that Fleet (1913–14), leading a company ashore in the fighting at Vera Cruz and later (1915–16) as aide to Adm. Augustus F. Fechteler, Second Division commander in the *Florida,* and briefly to Seventh Division commander Lt. Cdr. David C. Hanrahan on the destroyer *Balch* (DD-50); the *Pennsylvania* (BB-38) as fire control officer along the East coast (1920–21); and later the *Mississippi* (BB-41) as her captain in both oceans (1941). Again crossing the Atlantic with the armored cruiser *Tennessee* (ACR-10), he served in the Mediterranean (1914–15) aboard the *North Carolina* (ACR-12); as skipper in rapid succession (1921–22) of the Atlantic destroyers *Osborne* (DD-295), *Goff* (DD-247) and *Taylor* (DD-94) and later (1925–26) of the *King* (DD-242) in that ocean; as gunnery officer to Scouting Fleet (Force) commander Adm. Arthur L. Willard in the *Wyoming* (BB-32), *Arkansas* (BB-33) and cruiser *Augusta* (CA-31) in the Atlantic (1930–31); and twice on the *Indianapolis* (CA-35), as executive officer in both oceans (1934–36) and later (1939–41) in the Pacific as chief of staff to Scouting Force commander Adm. Adolphus Andrews. Ashore, Wilkinson studied ordnance engineering at George Washington University (1911–13), spent several weeks as assistant naval attaché in London (1914), headed the wartime and postwar Bureau of Ordnance's Experimental Section in developing depth charges and mine devices (1916–19, 1922–25); had tours of duty at the Bureau of Navigation heading the officer records section (1927–30) and the Planning Division (1936–39); and as secretary of the

General Board (1931–34) participated in the Geneva and London disarma-, ment activities. He returned to the Navy Department in October 1941 as Director of Naval Intelligence and the following January was promoted to rear admiral.

Appointed Commander Battleship Division Two, flagships *New Mexico* (BB-40), *Idaho* (BB-42) and *Pennsylvania* (BB-38), in August 1942 for South Pacific operations, Admiral Wilkinson trained in Hawaii, became South Pacific Deputy Commander at Nouméa, New Caledonia the following January, and in July took command of its Third Amphibious Force. Present aboard the stricken attack transport flagship *McCawley* (APA-4) during the Rendova landings in June, he raised his flag on that island in July for the New Georgia assaults, going on board the *Cony* (DD-508) for the Vella Lavella landing in August. Shifting his flag to Guadalcanal, he directed the surface forces protecting his beachheads and the Bougainville operation in November in which he was aboard the *George Clymer* (APA-27). In February 1944, flagship *Halford* (DD-480), he undertook the occupation of the Green Islands which virtually completed the neutralization of Rabaul and ended the South Pacific campaign. The following August he was promoted to vice admiral and redesignated Commander Third Amphibious Force of the Pacific Fleet to direct the landings in the Palau Islands and Ulithi in September, flagships the amphibious command ships *Mount McKinley* (AGC-7) and *Mount Olympus* (AGC-8). In the latter vessel he took the Southern Attack Force (Task Force 79) into the Leyte beaches from October through December and again into Lingayen Gulf in January 1945. Late that month Admiral Wilkinson flew to Pearl Harbor to begin planning for the invasion of Japan but instead ended up commanding the occupation landings at Yokohama in the *Mount Olympus* in September. Returning to Washington at the end of the year, in January 1946 he became a member of the Joint Strategic Survey Committee of the Joint Chiefs of Staff but shortly thereafter drowned when his automobile rolled off a ferry at Norfolk.

Winslow, Cameron McRae

(July 29, 1854–January 2, 1932).
USNA (At Large) 1875 (3/32)

National Cyclopedia of American Biography (reprinted by permission)

Early twentieth century fleet commander, Winslow followed his father, Cdr. Francis Winslow (1818–1862), Civil War commander of the screw gunboat *R. R. Cuyler* on the Gulf coast blockade, into the Navy just as the career of his second cousin, Adm. J. A. Winslow *(q.v.)*, was ending. He shipped out in the screw frigate *Tennessee* (1879–84) as well as the screw sloop *Kearsarge* in the Pacific (1877–78) and later in the Atlantic and Mediterranean (1885–86), the training frigate *Constitution* on her final cruise to Europe (1878–79), and the screw sloops *Despatch* along the Eastern seaboard (1884–85), *Pensacola* in Europe (1885), and *Galena* in the Caribbean (1886–87). He finally went ashore at the Naval War College (1887) and torpedo school at Newport (1887–89), which prepared him to command the Navy's first steel torpedo boat, the *N-1*, christened *Cushing* (TB-1). Lieutenant Winslow joined her fitting out at Bristol, Rhode Island, in December 1889, brought her into commission the next April, and experimented with her at Newport until March 1893, when he was transferred to the screw gunboat *Alliance* for Pacific and South Atlantic operations (1893–95). Equipment duty at the New York Navy Yard preceded service afloat on the monitor *Terror* (BM-4) (1896–97) and the new gunboat *Nashville* (PG-7), from which he led a boat expedition which cut the underwater cable off Cienfuegos, Cuba, during the summer of 1898; he was wounded in the action.

In the midst of a tour with the battleship *Indiana* (BB-1) (1898–99), Winslow was promoted to lieutenant commander, and subsequently spent several months on the staff of Adm. W.T. Sampson, flagship the armored cruiser *New York* (ACR-2), all in the North Atlantic. Reporting to the New

York yard late in 1899, the following February he took over the branch Hydrographic Office there and was thereafter (1901–02) flag lieutenant to Adm. Francis J. Higginson, Commander North Atlantic Station, flagship *Kearsarge* (BB-5). In March 1902 he became naval aide to President Theodore Roosevelt while assigned to the Bureau of Navigation and General Board, with promotion to commander in October 1903. Winslow, helping to refit the Presidential yacht *Mayflower* (PY-1), brought her back into commission in July 1905 and commanded her and the other vessels at Oyster Bay during the Russo-Japanese peace conference. In December he took command of the new protected cruiser *Charleston* (C-22), conveyed Secretary of State Elihu Root on good-will visits throughout South America, and then deployed to the Pacific coast until relieved in June 1907. Assistant to the Chief of the Bureau of Navigation, Adm. Willard H. Brownson, he was promoted to captain in January 1908 and given command of the *New Hampshire* (BB-25), which he brought into commission in March and operated in the Atlantic and Caribbean until transferred in November 1909 to be Supervisor of New York Harbor. Captain Winslow received his promotion to rear admiral in September 1911 and spent several weeks late in the year at the Naval War College.

Author of many professional essays, especially on navigation, Admiral Winslow commanded in succession three divisions of the Atlantic Fleet: from December 1911 the Second, flagship *Louisiana* (BB-19); from August 1912 the Third, flagship *New Jersey* (BB-16); and from January 1913 the First, flagship *Utah* (BB-31) and mainly *Florida* (BB-30). He reported to the Naval War College for special duty in January 1914 but had this tour interrupted by the Mexican crisis, during which, in the spring and summer, he commanded the Special Service Squadron, flagship *New York* (BB-34), off Vera Cruz. Leaving the College in August 1915, Winslow the next month became Commander-in-Chief Pacific Fleet in the *San Diego* (ACR-6) in the full rank of admiral, serving in this post until he retired in July 1916 as rear admiral. With the entry of the United States into World War I, he returned to active duty in September 1917 as inspector of naval districts on the Atlantic coast, flagship the patrol yacht *Aloha* (SP-317), retiring again in October 1919.

Winslow, John Ancrum

(November 19, 1811—September 29, 1873).

Captain of the *Kearsarge* in her celebrated victory over the *Alabama*, North Carolina-born, Massachusetts-raised Winslow became midshipman from the former state in 1827, spending the latter part of that year on the receiving ship *Fulton* at Brooklyn before joining the sloop *Falmouth* for her maiden voyage in the Caribbean (1827–30) and her transfer to the Pacific (1831–32). In the interval he attended the naval school at New York and afterward the Norfolk school (1833). He operated in the Brazil Squadron on the sloops *Ontario* (1835–36) and *Erie* (1836–37), on the latter rising to acting master then acting lieutenant. During duty at the Boston naval rendezvous (1838–40), Winslow was promoted to lieutenant and for a year (1840) was with the schooner *Enterprise* off Brazil until illness forced him to return ashore, to the Boston receiving ship. There, in October 1841, he distinguished himself in a fire on a Cunard steamer for which he received a gift from Queen Victoria. Joining the new sidewheel steam frigate *Missouri* in July 1842, he cruised in the West Indies until the following April. Four months later his ship sailed for Gibraltar, where it was destroyed by flames from an accident.

Lieutenant Winslow reported aboard the frigate *Cumberland* at the end of 1845 and spent most of the following year in the Gulf of Mexico. He led part of a landing party against Mexican forces at Tabasco and Frontera in November with such conspicuous success that he was immediately given command of the Revenue cutter *Morris*, which helped to blockade and capture Tampico, only to lose this vessel on a reef during a gale in December. Taken aboard the flagship frigate *Raritan*, he shared a room with Lt. Raphael Semmes, who had just lost his ship as well and against whom he would one day fight his most famous battle. Briefly on the sidewheel steamer *Mississippi,* Winslow was stationed at the Boston Navy Yard (1847–48) and as first lieutenant of the sloop *Saratoga* in the Caribbean (1848–49) and on the frigate *St. Lawrence* in the Pacific (1852–55). Promoted commander in 1855, he commanded the naval rendezvous at Boston (1855–57) and inspected lighthouses there (1860–61). In September 1861 he took command of the converting river gunboat *Benton* in the West, only to be forced to return home three months later after injuring his arm. His history of ill fortune continued with a case of malaria after he returned to duty with the Mississippi Flotilla late in the spring of 1862. He participated in the attack on Fort Pillow, led an expedition up Arkansas' White River to support the army in June, and was promoted to captain in July. Commanding the sternwheel casemate gunboat *St. Louis,* renamed *Baron De Kalb,* he patrolled the Mississippi during the summer and fall and put landing parties ashore to suppress Confederate guerrillas. A fanatical abolitionist, he criticized the government for failing to make the war a moral crusade and was ordered home in October to await further orders.

In December 1862 Captain Winslow was directed to take command of the screw sloop *Kearsarge,* then engaged in searching for Confederate raiders in European waters. He assumed command in April 1863 and hunted fruitlessly—handicapped by the loss of sight in an inflamed eye—until February 1864, at which time however the *C.S.S. Florida* managed to elude his vigil off Brest. He had better luck blockading the *Rappahannock* at Calais, and in June he trapped the famous raider *Alabama* at Cherbourg. She was commanded by Capt. Semmes *(q.v.)* who challenged Winslow for battle which he eagerly accepted. In the engagement, the last duel in history between single major wooden warships, the *Kearsarge* pounded the *Alabama* into a sinking condition. Immediately promoted to commodore, Winslow continued his patrol of the French coast with the *Kearsarge* then shifted to the Caribbean before returning home and being detached in November. After a lengthy hero's reception, he commanded the Gulf Squadron, flagship the sidewheeler *Estrella* (1866–67), and the Portsmouth Navy Yard (1869–70). Promoted to rear admiral in March 1870, he commanded the Pacific Squadron in the sidewheel steam sloop *Saranac,* the screw steamer *Pensacola* and the new screw sloop *California.* Forced by ill health to relinquish command in the summer of 1872, Admiral Winslow returned home, ending his naval career, although Congress refused to place him on the retired list because of his most singular achievement. A son, Rear Adm. Herbert Winslow (1848–1914), landed the first Marines during the Boxer Rebellion from his own ship *Solace* (AH-2) and, befitting his father's wartime command, went on to become captain of the new battleship *Kearsarge* (BB-5).

Worden, John Lorimer

(March 12, 1818–October 18, 1897).

Navy Department: National Archives

Commander of the *Monitor,* New Yorker Worden patrolled off revolution-wracked South America as midshipman (1834) on the Brazil Squadron flagship, the sloop *Erie* (1834–37), and in the Mediterranean on the maiden voyage of the sloop *Cyane* (1838–39). Seven months of training at the naval school at Philadelphia led to advancement to passed midshipman in July 1840 and assignment to the storeship *Relief* in the Pacific (1840–42). In between two tours of duty at the Naval Observatory (1844–46, 1850–52), he operated as executive officer of the storeship *Southampton* supplying warships on the West coast (1847–49), returning to the East on the ship-of-the-line *Ohio.* Receiving promotions to master in August 1846 and lieutenant in November of the same year, Worden served in the middle sea aboard the frigate *Cumberland* (1852–55), at the Observatory again (1855–56) and Brooklyn navy yard and with the Home Squadron until 1860.

Lieutenant Worden at the beginning of April 1861 delivered secret orders to the squadron at Pensacola defending Fort Pickens but on his return trip overland was arrested at Montgomery, Alabama, and held prisoner until exchanged in November. After a short recuperation from illness incurred in the South, in January 1862 he reported as prospective commanding officer of the revolutionary new ironclad *Monitor,* then building on Long Island, and superintended her completion and final commissioning at the end of February. Early in March he took his untried vessel to Hampton Roads where it engaged the equally-revolutionary ironclad ram *Virginia* (ex-*Merrimack)* on the 9th. Late in the battle an exploding shell wounded him in the face, thus impairing his vision and requiring his relief by his executive officer, Lt. Samuel Dana Greene, to complete the action. Promoted lieutenant commander in July, Worden, after a long recuperation, took command of the newly-launched monitor *Montawk* in October, brought her into commission in December, and led her in the bombardments of Fort McAllister, Georgia, in January and February 1863 and of Charleston in April, destroying the privateer *Rattlesnake* at the former place despite damage to his ship from a mine. His promotion to captain occurred in February and his relief in April, and he spent the duration of the war in New York assisting in the construction of ironclads.

Captain Worden commanded the screw steamer *Pensacola* in the Pacific (1866–67), took an extended leave in Europe in the rank of commodore (May 1868), and was Superintendent of the Naval Academy (1869–74). During the course of this tour—November 1872—he attained his final rank of rear admiral and also supported the creation of the United States Naval Institute, of which he was president (1874). As commander of the European Squadron (1875–77), flagships the screw frigate *Franklin* and the screw steamer *Marion,* he not only cruised European waters but operated in the Eastern Mediterranean during the Russo-Turkish War. Admiral Worden ended his career as a member of the Examining and Retiring boards, becoming president of the former in 1882 and of the latter in 1883, he himself retiring in December 1886.

Wright, Jerauld

(June 4, 1898——   ). USNA (N.J.)
1918 (93/199).

Supreme Allied commander in the Atlantic during the height of the Cold War, Wright graduated in June 1917 and spent World War I on the gunboat *Castine* in the Patrol Force out of Gibraltar while his father, Maj. Gen. William M. Wright, commanded the 89th Division in the Meuse-Argonne offensives of 1918. Ensign Wright received rapid wartime promotions to lieutenant (j.g.) in February and lieutenant in November 1918, the next month transferring to the destroyer *Dyer* (DD-84) at Gibraltar for Eastern Mediterranean cruising and Balkan relief until returning to Charleston late the next year and until mid-1920. During this time his father became Deputy Chief of Staff of the Army. Lieutenant Wright served along the Atlantic coast in the *Reid* (DD-292) (1920–22), on the Pacific coast on the *Breese* (DD-122), and in the Asiatic Fleet with the *John D. Ford* (DD-228), arriving with the latter ship in the summer of 1922 at Manila where General Wright had command of the Philippine Department. During young Wright's ensuing two tours of duty on the Presidential yacht *Mayflower* (PY-1) in the Potomac River (1924–26) and on the battleship *Maryland* (BB-46) in the Pacific (1926–29) he had additional duties as aide to President Calvin Coolidge and then to President-elect Herbert Hoover on the latter's 1928 goodwill trip to South America. Stationed at the Bureau of Ordnance to work on anti-aircraft devices, he was promoted to lieutenant commander in January 1931 and the following summer made first lieutenant of the cruiser *Salt Lake City* (CA-25) going from the Atlantic to the Pacific and advancing to gunnery officer (1932–34). After a year in the Executive Department at the Naval Academy, he was aide to Assistant Secretary of the Navy Henry L. Roosevelt (1935–36) and fitting-out officer of the Secretary of the Navy's yacht *Sequoia* (AG-23).

After more BuOrd duty (1936–37) and fitting out and assuming command of the *Blue* (DD-387), Wright was promoted to commander in June 1938 and then took his ship from the Atlantic to the Pacific for a year of operations as part of the Battle Force. He returned to the Academy as a battalion officer and in March 1941 to the Battle Force as executive officer of the *Mississippi* (BB-41), which soon deployed to the North Atlantic for escorting convoys to Iceland. Upon the outbreak of war in the Pacific, the ship immediately returned to the West coast. In May 1942 he joined the staff of U.S. Fleet commander-in-chief Adm. E. J. King to develop amphibious policy, with promotion to captain the next month, and moved to Gen. Dwight D. Eisenhower's staff for the North African landings in November, that month temporarily commanding the British submarine *Seraph* to successfully spirit French Gen. Henri Giraud out of southern France. He helped rearm the former Vichy French forces for service with the Free French in early 1943 and served also on the staff of Allied Mediterranean naval commander Adm. Sir Andrew Cunningham, RN. In March Captain Wright became assistant chief of staff to the American naval commander there, Adm. H. K. Hewitt *(q.v.),* for the Sicily and Salerno landings during the summer. Transferring to the Pacific in December, he took command of the *Santa Fe* (CL-60), fast carrier screening vessel, and fought her in the Marshall Islands, at New Guinea, and on various carrier strikes through early 1944, in the Marianas and Palau campaigns during the summer, and in the Leyte battle and operation in October. Late in that month he was promoted to commodore and a month later to rear admiral as Commander Amphibious Group Five in the amphibious command ship *Ancon* (AGC-4) for the Okinawa operation the following spring in which he led the Demonstration Group, Task Group 51.2.

Detached in August 1945, Admiral Wright commanded Cruiser Division Six, flagship *San Francisco* (CA-38), in Chinese waters in September and early October and superintended the surrender of Japanese forces in Korea. For the next three years he headed the Operational Readiness Section in the Office of the Chief of Naval Operations. He was Atlantic Fleet Amphibious Force commander (1948–50) with promotion to vice admiral in September 1950 and appointment in November to be Deputy U.S. Representative to the Standing Group, North Atlantic Treaty Organization. In February 1952 he reported to U.S. Naval Forces Eastern Atlantic and Mediterranean as Deputy Commander-in-Chief in London and in June as the Commander-in-Chief at Naples. Admiral Wright became Commander-in-Chief Atlantic Fleet and Supreme Allied Commander Atlantic in the rank of admiral in April 1954, headquarters Norfolk, and directed all NATO naval forces during the thermonuclear Russo-American Cold War of the Eisenhower era until his retirement in March 1960. He subsequently (1961–63) worked for the Central Intelligence Agency.

Yarnell, Harry Ervin

(October 18, 1875–July 7, 1959). USNA (Iowa) 1897 (4/47).

Navy Department: National Archives

Prewar Asiatic Fleet commander and aviation leader, Yarnell first joined the battleship *Oregon* (BB-3) and participated in her famous "dash" around the Horn in the spring of 1898, at the Battle of Santiago in July, and in the 1899 voyage to Manila. After examinations for commissioning as ensign at the Naval Academy, he fought in the Philippine Insurrection and in the Boxer

Rebellion relief expedition on the gunboat *Yorktown* (PG-1) and (1901–02) was aide to Asiatic Squadron commander Adm. George C. Remey, flagship the armored cruiser *New York* (ACR-2). In South Carolina aboard the torpedo boat *Biddle* (TB-26) (summer 1902), he brought the destroyer *Dale* (DD-4) into reserve commission and transferred to the *Stockton* (TB-32) for Caribbean cruising (1902–03), part of the time as skipper. He took the *Barry* (DD-2) back to the Far East via Suez and there transferred to command of the *Dale*. Lieutenant Yarnell served at the Indian Head, Maryland, proving ground (1905–06) before joining the commissioning crew of the *Connecticut* (BB-18), flagship of the Atlantic or "Great White Fleet," part of the time (1908–09) as her senior engineering officer. This Fleet was briefly commanded by his father-in-law, Adm. Charles M. Thomas, who however died soon after taking command (1846–1908). Two years at the Newport torpedo station were followed by staff duty as Atlantic Fleet engineer to the commander-in-chief Adm. Hugo Osterhaus, flagships *Connecticut, Washington* (ACR-11) and *Utah* (BB-31), and transfer to the *New Jersey* (BB-16) as navigator, mostly for Caribbean operations during the crisis with Mexico (1913–14). He attended the Naval War College (1914–15), served on its staff, and commanded the *Nashville* (PG-7) at Tampico (1916–17) and escorted convoys out of Gibraltar during the late summer of 1917. In the rank of commander, he commanded the naval base of Gibraltar and all U.S. naval vessels there from October to December, with brief additional staff duty with the Patrol Force. From then until September 1918 he was aide to America's European naval commander Adm. W. S. Sims and in his Planning Section at London, finishing World War I in the Office of the Chief of Naval Operations.

Captain Yarnell preceded his involvement with flying by commanding (1920–21) Atlantic Fleet Destroyer Squadrons One and Nine, flagship *Reid* (DD-292), and as chief of staff to Commander Atlantic Destroyer Squadrons Adm. Ashley H. Robertson on the *Rochester* (ACR-2). Reporting as commander of Naval Air Station Hampton Roads during the summer of 1922, he began flying activities himself the following February, one of the first senior officers to do so. He commanded the Aircraft Squadrons of the Battle Fleet at San Diego (1924–26) on the seaplane tender *Wright* (AV-1) and spent a year at the Naval War College studying and lecturing on naval aviation. He qualified during the summer of 1927 at Pensacola as naval aviation observer (100 hours of flight time, half that required for a pilot's wings) and thereafter fit out, commissioned and commanded the aircraft carrier *Saratoga* (CV-3) in both oceans until September 1928. Promoted rear admiral at that time, Yarnell became Chief of the Bureau of Engineering with additional duty as a naval adviser at 'the London Naval Conference early in 1930. He returned to the *Saratoga* as U.S. Fleet and Battle Force aircraft commander (1931–33) and then commanded the Pearl Harbor Navy Yard and Fourteenth Naval District. In October 1936 Admiral Yarnell became Commander-in-Chief Asiatic Fleet in the full rank of admiral, flagship the heavy cruiser *Augusta* (CA-31). This post required the utmost diplomatic tact following the Japanese invasion of China in 1937, especially when he refused to withdraw the Yangtze Patrol and then had to endure the sinking of its gunboat *Panay* (PR-5) that December. Detached in July 1939, he retired in the rank of rear admiral in November.

Exactly two years later Admiral Yarnell returned to active duty recruiting Reserve engineers and advising the Chinese Military Mission in Washington until January 1943. Again promoted to admiral in July 1942, he was appointed in the summer of 1943 to make studies at the Office of the CNO involving the future of naval aviation, the size of the postwar Navy, and the question of the unification of the armed forces. These studies were generally completed before the end of the year, and during the next he was briefly assistant to Secretary of the Navy James V. Forrestal before being released from all active duty in December 1944. Admiral Yarnell then (1944–49) headed the Navy's summer school at Culver Military Academy, Ind. His son-in-law was Vice Adm. John Sylvester (1904–   ), top man in the Class of 1926 at Navy.

Zumwalt, Elmo Russell, Jr. "Bud"

(November 29, 1920––   ). USNA (Calif.) 1943 (34/616).

Vietnam War leader and naval reformer of the 1970's, Zumwalt—whose father eventually became a physician at California's China Lake Naval Weapons Center—joined the destroyer *Phelps* (DD-360) after his June 1942 graduation for the Guadalcanal landings and support in August and September and the Attu landings in the Aleutians the following May. In August 1943 he went to San Francisco for instruction at the Operational Training Command and in January 1944 to the new *Robinson* (DD-562), on board which he supported the assaults at Saipan in June, Tinian in July, Palau in September, Leyte and the night action at Surigao Strait in October, Mindoro in December, Lingayen Gulf in January 1945, Mindanao in March and April, and Borneo from May through July. Promoted lieutenant (j.g.) in May 1943 and lieutenant in July 1944, Zumwalt was made prize commander of the surrendered Japanese gunboat *Ataka* in August and took her and the first U.S. flag up the Yangtze and Whangpoo rivers to Shanghai during the occupation until December. He then spent four months with the *Saufley* (DD-465) as executive officer on the voyage home to Charleston and thereafter (1946–48) as exec of the *Zellars* (DD-777) in the Atlantic. An NROTC instructor at the University of North Carolina, he was promoted to lieutenant commander in April 1950 and soon afterwards given command of the destroyer escort *Tills* (DE-748) in Naval Reserve commission at Charleston. As navigator of the battleship *Wisconsin* (BB-64), he participated in Korean War operations from March 1951 to June 1952. Following this were instruction at the Naval War College (1952–53) and later the National War College (1961–62) and two tours of duty with the Bureau of Naval Personnel (1953–55, 1957). Promoted commander in February 1955, he was skipper of the *Arnold J. Isbell* (DD-869) for two deployments in the Western Pacific (1955–57).

Commander Zumwalt served in the Office of Assistant Secretary of the Navy (Personnel and Reserve Forces) Richard Jackson as special assistant for naval personnel (1957–58) and aide (1958–59) and commanded the guided missile frigate *Dewey* (DLG-14) from before her December 1959 commissioning through Atlantic operations until June 1961. Promoted the next month to captain, he went to the staff of Paul Nitze, Assistant Secretary of Defense (International Affairs) (1962–63) and Secretary of the Navy (1963–65), at the former office as desk officer for France, Spain, and Portugal and then director of arms control and contingency planning for the Cuban crisis and in the latter as executive assistant and senior aide. In July 1965, at the age of 44, he became the youngest U.S. Naval officer ever to attain the rank of rear admiral and for a year commanded Cruiser-Destroyer Flotilla Seven, flagship the guided missile cruiser *Canberra* (CAG-2), operating along the West coast. Admiral Zumwalt directed the Systems Analysis Division at the Navy Department until mid-1968, that September becoming commander of U.S. Naval Forces in Vietnam and Chief, Naval Advisory Group, Vietnam, with promotion to vice admiral the next month. In this capacity he successfully completed the interdiction of all enemy waterborne logistics and reinforcements in the Mekong Delta area and transferred American riverine craft to the South Vietnamese Navy until his detachment in May 1970.

Two months later Admiral Zumwalt became Chief of Naval Operations in the rank of admiral—at 49 the youngest officer ever to attain that post and rank. As such, he sought to modernize the Navy's personnel practices by recognizing social realities, undertaking uniform, liberty, and watch changes, increasing enlisted men's rights and privileges, and dealing with such contemporary problems as service racial discrimination and drug abuse—all by CNO edicts known as "Z-grams." In so doing, he raised morale but at the sacrifice of some discipline. Admiral Zumwalt also initiated warship modernization policies aimed at meeting the growing challenge of the Russian navy. After retiring in July 1974, he authored an account of his years as CNO, *On Watch* (1976).

Appendices

SENIOR FLAG COMMANDS, 1776–1976

1. Normal ranks are given with each unit or post, although there was occasional variation.
2. Nineteenth century U.S. Navy squadrons also bore the title "station."
3. Also in those days turnovers of actual sea commands often took several months, therefore dates may overlap.
4. Temporary commanders are not normally included herein.
5. Early bureau chiefs could be commodores if they had previously held squadron commands; otherwise, they were captains.
6. Italicized names are persons with biographical entries in the present work.

APPENDICES—TABLE OF CONTENTS

APPENDIX I
DEPARTMENT OF THE NAVY

A. Secretary of the Navy, 1798–1976
    (civilian)

Benjamin Stoddert	1798
Robert Smith	1801
Paul Hamilton	1809
William Jones	1813
Benjamin W. Crowninshield	1814
Smith Thompson	1818
Samuel L. Southard	1823
John Branch	1829
Levi Woodbury	1831
Mahlon Dickerson	1834
James K. Paulding	1838
George E. Badger	1841
Abel P. Upshur	1841
David Henshaw	1843
Thomas W. Gilmer	1844
John Y. Mason	1844, 1846
George Bancroft	1845
William B. Preston	1849
William A. Graham	1850
John P. Kennedy	1852
James C. Dobbin	1853
Isaac Toucey	1857
Gideon Welles	1861
Adolph E. Borie	1869
George M. Robison	1869
Richard W. Thompson	1877
Nathan Goff, Jr.	1881
William H. Hunt	1881
William E. Chandler	1882
William C. Whitney	1885
Benjamin F. Tracy	1889
Hilary A. Herbert	1893
John D. Long	1897
William H. Moody	1902
Paul Morton	1904
Charles J. Bonaparte	1905
Victor H. Metcalf	1906
Truman H. Newberry	1908
George von L. Meyer	1909
Josephus Daniels	1913
Edwin Denby	1921
Curtis D. Wilbur	1924
Charles Francis Adams	1929
Claude A. Swanson	1933
Charles Edison	1940

Frank Knox	1940
James V. Forrestal	1944

Non-Cabinet Status

John L. Sullivan	1947
Francis P. Matthews	1949
Dan A. Kimball	1951
Robert B. Anderson	1953
Charles S. Thomas	1954
Thomas S. Gates, Jr.	1957
William B. Franke	1958
John B. Connally, Jr.	1958
Fred Korth	1961
Paul H. Nitze	1963
Paul R. Ignatius	1967
John H. Chafee	1969
John W. Warner	1972
J. William Middendorf II	1974
W. Graham Claytor	1976

B. President, Board of Navy Commissioners, 1815–42
   (Commodore)

John Rodgers	1815, 1827
William Bainbridge	1824
Isaac Chauncey	1837
Charles Morris	1840
Lewis Warrington	1841

C. Chairman, General Board, 1900–51
   (Rear Admiral, Vice Admiral)

George Dewey	1900
Charles J. Badger	1917
William L. Rodgers	1921
Joseph Strauss	1924
Hilary P. Jones	1925
Edward W. Eberle	1927
Andres T. Long	1928
Mark L. Bristol	1930
Jehu V. Chase	1932
George R. Marvell	1933
Richard H. Leigh	1933
Frank H. Clark	1934
Frank B. Upham	1936
Joseph Mason Reeves	1936
Thomas C. Hart	1936
Walton R. Sexton	1939
Arthur J. Hepburn	1943
Robert L. Ghormley	1946
Frank Jack Fletcher	1946
John H. Towers	1947

C. H. McMorris	1947
John F. Shafroth	1948
Harry W. Hill	1949
George H. Fort	1950

D. Aid for Operations, 1909–15
    (Rear Admiral)

Richard Wainwright	1909
Charles E. Vreeland	1911
Bradley A. Fiske	1913

E. Chief of Naval Operations, 1915–78
    (Admiral)

William S. Benson	1915
Robert E. Coontz	1919
Edward W. Eberle	1923
Charles F. Hughes	1927
William V. Pratt	1930
William H. Standley	1933
William D. Leahy	1937
Harold R. Stark	1939
Ernest J. King	1942
Chester W. Nimitz	1945
Louis E. Denfeld	1947
Forrest P. Sherman	1949
William M. Fechteler	1951
Robert B. Carney	1953
Arleigh A. Burke	1955
George W. Anderson, Jr.	1961
David L. McDonald	1963
Thomas H. Moorer	1967
E. R. Zumwalt, Jr.	1970
James L. Holloway, III	1974
Thomas B. Hayward	1978

APPENDIX II
UNITED STATES NAVAL FORCES AFLOAT

A. Commander-in-Chief Continental Fleet, 1775–77
    (Commodore)
        Esek Hopkins

B. Commander-in-Chief United States Fleet, 1919, 1922–45
    (Admiral)

Henry T. Mayo	1919
Hilary P. Jones	1922
Robert E. Coontz	1923
Samuel S. Robison	1925
Charles F. Hughes	1926
Henry A. Wiley	1927
William V. Pratt	1929
Jehu V. Chase	1930
Frank H. Schofield	1931
Richard H. Leigh	1932
David F. Sellers	1933
Joseph Mason Reeves	1934
Arthur J. Hepburn	1936
Claude C. Bloch	1938
J. O. Richardson	1940
Husband E. Kimmel	1941
Ernest J. King	1941

APPENDIX III
THE CARIBBEAN AND SOUTH ATLANTIC

A. West India Squadron, 1822–42, 1861–65
   (Commodore, Flag Officer, Rear Admiral)

James Biddle	1822
David Porter	1823
Lewis Warrington	1825
Charles G. Ridgely	1827
Jesse D. Elliott	1829
John D. Henley	1832, 1836
Alexander J. Dallas	1835, 1837
W. Branford Shubrick	1839
Joseph R. Jarvis	1861
Garrett J. Pendergrast	1861
Charles Wilkes	1862
James L. Lardner	1863
James S. Palmer	1865

B. Home Squadron, 1842–61
   (Commodore, Flag Officer)

Charles Stewart	1842
David Conner	1844
Matthew C. Perry	1847
Jesse Wilkinson	1848
Foxhall A. Parker	1849
John T. Newton	1852
Charles S. McCauley	1855
Hiram Paulding	1855
James McIntosh	1858
William J. McCluny	1859
Joseph R. Jarvis	1860

C. Brazil Squadron, 1826–61
   (Commodore, Flag Officer)

James Biddle	1826
John O. Creighton	1828
Stephen Cassin	1829
George W. Rodgers	1831
Melancthon T. Woolsey	1832
James Renshaw	1834
John B. Nicholson	1837
Charles G. Ridgely	1840
Charles Morris	1841
Daniel Turner	1843
Lawrence Rousseau	1845
George W. Storer	1847
Isaac McKeever	1850
William D. Salter	1853

Samuel Mercer	1856
French Forrest	1856
W. Branford Shubrick	1858
Joshua R. Sands	1859

D. African Squadron, 1843–61
    (Commodore, Flag Officer)

Matthew C. Perry	1843
Charles W. Skinner	1845
George C. Read	1846
W. Compton Bolton	1847
Benjamin Cooper	1848
Francis H. Gregory	1849
Elie A. F. LaVallette	1851
Isaac Mayo	1853
Thomas Crabbe	1855
Thomas A. Conover	1857
William Inman	1859

E. Gulf Blockading Squadron, 1861–62
    (Flag Officer)

William Mervine	1861
William W. McKean	1861

F. Mississippi Squadron, 1861–65
    (Flag Officer; Rear Admiral)

John Rodgers	1861
Andrew H. Foote	1861
Charles H. Davis	1862
David D. Porter	1862
Samuel P. Lee	1864

G. West Gulf Blockading Squadron, 1862–65
    (Rear Admiral)

David G. Farragut	1862, 1864
Henry H. Bell	1863
James S. Palmer	1864
Henry K. Thatcher	1865

H. East Gulf Blockading Squadron, 1862–65
    (Acting Rear Admiral)

William W. McKean	1862
James L. Lardner	1862
Theodorus Bailey	1862
Cornelius K. Stribling	1864

I. Gulf Squadron, 1865–67
    (Commodore)

Henry K. Thatcher	1865
John A. Winslow	1866

J.   South Atlantic Squadron, 1865–1905
     (Rear Admiral)

Sylvanus W. Godon	1865
Charles H. Davis	1867
Joseph Lanman	1869
William R. Taylor	1872
James H. Strong	1873
William E. LeRoy	1875
C. H. B. Caldwell	1876
Edward T. Nichols	1877
Andrew Bryson	1879
James H. Spotts	1881
Pierce Crosby	1882
Thomas S. Phelps	1883
Earl English	1885
Daniel L. Braine	1887
John G. Walker	1889
Andrew E. K. Benham	1892
William A. Kirkland	1894
Charles S. Norton	1894
Yates Stirling	1896
Colby M. Chester	1897
Henry L. Howison	1899
Winfield S. Schley	1899
Bartlett J. Cromwell	1901
George W. Sumner	1902
Benjamin P. Lamberton	1903
French E. Chadwick	1904
Charles D. Sigsbee	1904

K.   Special Service Squadron, 1920–40
     (Rear Admiral)

Henry F. Bryan	1920
Casey B. Morgan	1921
William C. Cole	1922
John H. Dayton	1923
Julian L. Latimer	1925
David F. Sellers	1928
Edward H. Campbell	1929
A. St. Clair Smith	1931
Clark H. Woodward	1933
Charles S. Freeman	1933
George J. Meyers	1935
Yancey S. Williams	1936
John W. Wilcox, Jr.	1938
H. Kent Hewitt	1940

L.   Fourth Fleet, 1942–46
     (Vice Admiral)

Jonas H. Ingram	1942

William R. Munroe	1944
(none 1945–46)	
Charles H. McMorris	1946
Daniel E. Barbey	1946

APPENDIX IV
THE NORTH ATLANTIC AND EAST COAST

A. Eastern Squadron, 1853
    (Commodore)
    W. Branford Shubrick

B. Atlantic Blockading Squadron, 1861
    (Flag Officer)
Silas H. Stringham	1861
Louis M. Goldsborough	1861

C. North Atlantic Blockading Squadron, 1861–65
    (Acting Rear Admiral)
Louis M. Goldsborough	1861
Samuel P. Lee	1862
David D. Porter	1864
William Radford	1865

D. South Atlantic Blockading Squadron, 1861–65
    (Rear Admiral)
Samuel F. DuPont	1861
John A. B. Dahlgren	1863
William Reynolds	1865

E. Atlantic Squadron, 1865–66
    (Commodore)
William Radford	1865
Joseph Lanman	1865

F. North Atlantic Squadron (Fleet in 1903), 1866–1906
    (Rear Admiral)
James S. Palmer	1866
Henry K. Hoff	1867
Charles H. Poor	1869
Joseph F. Green	1870, 1872
Samuel P. Lee	1870
Gustavus H. Scott	1873
Augustus L. Case	1873
J. R. Madison Mullany	1874
William E. LeRoy	1876
Stephen D. Trenchard	1876
John C. Howell	1878
Robert H. Wyman	1879
George H. Cooper	1882
Stephen B. Luce	1884, 1886
James E. Jouett	1884
Bancroft Gherardi	1889
John G. Walker	1892
Oscar F. Stanton	1893

Richard W. Meade	1894
Francis M. Bunce	1895
Montgomery Sicard	1897
William T. Sampson	1898
Norman v. H. Farquhar	1899
Francis J. Higginson	1901
Albert S. Barker	1903
Robley D. Evans	1905

G. Atlantic Fleet, 1906–22, 1941–76
   (Rear Admiral, Admiral)

Robley D. Evans	1906
Charles M. Thomas	1908
Charles S. Sperry	1908
Seaton Schroeder	1909
Hugo Osterhaus	1911
Charles J. Badger	1913
Frank F. Fletcher	1914
Henry T. Mayo	1916
Henry B. Wilson	1919
Hilary P. Jones	1921
Ernest J. King	1941
Royal E. Ingersoll	1941
Jonas H. Ingram	1944
Marc A. Mitscher	1946
William H. P. Blandy	1947
William M. Fechteler	1950
Lynde D. McCormick	1951
Jerauld Wright	1954
Robert E. Dennison	1960
H. Page Smith	1963
Thomas H. Moorer	1965
Ephraim P. Holmes	1967
Charles K. Duncan	1970
Ralph W. Cousins	1972
Isaac C. Kidd, Jr.	1975

H. Tenth Fleet, 1943–45
   (Admiral)
   Ernest J. King

I. Second Fleet, 1947–76 (Second Task Fleet, 1947–50)
   (Vice Admiral)

Arthur W. Radford	1947
Donald B. Duncan	1948
Robert B. Carney	1950
Matthias B. Gardner	1950
Felix B. Stump	1951
Thomas S. Combs	1953
Edmund T. Wooldridge	1954

Charles Wellborn, Jr.	1955
Robert B. Pirie	1957
Bernard L. Austin	1958
William R. Smedberg III	1959
Harold T. Deutermann	1960
Claude V. Ricketts	1961
John M. Taylor	1961
Alfred G. Ward	1962
Charles B. Martell	1963
Kleber S. Masterson	1964
Bernard A. Clarey	1966
Charles K. Duncan	1967
Benedict J. Semmes, Jr.	1968
Gerald E. Miller	1970
Vincent P. de Poix	1971
Douglas C. Plate	1972
John G. Finnegan	1973
Stansfield Turner	1974
John J. Shanahan, Jr.	1975

APPENDIX V
EUROPE AND THE MEDITERRANEAN

A. Mediterranean Squadron (1801–07), 1815–61
    (Commodore, Flag Officer)

Thomas Truxtun	1801
Richard Dale	1801
Richard V. Morris	1802
Edward Preble	1803
Samuel Barron	1804
John Rodgers	1805, 1825
James Barron	1806
Stephen Decatur	1815
William Bainbridge	1815, 1820
Isaac Chauncey	1816
Charles Stewart	1818
Jacob Jones	1821
Thomas Macdonough	1824
Daniel T. Patterson	1825, 1832
William M. Crane	1827
James Biddle	1829
Jesse D. Elliott	1835
Isaac Hull	1838
Charles W. Morgan	1841, 1849
Charles Morris	1843
Joseph Smith	1844
(none 1846–47)	
George C. Read	1847
W. Compton Bolton	1848
Silas H. Stringham	1852
Samuel L. Breese	1855
Elie A. F. LaVallette	1858
Uriah P. Levy	1860
Charles H. Bell	1860

B. European Squadron, 1865–1904
    (Rear Admiral)

Louis M. Goldsborough	1865
David G. Farragut	1867
Alexander M. Pennock	1868
William Radford	1869
Oliver S. Glisson	1870, 1871
Charles S. Boggs	1871, 1871
James Alden	1871
Augustus L. Case	1873
John L. Worden	1875
William E. LeRoy	1877
John C. Howell	1879
James W. A. Nicholson	1881

410

Charles H. Baldwin	1883
Earl English	1884
Samuel R. Franklin	1885
James H. Greer	1887
John G. Walker	1889
(none 1893–95)	
William A. Kirkland	1895
Thomas O. Selfridge	1895
(none 1898–1901)	
Bartlett J. Cromwell	1901
Arent S. Crowninshield	1902
Charles S. Cotton	1903

C. U.S. Naval Forces in Europe, 1917–29, 1940–76 (Twelfth Fleet, 1943–47)
(Vice Admiral, Admiral)

William S. Sims	1917
Harry S. Knapp	1919
Harry McL. Huse	1920
Albert P. Niblack	1921
Edwin A. Anderson	1922
Andres T. Long	1922
Philip Andrews	1923
Roger Welles	1925
Guy H. Burrage	1926
John H. Dayton	1928
Robert L. Ghormley	1940
Harold R. Stark	1942
H. Kent Hewitt	1945
Richard L. Conolly	1946
Robert B. Carney	1950
Jerauld Wright	1952
John H. Cassady	1954
W. Fred Boone	1956
James L. Holloway, Jr.	1958
Robert L. Dennison	1959
H. Page Smith	1960
Charles D. Griffin	1963
J. S. Thach	1965
John S. McCain, Jr.	1967
Waldemar F. A. Wendt	1968
William F. Bringle	1971
Worth H. Bagley	1973
Harold E. Shear	1974
David H. Bagley	1975

D. Eighth Fleet, 1943–46
(Vice Admiral)

H. Kent Hewitt	1943
(none 1945–46)	

Marc A. Mitscher	1946
W. H. P. Blandy	1946

E. U.S. Naval Forces, Northwestern African Waters (Mediterranean from 1946), 1943–48
   (Vice Admiral)

H. Kent Hewitt	1943
William A. Glassford II	1945
Jules James	1945
Bernard H. Bieri	1946
Forrest P. Sherman	1948

F. Sixth Fleet, 1948–76 (Sixth Task Fleet, 1948–50)
   (Vice Admiral)

Forrest P. Sherman	1948
John J. Ballentine	1949
Matthias B. Gardner	1951
John H. Cassady	1952
Thomas S. Combs	1954
Ralph A. Ofstie	1955
Harry D. Felt	1956
Charles R. Brown	1956
Clarence E. Eckstrom	1958
George W. Anderson, Jr.	1959
David L. McDonald	1961
William E. Gentner, Jr.	1963
William E. Ellis	1964
Frederick L. Ashworth	1966
William I. Martin	1967
David C. Richardson	1968
Isaac C. Kidd, Jr.	1970
Daniel J. Murphy	1972
Frederick C. Turner	1974
Harry D. Train II	1976

APPENDIX VI
THE EASTERN PACIFIC AND WEST COAST

A. Pacific Squadron, 1818–66, 1869–72, 1878–1907
    (Commodore, Flag Officer, Rear Admiral)

John Downes	1818, 1832
Charles G. Ridgely	1820
Charles Stewart	1821
Isaac Hull	1824
Jacob Jones	1826
Charles C. B. Thompson	1829
Alexander S. Wadsworth	1834
Henry E. Ballard	1837
Alexander Claxton	1839
Daniel Turner	1841
Thomas ap C. Jones	1842, 1848
Alexander J. Dallas	1843
James Armstrong	1844
John D. Sloat	1844
Robert F. Stockton	1846
W. Branford Shubrick	1847, 1847
James Biddle	1847
Charles S. McCauley	1850
Bladen Dulany	1853
William Mervine	1855
John C. Long	1857
John B. Montgomery	1859
Charles H. Bell	1862
George F. Pearson	1864
Thomas Turner	1869
John A. Winslow	1870
Roger N. Stembel	1872
C. R. Perry Rodgers	1878
Thomas H. Stevens, Jr.	1880
George B. Balch	1881
Aaron K. Hughes	1883
John H. Upshur	1884
Edward Y. McCauley	1885
Lewis A. Kimberly	1887
George Brown	1890
John Irwin	1893
John G. Walker	1894
Lester A. Beardslee	1895
Joseph N. Miller	1897
Albert Kautz	1898
Silas Casey	1901
Henry Glass	1903

Caspar F. Goodrich	1905
William T. Swinburne	1906

B. North Pacific Squadron, 1866–78
(Rear Admiral)

Henry K. Thatcher	1866
Thomas T. Craven	1868
William R. Taylor	1869
Roger N. Stembel	1871
Alexander M. Pennock	1872
John J. Almy	1874
Alexander Murray	1876

C. South Pacific Squadron, 1866–78
(Rear Admiral)

George F. Pearson	1866
John A. B. Dahlgren	1867
Thomas Turner	1868
David S. McDougal	1870
Roger N. Stembel	1872
Charles Steedman	1872
John J. Almy	1873
Napoleon Collins	1874
Reed Werden	1875
Charles H. B. Caldwell	1876
George H. Preble	1877

D. Pacific Fleet, 1907–22
(Rear Admiral, Admiral)

James H. Dayton	1907
William T. Swinburne	1908
Uriel Sebree	1909
Giles B. Harber	1910
Edward B. Barry	1910
Chauncey Thomas	1911
William H. H. Southerland	1912
Walter C. Cowles	1913
Thomas B. Howard	1914
Cameron McR. Winslow	1915
William B. Caperton	1916
Hugh Rodman	1919
Edward W. Eberle	1921

E. First Fleet, 1947–73 (First Task Fleet 1947–50)
(Vice Admiral)

Alfred E. Montgomery	1947
George D. Murray	1947
Laurence T. DuBose	1948
Gerald F. Bogan	1949
Thomas L. Sprague	1950

Calvin T. Durgin	1950
Harold M. Martin	1951, 1953
Arthur D. Struble	1951
J. J. Clark	1952
Ingolf N. Kiland	1952
Ralph A. Ofstie	1952
William K. Phillips	1953
Herbert G. Hopwood	1955
Robert L. Dennison	1956
Ruthven E. Libby	1958
U. S. Grant Sharp	1960
Charles L. Melson	1960
Frank Virden	1962
Robert T. S. Keith	1962
P. D. Stroop	1963
Ephraim P. Holmes	1964
Lawson P. Ramage	1964
Bernard F. Roeder	1966
Isaac C. Kidd, Jr.	1969
Raymond E. Peet	1970
Nels B. Johnson	1972
James F. Calvert	1972

F.   Third Fleet, 1973–76
   (Vice Admiral)

William T. Rapp	1973
James H. Doyle, Jr.	1974
Robert P. Coogan	1975
Samuel L. Gravely, Jr.	1976

APPENDIX VII
THE WESTERN PACIFIC

A. East India Squadron, 1835–61
    (Commodore, Flag Officer)

Edmund P. Kennedy	1835
George C. Read	1838
Lawrence Kearny	1840
Foxhall A. Parker	1843
James Biddle	1845
David Geisinger	1848
Philip F. Voorhees	1849
John H. Aulick	1851
Matthew C. Perry	1853
Joel Abbot	1854
John Pope	1855
James Armstrong	1856
Josiah Tattnall	1858
Cornelius K. Stribling	1859
Frederick Engle	1861

B. Asiatic Squadron, 1865–1908
    (Rear Admiral)

Henry H. Bell	1865
Stephen C. Rowan	1867
John Rodgers	1870
Thornton A. Jenkins	1872
Enoch G. Parrott	1874
Alexander M. Pennock	1874
William Reynolds	1875
Thomas H. Patterson	1877
John M. B. Clitz	1880
Pierce Crosby	1883
John L. Davis	1883
Ralph Chandler	1886
George E. Belknap	1889
David B. Harmony	1892
Charles C. Carpenter	1893
Frederick V. McNair	1895
George Dewey	1898
John C. Watson	1899
George C. Remey	1900
Frederick Rodgers	1902
Robley D. Evans	1902
Philip H. Cooper	1904
Yates Stirling	1904
William M. Folger	1905
Willard H. Brownson	1906
Joseph N. Hemphill	1907

C. Asiatic Fleet, 1910–42
(Rear Admiral, Admiral)

John Hubbard	1910
Joseph B. Murdock	1911
Reginald F. Nicholson	1912
Walter C. Cowles	1914
Albert G. Winterhalter	1915
Austin M. Knight	1917
William L. Rodgers	1918
Albert Gleaves	1919
Joseph Strauss	1921
Edwin A. Anderson	1922
Thomas Washington	1923
Clarence S. Williams	1925
Mark L. Bristol	1927
Charles B. McVay, Jr.	1929
Montgomery M. Taylor	1930
Frank B. Upham	1933
Harry E. Yarnell	1936
Thomas C. Hart	1939

D. Battle Fleet (Force from 1931), 1922–42 (under U.S. fleet)
(Admiral)

Edward W. Eberle	1922
Samuel S. Robison	1923
Charles F. Hughes	1925
Richard H. Jackson	1926
Louis R. de Steiguer	1927
William V. Pratt	1928
Louis M. Nulton	1929
Frank H. Schofield	1930
Richard H. Leigh	1931
Luke McNamee	1932
William H. Standley	1933
Joseph Mason Reeves	1933
Frank H. Brumby	1934
Harris Laning	1935
William D. Leahy	1936
Claude C. Bloch	1937
Edward C. Kalbfus	1938
J. O. Richardson	1939
Charles P. Snyder	1940
William S. Pye	1941

E. Pacific Fleet and Pacific Ocean Areas, 1941–45
(Admiral)

Husband E. Kimmel	1941
Chester W. Nimitz	1941

417

F. Pacific Fleet, 1945–76
    (Admiral)

Raymond A. Spruance	1945
John H. Towers	1946
Louis E. Denfeld	1947
Harold B. Sallada	1947
D. C. Ramsey	1948
Arthur W. Radford	1949
Felix B. Stump	1953
Herbert G. Hopwood	1958
John H. Sides	1960
U. S. Grant Sharp	1963
Thomas H. Moorer	1964
Roy L. Johnson	1965
John J. Hyland	1967
Bernard A. Clarey	1970
Maurice F. Weisner	1973
Thomas B. Hayward	1976

G. Naval Forces Far East, 1946–57
    (Vice Admiral)

Robert M. Griffin	1946
Russell S. Berkey	1948
C. Turner Joy	1949
Robert P. Briscoe	1952
William McC. Callaghan	1954
Roscoe F. Good	1956

H. Pacific Command, 1947–76
    (Admiral)

John H. Towers	1947
Louis E. Denfeld	1947
Harold B. Sallada	1947
D. C. Ramsey	1948
Arthur W. Radford	1949
Felix B. Stump	1953
Harry D. Felt	1958
U. S. Grant Sharp	1964
John S. McCain, Jr.	1968
Noel A. M. Gayler	1972
Maurice F. Weisner	1976

I. Southwest Pacific Area, 1942–44
    (Vice Admiral)

Herbert F. Leary	1942
Arthur S. Carpender	1942
Thomas C. Kinkaid	1943

J. Seventh Fleet, 1943–76 (U.S. Naval Forces Western Pacific 1947–49; Seventh Task Fleet 1949–50)

418

(Vice Admiral)

Thomas C. Kinkaid	1943
Daniel E. Barbey	1945
Charles M. Cooke, Jr.	1946
Oscar C. Badger	1948
Russell S. Berkey	1949
Arthur D. Struble	1950
Harold M. Martin	1951
Robert P. Briscoe	1952
J. J. Clark	1952
Alfred M. Pride	1953
Stuart H. Ingersoll	1955
Wallace M. Beakley	1957
Frederick N. Kivette	1958
Charles D. Griffin	1960
William A. Schoech	1961
Thomas H. Moorer	1962
Roy L. Johnson	1964
Paul P. Blackburn, Jr.	1965
John J. Hyland	1965
Walter F. Bringle	1967
Maurice F. Weisner	1970
James L. Holloway III	1972
George P. Steele II	1973
Thomas B. Hayward	1975
Robert B. Baldwin	1976

K. South Pacific Area and Force, 1942–46
    (Vice Admiral)

Robert L. Ghormley	1942
William F. Halsey, Jr.	1942
John H. Newton	1944
William L. Calhoun	1945
Paul Hendren	1945

L. Third Fleet, 1943–46
    (Admiral)

William F. Halsey, Jr.	1943
Howard F. Kingman	1945

M. North Pacific Area and Force, 1942–46
    (Vice Admiral)

Robert A. Theobald	1942
Thomas C. Kinkaid	1943
Frank J. Fletcher	1943
Ralph F. Wood	1945
Freeland A. Daubin	1946

419

N.   Central Pacific Force, 1943–44
(Vice Admiral)
Raymond A. Spruance

O.   Fifth Fleet, 1944–46
(Admiral, Vice Admiral)
Raymond A. Spruance	1944
John H. Towers	1945
Frederick C. Sherman	1946
Alfred E. Montgomery	1946

APPENDIX VIII
KEY ADMINISTRATIVE UNITS

A. Personnel

  1. Bureau of Navigation, 1862–1942
     (Rear Admiral)

Charles H. Davis	1862
Percival Drayton	1865
David D. Porter	1865
Thornton A. Jenkins	1865
James Alden	1869
Daniel Ammen	1871
William D. Whiting	1878
John G. Walker	1881
Francis M. Ramsay	1889
Arent S. Crowninshield	1897
Henry C. Taylor	1902
George A. Converse	1904
Willard H. Brownson	1907
John E. Pillsbury	1908
William P. Potter	1909
Reginald F. Nicholson	1909
Philip Andrews	1912
Victor Blue	1913, 1918
Leigh C. Palmer	1916
Thomas Washington	1919
Andres T. Long	1923
William R. Shoemaker	1924
Richard H. Leigh	1927
Frank B. Upham	1930
William D. Leahy	1933
Adolphus Andrews	1935
J. O. Richardson	1938
Chester W. Nimitz	1939
Randall Jacobs	1941

  2. Bureau of Naval Personnel, 1942–76
     (Rear Admiral, Vice Admiral)

Randall Jacobs	1942
Louis E. Denfeld	1945
Thomas L. Sprague	1947
John W. Roper	1949
Laurence T. DuBose	1951
James L. Holloway, Jr.	1953
H. Page Smith	1958
William R. Smedberg	1960
Benedict J. Semmes, Jr.	1964
Charles K. Duncan	1968
Dick H. Guinn	1970

David H. Bagley	1972
James D. Watkins	1975

B. Shore Establishment
  1. Bureau of Yards and Docks, 1842–1966
    (Captain, Rear Admiral)

Lewis Warrington	1842
Joseph Smith	1846
Daniel Ammen	1869
C. R. Perry Rodgers	1871
John Howell	1874
Richard L. Law	1878
Edward T. Nichols	1881
David B. Harmony	1885
George B. White	1889
Norman v. H. Farquhar	1890
Edmund O. Matthews	1894
Mordecai C. Endicott	1898
Richard C. Hollyday	1907
Homer R. Stanford	1912
Frederic R. Harris	1916
Charles W. Parks	1918
Luther E. Gregory	1921
Archibald L. Parsons	1929
Norman M. Smith	1933
Ben Moreell	1937
John J. Manning	1945
Joseph F. Jelley, Jr.	1949
John R. Perry	1953
Robert H. Meade	1955
Eugene J. Peltier	1959
Peter Corradi	1962
Alexander C. Husband	1965

  2. Naval Facilities Engineering Command, 1966–76
    (Rear Admiral, CEC)

Alexander C. Husband	1966
Walter M. Enger	1970
Albert R. Marschall	1973

  3. Office of Naval Material, 1942–66
    (Vice Admiral)

Samuel M. Robinson	1942
Ben Moreell	1946
Edward L. Cochrane	1947
Arthur C. Miles	1948
Edwin D. Foster	1950
Albert G. Noble	1951
Charles W. Fox	1952
John E. Gingrich	1954

Murrey L. Royar (SC)	1955
Edward W. Clexton	1956
George F. Beardsley	1962
William A. Schoech	1963
Ignatius J. Galantin	1965

4. Naval Material Command, 1966–76
   (Admiral)

Ignatius J. Galantin	1966
Jackson D. Arnold	1970
Isaac C. Kidd, Jr.	1971
Frederick H. Michaelis	1975

C. Ships
1. Bureau of Construction and Repair, 1842–1940 (and Equipment till 1862)
   (Captain, Rear Admiral)

David Conner	1842
Beverly Kennon	1843
Charles Morris	1844
Charles W. Skinner	1847
W. Branford Shubrick	1852
Samuel Hartt	1853
John Lenthall	1853
Isaiah Hanscom	1872
John W. Easby	1878
Theodore D. Wilson	1882
Philip Hichborn	1894
Francis T. Bowles	1901
Washington I. Capps	1903
Richard M. Watt	1910
David W. Taylor	1914
John D. Beuret	1922
George H. Rock	1929
Emory S. Land	1933
William G. DuBose	1937
Alexander H. Van Keuren	1939
Samuel M. Robinson	1940

2. Bureau of Engineering, 1862–1940 (originally Steam Engineering)
   (Engineer-in-Chief, Rear Admiral)

Benjamin F. Isherwood	1862
James W. King	1870
William W. Wood	1874
William H. Shock	1878
Charles H. Loring	1884
George W. Melville	1888
Charles W. Rae	1903
John K. Barton	1908
Hutch I. Cone	1909
Robert S. Griffin	1913

John K. Robison	1921
John Halligan, Jr.	1925
Harry E. Yarnell	1928
Samuel M. Robinson	1934, 1939
Harold G. Bowen	1935

3. Bureau of Ships, 1940–66
   (Rear Admiral)

Samuel M. Robinson	1940
Alexander H. Van Keuren	1942
Earle W. Mills	1946
David H. Clark	1949
Homer N. Wallin	1951
Wilson D. Leggett, Jr.	1953
Albert G. Mumma	1955
Ralph K. James	1959
William A. Brockett	1963

4. Naval Ship Systems Command, 1966–74
   (Rear Admiral)

Edward J. Fahy	1966
Nathan Sonenshein	1970
Robert C. Gooding	1972

D. Weapons
   1. Bureau of Ordnance, 1842–1960 (and Hydrography until 1862)
      (Captain, Rear Admiral)

William M. Crane	1842
Lewis Warrington	1846
Charles Morris	1851
Duncan N. Ingraham	1856
George A. Magruder	1860
Andrew A. Harwood	1861
John A. B. Dahlgren	1862, 1868
Henry Augustus Wise	1863
Augustus L. Case	1869
William N. Jeffers	1873
Montgomery Sicard	1881
William M. Folger	1890
William T. Sampson	1893
Charles O'Neil	1897
George A. Converse	1904
Newton E. Mason	1904
Nathan C. Twining	1911
Joseph Strauss	1913
Ralph Earle	1916
Charles B. McVay, Jr.	1920
Claude C. Bloch	1923
William D. Leahy	1927
Edgar B. Larimer	1931

Harold R. Stark	1934
William R. Furlong	1937
W. H. P. Blandy	1941
George F. Hussey, Jr.	1943
Albert G. Noble	1947
Malcolm F. Schoeffel	1950
Frederic S. Withington	1954
P. D. Stroop	1958

2. Bureau of Aeronautics, 1921–59
   (Rear Admiral)

William A. Moffett	1921
Ernest J. King	1933
Arthur B. Cook	1936
John H. Towers	1939
John S. McCain	1942
D. C. Ramsey	1943
Harold B. Sallada	1945
Alfred M. Pride	1947
Thomas S. Combs	1951
Apollo Soucek	1953
James S. Russell	1955
Robert E. Dixon	1957

3. Bureau of Weapons, 1959–66
   (Rear Admiral)

Paul D. Stroop	1959
Kleber S. Masterson	1962
Wellington T. Hines	1964
Allen M. Shinn	1964

4. Naval Ordnance Systems Command, 1966–75
   (Rear Admiral)

Arthur R. Gralla	1966
Mark W. Woods	1970
Roger E. Spreen	1972

5. Naval Sea Systems Command, 1974–76
   (Vice Admiral)

Robert C. Gooding	1974
Clarence R. Bryan	1976

6. Naval Air Systems Command, 1966–76
   (Vice Admiral)

Robert L. Townsend	1966
Thomas J. Walker III	1969
Thomas R. McClellan	1971
Kent L. Lee	1973
Forrest S. Petersen	1976

APPENDIX IX
COMMANDANT, U. S. MARINE CORPS, 1798–1978
(Major, Brigadier General, Colonel,
Major General, General)

William W. Burrows	1798
Franklin Wharton	1804
Anthony Gale	1819
Archibald Henderson	1820
John Harris	1859
Jacob Zeilin	1864
Charles G. McCawley	1876
Charles Heywood	1891
George F. Elliott	1903
William P. Biddle	1911
George Barnett	1914
John A. Lejeune	1920
Wendell C. Neville	1929
Ben H. Fuller	1930
John H. Russell	1934
Thomas Holcomb	1936
Alexander A. Vandegrift	1944
Clifton B. Cates	1948
Lemuel C. Shepherd	1952
Randolph McC. Pate	1956
David M. Shoup	1960
Wallace M. Greene, Jr.	1964
Leonard F. Chapman, Jr.	1968
Robert E. Cushman, Jr.	1972
Louis H. Wilson, Jr.	1975

APPENDIX X
COMMANDANT, U. S. COAST GUARD, 1915–78
(Commodore, Rear Admiral, Admiral)

Ellsworth P. Berthoff	1915
William E. Reynolds	1919
Frederick C. Billard	1924
Harry G. Hamlet	1932
Russell R. Waesche	1936
Joseph F. Farley	1946
Merlin O'Neill	1950
Alfred C. Richmond	1954
Edwin J. Roland	1962
Willard J. Smith	1966
Chester R. Bender	1970
Owen J. Siler	1973
John B. Hayes	1978

APPENDIX XI
CONFEDERATE STATES NAVY, 1861-1865
(Captain, Flag Officer)

A. Secretary of the Navy
    (civilian)
        Stephen R. Mallory

B. Virginia waters and James River Squadron
Samuel Barron	1861, 1862
William F. Lynch	1861
Franklin Buchanan	1862
S. Smith Lee	1862
Josiah Tattnall	1862
French Forrest	1863
John K. Mitchell	1864
Raphael Semmes	1865

C. North Carolina waters
Samuel Barron	1861
William F. Lynch	1861, 1862
Robert F. Pinckney	1864
James W. Cooke	1864

D. South Carolina waters and Charleston Squadron
Duncan N. Ingraham	1861
John R. Tucker	1863

E. Georgia waters and Savannah River Squadron
Josiah Tattnall	1861, 1862
Richard L. Page	1863
William A. Webb	1863
William W. Hunter	1863

F. Mobile Squadron
Victor M. Randolph	1861
Franklin Buchanan	1862
Ebenezer Farrand	1864

G. Mississippi River Squadron and New Orleans
Lawrence L. Rousseau	1861
George N. Hollins	1861
John K. Mitchell	1862
William F. Lynch	1862

H. Red River Squadron
Thomas R. Brent	1863
Jonathan H. Carter	1863

428

I. Texas waters
        William W. Hunter   1861
        Joseph N. Barney   1863

J. Naval Forces in Europe
        Samuel Barron   1863

K. Office of Orders and Detail
   (Captain)
        Samuel Barron   1861
        Lawrence L. Rousseau   1861
        William F. Lynch   1861
        Franklin Buchanan   1861
        French Forrest   1862
        John K. Mitchell   1863
        S. Smith Lee   1864

L. Office of Ordnance and Hydrography
   (Commander)
        Duncan N. Ingraham   1861
        George Minor   1861
        John M. Brooke   1863

M. Commandant, C. S. Marine Corps
   (Colonel)
        Lloyd I. Beall   1861

N. Engineer-in-Chief
   (Chief Constructor)
        William P. Williamson   1862

O. Chief Constructor
   (civilian)
        John L. Porter   1863

Further References

For the general reader interested in learning more about the U. S. Navy and of the men contained in this volume, the following sources—listed chronologically in historical time periods—are recommended:

Reynolds, Clark G. *Command of the Sea: The History and Strategy of Maritime Empires.* New York: William Morrow, 1974. The overall history of navies, Chapter 8 beginning the American experience, and including an extensive bibliography. For the U.S. Navy in the general American military experience, see the article, "American Strategic History and Doctrines: A Reconsideration," in *Military Affairs,* XXXIX, No. 4 (December 1975), 181–190, by the author.

Fowler, William N. *Rebels Under Sail: The American Navy During the Revolution.* New York: Charles Scribner's, 1976.

Sprout, Harold and Margaret. *The Rise of American Naval Power, 1776–1918.* Princeton: Princeton University Press, 1967.

Guttridge, Leonard F., and Jay D. Smith. *The Commodores: The U.S. Navy in the Age of Sail.* New York: Harper & Row, 1969. The Quasi-War, Barbary wars and War of 1812.

Bradlee, Francis B. *Piracy in the West Indies and Its Suppression.* Salem: Essex Institute, 1970.

Bauer, K. Jack. *Surfboats and Horse Marines: U.S. Naval Operations in the Mexican War, 1846–48.* Annapolis: U.S. Naval Institute, 1969.

Johnson, Robert Erwin. *Thence Round Cape Horn: The Story of United States Naval Forces on Pacific Station, 1818–1923.* Annapolis: U.S. Naval Institute, 1963.

Anderson, Bern. *By Sea and By River: The Naval History of the Civil War.* New York: Alfred A. Knopf, 1962.

Alden, John D. *American Steel Navy.* Annapolis: Naval Institute Press, 1972. The Mahan era, 1883 to 1909.

Freidel, Frank B. *The Splendid Little War.* Boston: Little, Brown, 1958. Against Spain, 1898.

Sims, William S. *The Victory at Sea.* Garden City: Doubleday, 1920. World War I.

Roskill, Stephen W. *Naval Policy Between the Wars,* 2 vols. London: Collins, 1968, 1976. The U.S. and Royal navies, 1919–39.

Morison, Samuel Eliot. *The Two-Ocean War.* Boston: Little, Brown, 1963. World War II.

Reynolds, Clark G. *The Fast Carriers: The Forging of an Air Navy.* New York: McGraw-Hill, 1968; rev. ed., Huntington, N.Y.: Robert Krieger, 1978.

Blair, Clay, Jr. *Silent Victory: The U.S. Submarine War Against Japan.* Philadelphia: Lippincott, 1975.

Cagle, Malcolm W., and Frank A. Manson. *The Sea War in Korea.* Annapolis: U.S. Naval Institute, 1957.

Hooper, Edwin Bickford, *et al. The United States Navy and the Vietnam Conflict,* Vol. I: *The Setting of the Stage to 1959.* Washington: Government Printing Office, 1976.

For the general researcher, the following published sources and a large number of biographies were utilized in the preparation of the present work:

Appleton's *Cyclopedia of American Biography* and supplements.

Current Biography, 1942–present, annual.

Dictionary of American Biography and supplements.

Dictionary of American Naval Fighting Ships.

Directory of Officers, U.S. Navy, annual.

Fasano, Lawrence. *Naval Rank: Its Inception and Development.* New York: Horizon House, 1936.

Hamersly, Lewis R. *The Records of Living Officers of the U.S. Navy and Marine Corps.* New York: By the author, 1902.

Morison, Samuel Eliot. *History of United States Naval Operations in World War II,* 15 vols. Boston: Little, Brown, 1947–62.

Naval Review, annual. Actually, the May issue of the U.S. Naval Institute *Proceedings.* Lists all current flag officers and billets.

Navy Register, annual. Also, *Register of Officers of the Confederate States Navy, 1861–1865.* Washington: Government Printing Office, 1931.

Notable Names in American History, 3rd ed. Clifton, N.J.: James T. White, 1973.

Register of Alumni. Annapolis: U.S. Naval Academy Alumni Association, annual. Includes addresses of living graduates, many of whom answered inquiries by the author.

Who's Who in America, annual.

Who Was Who in American History—The Military. Chicago, 1975.

For the serious scholar, two agencies in Washington, D. C. house the primary documents and photographs utilized herein:

The National Archives has on microfilm *Abstracts of Service Records of Naval Officers, 1798–1893* or "Records of Officers" (Microcopy No. 330) and in literally huge bound Bureau of Navigation volumes, *Record of Officers* for the period 1893 to 1917, both sources administered by the Old Army and Navy Section.

The Naval Historical Center of the Navy Department at the Washington Navy Yard maintains the Navy's Library, including all the reference and secondary sources listed above; helpful for general information is the head of the Historical Research Branch, for the present work Dr. William J. Morgan. But the main primary sources are housed in the Division's Operational Archives Branch headed by Dr. D. C. Allard. Within its "ZB" file of biographical summaries of prominent flag officers compiled over the years are indispensable mimeographed line biographies produced by the Navy between 1945 and 1975; Nina Statum handles this key repository.

General documents on the Navy from the Revolution to the pre-World War II years are deposited at the National Archives, although most available personal papers of twentieth century senior officers are in the possession of the Naval Historical Foundation, on loan at the Library of Congress. World War II and postwar documents are at the Operational Archives Branch of the Navy Department and are made available to individual researchers on the premises by Dr. Allard's team of tireless archivists who assisted importantly in this work: Barbara A. Gilmore, Bernard Calvacante, Nina Statum, Jeri Judkins, Mary Edmison and Kathy Lloyd. The author is indebted to them for their assistance.

Also helpful were R. L. Scheina, historian of the Coast Guard at its Headquarters; T. J. Lauer, Jr., deputy chief of the Commissioned Personnel Division of the National Oceanic and Atmospheric Administration; and C. Bradford Mitchell, historian of the Merchant Marine Academy.

Photographs were generously provided by the Naval Photographic Center in Washington or purchased from the National Archives, Library of Congress and private collections as credited.

Index

(Commissioning dates given for ships with identical names.)

435

436

439